MAKING AN EXHIBITION
OF MYSELF

By the same author

The Wars of the Roses
a book with John Barton on the
adaptation of Shakespeare's
Henry VI Parts I, II, III and
Richard III (1970)

John Gabriel Borkman
English version with Inga-Stina Ewbank
of Ibsen's play (1975)

Peter Hall's Diaries
edited by John Goodwin (1983)

Animal Farm
stage adaptation of Orwell's book (1986)

The Wild Duck
English version with Inga-Stina Ewbank
of Ibsen's play (1990)

PETER HALL

Making an Exhibition of Myself

SINCLAIR-STEVENSON

First published in Great Britain in 1993
by Sinclair-Stevenson
an imprint of Reed Consumer Books Ltd
Michelin House, 81 Fulham Road, London SW3 6RB
and Auckland, Melbourne, Singapore and Toronto

A CIP catalogue record for this book
is available at the British Library
ISBN 1 85619 165 6

Typeset by Falcon Graphic Art Ltd
Wallington, Surrey
Printed and bound in Great Britain
by Clays Ltd, St Ives plc

— CONTENTS —

FOR NICKI

AND FOR CHRISTOPHER
JENNIFER, EDWARD
LUCY, REBECCA
AND EMMA

— LIST OF ILLUSTRATIONS —

1. My mother in 1924.
2. My father when he had just been appointed Stationmaster.
3. At six years old.
4. *Albert Herring.* (*Guy Gravett*)
5. 3120201 Aircraftsman Hall.
6. At Cambridge.
7. Jill — my first love affair.
8. With Tom Bergner and my Austin 7.
9. As Hamlet at the Perse.
10. As Petruchio at the Perse.
11. As First Citizen in a Marlowe Society's *Coriolanus* at Cambridge.
12. With Leslie on our wedding day. (*Tony Armstrong Jones*)
13. Sir Fordham Flower. (*Shakespeare Centre Library*)
14. Charles Laughton as Bottom. (*Angus McBean – Shakespeare Centre Library*)
15. Mary Ure, Olivier and Edith Evans in *Coriolanus*. (*Angus McBean – Shakespeare Centre Library*)

— ACKNOWLEDGEMENTS —

Above all, I am grateful to John Goodwin. His help in the preparation of the manuscript was invaluable. He also encouraged me to be as candid as the law and reasonable courtesy allow.

My warm thanks as well to Maggie Sedwards for all her work in making this book happen, and for urging me on when I was flagging; and to Tim Goodwin who not only compiled the Index but searched out photographs – as did the Shakespeare Centre at Stratford-upon-Avon, Helen O'Neill at Glyndebourne, and Stephen Wood of the National Theatre.

Penelope Hoare and her assistant Roger Cazalet at Sinclair-Stevenson gave the text most generous care which I greatly appreciated; and Mike Shaw of Curtis Brown kindly provided bracing enthusiasm throughout.

I hope those I have known well in my life but who do not appear, or appear fleetingly, will understand that this has absolutely nothing to do with the depth of my affection or of my regard for them.

Peter Hall
London, 1993

PART ONE

Better Lucky Than Rich

− 1 −

I have a vision of a garden in long-shot and the lens of my worried young eyes makes it look enormous.

I was four years old and, after an upset with my mother, was running away from home. Rows were always with my mother, never with my father. She was handsome, genial and quick-witted. She was also the tempest – volatile and given to flying into rages. Yet she never disciplined me; she always asked my father to oblige.

I turned back at the end of the garden as I reached the gate, expecting to see two grown-ups begging forgiveness and imploring me to change my mind and stay with them for ever. Instead, I saw my father standing alone at the back door.

He was a kind man and did not know the meaning of cruelty. But he would not tolerate self-indulgence or dramatics. This made for frequent disputes, not only with my mother but with me, for we were both histrionically inclined.

I saw that he held my coat and large cap in his hand. 'Here,' he said. 'You will be needing these.' I burst into tears.

This taught me a valuable lesson: never threaten unless you are prepared to act.

*

3

My mother was alert to my temperament from my beginnings to the end of her days. She was a Suffolk country woman who lived by precept and aphorism. Her vocabulary was packed with comforting phrases: 'It is better to be born lucky than rich'; 'It'll all work out in the end'; 'A change is as good as a rest'. Some were less reassuring and induced alarm in a small boy: 'They're always out to get you' or 'They'll get you if they can'. In later years, she was much given to pronouncing these mantra grimly, usually after she had heard me sounding off on television or radio on censorship, or the teaching of Shakespeare, or the iniquities of the government's arts policy. 'I heard you, boy,' she would say pointedly, 'making an exhibition of yourself.' She became most anxious if I discussed politics. In her opinion, they would indeed then be out to get me. She was right in a sense: in the Thatcher years, they nearly did. She firmly believed that it was safer to 'keep yourself to yourself'.

She would certainly think that, by writing this book, I was making an exhibition of myself.

From earliest childhood I always took on too much and was what is called, in modern psychological jargon, an over-achiever. This made my mother proud, but also very anxious. When things went wrong, she would say triumphantly: 'You should have thought of that before'.

I have always worked too hard, played too hard, and taken risks. I have lived by obsession and enthusiasm and have always thought too little of the consequences. And when I was under intolerable pressure, or failing, my mother was always there to mutter her disapproval.

Being a director is not a safe job. Putting on plays is an unwise thing to do. The likelihood of success is small. It is better not to chance it. But I have always wanted to provoke, to startle, to challenge – and not much cared if I did. And I suppose it all started with provoking my mother. My father was wiser and warmer, and the man who tried to teach me balance. But I preferred to arouse my mother's anxiety. I have never

4

wanted to play safe. It has made for a bumpy and exhilarating ride, but I have not often been bored.

– 2 –

I once knew a BBC producer who turned his office at Television Centre into a serious health hazard by passing his whole life in it. Old socks, unwashed plates and coffee-ringed scripts were tumbled all over the floor. He obviously felt thoroughly at home in this mess, and I understood that. The place where I live and work is important to me because it gives me security. I am an untidy person, though I like tidiness. I am equally happy in two extremes: either a very precise environment where everything is carefully planned and placed – like a production awaiting its final dress rehearsal – or a complete shambles where I simply don't bother to see what isn't worth looking at.

I am a reckless traveller. I love nearly missing trains and just boarding flight-closed aircraft. But this recklessness does not extend to where I stay. Not for me the sudden arrival at the motel as the sun is going down. I need to know where I'm going, and I prefer to know what it's like. For thirty-five years I always stayed in New York at the Algonquin Hotel. It was a ghost of its great 1920s-self and had appalling service and hazardous, infrequent lifts. But it was the place where the staff, increasingly white-haired and puffing over heavy suitcases, always greeted me by name whatever time of day or night I arrived. Now they have gone, taken over by a Japanese corporation; and I have moved to the Wyndham where the staff remain cordial and constant.

So a sense of place is where I begin. When I think of the past, I think first of places.

*

Twenty-four Avenue Approach, Bury St Edmunds, Suffolk, is an unprepossessing little house in a row of early twentieth-century workers' cottages: two up and two down, with a kitchen at the back. The house has now sprouted a porch, a bathroom and an indoor loo. When I was born there, to Grace and Reginald, on 22 November 1930, the loo was outside and a tin hip-bath hung on the kitchen wall. The garden was tended by my father; not to grow food on decent soil would have been as unnatural to him as not breathing.

I was an only child and grew up cocooned by my mother's family who lived all around us. My father's relations were more widespread, and even more numerous, though most of them had emigrated to Australia. He was not obsessed with 'family'; he left that to his wife. 'Blood is thicker than water,' my mother would intone when we were faced with yet another family gathering.

Both families were close to the land and had been peopled by generations of farm labourers. Now, however, they were moving up into crafts and professions and becoming policemen or shop assistants. Nonetheless, they all had an innate ability to grow things and to look after animals. My maternal grandfather was a house-painter. My father's father, who died before I was born, seems to have led a roving, Dickensian sort of life, doing odd-jobs here and there, running a pub in Bangor, and ending up as a rat-catcher on the Royal Sandringham estate. My mother, who had a distinct aura of piss-elegance, as if she were clinging to respectability for dear life, always insisted that he was a 'vermin exterminator'. An old photograph shows a rather fly-looking man who would not be out of place on a racecourse. He looks the sort of helpful, convivial character seen by the score at Bury St Edmunds' weekly livestock market – men who might be small-time farmers, or odd-job men, or pillars of the church. They were certainly pillars of the pub.

My father was the only member of the family who

had achieved any academic distinction. He had won a scholarship to secondary school, secured his school certificate, and had then become an office boy for the London and North Eastern Railway. By the time I was born, he was a miserably paid clerk in the goods depot at Bury St Edmunds railway station – a huge, dusty, clanking place, smelling of bloaters and Jeyes' Fluid. I knew the pay was miserable because of the endless comments from my mother. She complained continuously about the lack of money and how hard she had to work to make ends meet. Even at that time, she castigated my father for his lack of push, his lack of ambition. Apparently it was his failings which made us so poor. I heard both of them talk enviously of the rich people who lived not in the Approach but in the Avenue itself. There you found the six-pound-a-week men . . . the men of affluence.

I can't pretend that any of this bothered me. I didn't feel deprived. I didn't mind being a working-class boy who could only bath himself once a week in a tin bath in the kitchen. It seemed a normal, if somewhat boring, thing to do. I was perfectly happy swathed in my parents' devotion, exploring the vast world of our tiny house and its neighbours. From the very beginning, my mother made me feel special. Perhaps this is the greatest gift a parent can give to a child. And I was, after all, the only child. When I asked why I didn't have any brothers or sisters, my mother, with a slight sniff, would produce one of her aphorisms: 'We couldn't do for two what we can do for one.' I believe now that this was a rationalisation which hid a great deal. I never knew the real reason. Perhaps she could not have more children; perhaps she could not face childbirth again. In any case, she was now hungrily ambitious for her only child. Circumstances had forced her into achieving very little for herself; and she knew early on that my father's sunny, untroubled temperament was not going to achieve it for her either. So all her ambition centred on me.

I loved both my parents. They seemed to me fabulous

creatures, expert in living and full of infinite strength and warmth. I would crouch under the living-room table, hidden by a long, red velveteen cloth which stretched to the floor. There I listened with delight as my parents went through a familiar routine. 'Where *has* he gone?' 'Has he run away?' 'Whatever shall we do?' At last my father would throw back the cloth and discover me doubled up in paroxysms of laughter. The huge figure would then lift me high in the sky and give me a colossal hug.

My parents were very physical and tactile. This surprises me now because their attitudes and morality were essentially late Victorian. They were very correct, very respectable. Looking back, it seems to me that Suffolk and East Anglia did not properly enter the twentieth century until the Second World War. But there was nothing prudish about my upbringing. I was cuddled and caressed. On Sunday mornings I would creep into my parents' bed, taking care, of course, to wriggle between them, and luxuriate in the sense of being physically at one with somebody else. This sense of recognition, of being seen by somebody else's eyes, of being appreciated and touched by another's hands, is the happiest sensation for a child. Out of it comes the first stirrings of a healthy sensuality. When I was three or four, I had a recurring erotic dream in which our next-door neighbour, her children and I all danced naked. We laughed as our willies bounced up and down. Our lady neighbour had, I noticed, a willy that was especially large. It was years before I knew there was any physical difference between boys and girls. It was also years before this stimulating fantasy faded.

I was taught to pray and believe in God. As a small child I prayed fervently for everyone I knew, especially my mother and father. I wondered, though, what God looked like. My mother could provide no clues. Vestiges of East Anglian puritanism made her chary of suggesting idolatrous images. So I settled on one for myself.

In my childhood, a poster was displayed everywhere. It

showed a maternal-looking peasant with a bonnet and an abundant, russet-coloured skirt. She held a large basket full of freshly reaped wheatstalks and brown eggs; she was the Ovaltine lady – a warm and cheerful earth-mother. I decided that she was God, and I thought of her when I said my prayers. My certainty was increased by regularly hearing a chorus of happy children on Radio Luxembourg. They sang in unison a catchy ditty beginning, 'We are the Ovaltinees, little girls and boys . . .' It was clearly a hymn of praise. My mother ticked me off roundly for being silly when, aged about five, I confessed to my secret God. I was hurt and indignant.

Religion was an automatic part of my life as a child, like a rather tasteless medicine administered regularly without explanation and without much hope of it doing any good. My parents went to church only for family rituals: marriages, christenings and deaths. My mother had a ready explanation: 'You don't need to be in a stuffy church to worship God. I can worship Him better outside in the fields, or in the streets when I look up at the blue sky,' she would announce. I said I felt exactly the same: I would much prefer to worship Him in the fields. But it didn't wash. I was packed off to Sunday School. I think now it gave them a chance to make love. I hope I am right.

Sunday School and children's services continued throughout my childhood. I liked them more after the age of eight. By then I had learnt the piano and was often asked to play the hymns. I realised when I was six that death is an experience all living creatures share, and that one day I would die. I was horrified, and the thought appalled me for days. Did this mean extinction? And if there was a heaven, where was it? The sheer *size* of space bewildered me. I was told that there were millions of stars, an infinite number of universes going on and on and on. Yet at some point, surely, space must stop? And then what? What was beyond it? What happened there and who was in charge? Was there another God in charge of God? Who started all this? I wasn't *sure* that it was God. And would it go on forever? As I grew older, I became more bewildered as I learnt about the evils men did in God's name. He seemed to change sides all the time. I comforted myself by playing the piano.

Our home didn't have much furniture and we didn't have much food – though it would be wrong to imply that I ever went hungry. My mother 'made do', but frequently reminded me that it was hard work. I don't think she exaggerated.

For my first twenty years, I constantly heard my mother boast that she always provided a good, cooked meal for my father's dinner. This occurred in the middle of the day. He would come home at about one o'clock, eat appreciatively and then go back to work. When he returned at night, there would be 'tea' on the table – large slices of white bread, home-made jam, home-made cakes and quantities of strong, sweet tea.

On Saturdays and Sundays, my father would visit the local pub and have a pint of bitter. Sometimes resources stretched to a pint-and-a-half or two pints. This would result in many complaints from my mother and the delay of dinner by a quarter of an hour. On Saturday nights, at precisely 9.15 p.m., he would return to the pub. He sometimes went on Sunday evenings as well, but it was not a routine – I think he believed that he should not make a habit of the pub on the Sabbath. Occasionally he bought ginger beer or a bottle of Guinness for my mother. These were frugal days.

I was a fussy child. I didn't like meat, but the weekly joint appeared in so many guises – roast, cold, minced, stewed – over its seven-day existence that the portions were tiny. We often had rabbit or hare given to my father by his country friends. When we ourselves moved to the country we snared rabbits; or thanked the local landowners effusively for the present of a partridge or pheasant. I hated milk and didn't want to eat eggs –

particularly the white of eggs. I was told off for my awkwardness. I could not bear fried food or fat in any form. My mother was bewildered. Fat and dripping were the stuff of life to her. She sobbed uncontrollably at the thought of my malnutrition. Some fifty-five years later I was tested for allergies and the doctors urged me to give up eggs and any product originating from the cow.

To a tiny boy, Bury St Edmunds was not a shabby little market town, but somewhere formidable and forbidding. I was overwhelmed by the rows upon rows of houses, by the frightening ruins of the Abbey – all sharp medieval flint – and by the enormous railway station where my father worked. I was proud of that; but even prouder to know that he had been a chorister at the forbidding church of St Mary's. The Playhouse cinema was more friendly. My father had appeared there as Giuseppe in *The Gondoliers* for the Amateur Operatic Society. This, I sensed, was the highlight of his youth.

The long walk from Avenue Approach across the town to the street where my grandparents and aunt had their houses terrified me. I don't remember traffic; I suppose there was little in those days. But I remember the multitude of houses – baleful houses that stared threateningly, united in keeping me out. My maternal grandmother's house was similar to ours – two up and two down with a kitchen at the back. But it was a place I hated visiting. There was a smelly loo in the backyard with a huge wooden seat which filled the entire wall. The loo paper was rough squares torn from the *Daily Mirror*. A smell permeated the house: the smell of age or decay or hidden dirt?

All the women of my family were fearsome cleaners, yet I suspect they were surface cleaners only. The hidden corners and the secret mouse holes went undetected. And the houses were always full of dogs – unwashed and spreading hair. My grandfather had a fine old collie whom I adored. Unwashed dog was the strongest smell of my childhood.

11

My grandmother's front parlour was loaded with gaudy porcelain knick-knacks and paintings of the Scottish Highlands at sunset. Amazingly there was a piano – not tremendously in tune, but with most of the keys working. My Uncle Bill, with Brylcreemed hair and engaging grin, would vamp the latest Fred Astaire hit. He added sheets of modern Gershwin or Cole Porter to the ancient music of *In a Monastery Garden.*

My grandfather had given up his job as a house-painter at fifty because of an attack of sciatica. He spent the next twenty years reading the *Daily Mirror*, smoking his pipe and listening to the radio. From time to time, he would keep an eye on his garden – though somebody else had to dig it for him.

My grandmother, huge and Victorian, was dignified, haughty and quick to take offence. She represented the past to me, the old days; just as Uncle Bill was modern and represented the future – a future, what's more, of cheerfulness and charm. But it was whispered (and I heard the whisper very early in life) that he was not a Pamment (my mother's family name). He had been a foundling, adopted gladly by my grandparents. He was not 'one of us'. That was doubtless why cheerfulness kept breaking in.

The rest of my mother's family were great moaners. They believed that life owed them a better living than it had provided, and were moody, introspective and always seeing implied insults in each other's behaviour. They loved to be proud of their grievances. 'They're not speaking,' I would be told of Uncle Ted, my mother's elder brother, and Auntie Gee, her elder sister. This would explain why another Sunday dinner at Grandma's had passed in inexplicable tension. Only Uncle Bill was always spry. But then he wasn't one of us . . .

The real 'us' was Uncle Ted – a brilliant, wayward man who could brood and sulk better than anyone. But he was also very funny, warm and generous. Like so many of his generation, he had left school at twelve or thirteen. But he was miraculous at making things. He had a lathe and all manner of brightly shining tools in my grandfather's shed. He took the *Model Engineer*, a magazine which displayed in each issue pictures of beautiful engines and machines in model form. I pored dizzily over back numbers and discussed them eagerly with him. He was the ideal uncle for a small boy. He promised to make me steam engines I could fire, model cars I could drive, model aircraft I could fly. I would dream great dreams. I would see the beginnings of these wonderful creations: little, beautifully-turned fragments of brass or small, spoked wheels that he had made with great precision. But nothing was ever finished. He never seemed to have the time.

One Christmas (it was 1935 when I was just five) Uncle Ted rigged a microphone in his outside workshop and, by ingenious wiring, hooked it into my grandfather's large wooden radio which stood by the window in the living room. On Christmas Eve, I was startled to hear a programme interrupted by a message from Father Christmas. He brought special greetings to Peter Hall of Bury St Edmunds. I was delighted, and either didn't notice or wasn't surprised that he had a strong Suffolk accent.

Uncle Ted earned a living as a car mechanic. Beneath his melancholy spirit and hypochondria (for he was always 'seriously' ill) was an instinctive understanding of mechanical devices that amounted to genius. In the late Thirties, he married Auntie Vera, a lovely and practical girl from Ipswich. A daughter and a son arrived, Jean and Roger, so I was soon, blessedly, no longer the only child in the family. But it was too late: I had been ten years without other children.

I still wonder what would have happened to Uncle Ted if he had had better opportunities and a slightly more positive approach to life. In middle age, much like his father, he gave up work for 'health reasons' and went on glowering at the world till he died of Parkinson's in his eighties, his marvellous talents sadly unfulfilled.

With his sister (Auntie Gee) and his father, he had started a small-holding for vegetables in the Fifties. It lost money. He and his father quarrelled cruelly, and ended up not speaking to each other. Many years later, his son would still not go to visit him, even when the old man was dying. At his funeral, I sat in the family car that followed the hearse, and noticed a figure standing alone at the grand iron gates of the cemetery. He clutched a battered bicycle in the pouring rain and was shrouded in a muddy, wet-streaked mac. It was Uncle Ted. As the car passed him I turned and looked back. He watched the hearse and its contents drive by without expression. Then he mounted his bike in the downpour and pedalled off in the opposite direction. We were not a forgiving family.

– 3 –

I showed a love of music early in life. I insisted on listening to the Salvation Army band in the Bury St Edmunds' marketplace every Saturday. And on Sunday mornings, I begged to walk by the military band from the barracks to great St Mary's as the Suffolk regiment went on its weekly church parade. I could hear nothing finer than the rattle of kettle drums and the crash of cymbals. My father or one of my uncles would walk with me. We never went into the church.

When I was six or seven I saw a brass band of toy soldiers parading in a shop window in Ipswich. I craved them with a passion that hurt. I told my Aunt Vera, who was an immediate friend to a small boy, all about the toy band. I told her of the wonders that would follow my possession of it. I could do counter-marches, tattoos and spectacular parades. It could figure on the stage of my toy theatre. I indicated that it would entirely change my life. I had little expectation that I would ever own this fine body of men, and I only half knew, in some recess of my mind, that I was begging Auntie Vera to buy the band – a box of delights that I am sure was far beyond her means. But I went on just the same. She encouraged me and I was obsessed.

On my birthday, the box of soldiers duly arrived, a present from Auntie Vera. I am still ashamed at the stratagems I used. Just before my thirtieth birthday, I fear I did the same thing. I was much taken by vintage motor cars and extolled their beauties to Leslie Caron, my wife, knowing that a friend had a 1922 Rolls-Royce he might be persuaded to sell. The open Rolls duly arrived on my birthday, with brass headlamps and a gearbox like a well-bred lorry. I felt as guilty then as I was when I cried with pleasure over the box of soldiers.

My Auntie Gee lived in the same road as my grandmother. I was always told that she and her younger sister, my mother, had been 'in business' together as young girls. They had actually been shop assistants at the local drapery store. They would sometimes take me to visit it. I loved to watch the change and the bills whizzing along the overhead wires. There are pictures of the sisters in their twenties, spruce in cloche hats, going out for the day on motorbikes with their fiancés: my father and Uncle Hugh Rainbird.

Uncle Hugh worked in a large corn-and-seeds shop on the outskirts of the town. He was an affable man but, sadly, an alcoholic, always 'out' at the Conservative Club or the Rotary Club, or having a drink with 'a valued client'. Aunt Gee spent her life sitting at home wondering when and in what state he would return. She prepared his meals punctiliously, but they were always spoiled because he was late. He would then mix everything – meat, vegetables, chopped Yorkshire pudding – into one great goo which he anointed with quantities of tomato sauce and vigorously stirred together. He said it was an aid to his digestion. I watched my aunt's face as this ritual proceeded and her cooking was systematically destroyed. The next day, she would produce another impeccable meal.

Aunt Gee had no children. She was a second mother to me, as encouraging and concerned as my real mother, and a trifle more lenient. When my mother was in hospital for a long period with an appendicitis which turned into peritonitis with complications, I lived with my aunt.

The only people we ever met were relations – 'family'. In the eighteen years I lived with my mother – from Avenue Approach to Cambridge and Whittlesford – I can't remember a single visitor who was not family coming into the house. I was allowed the occasional schoolfriend to play, but on a limited basis. My mother never had anybody call on her, nor did she wish it. Only with her own family, and particularly with Aunt Gee, was she intimate. 'Blood is thicker than water,' she would say grimly. 'You don't want other people putting their noses into your business and coming inside the house; better keep yourself to yourself.' Ironically, the only neat and tidy rooms in any of our houses – my mother's, my aunt's, or my grandmother's – were the front rooms which were never used. They contained the best furniture and awaited visitors who were never asked to come.

Our celebrations were always gatherings of relations. Every bank holiday, every Easter, every Christmas, we would make the journey to my grandmother's, where all the aunts and uncles assembled. This went for many weekends too. Once there, the men would leave for the pub, with Uncle Bill exuberantly in the lead, and my father, Uncle Ted and Uncle Hugh following. They often returned somewhat later than expected. Meanwhile, my grandfather would sit in his chair pulling on his pipe, and my grandmother, Auntie Gee, Auntie Vera and my mother all busied themselves with the cooking. As lunch got nearer, my dread increased: up to my tenth year, I found it impossible to eat anywhere but in my mother's house. I could sometimes manage fish and chips or bangers and mash in a café when we were on our annual week's seaside holiday. But I could not swallow my grandmother's cooking. Nor could I tolerate Aunt Gee's. The fatty flavours of the meat and the stale smell of the overdone vegetables nauseated me, though I suspect that the cooking must have been much the same as my mother's. I would try to force something down, but it wouldn't stay. Week after week I would sweat, feel sick, and then rush from the table and throw up. Sometimes this was real, sometimes it was the desperation of someone acting to escape a crisis.

The air was thick with reproach. I was told how rude I was, how indifferent to fine cooking, and how lucky my lot was compared with that of the starving millions of children all over the world. So every high-day and holiday, and many a Sunday, was a hell from which I longed to escape.

My stomach still turns as I remember the moment when the family prepared to sit at the table. My grandfather sharpens the carving knife and cuts the portions. Uncle Bill is ebullient and cheerful; Uncle Ted, watchful and wary. My father is talking to my grandfather about politics and the perfidy of management, while Uncle Hugh spreads tomato sauce on his goo. Meanwhile the women are tight-lipped and silent in their disapproval: the men, as usual, have been late back. The air is full of beer – and I am wishing that the floor would open and swallow me.

This nausea extended to school: I was unable to eat school meals until my early teens. I simply gagged on them. I have no memories of public holidays at twenty-four Avenue Approach because we were never there. I had no cousins or friends to play with at my grandmother's. What did I do on those endless days when the crisis of dinner had been lived through? I looked through the few books that my grandfather possessed. There was a shortened version of *Alice in Wonderland* – but with terrifying illustrations. All his books seemed to

have terrifying illustrations – engravings that belonged
to an old and forbidding age, like the ruins of Bury St
Edmunds' Abbey that always threatened me.

I looked through the books, banged on the piano,
and drew trains. My grandfather had quantities of lining
paper from his days as a decorator. These were cut into
long, seemingly endless strips, about eight inches wide. I
would draw a steam engine at the start of the strip and
then go on, adding truck after truck, van after van, until
I reached the end of the paper. Sometimes the drawings
were quite detailed. Goods trains, express trains, passenger trains, royal trains. They were always the LNER
– the London North Eastern Railway, my father's company – with apple-green locomotives and teak coaches.
This was the company of the Flying Scotsman and of
Mallard, the handsome 1930s Art Deco engine which
held the record for the fastest speed for steam. My
father was proud of his company, but ambivalent about
it. He longed, as a good union man and a supporter of the
Labour Party, to see the railways nationalised. I remember his jubilation after the war when it happened. And
his subsequent bitterness as pride and competitiveness
amongst railway men all but vanished, and standards
and investment declined.

Even so, he was a natural socialist, and remained
so all his life. He was gently radical, a caring man
who distrusted the ravages that a market economy
regularly produces. He believed in the rights of the
worker, but never trusted rules, dogmas, managers,
or politicians of any party. He was a staunch trade
union man until the Winter of Discontent in 1978. He
then developed as much scepticism about the unions
as he had naturally about every other institution. His
scepticism, though, was always understated, wrung out
of him reluctantly.

I once heard him protest vehemently at union behaviour. This was in the Seventies, in my early years running
the National Theatre. There was an agonisingly long

unofficial strike by the stage-hands. The union had no control of its more extreme members and was clearly frightened of them. It tried to preserve its position by not recognising the strike, but placated the militants by declaring the picket official. The theatre was therefore ringed by an official picket in support of an unofficial strike. The hope was that the actors would not cross the picket lines. Fortunately the actors ignored this absurd Alice-in-Wonderland situation and went on playing. My father was furious with the union's hypocrisy and angry that a minority could strike unofficially. 'They're bringing the whole Labour movement into disrepute,' he cried. 'The strike is unofficial so sack the lot of them.' I told him that Jim Callaghan's Britain had different principles from his.

– 4 –

At the age of five, my cosy, mother-filled existence was seriously disrupted. I was sent to the kindergarten just up the road – a mixed-sex establishment that was an appendage to the local, rather grand, East Anglian School for Girls. My parents believed (or at least my mother did, for she repeated it often) that what mattered in education was a good start. I cannot imagine how my parents afforded to send me to this school. They must have deprived themselves of all but the bare essentials.

I quickly liked school: the stories, the challenges, the competitiveness. And while I never much enjoyed the sports or the gym, I loved the percussion band. Anything to do with performing captivated me. I went to the theatre first when I was four. I saw *Robinson Crusoe* at the Playhouse, scene of my father's amateur operatic triumph. I was captivated by the darkness of the auditorium, the smell of the crowd, the music. It was a very erotic experience. I was particularly excited by all the blacked-up people in grass skirts.

Soon after I started kindergarten, a travelling puppet theatre visited the school and performed an entire *Sleeping Beauty* with string puppets, delicate sets, special lights, and a curtain that went up and down. I was transported and decided there and then to be a puppeteer when I grew up. That performance, and appearing as the 'Spider' in a dramatisation of *Little Miss Muffet*, set me on course. My costume was elaborate – made out of wire by my father and lovingly covered in black crepe paper by my mother. I was already addicted to making fantasies.

As I came to the end of my two happy years at kindergarten, we suddenly moved. My father had been promoted. He became a stationmaster, fifth class, at Barnham – a small railway station between Bury St Edmunds and Thetford. To us sophisticated townees (for that is how we saw ourselves) to go from Bury to Barnham was stepping back into the wilderness. The idea of living there raised wails of protest from my mother and from me. But my father, although proudly unambitious, insisted on being his own boss. He wanted to go to Barnham, so we went. And at Barnham, he came into his kingdom. It was a single-line railway station with a signal box and one goods siding. There were four passenger trains a day, two each way; and a goods train at noon. My father reigned over all this, wearing a gold-braided cap inscribed 'Station Master'. He had a staff of three – a signalman, a junior clerk, and an odd-job man. They were quickly very fond of him.

Our house was part of the station itself. It had two rooms downstairs, one a kitchen, and two bedrooms and a box room upstairs. There was an outside loo, no bathroom, and no gas, electricity or running water. The water pump outside froze regularly in winter, and we lived and breathed oil from the oil lamps. Our wireless was powered by large chemical batteries that were taken to the village each week to be charged. My father listened compulsively to the news; it was a passion of his. He chose his newspaper with care; first the *Daily Herald*, then later the *News Chronicle*. Finally, to my surprise, when I was in my early teens, he changed to the *Daily Telegraph*. When I questioned him about this, he observed that all newspapers were prejudiced and had no compunction about telling lies. The *Daily Telegraph* was no different except that it was so immoderately and invariably right-wing that he knew where he was. He also thought its news coverage was thorough.

Barnham was a very cold place. It was set just where the huge west Suffolk skies and tiny villages give place to the exotic brecklands of Norfolk, full of fern and pinewood and crying birds. The brecklands were like a jungle to me. I would not have been surprised to see a lion looking through the undergrowth. I collected birds' eggs and set them in labelled compartments in a crudely carpentered box. I climbed trees to look in the nests and learned to detect a cuckoo's egg – always a perfect match to the blue of thrush or green and beige of blackbird. It matched, but it was ominously too large. The mother bird would be reassured by the colour but not, curiously, worried by the size. I once saw a hatched-out cuckoo in a nest: a big triumphant bird with a hollow in its back. It had heaved out all the other young and they had smashed to death on the ground.

I fell in love with the huge spaces of Suffolk. It was an idyll full of violence and blood. I watched my mother skin a rabbit or yank the insides of a chicken out with her bare hands. Blood and offal and horse manure (always so good for the garden) were part of my everyday life. Understanding and accepting the violence of nature was, said my father, necessary 'if you were to be a man'.

At harvest time, we went gleaning. We picked up the ears of grain the binder had left in the fields so that we could feed them to our chickens through the autumn. All the village would be out: it was a party. The binder went round and round, and the square of corn in the centre became smaller and smaller as the sheaves were stacked up. Finally, there was a patch of wheat only some thirty feet square. All the living things of the field – the rabbits, the voles, the hares, the fieldmice – had taken refuge in it. We gathered round, the men with guns trained. At a signal, stones were thrown into the wheat and the first rabbit broke cover. The other animals, panic-stricken, followed. The air was filled with shots and shouts. The rabbits and hares hijacked into the air as the shots pierced them. The village cheered.

My father loved Barnham. We were still poor, but we managed. And he didn't have to work hard. He met each infrequent train and checked its arrival and departure with his large pocket watch. He dug his garden, saw to the flowerbeds on the station platform, tended his vegetables, talked to the farmers, and happily received tribute of game or rabbit from the local landowners. The Duke of Grafton's estate was the biggest in our area; his name was spoken with awe.

The crisis in my education had been solved in a way that I still do not quite understand. It was assumed that I would be condemned to the village school. But my father had been a pupil at the Bury St Edmunds' Secondary School for Boys. He still knew the headmaster and, I suppose, pulled some strings. After an interview and a test, it was agreed that, although I was only seven, I could join the class of ten-year-olds, commuting the five or six miles to Bury each day. I went on the train, in the charge of some older pupils. There were leather straps on the windows and brass catches on the doors. And the upholstery, even on this meagre little railway line, far outshone the furniture I was used to at home. I felt very privileged. There was a bookstall among the boxes of fish on the platform of Bury St Edmunds' station. I hoarded my pocket money and bought comics.

I was made to feel special at home. But there was a

disadvantage: any injury or illness, however slight, was seen as a disaster. So by the time I was six or seven, I was intellectually adventurous but physically timid. The school was tough, the boys big and boisterous; I was small and vulnerable, and also intelligent beyond my years. I was by far the youngest in the school – an oddity, an outsider. But being different did not make me feel un-happy. I had started to feel rather clever – though I didn't tell anybody.

My parents made me understand that learning was the one certain way to betterment. I was always allowed time to read and to listen to music on the radio, and was encouraged to ask questions. My mother would lament that she had left school early. She believed in books; but I never saw her read one. Housework gave her no time, she said. She was a terrible organiser, flitting constantly from one task to another. She was forever tired, forever worried, forever flustered. She scurried through life like an anxious hen. Our house was in a continuous state of chronic yet homely untidiness. There were odd bits and pieces of furniture, odd leavings of materials and orna-ments passed on to us or picked up. 'I can never sit down for a minute,' she would say. 'If only I could get the weight off my feet.' I was expected to help by running errands, going to the general stores or (when we moved to Cam-bridge) to the fish and chip shop. If I had no homework I occasionally dried the washing-up or shelled the peas. But men in our family did not help with the housework. It was not expected. They dug the garden, laid the fires and filled the oil lamps, but that was all. Reading a book let me off many a session of washing-up; but it had to be 'serious'. Comics would not do.

– 5 –

Barnham was a paradise for a small boy. My friend and mentor was Charlie Kent, the gamekeeper. He was old to the eyes of a six-year-old boy though he could barely have been fifty. He had been in the trenches in the First World War. He had no family and had never married. He lived by himself in one of a row of cottages which were reached by crossing the station yard and jumping a stream. His garden seemed always to be full of blooms – sweetpeas and roses and irises. Everything gleamed and shone in his cottage, polished like the toes of his splendid gamekeeper's boots. He was precise, though not in the least prissy.

He had three spaniels, brown and white with soft warm muzzles. They were great friends to a small boy. I grew up with dogs, and have tried to keep them later in life. For ten years at Stratford, in the Sixties, I had an Old English sheepdog named Simpkin (after an Elizabethan clown); and on my fortieth birthday, my children gave me a beautiful St Bernard puppy, who during his short life seemed to eat half a horse a day. He died of heart failure at ten months, his frame too big for the heart that sustained it – apparently a common failing in this huge breed. I have had no more dogs.

Charlie Kent was a man of few words – which is perhaps why I cannot remember his voice. I trailed behind him as he tramped round the Duke of Grafton's estate, both of us looking out for poachers or snared rodents. He tended the chick pheasants as they hatched out from under their foster hen. He always wore a flat cap, a greenish herring-bone jacket and jodhpurs with brown leather gaiters. He was reserved and respectful to his bosses and his betters; but there was a twinkle in the eyes

24

above his tiny sandy moustache. He gave me many rare pieces of information. I remember particularly the story of a bird seldom seen – the red-backed shrike. Charlie showed unusual excitement when we found evidence of it in a thorn bush. The nest was surrounded with a fearsome quantity of thorns and on each was a little blood-soaked mess.

Charlie explained that this was the 'larder' the mother had prepared for her offspring. She had placed flies, grubs and pieces of worm on the spikes and would later take them off to feed her young. When they got a little larger they would lean out of the nest and select juicy morsels for themselves. It seemed to me logical; better than a poor mother bird working her wings off to feed a monstrous baby cuckoo.

Long after I left Barnham, I heard that Charlie had been dismissed. He was old and ill, and died soon after. He received nothing for his lifetime of devoted work except his pension from the state. This wouldn't have surprised him. He expected nothing from the masters. 'There's "us" and there's "them",' he would say, 'and that's all there is to it.'

In 1970, I made a film based on Ronald Blythe's book, *Akenfield*, a portrait of a Suffolk village before and after two World Wars. The film was very near to my heart and one of the most directly personal things I have ever done. The characters in it were played by real people – local Suffolk people – improvising from their experiences and their knowledge of the place. I could hear my grandfather talking. I spent nearly a year on *Akenfield*; it took me back to Barnham and to Charlie Kent.

As well as the countryside, there was the station: another new world. I don't remember any school friends, but there were long hours spent in the signal box with the signalman. It was always overheated and had a huge stove merrily burning LNER coal. An impenetrable fug rose from the signalman's pipe. The cabin had a dozen white,

25

black and red metal levers standing upright. By tugging on one of these you could, with a mighty effort, shift the points or alter the signals. Each ticking telegraph monitor had a wooden handle that could be wiggled to and fro to send information to the neighbouring stations on the whereabouts of trains.

Trains then were steam trains. I still love them. They are fearsome, powerful and noisy, but somehow alive and unpredictable. A diesel engine keeps its power to itself, throbbing anonymously. But the old steam engines were proud of flaunting their power and seemed to have individual personalities. Even the little tank engines that served my father's station were noisy and particular. I was allowed in the driver's cabin, a rattling place of heat and smells. I was excited by the roar of the fire as the fireman piled on the coals. Each noon in the school holidays, I would ride on the tank engine as it shunted the goods trucks. I sang George Formby songs and played my ukelele.

I was given this ukelele one sea-side holiday. We had a week at St Leonards, made possible by my father's free travel as a railway man. We sat one morning in a large hall at the end of the pier. A band was playing – in my memory a huge Glenn Miller-like assembly, but probably some four or five musicians. There was community singing. The band leader, seeing this seven-year-old singing lustily, invited me up on stage to do a solo. I found myself singing into a large square microphone, lowered to match my height. I heard my own voice as the sea crashed outside. I was aware of many smiling faces, full of attention and approval as I sang.

> *Red sails in the sunset*
> *Way over the sea*
> *Oh carry my loved one*
> *Home safely to me*

The applause was tremendous. Or so it seemed to me.

We made further morning visits and I performed other songs: *Deep Purple* and *I Dream of San Marino*. Then one night there was a special treat. Abandoning our 'all-found' agreement at the boarding house, which provided us with a substantial, cooked high tea at the end of each day, we went to the pier for our evening meal. The band was now in tuxedos and couples were dancing. It was an altogether more serious and adult atmosphere. This was style.

I waited for my moment. Surely the band leader would call on me to perform? The audience, I was certain, would be delighted. The minutes went by and no call came. Eventually my father paid the bill and we left. I was heartbroken. I was a very vain little boy. It was an early and painful lesson on the fickleness of reputation.

My parents never mentioned then or later that there had been a possibility of me singing that night. But they bought me the ukelele banjo, with George Formby's signature on the drumskin, as a holiday present. I bore it back to Barnham and played it to the engine drivers.

My father's colleagues, the engine drivers, signalmen, firemen and porters, must have been very tolerant. I was without doubt precocious. Yet they were friendly and encouraging. I remember that generation of railway men as a remarkable breed. I see them as Edwardian gentlemen – impeccably turned out, with big moustaches, stiff white collars, and gold chains attached to their pocket watches. The convention was to be hardworking, proud of one's job, and to be seen to be doing it well. They probably had no more of these virtues than subsequent generations; but even if they were pretending, they convinced. Since the Second World War, the convention has changed. It is now smart to pretend to work as little as possible, and to affect not to care. It is clever to skive. In my father's day the trains were clean, and extraordinarily punctual. I can still recall his utter dismay when one was a few minutes late. And I can't

Making an Exhibition of Myself

remember one ever being cancelled.

To me, the railways were a world of power, of travel, and of change. I became an avid model railway enthusiast. My imagination was fed by the *Meccano Magazine*, *Hobbies Weekly*, and, above all, Uncle Ted's *The Model Engineer*, that awesome publication for real men, men with lathes. I made things compulsively. But the gap between my dream and the reality I could achieve was discouraging. I would quickly move on to the next project.

While we were at Barnham, my father presented me with two second-hand Basset-Lowke model steam engines, one a tanker, one with a tender. They were old, a little battered and very asthmatic, so their power was not to be relied on. But I loved them as they charged round an oval track on the kitchen floor hurling steam and water and methylated spirits in all directions.

Uncle Hugh noticed my passion. And although he was no handyman, he announced that he was going to make me a model station. On my birthday, he gave me a square-shaped package wrapped in brown paper. Inside was a strange-looking box open on one side with a ledge running along the bottom. It didn't look at all like a railway station, and I was very disappointed. Tactfully, I said nothing; I didn't want to appear ungrateful. I also had a secret thought: if I made a few changes, it would do very well as a model theatre.

My mother provided a stage curtain from a piece of green velvet trimmed with orange ribbon. I constructed a complicated system of rubber bands which, when connected to my Meccano clockwork motor, whizzed the curtain up and down at alarming speed. I made sets and painted them. The characters were mostly cut-outs from the Walt Disney magazine. I pasted the figures on thin plywood and then painstakingly fretted them out with my fretsaw. I did not tell Uncle Hugh what I was doing. Later, he attended a performance at my theatre, formerly his station. Tactfully, he said nothing.

28

My play-making was fed by films: *Snow White and the Seven Dwarfs* and Errol Flynn in *Robin Hood*. There was no theatre except for the annual pantomime and the amateur operatics. I went only to the pantomime. When I was ten or eleven, I sneaked through an exit door into *Gone With the Wind* – it was banned for children. I heard with terror the pain of Melanie's baby being born. I knew nothing of this because no-one had ever told me. Could this be why my mother often pointedly referred to what she went through when she gave birth to me? I was bewildered. I couldn't feel responsible.

There was one miraculous Christmas at Barnham, with thick snow and very low temperatures. When I crept out of bed in the middle of the night to use the chamber pot, its contents were frozen solid. I tobogganed in the fields on a tin tray and the uncles built a huge snowman in the station yard. I had a batch of ducklings which hatched out under a broody hen. I kept them warm with an oil lamp. Everything was secure.

Then, suddenly, it was all change again. My father was promoted. He was given a job on the 'Relief' – which meant he replaced stationmasters who were on holiday, or sick, at a variety of stations over a large area of East Anglia. It was necessary to live in Cambridge – a world away and a huge city. My mother, who had raised great objections to the primitive backwardness of Barnham, now went into floods of tears about leaving it. She didn't want to leave Suffolk, she didn't want to go to the city, and she certainly didn't want to go to Cambridge. Consequently, neither did I. We both cried loudly throughout the whole of one night. But my father was adamant. This was the next step, and he was going to take it. In any case, he thought it would be good to get me away from a country atmosphere. Cambridge might be more of a challenge.

Though he rarely expressed strong feelings, my father could be suddenly firm. I think this came from his extraordinary common sense and self-containment. He didn't dramatise; he had great dignity. My mother was always seeing disasters – real and imagined – on the horizon. I'm sure she must have worried him continuously. But he spent a large part of his life successfully refusing to be provoked while my mother did her utmost to provoke him.

There may have been another reason for our move. The family thought that Barnham would be a dangerous place if there were a war. Near to it, buried in the brecklands, was a large underground storehouse for explosives. Occasionally my father would work long hours because a 'special' was coming through. A dark train, bearing bombs, would arrive in the middle of the night and my father would anxiously shepherd it to its objective. In those Barnham years, I heard a great deal about Hitler and a great deal about Mussolini. And I remember Munich. No-one in our family thought there would be peace in our time.

– 6 –

Our new home was on the outskirts of the city of Cambridge, a semi-detached house at twenty-two Blinco Grove. My mother stopped protesting for a while; it appeared that we had come up in the world. The house was painted green and cream and actually had electricity. There was no bathroom, but the loo was, for the first time, part of the house, though still outdoors. For the first time, too, I had a room of my own which was warm enough to work in during the day. I did not notice that the house was built on the cheap, that its garden was puny, its environment dull. When it rained heavily, the bend of Blinco Grove flooded the road to a depth of two feet or more. I always hoped that the water would engulf the front parlour; it was still never used.

Cambridge itself thoroughly alarmed me. The colleges reminded me of the frightening medieval ruins of the Abbey at Bury St Edmunds. There were other monstrous things: the long single platform of the station; the endless windy loneliness of Hills Road that had to be travelled to reach Blinco Grove. The maze of streets made me nervous too. There were no trees and no fields. I fell into a deep depression which lasted for months. I wanted to be back at Barnham with Charlie Kent. Children weren't supposed to have depressions in those days; it was considered an indulgence even in an adult. To everyone's consternation, I frequently burst into tears. There were family councils at Bury St Edmunds at the weekends. We journeyed there on the train, using my father's privileged rail travel. The aunts and uncles shook their heads and feared that I had always been highly strung. They thought I read too much: it tired the brain, and then the imagination became feverish and took over. I suppose that it would have been easier if I'd had brothers or sisters. At least there would have been someone to share my problems with. And my mother would certainly have been happier with three or four children to look after. She was a natural mother.

I have felt suicidal several times. A passion not to go on has overwhelmed me on many key occasions in my life. This was the first time it struck and, because I had fewer inner resources and less to distract me than when I was grown-up, it was perhaps the worst time of all. I was very near the brink.

I was sent to the Morley Memorial, an elementary school just round the corner from Blinco Grove. I found a good deal of bullying there. The classes were large and the discipline strong. I, an only child of eight and a loner from the wilds of Suffolk, was mocked by brawling boys and giggling girls. Perhaps it was because I had a thick Suffolk burr. I remember how the children listened to me and then burst out laughing. But at the time I wasn't aware of any accent. My mother was certainly keen that I should speak properly, but nothing was ever done about it. She primly corrected my more outrageous expressions; but though she saved from the housekeeping money to pay for me to learn the piano, the resources mercifully didn't extend to elocution lessons. The real Suffolk sound has long gone from my voice, my accent settling in to the not-quite-U that I have carried with me since my teens. But I can still hear the original vowels and inflections in my voice, as I can hear them in my fellow Suffolkmen, David Frost and Trevor Nunn. My parents kept their Suffolk voices until the end of their days. I loved their sound. But if I return to Suffolk now, the speech soon depresses me. I think of family gatherings and constraint.

My depression was acute and today would be considered very dangerous. Cambridge continued to be full of alarming foreign things: flatness; the cold of the Fens; crowded buses; huge recreation grounds with swings and wooden roundabouts that hurt my ankles and knees. I walked through the Mill Road district and noticed poverty for the first time. Deprivation is always more evident in the town than in the country. I survived, as I was always to survive, by frantic activity. I gradually came back from the brink.

The school was bearable because it was just round the corner from home; if the worst happened, I knew it would only take me two minutes to reach the safety of my mother. Further up the road, I found the delights of the public library. There I could escape into richer and richer fantasy.

Richmal Crompton's William enthralled me; I laughed and laughed at his anarchy and independence. I discovered Bulldog Drummond and the adventure culture of the *Boy's Own Paper*. I never felt part of Imperial Britain because I belonged to the wrong class and went to the wrong schools. But it was thrilling nonetheless to see how much British pink there was on the map of the world. And I discovered Dickens. His melodrama excited me; he seemed to capture the terror of living. My father gave me a complete edition in tiny print and uncertain binding which he had obtained cheaply by cutting coupons from a daily newspaper – I think it was the *News Chronicle*.

My mother said she had read most of the major novels, but I was perfectly sure she hadn't. I loved her pretensions and the fact that I could see right through them. She was always ready with a fluent speech of appreciation about Fagin or Pip or Mr Micawber. This was her talent: she accumulated knowledge and critical opinions by some kind of osmosis. If a judgement was in the air, she would pick it up. She was one of those people who didn't need to see the play or read the book or see the film. She already knew what it was like.

On my ninth birthday, my parents gave me a full-size bicycle. It looked huge. It had wooden blocks on the pedals so that my short legs could cope with its height. I would grow into it, they said. I took to cycling all over Cambridge. Somehow the streets seemed less threatening if I could cross and recross them on my huge black Raleigh steed. This bicycle served me all the way through university as well as school. It was finally stolen from outside my college in my last year.

The longing for Barnham began to fade. I made the first friends that I can remember. I joined a gang of four or five other boys. We did everything together. Our model was, of course, William and the Outlaws.

I fell in love too. She was a fragile-looking blonde with blue eyes called Monica. I watched her all day in my class at school. I kissed her during Postman's Knock at a party. She seemed to find me absurd, and I suppose I was. She giggled at my intensity.

— 7 —

I was sitting on the back steps shelling peas for my mother on a Sunday morning in September when Chamberlain announced on the radio that we were at war with Germany. It had been long-expected, but it was still a terrible shock. We thought there would be immediate change in our lives, but it didn't come, at least not at first. Our family unit was more secure than most. My father was in his late thirties and as a railway man was in a reserved occupation, unlikely to be called up. We already had air-raid shelters at school. They were right in the middle of the playground, as if playtime were permanently over. But air-raid practice and gas-mask drill were treats. They were not only a welcome escape from lessons but an opportunity to tickle the girls in the half-gloom.

At home, when the air raids eventually came, we sheltered under the table. Sometimes we put blankets down and spent the whole night there. It was a monumental Edwardian table, in light oak, that filled our tiny room. My father had bought it for very little at a sale. I believed it was thick enough and strong enough to protect us from any bomb. We heard the German aircraft throbbing overhead on their way to London or to Coventry. Occasionally, an unused bomb would be unleashed on the way back. I saw a Cambridge house with its front sliced off about three streets away from us. All the people had been killed. Their home was exposed indecently, like a tatty doll's house. I was very frightened. But the war made me feel closer to my parents and more a member of my school. I was now proud to be part of Cambridge; and my depression began to lift.

I watched the Battle of Britain from our back garden and saw Spitfires chasing Messerschmitts through the clear blue sky while my mother yelled at me to take cover. I was feeding my rabbits: they were part of my war effort. I bred them and took them to market to sell for meat. I built a box trailer on pram-wheels to fasten to the back of my bike, and cycled out into the countryside to pick grass and clover from the roadsides to feed the ravenous horde. At my peak, I owned sixty-nine rabbits. I listened awestruck to the screams of the doe when I introduced a buck into her cage. It was fascinating. Were the screams pain or pleasure? My mother watched too and, with an air of putting somebody right, said, 'It's not very pleasant, you know.' We did not eat my rabbits. The rabbit meat that regularly appeared at our table was the wild variety given as presents to my father as he journeyed round the country stations of East Anglia: 'A brace of rabbits for the stationmaster . . .'

My father took an allotment and I dug for victory with him. I helped him make black-out frames for all our windows – squares of wood battens with black roofing felt stretched over them. I had a map of Europe and little flags with which I tried to keep track of what was happening. I gave up when we were swept out of France.

The night after Dunkirk, Blinco Grove was filled with grimy, exhausted soldiers, some of them alarmingly bloodstained and bandaged. They sat on their kit bags on the kerb in the evening sunlight. Each house took in one soldier and gave him a bath and a meal. Our soldier was grateful for the tin bath in the kitchen. But he wasn't very communicative.

By the autumn of 1940, it seemed as if the war would never end. Or if it did, that we would lose it. I was mightily impressed by Churchill's radio speeches. He sounded like a leader and gave me hope. I was shocked to find that my father didn't share my enthusiasm; nor did my grandfather, nor the majority of my uncles.

Churchill, they said, was a Tory and his Tory past and treatment of the working man could not be easily forgotten or forgiven. He might be doing a good job now – he had always had the gift of the gab – but he should not be trusted in the future.

I did better and better at school. I was selected to be one of the pupils who took the scholarship exam. If I did well, I would go to the Cambridge County Council Secondary Modern School. If I did very well I might win a place at the Perse – an ancient grammar school that had been going since the seventeenth century.

I sat the exam and was interviewed by the headmaster of the Perse. He was the tallest man I had ever seen. He had a cavernous bass voice and a threatening manner. He was reputedly a monster who shouted at boys with unbridled ferocity before caning them. He smiled at me under his thick black moustache and asked me what I wanted to be when I grew up. Like every other boy at that time, my head was full of Spitfires, Hurricanes, Lancasters and Heinkels. 'An aeronautical engineer,' I replied. Fortunately he didn't ask me what the job entailed, and he awarded me a scholarship.

In the autumn of 1941, I began my progress through the school as a Minor Scholar, together with three other boys. We were paid for by the Local Authority. Major Scholars (of whom there were even fewer) were funded by the school itself. We Minor Scholars had dirty, dog-eared books covered with the notes and protests of previous generations. On each flyleaf, stamped in big letters, was the slogan: 'Minor Scholars' Book. This book is the property of the Perse School and must be returned on demand'. I have always loved books, particularly their physical nature – their colour, feel and smell. It infuriated me that such worn-out rags should be given to the scholarship boys. The other boys had shiny new books, bought for them by their (no doubt) well-off parents. I knew I was an outsider, but I didn't want to be reminded of it every time I opened my books.

Better Lucky Than Rich

In the Thirties, the Perse boasted a remarkable teacher called Caldwell Cook. He had pioneered a method of teaching English – and particularly Shakespeare – by 'playing' it. He wrote a book which, in its day, was the herald of much that was to follow in the Fifties and Sixties. It was called *The Play-Way*. When I arrived at the school, Caldwell Cook was long dead. But something of his pioneering tradition survived. My earliest memory of Shakespeare is of a group of eleven-year-olds, armed with wooden shields and swords and cloaks, shouting *Macbeth* at each other. We played on a minute stage which Cook had installed in a basement. It was known as the Mummery; it smelt musty and was falling apart. The experience of acting the play was immediate and exciting. It never occurred to me not to love Shakespeare. He was thrilling and blood-soaked and full of witches. I wanted to know more about him.

In spite of the war, life developed a stately rhythm at Blinco Grove. The diet was predictable because of rationing. There were very few sweets and no toys. My model railway was not what it might have been in peacetime. I cycled to and from school each day down the wet and windy Hills Road. I worked hard at my lessons, and enjoyed cricket, tennis, athletics and swimming. I was becoming more of a sportsman. I liked the summer sports. I did *not* enjoy rugby, which seemed to me to involve either standing around in the cold, longing for some action or, if I finally got the ball, being violently and painfully attacked by a mob of opponents.

A family of evacuees, bombed out in London, moved into the house directly opposite. Edith was the daughter of the family and I fell passionately in love with her. I kissed and kissed her in the darkness of the autumn garden. She tired of the activity but I wanted to go on and on. Sexual passion is agony before we have the means to assuage it.

My mother was delighted to discover that our next-door neighbour, Mr Spink, gave piano lessons at 6d a time. By very careful management, she and my father purchased a second-hand piano. I was then introduced to Mr Spink and began work. I had a great facility for the piano, and by the time I was twelve was playing Mozart and Beethoven with an ease I find frustratingly impossible now. On my tenth birthday I was taken to Mozart's *Requiem*. The following week, I stood at the back at the Arts Theatre with my mother and heard Sadler's Wells perform *The Marriage of Figaro*. It was my first *Figaro*. I loved the music, but I thought the drama sugary and affected. Perhaps the production wasn't very sexy.

Life is largely about luck – and, when you are young, the luck of having the right stimulus at the right time. Long before my adolescence, Shakespeare and Mozart were firmly lodged in my heart.

I loved jazz as much as I loved classical music. I still do. The average classical musician (and I stress average) is not allowed to make music in the committed way of a jazz musician. He too often just plays the notes – accurately no doubt, but without personal inflection. The style of the great jazz-man is uniquely his own.

A group of boys shared this interest. We listened to the radio and passed the rare record from hand to hand. I had to listen at other people's homes because we had no gramophone. Out of these enthusiasms came, in the early years of the war, Peter Hall and His Band: I played the piano, and my friends supported me with trumpet, accordian, drums and clarinet. We played our repertoire in village halls around Cambridge in aid of the Red Cross.

This was the first time that life cast me as a leader. Being an only child can make you shy or assertive; I was by turns both. I hadn't had many friends in my early years. Friends began at Blinco Grove – and particularly when I reached the Perse. The old grammar schools were very clear in their system. Leaders – to be captain of cricket or a prefect or (the ultimate accolade) head of

school – emerged by talent. Often a fledgling talent was
encouraged by the staff. I was a maverick but the system
could still use me. I always felt an outsider, by birth
and position. But my confidence grew as more and more
responsibility was given to me. I don't think I was
ambitious – but by my early teens I knew that I could
lead a group, and that people seemed to accept me. As I
prospered, won prizes, performed this and was appointed
to that, my mother's pride swelled. It was her view that,
provided I didn't do something silly, I was on my way to
being somebody. She already saw me as a grammar-
school teacher with a suitable wife and family, security
and a pension. 'It's better to be born lucky than rich,'
she would say, smiling in approval. I didn't like that: I
didn't feel particularly lucky. But I was of course wrong.
I was lucky to have her unswerving belief, and her
courage and support.

– 8 –

About half-way through my time at the Perse, my father
gave up his peripatetic life as a relief stationmaster. I
regretted this. I had travelled all over East Anglia with
him during my school holidays. I had seen Ely Cathedral,
the endless blackness of the Fens and the rich textures of
Constable country. It was an area of great variety and it
was where I belonged.

He now moved up a class, and became stationmaster
at Shelford, some four or five miles outside Cambridge.
Once more we lived over the shop; but now forty or fifty
trains went thundering past the bedrooms every night.
This was a busy line – Cambridge to Liverpool Street.

Shelford was already virtually a suburb of Cambridge,
but you could still see the village. There were a few shops,
a post office and a church; and fields where I could fly

the model aeroplanes I built. The rabbits were no more, but we kept a goat, and it was my daily responsibility to milk it. Our home, brown and dark and airless, was attached to the station booking hall and office on one of the two platforms. The plumbing in the house was basic. There was the usual outside loo, but because it was part of the station building, it was mercifully not as cold. I associate defecation in my youth with being chilled to the bone. There was a bath, but it was in the kitchen and covered by a wooden top which my mother used as a working surface for her cooking. Once a week, this top was cleared and lifted, kettles were heated and poured, and we all took a bath. This was a luxury. When I first went to Russia in the late Fifties, I was struck by a familiar smell – fusty, heavy and woollen. It belonged to my childhood. It was body odour – something we all lived with before bathing became a daily habit.

The garden at Shelford butted straight on to the back of the platform and ran practically the length of it. It was full of flowers. My father grew his vegetables across the road in a plot just opposite the signal box. It was a time of shortages, so we cultivated and reared everything we could. In addition to the goat, we had a flock of Rhode Island Red chickens led by one proud cock. They ran wild in the tiny goods shed. As one of the main commodities brought to the station was grain for the local mill, they waxed very fat and laid many eggs. My father was delighted. He always remained a peasant, despite his reasonable education. He could make things grow anywhere, and would have kept chickens on the moon. He was the perfect father for a country boy. I would tag along happily behind him, collecting the eggs, picking wild mushrooms, counting the ducks. But my other self, the grammar-school boy with artistic pretensions, was finding it harder and harder to talk to him.

He still sang occasionally while I accompanied him on the piano. His repertoire was the Savoy operas and ballads such as *Until* and *The Road to Mandalay*. My

40

mother also sang, in a reedy, tremulous voice. She was particularly fond of *Because*:

> *Because I come to you with accents sweet*
> *I feel the roses growing round my feet*
> *Because . . .*
> *I COME TO YOU*

I became more and more condescending about their Edwardian songs and about Gilbert and Sullivan. I found the operas sentimental and winsome, and the years have not converted me. The flippancy and sexlessness of Gilbert and Sullivan has done much to inhibit British taste. Facetiousness breaks in every few bars, and they seem to me a form of arrested development, prep school opera, full of jolly tunes, but without sex or ambiguity.

When I was thirteen, I supplemented my pocket money by hand-pumping the organ in the village church at Stapleford, a short bicycle ride from Shelford. It was a strenuous occupation if the hymns were long, especially if the organist became over-excited in the last verse and pulled out all the stops. The wind required then was alarming and needed double-quick action with the wooden handle. I was soon trying to play the primitive but sweet-toned instrument myself. One of my friends pumped for me; not very willingly and not for very long. After a few lessons, I was allowed to practise alone at Little Shelford Church. The organ there boasted an electric pump.

Each practice terrified me. Twice a week, on cold, dark winter evenings in the half-light, my cycle lamp bobbing, I pedalled my way along the lanes to the church, stood my bicycle against the wall, and walked across the graveyard to the church door, closing it behind me with a crash that seemed to reverberate all round the village. I was not permitted to turn on the lights. I picked my way down the aisle, my torch beam jumping among the pews, before climbing up the spiral staircase to the organ. All the time,

I was aware of creaks and groans, sudden cracks, and hisses that seemed like distant whisperings. An empty church at night is a very noisy place. And every noise has an echo.

After unlocking the keyboard, and turning on the one small light on the music stand, I tried to thaw my hands. They were by now so frozen they were incapable of feeling the keys. The first note of the organ was a violation of the silence. It seemed it must wake the village, if not the dead: organ notes from an empty church in the middle of the night. In fact, it was about 7 p.m. and I was a frightened teenage boy sitting in the organ loft with one tiny bulb illuminating me in a sea of darkness.

As I practised and the sound of the organ rolled on, I felt safer. I loved mixing sounds, combining the stops. And I loved the loud grumble of the deep bass notes. The pedal keys quivered under my feet as I played and the sound went right up through my body. The trouble always was the final climactic chord. As it echoed away into the church, I was left with a deafening silence. And then the church noises began again. The only solution was to start another piece as quickly as possible.

I continued my organ practices doggedly, was confirmed, and at sixteen became, for a year or more, the organist for the weekly children's service. Then, in my last two years at school, reason consumed me and obliterated my faith. Ten of Bernard Shaw's plays had been issued in a collected Penguin edition; also ten books by H. G. Wells, including his *History of the World*. I read all these, and *The Life of Christ*, and Samuel Butler's *Erewhon* and *The Way of All Flesh*. With a feeling of enormous relief, I gave up religion. It has worried me ever since. I stopped playing the organ too. I haven't played in a church for forty-five years.

I came to man's estate at Shelford. The outward signs were pimples, razor cuts, and worrying stiff patches of

dried semen on my pyjama trousers. My mother sym-
pathised delicately over these constant night emissions,
not realising (or so I hoped) that they were largely self-
induced. I worried about masturbation, of course. School
was always rife with rumours about the madness, disease
and death that it brought on. But I didn't worry enough
to stop. I was completely obsessed by dreams of women
and sex – the unknown mystery. There was no talk of
the facts of life in my family. I remember my mother
once dealing with the subject of contraception; it had
come unexpectedly into the conversation because of an
item in the newspaper. 'I don't think we need talk about
it,' she said. 'I always think that if you've been brought
up properly, you know what to do.' I was baffled. She
would say no more.

Now I was grown-up, my father asked me each
weekend to join him for a half of bitter or a half of cider
at the Railway Tavern by the level crossing. I went out
of duty, but I hated it. The English pub in those days
provided drink cheerlessly. There were few women, and
of course no children.

I'm afraid that my lack of enthusiasm for the chilly
cordiality of the English pub must have disappointed
my father. We still shared a few activities. We turned
a room which had once been part of the station into a
small workshop for us both, full of tools. We listened
to the wireless together. But my father and mother still
deferred to me, gladly giving up *Old Mother Riley* if I
wanted to hear a Promenade Concert. Selfishly, I always
took advantage of their generosity.

Cambridge was awash with the arts during the war.
Many institutions performed regularly out of London:
symphony concerts from the BBC; opera productions
from Sadler's Wells and the Guildhall School. The
university showed classic films from Russia, France
and Germany. And there was constant drama – whether
from the Marlowe or other university societies, or the
perpetual stream of plays on tour. I saw John Gielgud's

Hamlet at the Cambridge Arts Theatre. I also saw
William Devlin's Lear and Robert Eddison's Hamlet; and
all the repertory of Donald Wolfit's company. His Volpone
and Lear are still vivid in my memory. I went to the Arts
and stood at the back each Monday night for 6d. It was
a sizeable bite out of my 2s 6d a week pocket money but
my appetite for theatre, music and film was voracious. I
bullied my parents into taking the *Sunday Times* so that
I could keep up with events in the arts. I read James
Agate on the theatre and Ernest Newman on music.
Newman taught me about *The Ring* long before I heard
a note of it. I saw the Ballet Rambert and the Ballet
Joos. One afternoon, after a concert, I chased a surprised
Sir Adrian Boult all the way up Petty Curie. He was
trying to catch a train back to London. I was eager for
his autograph.

I wasn't at home much. If I weren't attending a
performance, I was earning money doing odd-jobs to
help me buy tickets. I did a paper round; I was a part-time
postman at Christmas; I picked cherries, strawberries
and apples in the fruit fields of the fens; and my back
ached with picking up potatoes. My parents gave me
not only the time to be myself, but all that they could
spare in the way of money. My development and enthusiasms were what mattered. Yet inevitably I was growing
apart from them. My tastes, my reading, even my understanding, were becoming different. I talked to them less
and less. They had less and less to say to me. It was
a problem with no solution.

My father's sister, Aunt Mahala, lived in Lewisham.
With a free bed from her, and usually a free railway
ticket from my father, I could afford every school holiday
to hurl myself into the London theatre. I often saw six
or seven plays in one week, combining them with art
galleries and films in the mornings and afternoons. The
tram from Westminster to Lewisham was extraordinarily cheap. So was the theatre. I could stand at the back

or perch in the gallery for next to nothing. If funds were not too short, I could buy a seat in the pit – known grandly today as the back stalls – having reserved my place with a camp stool, placed in a queue of stools outside the theatre in the early morning. Thus I was able to see Richardson's Vanya, Falstaff and Cyrano; Olivier's Richard III, Hotspur and Astrov; Peggy Ashcroft as the Duchess of Malfi; and John Gielgud as Hamlet for the second time. It was still wartime and there was the danger of bombs, sometimes buzz-bombs or V2s. Nobody seemed to take much notice of them. There was a determination that life must go on. London was outwardly grey and boarded up, with deserted streets and a few noisy cars; but inside the buildings there was a sense of an immense party in full swing. The variety of entertainment expressed a great desire to go on living. My mother occasionally accompanied me on my jaunts to the theatre. But mostly I was on my own and glad of it, taking in a quantity of theatre and film and art that only someone truly obsessed could assimilate. I would return to Shelford with my head ringing. What drove me? Why did I fill my life with performances? I loved fantasies, images, metaphors, whether expressed by words, or music, by colour or by form. They excited me more than anything in life.

There were also occasional school outings either by bus or by train. I went in a party to Stratford-upon-Avon and saw a ravishingly beautiful production of *Love's Labour's Lost* by a twenty-year-old genius from the Birmingham Repertory Theatre, Peter Brook.

I was furious and envious. How could he have done this at such an early age? I decided that somehow or other I would work at the Stratford theatre. I vowed that one day I would run it. I was sixteen, and not at all hopeful that I would realise my ambitions.

A more urgent need was to pass my school examinations. Exams had always been the way on, the way out. They had also been times of terror, because I was well aware that I only needed to fail once. I couldn't afford to slip on this particular greasy pole.

My aim was to win a scholarship to university. I knew it would need a great deal of hard work and not a little good luck. Education is not so much a matter of which schools you go to; it is more whether you have the good fortune to meet two or three special teachers who light up your mind and encourage your spirit. The Perse, perhaps because it was in an agreeable university town, or perhaps because of the war, had collected a group of brilliant eccentrics among its staff.

In my very early years at the school, my history master was Vivien Richards. He had been a close friend of T. E. Lawrence and his stories about him were like episodes from the *Boy's Own Paper*. They excited at the time, but then palled. I disliked Lawrence. I didn't believe in him. There was something about him that wasn't real. Vivien Richards, however, instilled in me a lasting passion for architecture. He took groups of boys round the Cambridge colleges and taught us how to read a building as a piece of history. Medieval buildings at last stopped threatening me. He also asked us to his lodgings to listen to records. He had a collection of classical music which he played through an enormous black horn. He used fibre needles, of which he was very proud, and the gramophone itself was clockwork, wound by hand. No electricity for him. Four or five boys would group around the mouth of the horn and listen to the music, sipping cocoa in an untidy room that was stacked with 78 r.p.m. records and books.

I realise now that Vivien Richards was homosexual and I suppose had been in love with Lawrence. It is curious to realise how many of my school teachers must have been homosexual. It was, of course, a hidden matter in those days – a criminal offence that could destroy a career. Several of my teachers lived solid bourgeois lives, sharing a house with a companion who was a business man or a local authority official. They were good men who just got on with their jobs. And though my mother would designate one or other of them as 'not a ladies' man' with a meaningful look, she clearly never felt the need to warn me. I have a vague guilty memory that we boys would giggle and mock these men like flirtatious young women. We did it by instinct. We certainly felt no danger.

My art master, Mr Crouch, was dry, witty, wise and a superb pianist. Where the arts were concerned, he had seen it all; and yet he was adamant that it should be seen again by each new generation. He loved the theatre and directed a school production of *The Taming of the Shrew* in which I played an assertive and fiercely bearded Petruchio. In preparation, he took a party of us to an Old Vic Company production of the play. Trevor Howard was the Petruchio. I thought he underplayed the part.

My history master after Vivien Richards had been, wonder of wonders, a professional actor. John Tanfield actually *knew* what it was like to be on the stage, to sit in dressing rooms, to be part of the professional theatre. I grabbed every bit of theatrical gossip he could remember and chewed on it eagerly. He had not been a successful actor and, armed with a double first, had returned to teaching. I sat with him over innumerable meals while he talked theatre, his wife watching him with an ironic and understanding smile.

He directed me as Hamlet. 'If you speak Shakespeare quickly and rhythmically, the complications mostly take care of themselves,' he said. 'If you understand it, the audience will understand it too.'

He was a tall, gangling man, with an actor's delivery and a long horsy face. He chain-smoked in class. And he was an iconoclast to the end, always wittily suspicious of authority.

Maurice Wollman was ruthless yet benign, and trained the brighter boys hard to pass exams. I always feel I owe my success in major examinations to his organisation of my memory. It wasn't education, but method. But that is what examinations demand. Until I was in my thirties, I had a photographic memory; I learnt things quickly, but I also forgot them quickly.

The inspirer of my last years at school was Douglas Brown. He was a famous old pupil of the Perse who, after his war service, had returned as an Exhibitioner to St Catharine's, where he had taken a double first starred with distinction. He was now supervising at the university, combining it with a job at the Perse teaching Caldwell Cook's *Play-Way* to the juniors. He also coached the seniors for university entrance.

He was a small tense man with fierce concentration and an engaging grin, a zealous scoutmaster and a teacher who could inspire. He set aside a weekend each year in order to read Keats's letters from cover to cover so that he could, as he put it, 'experience the man's life'. I was impressed and tried to emulate him. The senior pupils spent the summer holidays painting and decorating the Mummery for him so that it could once more resound to the cries of little boys shouting Shakespeare at each other. Douglas kept open house every Friday night: sandwiches, coffee and music. The records were still 78s, but the reproduction was electric by now. Here I first heard Britten, and was excited beyond belief by a British Council recording of Tippett's *Child of Our Time*. I heard modern music which was sensual, and which appropriated Bach as readily as negro spirituals.

Douglas was a sceptical Leavisite – by which I mean that while he respected the acumen and moral integrity of the Cambridge sage, F. R. Leavis, he was critical of his more extreme and negative opinions. Leavis sneered at talents he did not approve, such as the Georgian poets or Tennyson; but Douglas would not permit us to sneer at the great. Nonetheless, we all read *Scrutiny*, the magazine edited by Leavis and his wife, Queenie. And from Douglas and Leavis we learnt two important things. First, that the integrity of any artist can be judged from a close analysis of the way he expresses his work. Sloppy writing is the result of sloppy thinking; over-decorated prose or verse betrays a lack of confidence, a desire for effect. Close textual analysis therefore will always reveal the basic quality of the art. The second lesson was the importance of art itself. In an increasingly secular age, the artists were really our prophets and our priests, helping us to learn how to live. Art therefore had an absolute social purpose and an awesome responsibility to be honest. It could also improve our lives. Trashy art could well be seen as a reflection of a trashy age.

Then there was obscenity and violence to consider. I first read James Joyce's *Ulysses* when I was seventeen. I didn't realise that I was still an East Anglian prude. It shocked me. I was violently against it. Douglas pointed out to me that the obscene, the violent and the disturbing must necessarily be part of an artist's vocabulary. We must judge only the integrity with which they are used.

Douglas was a great man who always made me feel inadequate. Compared to him, I hadn't read enough, done enough, or used my time well enough. My mother liked him but was wary. She found him bookish. He could, in her opinion, have done with a little life. He loved the theatre, but made me feel that it was impure and, compared with the precision of music, recklessly generalised in its interpretations. I believe he would find the theatre has more intellectual honesty now, intermittent though that can still be.

After a brilliant period supervising at Cambridge, Douglas went as a lecturer to Reading University. From there, in the early Sixties, he was appointed Professor of English at the new University of York. As he took up the post, he died of leukaemia. It seemed as if his passion for learning had consumed him. He left behind a distinguished little monograph on Thomas Hardy; not very much to mark the passage of a great man.

*

In my last two years at school I was so active I nearly burst. I acted, edited the school magazine, and read and read and read. I also became head boy. It was a joy to help run the place. I discovered that administration could be exciting. I wasn't an outsider any more – almost. I was so greedy for experience that it hurt. Most of that experience came through the performing arts.

Did I know what I wanted to be? I most certainly did; and I had known it in my soul since I was fourteen. I was going to be a director in the theatre. I was going to be the man who organised the fantasies, and who sometimes, perhaps, invented them. I must have had a confused idea about what a director in the theatre actually did. I went out of my way to act, but I never wanted to *be* an actor. I just wanted to know what it felt like. The job I wanted was to make all the fantasies happen. And I kept my ambition secret.

When pressed, I would confess that I would like to go into the theatre. People reacted with pain or horror or surprise: they thought I wanted to be an actor. I had read Gordon Craig's *On the Art of the Theatre* (which is still the best job description of a director that I know); and, with a certain amount of bewilderment, the books by and about Stanislavsky. I read Granville-Barker; I read about Shakespeare's Globe; and I read every book I could find about Lilian Baylis at the Old Vic, Miss Horniman in Manchester, Barry Jackson in Birmingham, Terence Gray at the Festival Theatre Cambridge, and Norman Marshall at the Little Theatre in London. I devoured theatre magazines and every scrap about drama in the newspapers. I lived in the public library. I was following a secret agenda which was mapped out partly by plan and partly by instinct.

My parents always wanted me to be a teacher. It is therefore hardly surprising that in my adolescence I was already indifferent to what is one of the most crucial jobs in our society. I thought that the best way to launch myself into the theatrical profession would be from the amateur theatre world of university – Oxford or Cambridge. Many, I knew, had done just that. If I failed, I could then become a teacher. But Michael Redgrave, Marius Goring, Robert Speight, Hugh Hunt, George Devine and Peter Brook hadn't failed; perhaps I wouldn't either.

I still have a recurrent nightmare. It visited me first when I was twenty-seven and had just been appointed the Director of the Stratford theatre. In my dream, I am indeed a teacher. As English master, I am directing the school play. It is usually *Julius Caesar*, with a rabble of small boys I can neither control nor inspire. During a particularly noisy riot, I overhear one whispering to another: 'They say he used to direct at Stratford, but I don't believe it.' I wake up sweating . . .

It is a great blessing to know what you want to do and to have the passion that makes you do it. That certainty, however, has an undertow of agony; perhaps you will not get the chance to do what you want to do; or worse, perhaps you will be incapable of doing it. So to be *able* to do it when you are at last given the chance is the greatest blessing of all. But this ability is never certain, never constant; it is always in doubt. The most talented seem prey to the worst fears. Peggy Ashcroft always had something very near a breakdown before she achieved her great performances – it only lasted a few hours, but it was an intense collapse. Laurence Olivier suffered paralysing stage fright for many years. And all the writers I know are haunted by the spectre of the blank page.

The theatre keeps you humble and it keeps you young; you learn your job to the very end, and always feel unsure with every new job: 'Can I still do it? Shall I be found out?'

Ralph Richardson defeated the fears; he liked long runs: he was able to go on practising. He often told me that he loved the nightly expectation of going down to the theatre. He felt like a woodcarver trying to repeat an ever more delicate decoration. He would re-carve his performance each night, making it a little finer, a little more economical. Some nights, the knife would slip and he would spoil a whole section. He knew that perfection was impossible, but the important thing was to continue carving. If the run was happy, the carving would improve, though the improvement might be hardly discernible from performance to performance.

The end of the war and the election of a Labour government in 1945 gave new hope to families like mine. My father thought that a golden age had come: a welfare state where people cared for education and for health and where the railways were nationalised. I noticed a renaissance in the arts too. The Council for the Encouragement of the Arts became The Arts Council, and the Third Programme arrived. I sat in my little room under the eaves of Shelford station and listened eagerly to the radio, my own now, bought from my earnings from odd-jobs. I feasted on music and drama – Shaw, Shakespeare, John Webster. Nothing widened my horizons so much as the Third Programme. It was frequently demanding and difficult, but it challenged, and I was stimulated as well as entertained. There was a jibe current at its foundation that it was merely dons talking to dons. I would love to hear it again instead of the current inanities which move ever down-market in the desperate pursuit of popularity.

In my last three years at the Perse school, I set a pace which has continued all my life. I have frequently been called a workaholic, though I have never been able to understand why an obsessive pleasure in work should be seen as an indulgence. I love high activity; I enjoy being extended. I have always worked on many things at once. Whatever abilities I lack, I know I have the gift of complete concentration on the thing in hand at the moment I am doing it. I can then forget about it and move on with equal concentration to something else. The variety itself generates energy. I discovered in the

Sixties, through a routine medical examination, that my body has a tendency to manufacture too much adrenalin. I have consequently developed an adrenalin addiction; consciously or unconsciously, I put myself into situations where high quantities of adrenalin are produced. I'm sure this is why I like constant work, and why I don't much enjoy my rare holidays unless I have a task: something to write or something to study. Otherwise, I am apt to sit staring morosely at the horizon. My engine either functions at full speed or it stops altogether, and then I suffer a truly terrible depression.

My eldest son, Christopher, who was born with an altogether more phlegmatic temperament, asked me when he was ten why I worked so hard. 'What are you trying to prove?' he said. I told him I was not trying to prove anything: I like working hard. A hard day's directing gives me a peace that I still enjoy, a physical satisfaction.

I enjoyed myself so much during the intense activity of my last years at school that I began to question all the hours spent sleeping; they seemed an awful waste of time. I tried systematically to cut them down, but I couldn't get below five hours; four induced collapse.

The last major hurdle at school was the Cambridge scholarship examination. I sat it before my Higher Certificate rather than after. It was regarded as a trial run. If I failed, I could always have a second chance. After the examination, I was called for an interview at St Catharine's College. The senior tutor there was Tom Henn, the distinguished Yeats scholar. He could easily reduce himself to tears by intoning great verse. This seemed surprising in an Anglo-Irish military man.

His rooms were filled with dogs and pipe smoke. I remember him dressed in baggy tweeds in an environment that was more like a country gentleman's study than a Cambridge don's. Fly-fishing rods and double-barrelled guns nestled alongside the letters of Maude Gonne and the journals of Lady Gregory.

At the scholarship interview, he questioned me about the theatre – and the floodgates of my enthusiasm opened. He had heard of my exploits as Petruchio at school, and asked me to deliver the wooing speech. I launched into 'You lie in faith, for you are called plain Kate . . .' My ringing voice woke up the spaniels.

I was also asked about my literary and critical enthusiasms. Douglas Brown had schooled me carefully; I was not to mention Leavis. Tom Henn was of the other camp – the King's group centred round F. L. Lucas and George Rylands. Their approach to literature was romantic, not social, and much less based on textual analysis. Their reactions were personal and emotional, and they distrusted Leavis.

I was awarded an Exhibition in English to St Catharine's. Tom Henn supervised me during my first year, and I visited his rooms once a week with two other students for an hour's discussion on the essays we had written and the books we had read. I remember him elucidating an image in a Yeats poem. 'Have you ever,' he intoned, 'made love – to a girl – in a cave?' Since we had never made love to anybody, in a cave or anywhere else, we shifted in our seats uncomfortably. Men outnumbered women in Cambridge at that time by eight to one.

I loved Tom Henn because he was eccentric and emotional. He spoke in a strange liturgical baritone chant, with Irish *r*'s and over-meticulous vowels. He worshipped literature and heroic achievement. He was a military man with a poet's soul. His high emotions couldn't comprehend the rigorous critical zeal of Leavis. I secretly attended Leavis's lectures; but since I was directly supervised by Tom Henn, it was rather like a devout Catholic finding his day-to-day inspiration from the sermons of Luther.

Leavis was a familiar figure in the Cambridge streets. He rode an absurdly old-fashioned tall black bicycle. His shirt collar was always wide open, even in the worst weather, and he was the original corduroys-and-open-sandals man. He wore socks with his sandals.

His delivery at lectures was dry and witty, with an in-built sneer in virtually every phrase. We attended in order to be shocked and outraged at his judgements, though actually we were delighted to hear all the great reputations overturned. T. S. Eliot was suspect; so was Bloomsbury and all its works; so also, at that time, was Dickens. I consequently neglected one of my great childhood enthusiasms and substituted for Dickens the authors in Leavis's current Great Tradition: Jane Austen, George Eliot, Henry James and D. H. Lawrence.

With my scholarship secured a year early, I was able to restructure my last twelve months at school. Douglas Brown gave me a huge reading programme. And I was to play Hamlet in the school play.

Hamlet obsessed me. I read a mountain of books about it. Granville-Barker's remains the best. He never forgets that the play is a play and must be judged as something that communicates on the stage.

I never could act. In my performances, I merely drew diagrams of acting – indications of how a performance could be shaped and what it should mean. I was giving a lecture on the part; I wasn't *being* it. Nonetheless, the lecture was clear, some people mistook it for acting, and my Hamlet was certainly more than the audience had been expecting at a school play. I was a success and received my first fan letters. I was gratified. But for me acting was only a means to an end.

As term ended I was aware that the first chapter of my life was closing. I was due to begin my National Service. All my plans would have to be put in suspension for two years. University seemed a long way off. Even so, I worried; I knew I must get through Cambridge as well as I had got through school. I was a scholarship boy of whom a great deal was demanded. There was still no money and this added to the tension. I felt I would be scrambling by my finger-nails over a wall into an alien, well-educated, well-heeled world, where I was neither expected nor welcome. And after that? I had no contacts in the theatre, nor did I have any knowledge of how to begin a career in it.

The day after school finished I set off to West Kirby, near Liverpool. Suddenly I was 3120201 Aircraftsman Hall. Up to this point in my life, I had believed that you made your own luck by grasping every opportunity offered, however dangerous and however demanding. Whatever happened, it was up to you. But as I looked round the hut at the other eighteen-year-old trainees, who were all fucking and blinding at me as I tried to read, I felt that my luck had run out. I wasn't going to make much of this.

– 9 –

RAF West Kirby took in boys and made them men; that's what the NCO said. It was a brutal place, and the transformation took eight weeks. A boy in the next hut committed suicide by cutting his throat with a razor. I don't recall any newspaper reports, scandals, committees of enquiry or questions in the House. I suppose it was hushed up. Certainly the conditions were mindless enough to induce terrible despair.

My home was a hut occupied by thirty other lads. It was presided over by an irascible and threatening corporal who was foul-mouthed and had a natural hostility to anything that was out of line, humorous or nonconformist. The food was awful, the physical demands extreme, and the intellectual stimulation nil. We were made fit: that was the only achievement. But our spirits were broken in the quest for discipline. And I became aware that a high proportion of the male population have no descriptive adjective in their vocabulary other than the word 'fuck'. I had no moral objection to this; it just made conversation monotonous.

We were confined to camp for the first two weeks; then we burst out, like prisoners suddenly freed. I was a wartime child, so I had still not been abroad. Even the North was another country to me. Liverpool I found very exciting – black, grimy and full of clouds, rain and steam. It was spring, but it always seemed dark. During my basic training, I went to the Liverpool Playhouse three times. I saw *Uncle Vanya, The Tempest* and *The Schoolmistress*. John Fernald was the director and he had a fine permanent company that included Gladys Boot, Cyril Luckham, Michael Aldridge and Rosalind Boxall. I watched enchanted. I could not know that I would work with all these actors; or that I would work for John Fernald himself in a little over four years.

I felt that doing plays with the same company on the same stage in the same town was a definition of what civic theatre ought to be. I knew all about the golden age of William Armstrong at Liverpool and I yearned to spend my days at a theatre linked, as his had been, to its community. This, I suppose, is a theatre person's dream of life before the fall. If someone offered me a regional playhouse now, with a subsidy that allowed the highest standards (by which I mean paying the actors properly), I would find it irresistible. Unfortunately, it will never happen. No regional repertory now has enough funds to hire a company of top talent.

I hoped to spend my National Service in the Education Corps. I could not be considered officer material as I did not yet have my degree. But on the strength of my Cambridge scholarship, I was sent from West Kirby to the RAF School of Education at Wellesbourne Mountford in Warwickshire to be trained as a Sergeant (Acting) Instructor.

Things became far more civilised. We were only three or four to a room; and, best of all, it was only a short bus ride to Stratford. I was able to board the six-thirty bus outside the camp gates and be deposited near the theatre in time to buy a standing place at the back of the stalls. I never failed to get in; the great Shakespeare boom was only just beginning.

By seeing each play that summer many times, I learnt another lesson about the nature of repertory theatre. What is good to start with gets better and better. What is uncertain or bad tends to get worse.

This was my third consecutive summer of seeing everything in Stratford. The two previous summers I had cycled over with a schoolfriend from Cambridge. It was nearly a hundred miles; most of the journey was blessedly on the flat, but we prayed for no head-winds. We pitched our tent up river from the theatre, on the municipal camping ground, where the Avon, as yet unpolluted, served as the town's swimming pool. It rained a good deal, and we were cold. We lived on fish and chips and the occasional visit to the town's British Restaurant, a place of basic food, the product of the war. And we saw the plays every night. I remember the young Paul Scofield alternating with Robert Helpmann in a mid-Victorian staging of *Hamlet*. Scofield was a brooding, difficult, Byronic Hamlet. I was transported despite a duff production in which Elsinore became Saxe-Coburg. But it gave Scofield a middle-aged society to fight. I remember, too, Diana Wynyard and Tony Quayle in *Much Ado*; and a baleful *King John* with Helpmann in full chrome make-up. In the RAF year, I met *Cymbeline* for the first time and, by seeing it frequently, learnt to love its tangled complexities. Stratford – a little rundown Midlands market town then, with its large 1930s cinema-like theatre slapped incongruously by the river – was more and more the focus of my ambitions.

During the day, I was trying to turn myself into a Sergeant Instructor who could teach current affairs. It was a difficult role for someone just out of school, because it demanded at least the appearance of maturity. Gradually, I began to enjoy teaching. School had given me many opportunities for public speaking, and I knew I liked this elemental form of communication. To some extent, too, a teacher (like a director) thinks on his feet and lives in public. This was all useful experience.

By the end of the summer of 1949, I had hopes that my National Service years were not going to be entirely wasted after all. Then came another upheaval. I was posted to Germany.

– 10 –

We crossed the border. I looked out of the train window and saw people working in the fields: farmers ploughing, women weeding. It looked much like anywhere else. But it wasn't anywhere else – it was Germany and these were Germans. I rushed down the corridor to the lavatory and was violently sick.

I had been conditioned throughout my adolescence to think of Germans as the beasts who produced Belsen and Auschwitz. They were not human. I found it hard to look at them. It took me a long while to get over this, to realise that we all have the same beast within us and that hatred can only breed hatred. I am now a fervent European: it gives us at least the chance to develop tolerance.

I was posted to the RAF Headquarters for Education at Bückerburg. A demobilisation school was attached to it, providing one-month refresher courses for students returning to civilian life. The rush of people being demobilised was over, but there was still a trickle. I expected, like all my companions, to be sent on to some air base in Germany where I would be the Education Sergeant running the library, teaching current affairs, and presiding over the Gramophone Society. But I was made to wait at headquarters. A Squadron Leader who had been teaching the course in economics had just been hurriedly posted for fraternising with a German girl. The Commanding Officer called me into his office. 'I see you did economics in Higher Certificate, Hall?' he began. 'Yes, sir, but only as a subsidiary subject.' The CO considered this for a moment. 'Never mind,' he said. 'I'm sure you can get up a course in economics and business management that will satisfy our applicants.'

I tried desperately to meet his demands. I dreaded giving refresher courses to veterans who had gone through the war and who held pre-war BScs at the London School of Economics. But these turned out to be the easy ones; they were happy to have time for a month's reading and a few seminars on general subjects. The difficult customers were the people who wanted to be taught from the beginning. They had to learn with me, at the same time as I learnt.

Our courses took place in the requisitioned Bückerburg Schloss, an amazing confection of cheap nineteenth-century rococo, with painted ceilings and rampant cupids. My office was an over-decorated salon which I shared with a young Pilot Officer and a pair of Bechstein grands, washed up by the Occupation. The pilot officer was also a pianist, so we whiled away the hours playing music for two pianos. Then the pilot officer changed. Unfortunately, the new man, Kenneth Ewing, was no pianist. But he was almost as mad on the theatre as I was, and subsequently became a leading play agent.

I only had to teach for a few hours each week, so I spent most of my time reading. Douglas Brown had given me one list, and St Catharine's had given me another; I was determined to be well prepared before I went up. I was planning to spend my time not studying, but in the university dramatic societies.

I think I finally wasn't a bad teacher. I learnt to lead a group, and to handle people. And mapping a journey through a subject on which you have only a general grasp is no bad training for leading a group of actors in the discovery of a play.

Germany then was still war-torn and miserable. Our weekly cigarette ration was worth more than our pay. As conquerors, we were rather better off than we were in England. There was meat, plenty of food, and we had centrally-heated barracks. I was surprised to be warm for the first winter in my life. But it was disturbing to be living so comfortably in a land of deprivation and rubble. I also found, unsurprisingly, that Acting Sergeants of eighteen were not on the whole very popular with their fellows. The next youngest member of my Sergeants' mess was thirty-eight. The older men were mostly advanced alcoholics who had sweated for years before being rewarded with their three stripes. They were not at all pleased to see a boy quickly reaching their rank simply because he had passed a few exams.

For a time, I shared a room with a Sergeant in his late forties. He got drunk every night and never returned from the mess to our bedroom until two or three in the morning. One night, the sound of running water invaded my sleep; I dreamt of brooks and little waterfalls. It was a lovely sound except that I seemed to hear, amongst the gentle splashing, a man's voice muttering imprecations. As I became conscious, I saw my fellow Sergeant solemnly pissing into my wardrobe. He had opened the door either because he thought it was the lavatory, or because he wanted, in his drunken animosity, to fill up my boots. His performance was abundant. As he pissed, he muttered, 'Who does this young fucker think he is? Coming here pretending to be a Sergeant. Pretending he knows better than us . . .' I woke him as much as the drink permitted, undressed him and put him to bed. I left my piss-filled boots unemptied until the morning.

The Sergeants had their revenge on me: they appointed me mess barman. For some four months, I served drinks from 8 p.m. until three or four in the morning. There was one night off a week. Otherwise, I had the torture

61

of listening every night to the Sergeants' wondrously bigoted, reactionary talk as they travelled inexorably into their accustomed drunken stupor. When they were all completely pissed, I could close the bar and go to bed. I think they only stayed in the RAF for the mess. It was a place where drunkenness was a sign of virility, and costs were low. To me, it was a grotesque version of the English pub. Its nightly purpose was oblivion.

Eventually, I was given a room on my own. I solemnly covered all the available wall space with postcards from the National Gallery and the Tate. One of my teachers had said to me early on that he wasn't sure about the strength of my visual sense. The criticism stayed in my head. I consciously trained myself to look at form, pattern and colour. Art galleries, art books and postcard reproductions became part of my discipline. Looking at paintings is now an intense pleasure, and it developed from making myself do it. But I still believe that I hear more keenly than I see. The sound of words and of music are the immediate stimulations.

Despite the ruined towns and the chronic shortage of food, the Germans poured money into the performing arts. They still had subsidised music, drama and opera because they needed them. I was very impressed. Hanover's opera house had been destroyed by bombs, but at the Herrenhausen, the old stables of the Elector of Hanover's palace, a temporary theatre had been constructed. There, I saw Wagner for the first time in my life. It was *Tristan und Isolde*. The sensuality overwhelmed me: it was a physical experience.

I went also to the first German production of *Albert Herring*. It was a very Teutonic view of East Anglia. I had seen the original Glyndebourne production when it toured to Cambridge and had been mystified by the dismissive tone of the critics. It seemed that the comic was thought less worthy than the tragic.

Sung lines such as:

I am sorry Miss Pike,
But I punctured my bike

aroused particular fury. I thought that the naiveté
of the opera, and the pretensions of its characters,
expressed the heart of Suffolk. When I directed a revival
at Glyndebourne in 1985, Britten, alas, was dead, though
Peter Pears, the original Albert, and Eric Crozier, the
librettist, saw it. The piece, I like to think, emerged
as what it is: that rarest of things in opera, a genuine
social comedy. It has a serious heart which defines its
mirth: witness its depiction of the pain of adolescence;
witness the great threnody on death in Act III. None of
this was visible in the facetious German production.

Hamburg was further away than Hanover, but I
went there too. The bomb damage was still apocalyptic. I walked through streets piled high with rubble
to performances at the bombed opera house. Only its
stage had survived, and a temporary auditorium and
stage had been built on it. I saw Verdi and Puccini
and more and more Wagner. I went by train across
Germany to Oberammergau where I saw one of the ten-
yearly manifestations of *The Passion Play*. It was a
dreadful text and the production had more nineteenth-
century religiosity than a bad production of *Parsifal*.
But I was excited to see an entire village on the stage
– a cast of 1,000 people. Their behaviour was precisely
drilled and precisely defined; I had some sense of what
Max Reinhardt's meticulous theatre must have been like.
There were frequent Bavarian rain-storms which soaked
the actors. The audience was under cover; the stage
was not.

In Germany I saw the great clown, Grock. He stood
on a chair playing a diminutive violin that exploded at
irregular intervals. His act was a tragic farce, and had
a private mystery all of its own as disaster crept nearer
and nearer to him. I will go anywhere to see a superlative

comic. I love the direct one-to-one relationship with the audience as the comic flatters and then abuses them. It is a contest as acute and as basic (and sometimes as terrible) as a bullfight. It is also in the great tradition of direct dramatic storytelling and has lessons for every actor. All Shakespearean soliloquies are directly addressed to the audience. The actor does not commune with himself, unaware that the audience is overhearing. Instead, he shares himself with his audience. He always tells the truth, from the heart, and asks the audience to share his predicament. Similarly, the baroque aria and the Mozart aria are also direct revelations of self. It is only since the naturalism of the late nineteenth century that the theatre has grown shy of soliloquy, or aria, or aside. The great stand-up comics still show us the way: Max Miller, Ken Dodd, Frankie Howerd, Mort Sahl, Lenny Bruce, Barry Humphries – these lewd and anarchic men are my heroes. We *know* them.

One Christmas, just before the war, my mother and father took me to the London Coliseum to see the Crazy Gang: six wayward clowns who appeared to be always just about to do something awful, which would almost certainly be dirty. Yet somehow they never got round to doing it. With a detached air, they papered a room, paste flying, ladders collapsing, buckets spilling their paint everywhere. My mother was rather sniffy about these alarming old men. 'Stoopid,' she said, in her best Suffolk accent. But I was their slave from then until their last Victoria Palace shows.

The RAF had an amateur dramatic club at Bückerburg. It was frequented mainly by the bored wives of the officers, or those who had been on the fringes of show business in civilian life. Putting on a play was done in an atmosphere of joyous camp, as if we were all about to enjoy an outrageous party. There was no hope of me directing. The productions were safely in the hands of an enthusiastic and queenly Sergeant, whom I liked very much. I acted, among other parts, a romantic lover in a historical farrago called *The Rose Without a Thorn*. My entry through the mullioned window of the bedroom at the dead of night produced loud wolf whistles at the Bückerburg Garrison Theatre. I also played Robert Browning in *The Barretts of Wimpole Street*. I still had no intention of being an actor.

I tried to learn German, but achieved only moderate success. I have no ability in languages. At various times I have also attempted, with fairly dismal results, to master Italian for my Cambridge degree; and French because I became part of a large French family by my marriage to Leslie Caron. I can read a little in all three languages, but trying to speak them becomes an abominable embarrassment – because, I suppose, I hate making a fool of myself.

This is a great regret to me. I have never resolved it and deeply envy friends who can easily speak another tongue. They have full access to another culture. There is a kink in my brain – or more probably a deep conceit in my nature – which makes learning languages impossible. Yet I can give a lecture for an hour without notes; it is rare for me to encounter an unfamiliar word in English; and I can write without inhibition. I delight in words, and when directing plays I am keenly responsive to the music and rhythm of dialogue. But I am no good at foreign languages.

I fell in love in Germany. Her name was Jill and she was a porcelain-faced member of the WRAF in which she was intending to make her career. She was private and shy, and as young and virginal as I was. We had good times together for an entire summer, boating and swimming, and visiting the Harz mountains. We cuddled and I groped feverishly. This, remember, was the pre-Pill age when how far you could go with a girl was a clear indication of her morality. I masturbated lustily in my bed and dreamt of making love to Jill. Being a romantic, I took the whole thing terribly seriously – much more, I suspect, than she did. Just before I was demobilised, we became engaged. As a consequence I recklessly cancelled all my plans and all my ambitions. I forced myself to think that a career in the theatre would not be wise for a young man about to marry. It was all far too hazardous. I resolved to become a teacher and settle down. I was very tortured and very sad. This decision marked my arrival at university.

Soon after, Jill and I at last went to bed. This momentous happening was possible because I had celebrated my demobilisation by buying a 1929 Austin Seven for forty pounds, money I had saved in the RAF. It was held together with wire and made driving a real craft for it was totally unreliable. It took us off on a winter's holiday to the Welsh mountains. On the way, we stopped the first night at a hotel in Leamington Spa.

How and why our love-making worked, I cannot imagine. I was totally inexperienced and so was she. My knowledge of sex and of a woman's body was confined to chatter and gossip, my avid reading of Penguin sex-education books, and a great deal of D. H. Lawrence, whose rhapsodic descriptions were, at best, rather unclear. Since both of us had remained virgin until nineteen, we had very little objectivity about our sexuality, or how basically suited we were. Our pleasure in each other seems to me now a wonderment. Certainly one of the great physical sufferings of my youth was being a virgin for so long. Others I knew had by my age been with experienced girls, or had paid for sex. But I was always reluctant to cheapen something precious. That sounds priggish. But I wasn't a prig; I was passionate. I would have fallen in love with the first whore I laid.

Sex is the great mystery, as great as death. Yet we commercialise it, and destroy it with fear, prudery and envy. It is the expression of our love, and the means by which nature ensures our future. It gives the greatest pleasure and the greatest pain. At nineteen, I had been given absolutely no education, no counselling and no help in this crucial part of life. Is it really much better for young people now? Knowing how to give pleasure to a woman by loving her is the nearest most men get to being an artist. It is something that should be helped and cherished.

I had hardly been near an aeroplane or an airfield during my time in the RAF. I'd felt very much like a visiting civilian. I flew far more at school in the Air Training Corps when I loved the physical sensation of small aeroplanes, and particularly the skill of gliding: the silence, the waywardness, the uncertainty about where the air currents would take you. Life in the Education Corps was pedestrian, run by a lazy bureaucracy, full of sloth and predictable narrow-mindedness. I believe that National Service had a seriously debilitating effect on the youth of Britain. Far from making men of several generations, it taught them how to be idle. To skive became a habit. Conscripts always managed to look busy because we had been trained to look as if we were doing something when in fact we were doing nothing. Most of the time, there was nothing to do. At the height of the war, the Services must have been very different, when there was purpose and energy, and everyone shared the urgent need to win. In peace, the Services were concerned not with necessity but with method – the *way* something was carried out. Custom and pomposity triumphed. Great soldiers are as stimulating to meet as the top of any profession – great bankers or businessmen or surgeons – but God preserve me from the average military mind, obsessed with detail and precedent. I often remembered that I was engaged to a girl who had intended to make her life in one of these alarming institutions. Should I really give up the theatre and become a teacher? Would she really give up the WRAF and become the wife of a teacher? The future was increasingly uncertain.

I flew back to London from Germany in an unpressurised Dakota and was airsick most of the way. I was due at Cambridge University within weeks. I would be a civilian once more.

– 11 –

My first action when I arrived at Cambridge was to book the Amateur Dramatic Club theatre for the October two years following – the start of my third year. I said in my letter that I wanted to do an independent production. It was a contingency plan. For the sake of Jill and my engagement, I still intended to give up the theatre and my secret aspirations. But I booked the theatre, just in case things changed. I had no money to pay for an independent production, so I was by no means sure that I could honour the booking. My action was instinctive and a kind of madness; I didn't think about it very much. It was born equally of calculation and desperation.

On my first day at Cambridge, I checked into a forbidding semi-detached house on the western outskirts of the city. It was much like Blinco Grove, but less friendly, freezing cold and on the other side of town. It was not quite what I had in mind as the start of my university career. But first-year men at St Catharine's had to stay out in lodgings; there was no collegiate life for them.

It was foggy – a fenland October day. I went back to the college and presented my ration book at the Bursar's office. Rationing was still in full swing and most freshmen had just done their National Service. A few had come up straight from school and seemed extraordinarily young. This was the pre-jeans society; and we certainly would not have worn army surplus garments, even if we'd owned any, since most of us had just escaped with relief from conscription. We dressed in flannels and sports jackets – if possible with large leather pads on our elbows.

I walked from St Catharine's, through King's, across to Clare and then across Clare Bridge. These places were all familiar from my school days. Now I was part of them. Or was I? I felt lost. I carried my gown in my hand. We had, I knew, to wear gowns in Hall, after dark, and for lectures and supervisions (the visits to our supervisor in his rooms to discuss our essays). I knew, too, that we had to be back in college at 10 p.m. and that women were not allowed on the premises after seven, unless by special permission. As time went by, and I noticed how busy people were in the afternoons, this rule appeared sillier and sillier.

On this first day, I stood and looked at the misty river. I felt inadequate. Obviously you needed a private income to enjoy this place, mutual friends from the right school and a confidence bred of your class which I simply didn't have.

A figure crossed the bridge in the mist, and came towards me. Like me, he carried his gown, new and untorn; and like me he looked anxious. He introduced himself. His voice was reassuringly cockney. His name was Tony Church and he was bent on being an actor. We fell upon each other's enthusiasm for the theatre as if it were a secret religion in a pagan land; and began an intermittent friendship which has lasted to this day. I have directed Tony more times than I can remember: at Cambridge, at the Oxford Playhouse, at the RSC and at the National Theatre. At Cambridge I met many people who have remained colleagues all my professional life.

My first year was a disappointment; but then I was trying to give up the theatre. I hung sulkily around the fringes of the university dramatic societies. I was involved, but always half-heartedly, because of Jill and my ideas for a career. I tried to believe in them, but couldn't. I also wished that I was living in college; I needed a strong new sense of place; I hated my digs. I spent a good deal of time at home, at Whittlesford, where my parents had moved, one station up the line from Shelford; another slight promotion for my father.

In the late Forties and early Fifties, Cambridge drama was highly organised and offered amazing opportunities. The productions were regarded by the arts editors of the national papers as news, and the first-string critics often travelled from London to see them. It was thought, I suppose, that anyone who survived the university rat race stood a good chance of making a mark in the profession. But drama at Cambridge was not a university department; it was run by the students and was as important for those with theatrical ambitions as the Union for would-be politicians, or *Varsity* and *Granta* for journalists. The Amateur Dramatic Club, whose productions I had often seen as a schoolboy, had a small theatre. Its stage was frequently let out to other societies, chief among them the University Actors.

The Marlowe Society put on plays (usually Shake-speare) at the Arts Theatre in the Lent term; and other productions as part of the Cambridge summer festival. The Society had a strong tradition of verse-speaking upheld by George Rylands, an English don at King's and one of the last surviving members of the Bloomsbury group. He had been the office boy for Leonard and Virginia Woolf when they started the Hogarth Press. Now he was on the board of H. M. Tennent Ltd, the main West End producing management. He also directed professionally – John Gielgud in *Hamlet*, for instance, or Peggy Ashcroft in *The Duchess of Malfi*. If Cambridge had a link with the professional theatre, George Rylands – always known as 'Dadie' – was it. He was an enthusiastic amateur actor and I had seen him play Oedipus and Antony and Macbeth. He had a musical, emphatic voice, whose constant upward inflections sustained the sense if not the emotion. We were all given to imitating him. He was a golden man, with piercing blue eyes and a mischievous wit. At the most solemn moments he had an endearing habit of breaking into giggles. In the lecture hall a half smile would be quickly suppressed when he found the paradoxes of his own scholarship amusing. He was a gossip, a wit, a delight: an inspiration to us all. He still is – as, in his nineties, he trots round King's.

Drama standards at Cambridge were also set at that time by John Barton. As a freshman, I was in awe of him, but he soon became a very close friend and a colleague whom I have admired throughout my life. He is one of those extraordinary originals who give a good name to Eton – no stereotype, but an eccentric, individual and unique. The son of an extremely English family whose father was a top civil servant, he developed at school a passion for words and for play-making and performing. When I first met him, he had already wrecked his back in a legendary and dangerous duel in an ADC production of *Macbeth*. As I went up, he was presenting and directing his own play, *That's All One*, a whimsical, comical piece, a blend of Lewis Carroll, pastiche Shakespeare and Jerome K. Jerome, with a good deal about cricket. It had music by Julian Slade and was designed by Timothy O'Brien.

John was already a fiercely professional director, expert at staging and lighting. He dominated the ADC and Marlowe committees with his rigorous demands, and would have no truck with amateurism. He was completely obsessed by the theatre and would work round the clock, without thought for sleep or food. He smoked continuously, fell over things, dropped cups of coffee and, to ease the enthusiasm which threatened to possess him, would chew razor blades throughout rehearsals by gently flopping them over and over on his tongue. I have seen many actors and actresses, at Cambridge and, later, at Stratford, mesmerised by that revolving blade. Occasionally, a tell-tale trickle of blood would seep out of the corner of his mouth as John elucidated a particularly difficult textual point.

Without John, I don't think my Cambridge theatre generation would have achieved so much. He not only set standards himself, he expected others to do the same. His

71

influence lasted for many years, even after he had gone – from Peter Wood to Jonathan Miller and from Trevor Nunn to Richard Eyre.

Peter Wood was already a fine director by the time he left Cambridge. I remember him wearing an imposing camelhair coat draped like a cloak from his shoulders. He had blond wavy hair, a superior laugh and a speedy wit. I hated him on sight. He made me feel that I was a boy from the backwoods of Suffolk with little confidence and a very uncertain style.

Peter left Cambridge at the end of my first year and obtained, through the influence of Dadie, a job as assistant stage manager and understudy with H. M. Tennent. He was engaged for *Seagulls Over Sorrento*, a farce with Ronald Shiner at the Apollo Theatre in Shaftesbury Avenue. We were all very impressed. But there was a catch. Peter had been made to sign a run-of-the-play contract. As the play was an enormous hit he had to stay on at the Apollo for some three or four years, by which time I was already a successful director. He then rapidly established himself as one of the most expert talents of his generation. I know nobody with a greater knowledge of comedy, comic timing, and how to place and obtain a laugh. We have been friends and worked together on and off for forty years.

I studied hard during my first year at Cambridge and resentfully kept the drama to a minimum – like a man having the occasional deep drag on a cigarette while purporting to give up smoking. I was a terrible Magnus in a freshman's production of Shaw's *The Apple Cart*, a round-faced boy pretending to be a mature, middle-aged man. I had a small part in *The Enchanted Isle*, Dryden's adaptation of *The Tempest*, and fell in love with Purcell's music. I played the First Citizen in the Marlowe Society's *Coriolanus* and watched, fascinated, as Dadie directed with his nose firmly in the text. He was more concerned with our line endings and our iambics than with whether we were bumping into each other. John Barton compensated by being in charge of the battles.

My engagement to Jill jogged along. We met whenever we could, but her life and mine were moving separate ways. She was now a Pilot Officer and her career was flourishing. We still had a passion for making love, but seldom found anywhere private. A spring and summer of cramped cars, cold tents and rain-soaked trees and bushes failed to diminish our ardour. But by the time autumn came, we both knew our engagement was going to end. There were too many pressures on both sides pulling us apart. It was a sad break-up.

I became introspective and alarmed. I took a summer vacation job as a level-crossing keeper. My father had recommended me to British Rail and I had been successfully tested for my knowledge of the railway telegraph system. The crossing I looked after was on the main line from Cambridge to Liverpool Street. Trains were fast and frequent, but the crossing was an anomaly because its gates were normally locked against the very minor road. I sat in a hut by the railway for twelve hours at a stretch – either from six in the morning, or from six at night. A large bell mounted on the outside of the hut clanged in code the type of train that was about to pass.

On fine days, I sat in the sun and studied. It was an ideal job for a student, though I found it hard to get my mind off Jill. The road was little more than a made-up farm track. If any form of vehicle arrived, I rang up the nearby signal box to check if there were any trains about. I had to take this precaution because I had usually silenced the bell with a sock, so that it would not disturb my concentration. On the night shift, I was even more out of order. I dismantled the bell completely and slept soundly, though express goods trains constantly rushed by, six feet from my head.

One night, I was awoken by a loud banging on the door. A man's furious face was visible through the small panel of glass, shouting. It was clear from his pounding on the door, which I had locked before going to sleep, that he was in a hurry to get his car over the crossing. It stood, lights glaring, by the gates. As I picked up the telephone to ask my friend at the signal box if it was safe to open up, two or three police cars screeched to a halt and the man ran across the fields, chased by the law. He had burgled a house, then stolen the car. I was commended for my sleepiness; I had given the police time to catch up with him.

In that same long vacation, armed with sixty pounds, an old battered tent, a primus stove and a great number of books, Tom Bergner and I set off for Italy in my beloved old Austin. Tom was a wise and witty fellow scholarship man at Caths. He had a sharp Jewish sense of humour and a great ability to mock British crustiness. He was a friend whom I would have liked to keep. He went into the Coal Board and I went into the theatre. We haven't met since Cambridge.

Our trip lasted six weeks. We camped on a football pitch on the outskirts of Paris; we drove down the Rhône valley, explored Provence, and puttered along the Côte d'Azur into Italy and on to Florence. Money was so tight that we lived mainly on spaghetti and tomatoes cooked on our stove. I was 15 lb lighter when I returned home.

The cobblestones of northern France played hell with the Austin's springs. The engine broke down frequently, the radiator sprang a score of leaks – so did the tent. But I saw Paris for the first time; and *The Winter's Tale* at the Comédie Française, the Louvre, and *Boris Godunov* at the Paris Opera. The richness of the French country-side made me dizzy. As we drove south from Paris to the sea I saw the colours and felt the heat of the Midi. It was a completely new experience for me. I worshipped Provence. The Côte d'Azur was a little run-down and rather empty. It felt old-fashioned – what was modern belonged to the Twenties and Thirties. The post-war boom had not yet begun.

We reached Florence and I discovered my favourite city in the world: so much human genius in so small an area, and displayed on a perfect human scale.

I had the good luck to wander round southern Europe before mass tourism began. The roads were bad, but there were very few people about. Now there are too many, and national differences are consciously emphasised to delight the package tourist. It is, alas, a world of theme parks, and tourism is a branch of show business. Our trip was primitive but as important to me as learning music or my obsession with the theatre. Sadly, though, I was still in love with Jill. She wasn't that easy to forget. Although we had agreed not to write to each other, I haunted every poste restante office on our journey, just in case she had changed her mind. But no word came. Sometimes I was glad, sometimes devastated.

I returned to Cambridge full of determination. I presented myself to the drama groups with the energy of a phoenix confidently expecting to rise. But they could see no difference in me; I was the same sulky young man. It took me a couple of terms to get going in university theatre; and it wasn't until my third year that I really flew. As the theatre activity increased, I did academically less and less. My degree results reflected the loss of Jill and my return to the theatre. I was assessed at the end of my first year as a First; at the end of my second year, I received a 2:1; in my third, a 2:2. Had there been a fourth year, I believe I would have failed.

My parents watched anxiously as I worked harder and harder, not to land a decent, well-pensioned job, but to become a director. Tom Henn and Douglas Brown were equally alarmed as one of their academic high-fliers threw all his prospects away.

I dug deeper into Shakespeare, with one eye more on my future needs than the needs of the examination. I learnt about the texts – about contemporary typography and printing, the validity of the Shakespeare editions and Elizabethan spelling and pronunciation. The Marlowe Society mounted a production of *Julius Caesar* in which we all attempted to speak Elizabethan. We were trained in the accent by the expert scholarship of the day, and the play was directed by Dadie and John Barton. We were hardly good enough to play *Julius Caesar* in our own voices, much less good enough to speak it in a foreign language; for it *was* foreign – as a sound, like Belfast crossed with Devon. But how could our experts be sure they had it right? There was, after all, great latitude in the scholars' pronunciation of Chaucer's middle English. I worried that it could be the same with Shakespeare. Yet even for those of us who had only small roles (I doubled Marullus and Metellus Cimber) it was an unforgettable experience. Learning the accent gave living proof that the resonance and assonance of Shakespeare's text were richer and more complex than the clipped grey sounds of modern English.

When I am preparing a Shakespeare play, I still mutter the text to myself in Elizabethan. It reveals the shapes and the colours. It *always* makes the words wittier. Sometimes, to the incredulous delight of actors, I can be persuaded to demonstrate this arcane ability. I sound like a pedantic imitation of Ian Paisley, except the *k*'s are all pronounced. For instance,

> *Doth not Brutus bootless kneel?*

becomes

> *Doath nut Brewters bewtless kerneel?*

I nurse an ambition to direct a Shakespeare play with a completely American cast. I would like to use the richness of their vowels. Their sound is much nearer Elizabethan pronunciation than our restrained modern English. Americans usually take one of two courses with Shakespeare: either they speak Shakespeare as if they were pretending to be English, which is false and unendurable; or they ignore his shapes and try to speak him naturalistically, as modern Americans. If they learnt the rhythm and the form, and spoke the words with full-blooded American vowels, Shakespeare would live powerfully in American.

In time I began to understand more and more the nature of Shakespearean speech. I had learnt much from the textual analysis of Leavis; and much from Dadie, who had an instinctive understanding of breathing and form. In my early years in the profession, I worked with Edith Evans. She passed on to me the verse techniques that had been taught to her by William Poel, the great revolutionary director whose work had inspired the Marlowe Society when it was founded in the early 1900s. He reinstated the fleet ideals of Elizabethan speech and ousted the slow romantic rhetoric of the late Victorians. He believed that his way was Kean's way and even Garrick's way. The need to speak the speech trippingly on the tongue, combining a sense of form with a keen emotion, goes back all the way to the sixteenth century.

The rules of Shakespearean verse can be learnt in three hours. But then the actor must make them his, and apply them in his own way. The essence is to speak the lines rather than the individual words. The five-beat iambic line is the unit of communication. By the way he structures his lines, Shakespeare tells the actor when to go fast, when to go slow; where to come in on cue, where to pause. If you observe what he wrote, the scenes orchestrate themselves, their literal and emotional meaning is released and easily communicated to the audience. But, as in music, you must learn the notes correctly before you start to express the emotion. All this began to excite me at Cambridge. I already knew that you should never, never take a breath on the middle of a Shakespeare line, even if there is a full stop. You breathe on the end of the lines, often with tiny top-up gulps, so that the lungs are acting like the store of air in bagpipes – breath is always available to control the line and form it. And so the line is preserved.

I went several times to Stratford to see the 1951 History Cycle – Tony Quayle's greatest achievement – with Michael Redgrave as Richard II and Hotspur, Alan Badel as Poins and Justice Shallow, and Quayle himself as Falstaff. Above all, there was Richard Burton as Prince Hal and Henry V. Every generation has its new actor, somebody who redefines to his own age what acting is all about. He is usually thought of as more 'real' than the previous generation, who suddenly appear old-fashioned and stagy. Richard Burton in 1951 was, for me and countless others, that new actor. He spoke 'true'; but he still spoke Shakespeare. The critics at the time were greatly struck by his charisma and his obvious star quality. But many were disappointed by his understatement, his 'throwaway' naturalness. As members of the previous generation, they found him deficient in rhetoric. They were both right and wrong; they were not judging him by the emotional tastes of the new generation, but by the standards of Gielgud and Olivier. I noticed exactly the same response to Gerard Philippe a few years later in France. His performances in *Richard II* and *Le Cid* enraged the French critics. But neither he nor Burton denied the form; they simply adjusted the emotion, so that the rhetoric seemed less. Philippe was the new voice. Today, he and Burton would seem artificial.

My trips to Stratford owed much to Michael Birkett, a colleague in the Cambridge drama groups, and a hugely generous and enthusiastic spirit who was determined to have a career in the arts. He had a magnificent set of rooms in Trinity Great Court, and a car which would speed three or four of us from Cambridge to Warwickshire. We passed the journey doing bad imitations of Harry Andrews, the definitive Henry IV. Michael is still a loved friend.

I went on learning about Shakespeare: the Globe

Theatre and the articulation of the plays; how scene must follow scene like a well-cut film, slow scene following fast scene, lyrical scene following violent scene. The stage must never be allowed to go cold. I had seen a London production of *Richard II* with Alec Guinness in the title role. It had a plain wooden set by Michael Warre which became everything and everywhere. This was a revelation to me. The set was like a mask and took on all the various moods of Shakespeare's text. Tanya Moiseiwitsch's great design for the Stratford Histories did the same. I read more of Granville-Barker. I read Ronald Watkins's books about plain stage Shakespeare – especially *Moonlight At The Globe*. I began to dream of a plain stage and a fluent succession of contrasting scenes. I had still not directed a Shakespeare play; I had still not directed anything.

As my second year at university ended, theatre began to take over my life. The Marlowe Society presented *Romeo and Juliet* at the Arts Theatre as part of the Cambridge summer festival. John Barton played Mercutio; I played Tybalt. We rehearsed throughout the long vacation. I loved the control and precision of fencing. John and I devised the most impossibly dangerous (and long) rapier and dagger fight. It stole all the notices and was much praised, but I suspect that it brought the play to a complete halt. As the Prince of Cats I wore too much chrome make-up and had a very flat voice. But the performance worked. I was a success.

Even better, I started to direct, co-staging *The Browning Version* with John Barton. At last I found myself analysing the acting process. John was much more experienced than I, but from the first we were good for each other. He pushed me to be more precise; I urged him to be less dogmatic. I still love the play; perhaps it is Rattigan's finest. It never manipulates its characters and it is economical and heart-breaking.

Romeo and Juliet was transferred to the old Scala Theatre, London, for a fortnight's run and then went on to the Phoenix for a further two weeks. Winston Churchill came to see us and, after the performance, we were presented (one has to use the royal word) to the great man. He was, I suppose, nearly eighty. He gazed at us vaguely and cherubically. It was very awkward. He smiled and said nothing except a mumbled thank you. He seemed disappointingly old.

That undergraduate summer in London was a heady time. We were amazed to find ourselves playing in the West End. Those of us with professional ambitions joined Equity immediately (there was no closed shop in those days). There were perpetual parties and chattering that went on all night. And there were girls. A tiny house in Tryon Street in Chelsea which belonged to Judy Birdwood, the Marlowe Society's motherly wardrobe mistress, was where a group of us were allowed to doss down. A theatre company can, at its best and however briefly, become a Utopia in which everyone works and lives and believes together. We achieved such unity that summer, despite a little quarrelling and bitching, and a great deal of falling in and out of love.

– 12 –

Just before we left for London, the ADC committee had noticed to its surprise that it was booked to present an independent production by P. R. F. Hall as the first play of the coming autumn term. They called me in to ask if it was me and what I intended to do. They had a say in the choice of play, since it would affect their share of the box office. I was, like all my contemporaries, keen on modern French drama – particularly of the more perfumed kind. I proposed *The Infernal Machine* by Jean Cocteau and *The Master of Santiago* by Henri de Montherlant. Fortunately, the committee didn't think

much of either choice; and I doubt if I made the case
strongly, as I had at this stage no idea where the money
was going to come from to mount the production. I had
one more suggestion: *Point of Departure*, a translation
by Lucienne Hill of Anouilh's *Euridice*. To my surprise,
the committee agreed enthusiastically.

I had seen the play the year before in London at the
Duke of York's, with Dirk Bogarde and Mai Zetterling.
It seems manipulative now, but at the time I thought
that the theatre had at last caught up with the French
cinema and all those moody Jean Gabin films. It was
funny and haunting and sexy; and it gave a director
ample opportunity to show his surrealistic paces.

I collected a cast as fine as Cambridge could offer,
including one of the most original actors, amateur or
professional, that I have ever worked with – Donald
Bevis. He was a French don at King's and his acting
had a quality which marks all great actors – surprising
and unpredictable timing. He never said a line as you
expected it.

I hustled to find money for the production. I had
no resources and no prospect of an overdraft. Two of
my teachers from the Perse, John Tanfield and Cecil
Crouch, came to my rescue, and jointly lent me eighty
pounds – a great deal of money in those days and a sum
that I am sure they could ill afford.

There is always a tang of expectation in the air at
the start of the new university year – especially if it is
your third and last. Students in their third year inherit
the world. I was as happy as I have ever been when I
came back from the vacation. I was lucky enough to have
rooms in the roof of the central court of St Catharine's,
looking out towards King's Parade. I had installed my
only precious possession – a 1793 Broadwood fortepiano
which I had found mouldering in an old piano shop some
months before and had recklessly bought for the idioti-
cally high price of forty pounds. I still have it. It belongs
to that brief period when the English could do no wrong

in furniture design, architecture or the perfect turn of a sentence. And it has the sound that Mozart heard for his piano sonatas.

Best of all, I was about to rehearse *Point of Departure*. Becoming a director was a deeply pleasurable physical experience – like being dropped into a warm pool and finding I could swim. I had never felt that life was so easy, so relaxed, so assured. Thus must a duck take to water. I knew I had much to learn, but the practised amateur actors in the large cast supported me and seemed pleased at the help I could offer. I quickly forged the group into a company. The play was a success with the public and the university reviewers. John Tanfield and Cecil Crouch got their money back.

It was at this time I discovered, at last, that I could direct. My relief was acute and produced tears. I remember precisely the moment that I knew: we were rehearsing in a large room in the Bull Hostel, an annexe of St Catharine's which had formerly been a seedy hotel. The gas fire popped and the traffic on King's Parade went by the windows. We were in our third day of work and were trying to define a particular scene's purpose in the pattern of the play. The analytical training I had received in the English faculty was proving useful – I was asking the right questions. In addition, I now understood something about actors, something about teaching and something about leading a group. I was on my way.

There is no accepted way to become a director. You have to believe that you can do it, and by training in other disciplines, by practice and watching others, you become what you have it in you to be. You can learn how to break down a scene into units, you can learn how to stage, how to light, how to help actors create a character. But no amount of learning will make a director, any more than intensive training will make a conductor. During my career, I have been the impresario – or producer, to use the American term – for the greatest directors in the English-speaking theatre, from Peter Brook to Franco Zeffirelli. I have watched them all at work. My conclusion is that there are as many ways of directing as there are people. I have seen bad directors talk obvious sense to actors and achieve appalling results. I have seen good directors utter palpable nonsense and provoke brilliance.

A director must like actors and they must trust him. He must not abuse his power, for even the greatest actor – even Laurence Olivier – can have his confidence badly damaged for days by an unguarded remark. Directors should guard against their subjective reactions leading them into expressing their own fantasies about a play. An author should be present at the rehearsals of a new play and should collaborate fully with the director. If the director is working on a classic, he has to try to understand the author's intentions and express them in a way that a modern audience can understand. His work with the designer is crucial; no production ever survived a set which had an atmosphere at odds with what the production was trying to say.

The director provokes the talent around him to give of its best; and then he edits what has been created so that the production makes a coherent statement. This is the moment when his personal stamp is visible, when the concept of the production is defined. The director is the leader of a group who are on a journey to discover the play; neither he nor the group members know necessarily where that journey will lead them. To start out rehearsing with a concept which is imposed inhibits creation and prevents discovery. A good rehearsal has the excitement of the unexpected.

All the director's decisions have to be endorsed by the actors, since they have to recreate the play with conviction at every performance. He is part guide, part philosopher, part friend; he is also part conspirator, part psychiatrist, part actor, part scholar, part musician, part editor, part guru, part politician, part lover. He is occasionally part servant. He has to wear a different mask to satisfy the needs of many different people. He should not be a liar but sometimes he cannot tell all of the truth; confidence is too frail to withstand it. He has to nurture with the care of a good teacher, and reassure with the love of a good parent. It is a job of great power and influence, and can easily breed megalomaniacs and manipulators. It tempts the weak to be cruel to the insecure or the inexperienced.

Success is transitory; and finally only attractive because it means that this time the director hasn't failed. I personally don't do it for success, nor for money, nor for the audiences. Nor do I do it for the critics. I don't even do it for the playwrights – though of course I like it when Harold Pinter or Samuel Beckett or Tennessee Williams praise me for realising their play; it makes me feel fulfilled. But my chief satisfaction is the special time in every rehearsal period when the group becomes collectively inspired. The actors, the director and everyone concerned take strength from each other and, by working together, make themselves better, more perceptive and more talented than any of them knew they had it in them to be. It is a sensation that is very near ecstasy. With luck, it happens two or three times in every production.

– 13 –

John Whiting's *Saint's Day* was my next production at Cambridge. I had seen it in London in 1951 and responded to its haunting, apocalyptic power. It had the excitement of being a contemporary play – it defined the mood of the late Forties. For my revival – the first since its premiere – several national critics trooped down to Cambridge to argue once more in their reviews what John Whiting actually meant. In those days of the well-made play, critics expected simple statements, not

1. *top left* My mother in 1924.

2. *above* My father when he had just been appointed Station Master.

3. *left* At six years old – a hesitant cowboy.

4. *Albert Herring* (Glyndebourne). The opera is set in East Anglia where I was born. I directed this production in 1985.

5. *below left* 3120201 Aircraftsman Hall. I hardly went near an aeroplane or an airfield during my National Service in the RAF. **6.** *below right* At Cambridge.

7. Jill – my first love affair.

8. With Tom Bergner and my Austin 7. It took us through France and Italy in the long vac.

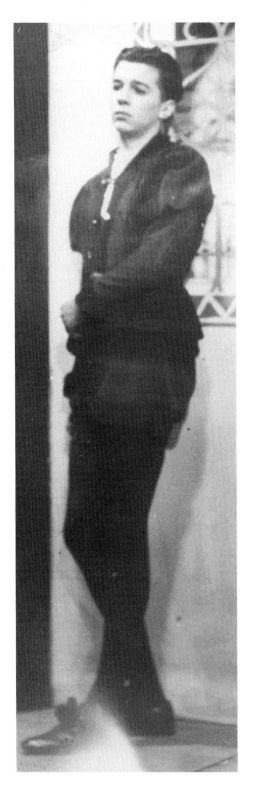

9. As Hamlet at the
Perse.

10. As Petruchio at the
Perse, with a boy
Katharina.

11. As First Citizen in a
Marlowe Society's
Coriolanus at Cambridge.

12. With Leslie on our
wedding day.

13. Sir Fordham Flower – Fordie. The RSC would never have happened without his courage.

14. Charles Laughton as Bottom (Stratford's 100th season). His huge moon of a face appeared to be much larger than anyone else's. The audience watched only him.

15. Mary Ure, Olivier and Edith Evans in *Coriolanus* (Stratford's 100th season).

16. A starry line-up in the gardens behind the Stratford theatre during the 100th season in 1959. All except Leslie were taking part. From left: Charles Laughton, Mary Ure, Laurence Olivier, Paul Robeson, Edith Evans, Glen Byam Shaw, Angela Baddeley, Harry Andrews; and Leslie with me.

17. With Leslie, Christopher and Jenny on holiday in France.

18. Leslie and Christopher do the twist. Jenny is bored.

ambiguity or contradictions. I learnt for the first time that controversy doesn't always stimulate: it can quite easily frighten people away. The play was a box-office failure (the loss borne by the society – University Actors – not, thank goodness, by generous schoolmasters); but it started a friendship with John Whiting which lasted until his death in the mid Sixties. He was a cryptic, kindly man with a passion for the theatre and for Byron. He had a blazing wit he too often buried in his work in tortured ambiguities. He was an actor, like many of the new dramatists – Ustinov, Pinter, Osborne – and he knew his craft. But it wasn't quite his time, though *Saint's Day* and Rodney Ackland's *The Red Room* are in my view the only two plays which express the exhausted, chaotic atmosphere of the immediate post-war period. Failure affected John deeply. He became one of those obscure yet prosperous people who doctor other writers' films scripts. He gave up the theatre.

I contrived to get him back in the early Sixties. First, I went to Hollywood and saw Aldous Huxley. He was virtually blind and only distantly interested in what I wanted – the rights to adapt his book, *The Devils of Loudun*, into a play. After a lot of discussion he agreed, and I sent the book to John. I told him that Dorothy Tutin and Richard Johnson, on the strength of reading it, had already agreed to appear in the main parts. I also said that we were starting rehearsals in six months with Peter Wood directing and Sean Kenny designing. It was to be the first new play commissioned by the Royal Shakespeare Company for the Aldwych Theatre. The plan worked. *The Devils* was a success and John began writing again for the theatre.

The third play I tried to direct at Cambridge was an undoubted masterpiece – *Uncle Vanya*. My production was certainly not extraordinary but I felt I had uncovered something fundamental about Chekhov. His characters dramatise the essential selfishness of human beings. They are all monuments of egocentricity. A character announces that he is contemplating suicide. The person to whom this alarming news is addressed takes no notice, merely observing that it is time for lunch. This inability to sympathise or even notice other people's problems is the essence of Chekhov's comedy. It makes his characters funny, anarchic and bracingly unsentimental. The English tend to temporise this self-ishness with good manners and gentility; this blunts the edge and makes the cruelty less comic.

A director is privileged for a time to live inside the head of the genius he is serving. I may well not be capable of understanding all that I find, but while I am examining every detail of the masterpiece I am staging, I feel very close to Mozart, to Wagner or to Shakespeare. To direct a work is a far more searching experience than simply studying it or going to a performance. My definition of paradise is to be always rehearsing: a Shakespeare play, followed by a Mozart opera.

After *Uncle Vanya*, I wrote a long and careful letter to Dadie. I asked him what hopes I had of being a professional director. He replied with a terse postcard. 'My advice to those wanting to enter the theatre is the same as the advice Mr Punch gave to those contemplating matrimony: Don't.' But I would not be put off. I went to his rooms and had a long talk with him. I was so persistent he offered to try to get me an assistant stage manager's job with H. M. Tennent. Remembering that Peter Wood was still stuck at the Apollo Theatre after three years, I politely refused. He was, I think, amazed at my arrogance; and I was very frightened at what I had done. Though I was now the proud possessor of a batch of good national reviews, and in John Whiting had a professional friend and supporter, these would hardly win me a life in the theatre.

I didn't let up on the pace I was setting myself, however. I directed *Winterlude*, a strange Ruritanian

86

comedy by John Barton, which didn't succeed but was my first attempt to work with a writer on a new play. And I rounded off my three terms of continuous directing with a May-week production of *Love's Labour's Lost* at the ADC. At last I was doing Shakespeare.

All that I had learnt from Dadie, all that I had eagerly discussed with John Barton (a scholarly King of Navarre) was now put to use. It was a very Elizabethan production – big ruffs and formal costumes. In my memory, it looks lovely – like a Nicholas Hilliard come to life. Raymond Leppard selected the music, and he and I played it on alternate nights on a harpsichord. He played it brilliantly.

I loved the melancholy heart of the play and its long dying fall. I think the production was atmospheric and well spoken. I now knew by experience that Shakespeare could never be fully released in the theatre unless his words were allowed to live. I also found out that artificial costumes can dehumanise a production. A lot of the subtle emotions and wit we had discovered were lost when the cast donned the ruffs and the panniers.

As the end of my time at Cambridge drew nearer, I became only too aware that I had directed rather more productions in my last year than a professional could reasonably have expected to do in the same period. I had done next to no studying and had been warned of the consequences. Douglas Brown was especially clear-headed. He told me I was risking my degree and my future, but if the theatre was what I wanted, he would not try to stop me. I said I would take the risk. He then allowed me to miss supervisions and forget my essays. He was a real friend.

I was completely unprepared for the examinations, and stayed up night after night studying. I nearly broke down in the middle of one paper. Somehow the adrenalin kept me going. Immediately afterwards I continued the rehearsals for *Love's Labour's Lost*.

Once the production and the term were over, I suffered the inevitable collapse. But Cambridge hadn't quite finished with me because I had three plays to direct for the Marlowe Society's summer festival: Anouilh's *Antigone*, Whiting's *Penny for a Song* and Pirandello's *Henry IV*. These would all be played at the Cambridge Arts Theatre during late July and August. But after that? In the night watches, I wrote sixty-eight anxious letters to people in the theatre asking for any kind of work. They were all hand-written and all (I thought) precisely judged to interest the recipient. I had five replies, each regretting that there were no openings. Since then, I have always answered every letter sent to me – unless it was from an obvious madman.

I sank into a deep depression. John Whiting was a staunch friend and gave me one or two introductions; but they led nowhere. I had little to my name but some university debts. The future was bleak.

The exam results came. I breathed a sigh of relief at my 2:2. It was a second-class degree but I had deserved to fail.

Cambridge had given me a great deal, but above all it had given me the opportunity to be a director. And I had found there a stimulating and loyal group of friends who were as keen on the theatre as I was. John Barton had decided to become an academic, but a galaxy of other people from my time, Peter Wood, Timothy O'Brien the designer, Toby Robertson, Tony Church, Tony White and Michael Birkett among them, were all bent on the profession.

Cambridge had also given me a measure of confidence when I tried to write or speak. I had been an invisible member of St Catharine's, for I had used my college as a lodging house, spending all my time in theatre circles. My attic in the roof of that lovely quadrangle had been largely uninhabited. The college had little connection with the drama. But the seventeenth-century dramatist James Shirley had been a student, and there was a Shirley Society which held Sunday-evening lectures. I didn't go very often, but I once heard Michael Ayrton

speak without a misplaced word for an hour on his belief
in art. His courage in speaking without notes, in actually
thinking aloud, had held the audience and made them
follow him thought by thought. I resolved then always
to direct, always to lecture, without reference to notes.
I would try to think it out with the people I was talking
to, whatever the dangers. I have stuck to this resolution.
I have talked to actors about Shakespeare, to singers
about Mozart and I have lectured regularly in univer-
sities. I have given Memorial addresses in St Martin-in-
the-Fields and Westminster Abbey; and I have never
used notes.

Now, though, with a career to make, I had to face
up to a number of negatives. My love affair with Jill
had been intense; but it had gone wrong simply because
of the extent to which my ambitions consumed me – a
taste of terrible things to come. I had put my parents
through a deeply anxious time; I was in debt and worried
about money; I was always in top gear, overworked, over-
stretched, overenthusiastic. Part of me would have liked
to take things easily and wait – but I couldn't. Sometimes,
too, I felt an incompetent, with only a glancing knowledge
of many things. I was an unfulfilled, unsuccessful scholar,
an unfinished musician, an untrained administrator and
an appalling linguist. I knew how to act, but knew I had
no talent for it. I knew I could talk to amateur actors and
help them develop; but could I talk to professionals? I was
also aware that I was a cliché: the working-class boy who
had turned himself into a phoney member of the middle
classes. I didn't belong with my parents or relations, but
I didn't quite belong with my new friends. I knew I would
only feel confident if I made a success of my profession.
For the second time, I contemplated suicide. I was desperate.

I threw myself into rehearsals for the summer festival
and tried to forget the black void that awaited me once
it was over. The plays earned me some more London
notices. Reports of Pirandello's *Henry IV* caught the eye

of Alec Clunes, the director and actor who ran the Arts Theatre Club in London. In those days there was no fringe, but there were a number of club theatres which worked outside the licensing authorities or the writ of the censor, the Lord Chamberlain. These theatres did provocative or banned plays and difficult classics. The Arts was the best; in fact, a critic had dubbed it 'our pocket-sized national theatre'.

Alec Clunes was a talented and scholarly man, an excellent actor and an able director. He invited my *Henry IV* to the Arts Theatre for a fortnight at the end of August. Even then, I knew that this was incredibly, not to say indecently, lucky. Our reception was good, and the morning after the first night, I had a phone call from John Counsel, the director of the Windsor Rep. A fortnight later I was directing Somerset Maugham's *The Letter* for him. I had jumped the abyss, made the leap from amateur to professional. To my surprise, the actors didn't seem that different in their methods or in their attitudes. They were less likely to want to work all the hours God made – but I thought that was sensible. They listened to me; they allowed me to shape the scenes; I was accepted.

It had been a near thing, though. If the invitation to London hadn't come, what would have happened? Would I have survived? Would I have persevered in the theatre? In the early years, you need enormous luck. I had been granted it. As a consequence – and however foolish it may appear – I have always felt guilty.

Alec Clunes was in the process of selling the Arts. The new owner was Campbell Williams, formerly chairman of Keith Prowse, the ticket agency, and an investor in theatre productions. He had engaged John Fernald to be his new director. Alec, as a leaving gesture, suggested that I be kept on to assist by reading scripts and being a general dogsbody. Campbell Williams proposed a salary of seven pounds a week and luncheon vouchers – just enough to live on. But the miracle (and I believe this too was suggested by Alec) was that I was also to be allowed to work in regional repertory theatres if I could get guest jobs, which from time to time I did.

The black hole was no longer at my feet. I have often approached it in subsequent years, but have seldom been so close to its brink. Nor have I been out of work since, though I still fear it could happen; it is the common condition of my profession.

– 14 –

I found a place to live in London. Felicity, the mother of Toby Robertson, had a basement in a large house off Kensington Church Street. I moved into it for a minimal sum and lived with a large anthracite boiler, rancid and acid smelling, which made it difficult to sleep, even to breathe. Felicity fed me and encouraged me and my luck held. She was, among other things, a writer and adaptor of radio plays. Most of all she was an enthusiast, with a warm heart and many eccentric loves and hates – one of those life forces that the theatre seems blessedly to attract.

At Worthing I did an obscure American thriller called *The Man*, and found that I had seven days in which to stage it from start to finish. In weekly rep the actors not only performed this week's play every night, they also rehearsed next week's play from the Tuesday. It was read in the morning and Act I was staged in the afternoon. Acts II and III were staged on Wednesday. On Thursday morning the company worked through Act I, which by some miracle was now approximately learnt; but Thursday afternoon was a matinée, so it was useless to the director because his actors were otherwise engaged. On Friday Acts II and III were worked through; and on Saturday morning the whole play had a run-through. The actors then did a matinée and evening performance of this week's play. On Sunday the company had the day off, though in reality they would be desperately learning their lines; also, last week's set was taken down and next week's set put up – often being built and painted at the same time. On Monday morning the director lit the play; on Monday afternoon there was a dress rehearsal; and on Monday night the play opened. The whole process then began again.

Most British theatre in the Forties and Fifties was weekly rep. Though ruthless, it produced a whole generation of expert actors who survived by constantly refining their craft. Perhaps Paul Eddington should stand as its hero, for he is the most consummate craftsman I know. Weekly rep had the energy of theatre at its rawest. It also had immediate judgement from its audience. I once asked the distinguished film and television writer Ken Taylor how he had developed such a strong sense of narrative in his scripts. He said he had been on the book as stage manager at Leatherhead for many long years, so was at once aware, by listening, when a play lost its audience and the story died. He always tried to analyse why. The narrative sense he gained from this gave us *The Jewel in the Crown*.

But for a director, weekly rep was another matter. Keeping order was about as much as could be done. The cast couldn't cope with ideas (they hadn't the time), they just needed to get the play on. I learnt nothing from the experience except compassion for the actors.

I was busy throughout 1954, eking out a living at the Arts, and directing now and again at the Oxford Playhouse, Windsor and Worthing. As my prosperity increased, I left my anthracite boiler in Kensington and moved to a pleasant basement room by the canal in Little Venice; then to two rooms behind St Thomas's Hospital on the south side of Westminster Bridge; then finally to a rather grand flat in Montague Place which

I shared with John Barton. On leaving Cambridge in 1953, John and Toby Robertson, Peter Wood and myself, with Colin George and Gordon Gostelow from Oxford, had formed the Elizabethan Theatre Company. We toured small theatres and school halls giving plain, well-spoken Shakespeare. So in addition to my part-time work in London and the reps, I was able to direct frugal productions of *Twelfth Night* and *The Merchant of Venice*.

I also managed to combine my job at the Arts with six happy months, towards the end of 1954, as director of the Oxford Playhouse. I had an extraordinarily talented company, including Billie Whitelaw, Ronnie Barker, Michael Bates, Derek Francis and Tony Church. There were also two assistant stage managers with acting ambitions. Their names were Maggie Smith and Eileen Atkins. Both now claim that I gave the best parts to the other. Eileen also maintains that I sacked her for having a continuous cold. In an extravagantly praised Christmas show I directed, entitled *Listen to the Wind*, with music by Vivian Ellis, Maggie Smith played the damp West Wind in green make-up and with drooping inflections. From the very beginning, she had a lethal sense of the ridiculous. I also accompanied her on the piano when she sang 'The boy I love is up in the gallery' as part of our Victorian Music Hall programme. She was clearly going to be a star.

Oxford in the mid Fifties was not unlike Cambridge. I was always either in the theatre or, rather unwillingly, in the pub that conveniently butted right up to the stage door. A diet of Scotch eggs, cheese, pickled onions, and late-night curries at the local Taj Mahal kept my digestion in a state of turmoil. In truth, I was hardly aware of Oxford itself. But that goes for directing anything anywhere: if you are immersed in a production in London or Stratford, New York or Los Angeles, Bayreuth or Glyndebourne, there is little time to appreciate much else.

By now, I was not just the script reader at the Arts; in the spring of 1954, I was invited to do a production. Mindful of Alec Clunes's great days there, I chose an international classic, Lorca's *Blood Wedding*. I loved Lorca's ability to mix surrealistic poetic theatre with the concrete depiction of peasant life. I can't have had any idea of the risk I was running in putting on this difficult play. I surreptitiously rewrote the only translation – an appalling mixture of windy poetics and American slang – and hoped for the best. It was enough of a success to fill the theatre for a month, and to my delight Harold Hobson in the *Sunday Times* noticed a new director. He described how I had created a living forest on a tiny stage: the entire cast held freshly cut tree branches which they swayed gently in a mass of backlight. Lionel Jeffries made his name playing the father. He had been out of work for months and told me that if I didn't give him the job he was going to become a policeman. He hasn't stopped working since, mainly on the screen. He is that rarity in England, an eccentric, sexy character actor who takes enormous risks. I wish he had appeared more often on the stage.

I felt passionate about the position of the Arts Theatre. I had seen great performances there: Shaw's *Back to Methuselah*, Jean Forbes-Robertson as Hedda Gabler, Wilfrid Lawson as the Father.

John Fernald – buoyed up by my enthusiasm for little-known foreign drama – let me direct as my next production a Goldoni play, *The Impresario from Smyrna*. This again was an awful translation but it could, I thought, take the audience into a world of classic comedy which, with my Third Programme zeal, I wanted to bring to the notice of the English. However, things did not go well, and I learnt a nasty fact about a director's life.

A director has little idea at any stage of the proceedings just how successful a production is going to be; but by the end of the first reading, he has a very clear idea if he has made a mistake – an irrevocable mistake, I mean, in the choice of play or the choice of actors. But however awful this revelation, there is absolutely nothing he can do about it except compose his features into a let's-get-on-with-it smile and pretend that everything is going to be all right. He is then in hell for the next four or five weeks, for he knows that everything is certainly *not* going to be all right. Yet there is nobody in the cast he can share his feelings with because the actors expect him to be optimistic and positive, even though they too realise in their heart of hearts that they are working on a failure. I knew that *The Impresario from Smyrna* was a disaster from day one. The cast was wrong for it, and the facetious and silly translation made a slight play slighter. But I battled on because I had to.

I then experienced a delusion that afflicts all directors. Confidence rises even when you are working on the most obvious dog. Perhaps, you think to yourself, the dedication and hard work of the cast has turned the awful enterprise round? Perhaps you have been unduly pessimistic? A self-deluding hope fills the company as they approach the first night; maybe if it didn't, they would never find the nerve to open their mouths. By the end of the Goldoni rehearsals, I was afflicted with this hope. For the first and only time in my life, I stayed up all night after the opening and went at dawn to collect the newspapers from Fleet Street. Once a professional tradition, this is no longer possible. The speed of modern technology means that most newspapers now print their reviews two days after the first night.

I stood in Fleet Street that morning in the dawn light and read the most terrible set of notices imaginable. They winded me, and I had to admit they were deserved. I should not have done the play because I clearly had no idea what style it required. It is a cliché that comedy is a very serious business. And it is certainly true that you cannot direct comedy without being in touch with the heart of the play, which must be believable and recognisably human if the comedy is to have any truth.

I had completely failed to find that heart. I wondered if I should ever work again.

Flops are inevitable in any theatre career. Sometimes they are from circumstances outside your control; sometimes they are bred of your own inadequacies or miscalculations. The trick is to learn from your failures. To be recriminating or self-pitying is pointless. And since critics can only talk about *what* you did, and not *why* you did it, their comments, whether in praise or condemnation, can be very misleading. In fact, imputing motives to me is the only thing that makes me lastingly angry with critics. They cannot know why I made one choice rather than another. They can only know that, for them, I was wrong.

I like to keep moving. I have always striven to be booked up so that I can go briskly from one job to the next, whatever might be the outcome of the present piece of work. There is a great deal to be said for this. I am a director; each day I want to direct, not wait for the phone to ring or meditate on my failings.

I was always in love during my early years in London, just as I had been in my two last frantic years at Cambridge. I fell in love easily and regularly. I seemed incapable of having casual affairs. It was all or nothing. My intensity, I think, put girls off or, if it didn't, landed me in serious relationships immediately, before either of us was ready. I loved women but, as an only child who had grown up in a single-sex school, I knew little about them. If a girl was very pretty, I naturally believed that she was very clever as well. I was an out-and-out romantic.

Before the Pill and before the permissive society, it was difficult to develop a stable sexual relationship. Frustration was the norm. When I was at Cambridge, competition was fierce. Cycling through the cold fenland rains to have tea at Girton became an erotic experience. What surprises me now is not that my generation had so little sex in the Fifties, but that, given the circumstances, we had any at all.

I have been married four times and had two other long-term serious commitments which were marriages in all but name. I don't wonder that people doubt me when I say that I believe passionately in marriage, in the sharing of life completely with a partner, where each supports the other through the difficulties as well as the excitements. When I was shooting the film of *Akenfield*, with local East Anglian people improvising the parts, I found a fine old Suffolk character with flint-blue eyes, lantern jaw, and a faint mocking smile. He must have been in his late seventies. I asked him to have a chat with the hero, Tom, who was planning his marriage. There was no rehearsal; we rolled two cameras as they talked:

OLD MAN: I hear y'are gettin' married, boy . . .
TOM: Yeah . . .
OLD MAN: Well, if there's onything better in this life, then oiv never hed it.

I agree. The problem is that it is a part of life where compromise is difficult. If a relationship is not completely right, then in my case it very quickly seems to go completely wrong. The deficiencies feed on each other until finally there is nothing left. This is not to say that until I married Nicki Frei there were not spells of intense happiness and fulfilment. But it has taken me nearly a lifetime to achieve the marriage I hoped for.

After Jill, there were many attempts to get it right. Until Nicki, they all ended in pain.

– 15 –

I waited after the failure of the Goldoni to see if my career was over. I detected a slight coldness mixed with a dash of sympathy among my colleagues. I was no longer the golden boy who could do no wrong. Infallibility like that only comes once in a career – after the first success. Ever after, whoever you are and whatever you have done, you are to some degree only as good as your last play.

I waited and waited. Had John Fernald lost his trust? Blessedly he gave me another production and handed me a script based on André Gide's *The Immoralist*. The play was a Broadway adaptation, and made a banal novel even more banal. It used secret homosexuality as a melodramatic titillation, much like the Victorians used drink and drunkenness. The play told the story of a bisexual – a man who on his honeymoon in North Africa found his homosexuality awakened by watching an Arab boy dance. We can smile at the melodrama now, but in 1954 the subject was taboo and it seemed important and immensely daring to stage it.

The play was of course banned. Strict censorship by the Lord Chamberlain meant that public theatres were not allowed even to mention the existence of homosexuality. But club theatres like the Arts were outside the Lord Chamberlain's aegis. Providing you joined a theatre club, you could have your morals corrupted – and be burnt to death, for clubs were also outside the official fire regulations.

I was indignant that the theatre should be censored in a way that did not apply to publishing, broadcasting or the press. The Lord Chamberlain's readers were mostly ex-Service officers picked, apparently, for their extremely dirty minds, since they often found filth where none was intended. I was shocked, too, by the prejudice at that time against homosexuals and by the fact that they were still, in the eyes of the law, criminals. These were causes worth joining. Plays by Ibsen, Shaw and Granville-Barker had all been banned; and how many plays had been aborted before even a word was written because the dramatist knew that he would be censored?

It wasn't easy to get actors to come to the Arts. Agents were definitely not interested in a young director who was offering no money for rehearsals – just luncheon vouchers – and eight pounds a week when playing. I discovered that the only way to cast a play was to speak directly to the actor. Through a mutual friend, I found Yvonne Mitchell's phone number and asked her if she would do *The Immoralist*. She was then a considerable star of screen and stage. She agreed, and a lifelong friendship began with her and her husband, the critic and author Derek Monsey. Then another favourite actor, Michael Gough, joined the cast.

In the event, *The Immoralist* was a big success, though of course its subject matter meant it could not transfer to the West End. Heterosexuals swarmed to it to show their tolerance. So, naturally, did homosexuals.

I was happy with the production: I could sense that my work was maturing. I was beginning to know by tempo, pause and timing how I could create atmosphere.

My next production at the Arts was a much finer play, Julien Green's *South*. Set at the beginning of the American Civil War, it was another homosexual tragedy, and the first production I was completely proud of in my own heart. It was a delicately written piece, hardly daring to verbalise its feelings. I found what lay under the words and orchestrated it.

In the early stages of rehearsal, the shape and pace of a scene must not be imposed. The actors should be free to create while the director helps to release their imaginations; and if that means going very fast or very

slow, or taking enormous pauses, it must happen: everything must be allowed. But once the truth of the scene
is found, the director becomes the editor. He must shape
what has been discovered in the certain knowledge that
an audience's collective apprehension is quicker than an
actor's instinct or a director's desire to linger over the
finer moments. He must make sure every second of
action earns its time upon the stage. At this point,
he shapes the scene as a conductor shapes a piece of
orchestral music – quickening here, slowing there, so
that the audience is given variety. Not only does this
give form to what the actors have created; it also provides
a map which the actors can follow on those evenings –
and they will happen – when inspiration is not present.
By following the map, it is possible to induce creativity
when none was there. *South* was my first production
which achieved a full and justified shape. A new young
critic called Bernard Levin, writing in *Truth*, understood
what I had done. I was very pleased.

The Goldoni was now almost forgotten; it had certainly been forgiven. If I had done it after *The Immoralist*
and *South* instead of before, I might not have had my
next stroke of luck. John Fernald was offered the job
of principal of the Royal Academy of Dramatic Art, so
he decided to give up the Arts. Campbell Williams, the
owner, called me into his office and asked me to run it.
Suddenly, I had my own theatre in the centre of London.
I was just twenty-four.

– 16 –

John Whiting was my guide to what was happening
in world drama. He told me about Eugene Ionesco's
work, particularly *The Bald Prima Donna* and *The
Lesson*. Their surrealistic comedy was very attractive; it

struck a blow at the British theatre which often looked bogged down in time-wasting naturalism. As John Fernald left, we shared a double bill at the Arts in which I directed *The Lesson* and John an André Obey play about the Trojan War called *Sacrifice to the Wind*. The Ionesco, the first to be seen in London, brought abuse, laughter and rage. The author came over and gazed at the production like an amused gnome who wanted to blow everything up, not because he particularly disapproved of it but because it would be fun. It was the first time I had met a complete anarchist and I greatly enjoyed the experience. For thirty-five years, Ionesco told this story: 'When the young English director Peter Hall was directing *The Lesson*, he objected that the Professor kills forty pupils during the day. The girl who arrives for her lesson in the play is the forty-first. "Wouldn't it be more credible," asked Peter, "if he'd only killed three or four?" This, Ionesco would say, is an example of the English love of understatement.

There is no truth whatsoever in his story. But I appreciated Ionesco.

After *The Lesson*, I took a deep breath and directed a revival of *Mourning Becomes Electra*, O'Neill's great but finally earthbound attempt to write a modern Greek tragedy. It was my first try at an epic event. Ever since I had seen Richardson and Olivier do the two parts of *Henry IV* in one day, I had believed in big occasions in the theatre. It was a belief that later led me to *The Wars of the Roses* trilogy and to the seven History Plays at Stratford; and, at the National Theatre, to both parts of *Tamburlaine the Great*, to *The Oresteia* and to the cycle of the three Late Plays of Shakespeare.

Mourning Becomes Electra disappointed the critics; they objected not to the production but to the play. O'Neill is a great architect of drama, but not often a great writer of dialogue. He seems to half realise his deficiencies and loads the page with long stage directions describing the high emotions of the characters. The actors are instructed to be scornful, to make their voices quiver and to look sad and angry at the same time; all these instructions betray O'Neill's anxiety. Descriptive stage directions are dangerous for actors; they encourage applied results – not acting processes. I would like to see *Mourning Becomes Electra* with the stage directions ignored and the emotions underplayed. A realistic approach might well reveal far more, and be more in tune with the under-stated naturalism of O'Neill's dialogue.

By now it was time for a holiday. I had no current girlfriend, so I went alone to Spain. I have always found a holiday without a purpose unendurable, and packed my bag with all twelve volumes of *Remembrance of Things Past* – a work I had not read. I lay on a beach and surrendered myself to this intricate marathon. I was in the middle of book ten when a telegram arrived: 'Business on *Mourning Becomes Electra* failing. Please return immediately to begin rehearsals of next production.' I have still not finished Proust's masterpiece.

I returned to direct *Waiting for Godot*, the world premiere in English of Samuel Beckett's play. I, and everybody else at the Arts, thought the enterprise was a huge gamble. The text had arrived in my little cupboard of an office several weeks earlier and in the most conventional way possible – through the post. With it was a letter from Donald Albery, a leading West End manager, asking if I would like to stage it. Attempts to set it up in the West End had completely failed. Many luminaries, Gielgud, Richardson and Guinness among them, had refused to appear in it.

It was at that time running in a tiny theatre in Paris. As director of the Arts, I went to Paris every three or four months because it was then the centre of theatre. I had met Julien Green and Jean Anouilh there; also Henri de Montherlant, in a pretentiously empty room on the Quai d'Orsay furnished with busts of

Roman emperors which looked much like his own head. But I hadn't met Beckett. Nor had I seen *Waiting for Godot*. To be truthful, I had only just known of him and his play.

I had read it during a long meal-break at the technical rehearsals for *Mourning Becomes Electra*. It needed four men, a boy, and a tree that was bare in the first act but sprouted leaves in the second. I found it enormously appealing, and written by a master. This was poetic theatre. What do I mean by poetic? Well, it wasn't sequinned with applied adjectives like Christopher Fry, or with dry ironic platitudes like T. S. Eliot. Here was a voice, a rhythm, a shape that was very particular: lyrical, yet colloquial; funny, yet mystical. Though expressed in natural speech, unpretentious and believable, it was much *more* than natural speech: there was a haunting sub-text.

Waiting for Godot is an inversion of a normal play: for the first time, lack of action becomes the action. And the play is a rich metaphor: all of us are, by the act of living, waiting; certainly waiting for death and, perhaps, waiting also for some answer to our existence. I didn't think whether it would be a success or not; I certainly didn't worry about whether it was important or not. I just felt a strong desire to try to realise it on the stage. All the time, I came back to the sensual pleasure of the evocative writing, to its unique rhythm and tone. I have nightmares, even now: suppose I had turned the play down and then lived to realise what I had rejected?

It wasn't easy to cast. Actors were baffled by the long passages of seemingly inconsequential dialogue. They did not see that it was funny and human. I finally engaged Paul Daneman, Peter Bull, Peter Woodthorpe and Timothy Bateson. It would be an exaggeration to say they were enthusiastic. They worked hard, but sometimes they thought they were in a kind of con job – that Beckett was having us on; that the play was a suit of Emperor's New Clothes. Rehearsals, though, revealed in it much comedy and a dark seam of terror. I had from the start thought of Vladimir and Estragon as tramps. It has been pointed out since that there is nothing to indicate this in the text and the observation came as something of a shock. They seemed then – and they still seem – tramps to me: two men waiting in a limitless landscape for something to turn up while chewing the odd carrot to pass the time.

On the first night, very little went right. After half an hour, there were yawns and mock snores and some barracking. Later on, the audience nearly erupted into open hostility but then decided not to bother and settled instead into still, glum boredom. A few people laughed with genuine recognition; and the same few applauded enthusiastically at the end. It was a mixed reception, with the mixture very definitely on the side of failure.

When the performance finished, I met my new and extremely smooth international agent, a man who had promised great things for me in London and America. He was puce with rage and for the first time in our relationship expressed a strong opinion. 'Well, you've done it now,' he spluttered. 'We were just getting you going, we have the meeting with Tennents, and the possibility of Broadway, and you go and do an awful thing like this.' I decided then and there that he was not for me. I've never been very good at hiding my feelings if my beliefs were threatened. By now, I believed passionately in Beckett and in *Waiting for Godot*. Nonetheless, I was suddenly frightened – which I had not been as the curtain fell.

The next morning's press was dreadful. The notices were outraged or uncomprehending or patronising. The *Guardian* reflected that this was just the sort of nonsense that could be seen in smoky basements in Berlin in the Twenties, but that we really didn't need it now. Among my new friends who hung around the bar of the Arts was a forthright agent just starting out called Peggy Ramsay. She was already a doughty fighter who treated the world as a nest of fools that had to be manipulated either covertly or blatantly if there was to be any hope of right being done. Subsequently, she was to represent practically every important British dramatist. She knew a little about Beckett, and during my preparation for *Godot* had helped me find out more. I had read his novel, *Watt*, and had discovered something of his Irish background and his connection with James Joyce. I discussed the notices with her: the actors and I came out of the occasion well enough – but Beckett was largely derided.

Peggy urged me to send at once, that day, to Harold Hobson, the *Sunday Times* critic, a copy of *Watt*, saying that if last night's performance had interested him he might be intrigued by this book. I did as she suggested and crossed my fingers.

Meanwhile, Campbell Williams called me into his office and announced that the play would have to come off immediately as nobody wanted to see it. I asked him to wait at least until the Sunday notices, and, after a lot of persuasion, he agreed.

Hobson's notice began with a reference to *Watt*, and then developed into the kind of panegyric that theatre people imagine in paradise. He understood the play and acclaimed the arrival of an extraordinary talent who was changing the nature of drama. He then went on writing about *Godot*, week after week, for the next couple of months. Kenneth Tynan in the *Observer* liked it too; but he took time to work up a full enthusiasm.

Hobson was a Christian, though this did not prevent him being on occasion a virulent critic. He had an inclination to assess the metaphysical weight of a play; he also liked to isolate key moments of redemption or forgiveness. One of his articles on *Godot* defined what he took to be a deeply Christian moment – when Vladimir took off his battered bowler hat and said, 'Christ have mercy upon us'.

When we were rehearsing, Paul Daneman had told

me he was having enormous difficulty with Vladimir's long philosophical speeches in the second act because he felt engulfed in his hat. We ran the scene again, and on reaching 'Christ have mercy upon us' I stopped him and, without much directorial originality, asked him to remove his bowler.

After Hobson's spiritual experience had been published, I found a distraught Daneman in the theatre. 'I can't take my hat off on that line now,' he said. 'The audience will be waiting for it and will feel let down.' I urged him to continue. The notice would be forgotten in a few days, I said, and the audience would receive the moment for what it was – a plausible human action that would mean different things to different people.

Hobson saved *Godot*. The play quickly became the talking point of London and then an international success. It featured in cartoons and radio programmes as well as newspaper articles. I was interviewed on *Panorama* by a bewildered Malcolm Muggeridge who asked indignantly, on behalf of the British public, what it all meant. People abused it, walked out of it, loved it, laughed at it and wrote letters to the papers about it. It shifted people's expectations of what a play was. Some found the change exciting, some appalling. But nobody was indifferent.

The play transferred from the Arts to the Criterion Theatre, where it had a long and successful run. And I earned my first real money. Ever since, I have believed that if you do what you like, and do it with conviction, you will finally make money in the theatre. All the evidence suggests that this is not true; in our age, it is usually trash that makes real money. But it has been a sweet delusion to live by.

I now became, for the first time, a little bit famous: the new young director, interviewed by *Vogue*, photographed by Tony Armstrong Jones, and asked by Sunday newspapers how he proposed to spend Christmas.

What was my production like? I suspect that I was

very near the heart of the play. It had humanity without sentimentality and a bleakness that coexisted with tenderness. It was also funny. I regret the music: there were little wisps of Bartok in the air now and then. They were underplayed, but even so they were competing with the music of one of the greatest writers of the century. I was definitely gilding the lily.

Beckett hadn't come to the first night. He disliked going to public performances of his own plays. But once our production was well established, he slipped into the audience. He said he was pleased. He was certainly pleased that *Godot* had become part of people's consciousness. The play is the major drama of the mid twentieth century. *Look Back in Anger* was a social and English phenomenon, and it started a national revolution: the young for the first time wanted to write plays, not novels or poems. But it was old-fashioned in its structure and technique. Beckett widened the scope of theatre for ever and the effect was international.

Sam was in no way a typical dramatist. He was neither paranoid nor arrogant. I understand very well why writers are the most difficult people to deal with in the theatre. They make something out of nothing and are haunted by that blank white page. They are also the victims of all the crazy interpretative ideas that are pushed at them; and all the vanities and insecurities, and sometimes stupidities, of the actors, directors and designers. Sam was never defensive. He was courteous, kind and had a twinkle in those cryptic Irish eyes which mocked his own opinions and everybody else's. He was meticulously well-mannered in rehearsal, very understanding of actors and knew exactly what he wanted.

I remember the grace and precision with which he tutored Peggy Ashcroft, showing her how to hold Winnie's powder compact in *Happy Days*. He had a great interest in the meaning of mime and exact physical gesture. So when I directed the play, I asked him to come for a fortnight to teach Peggy all the physical business before we began rehearsals. It is detailed in the stage directions, but could not be anything like as subtle or as intricate as his imagining.

Towards the end of my time at the National Theatre, I asked Sam if he would direct a new production of *Godot*. He said that he couldn't. He had done a production at the Schiller Theatre which had taken him six months to plot, writing out the action step by step, gesture by gesture, as if he were writing a novel. He then dictated it to the actors; and they then had to make this imposition their own. They told me it had taken them many, many weeks. Paradoxically, the result was a masterpiece, though by the rules of direction it shouldn't have been. In the Beckett archives at Reading University is an entire volume describing the precise gestures of Vladimir and Estragon in this Berlin *Godot*. As he said, he was a writer, not a director.

Sam's face is one of the icons of the century. We all know the gaunt bones and the ravaged cheeks. And we know from his drama the bleak sense of isolation and despair – modern man waiting in an indifferent, uncaring universe. But in life, Sam was the warmest, most humorous person you could meet. He seemed a nihilist, but humanity would keep breaking in. He helped us pass the time realistically and unsentimentally; but he provoked a great deal of laughter.

Amazing things came out of *Godot*. One morning, the phone rang and a gentle, cultured American voice with a beautiful drawl asked if he could speak to Peter Hall. He said that his name was Tennessee Williams. I thought for a moment that it was a practical joke. He asked if we could have a drink together. He had seen my production and wanted to tell me that he would be happy, indeed honoured, if I would direct his plays in London. This was a gift indeed, and led quickly to stagings of *Camino Real* and *Cat on a Hot Tin Roof*.

I received, too, a script from a young unknwon play-

wright. He felt, having seen *Godot*, that I might be in
sympathy with his work. The play was *The Birthday
Party* by Harold Pinter. I was very taken with it, but
by this time, alas, my calendar was completely full; and
when it opened at the Lyric Theatre, Hammersmith, I
was directing in New York. Flying home on the Sunday,
I read Harold Hobson's review, hailing a brilliant new
dramatist. I resolved to go and see the play the following
week. But I found that it had closed that Saturday
evening, after four performances. Hobson had once again
been the lone voice of enthusiasm. This time he had come
too late.

I was also lunched by Anthony Quayle and Glen
Byam Shaw. Would I, they asked, do the occasional
Shakespeare production at Stratford-upon-Avon? It was
a very satisfying moment as I said yes; and between
1956 and 1959 I staged five plays there as a visiting
director.

In the meantime, I had a theatre to run myself. The
most successful play I did at the Arts after *Godot* was
Anouilh's *Waltz of the Toreadors*. It had flopped badly in
Paris and Anouilh had forbidden any more performances.
But I had seen the play and liked it very much. I sent him
a letter maintaining that it would be successful in London
– particularly if the central part were played by Hugh
Griffiths, a wonderfully sensual Welsh actor whose work
he knew from *Point of Departure*. I added rashly that I
thought the play had failed in Paris because it had been
misdirected. I elaborated the faults of the production at
some length. Anouilh responded by giving me the rights
for London. He also agreed about the bad production; he
had, he said, done it himself.

That letter, and many others from my early years
– from Sam Beckett and Tennessee Williams, from
Harold Pinter and Peter Brook – were all destroyed
in a fire a few years ago. I have never kept any scrap
books, designs, photographs of productions, or reviews.
I have always wanted to live in the present. The only

things I had kept were letters. They were stored in boxes in a loft at my parents' last home. When the house stood empty, while I was trying to sell it after their deaths, it was broken into – perhaps by schoolchildren seeking to smoke in private. They started a fire, and everything in the loft was destroyed. Sadly, therefore, this book can contain no quotations, only memories.

– 17 –

By 1956 I was getting restless. I was still at the Arts, but was brooding on how to develop what I was doing. I wanted to gather a group of actors who could work together over a substantial period and so achieve a style. But I wasn't able to employ them for long enough on the money the Arts could afford, and despite the support of young talents, including Eric Porter and Ronnie Barker, it wasn't possible to make it happen. So I resigned; I needed a change.

Donald Albery engaged me to direct Anita Loos's stage adaptation of Colette's novel *Gigi* in the West End. The name part was to be played by Leslie Caron. At that time, she was a big Hollywood star, known everywhere for her performance in the film *An American in Paris*. I had seen her first when she was fifteen, a star even then, dancing in London with Roland Petit's Ballet des Champs Élysées. In *Les Rencontres*, she was the Sphinx set in the middle of an extraordinary design by Christian Bérard – it was as if a Renoir waif had strayed onto the stage and surprised us with her animal ferocity.

Then I saw her films. I was half in love with her before I met her.

I enjoyed the rehearsals. I liked Leslie's sense of humour and her tenacity. Ballet dancers are trained to work with a doggedness that is not found in actors or opera singers, and she would work until she dropped. We got on wonderfully. She brought me Europe and America; and I brought her music and literature and some of the riches of English culture.

The play did a long pre-London tour. By the time it reached Oxford, we knew we were very much in love. It was glorious – and worrying. I wasn't sure I could deal with Hollywood and her international stardom; I wasn't even sure I could deal with French in-laws. I felt provincial again.

Gigi was a reasonable success, continuing for six months, and we married during the run. At a lunch we had after the ceremony were a few friends and relations: Leslie's small feisty grandmother over from France; my parents; John Barton; and Tony Armstrong Jones who took some pictures on the understanding that he could flog one of them to Fleet Street. Then Leslie left to do the evening performance.

Our first home was the Montague Place flat which I had shared with John Barton. Later we moved to Hyde Park Square where we had our first baby, Christopher. And in 1957, we settled in a beautiful house in Montpelier Square, which we bought freehold for the huge sum of £14,000; there Jennifer was born.

The positive side of our marriage was the excitement and the fun and the joy of having two bright and beautiful children; the negative was the anxiety produced by two hyperactive people leading diverse and demanding careers. I was always in a great hurry; and Leslie, quite understandably, was equally worried, mainly about keeping her position as an international film star. She had to be in Hollywood; I needed to be in England.

MGM offered me a job in Hollywood as a trainee director. Whether this was real, or just a ploy by the moguls to keep Leslie happy, I never tested, because in 1958 something extraordinary happened. It was a dream

111

realised. I was asked to succeed Glen Byam Shaw at Stratford, taking over from the 1960 season. I could not say no to that.

I told Leslie my news and she begged me not to do it.

– 18 –

France was central to my life while I was married to Leslie. It didn't help my stumbling French to be suddenly part of an haut-bourgeois family who to my surprised ear spoke their language with a shrill upper-class English accent. But Leslie brought me new friends. Lila de Nobili, the great designer, was among them. Her work was supremely romantic, but never camp. She had a child's vision, an ability to look sadly at the world as if it were disintegrating into an over-ripe autumn of browns, yellows and golds, with the occasional splash of blue or orange to show where the energy had been before the fall. Her sets were a cunning amalgam of painted cloths and gauzes. She knew all the tricks of the classic Italian scene painters; hers was a theatre of illusion, dark shadows and glowing highlights.

I brought Lila to Stratford in 1957 and she designed *Cymbeline* for me. In subsequent years, she did *Twelfth Night*, *A Midsummer Night's Dream* and *The Two Gentlemen of Verona*. She did not, as was normal, have her backcloths painted on the frame at the back of the theatre. She painted them herself on the floor of a village hall on the outskirts of the town. Armed with endless buckets of brown, beige, and cream pigment, and wearing dirty pink bedroom slippers with pink pompoms thickly encrusted with paint, she walked over the spread-out cloths, making great puddles of colour, and occasionally splattering the shadows with gold. It was alarming to watch her because I could see no picture, no coherence and no shape. Yet hung on the stage, and at the right distance from the audience, these cloths became a magic world.

I loved Lila, and she, I think, loved Leslie and me. She appeared to be not in this world; but she was actually a shrewd observer of other people's follies. She loved to giggle with us while she sketched our two children. She was a recluse, living only for her occasional forays into the theatre, and for her few friends – Raymond Roulleau, the French director, Visconti and Zeffirelli, and Maria Callas. I met them all with her.

Callas, to meet, was shy, sweet and unsure. The shy personality only became a tiger in performance, appearing to appropriate the orchestra so that all its force and passion seemed to come out of her still, relaxed body. She, more than anyone, revolutionised operatic acting with her concentration.

Lila was a great painter: she turned paint into light. She still lives, but she leads an isolated nun-like existence in Paris, doesn't answer letters or take phone calls, and for many years has resolutely avoided the pressure of theatre work.

I was walking along the Quai d'Orsay recently with Nicki when an old woman with a shawl over her head and a shopping basket in her hand brushed past me, turned and ran down the next street. She was hunched and private, and I hardly noticed her. But I thought the face was familiar and paused. Suddenly I was sure it was Lila. I ran after her, but she had vanished.

When Peggy Ashcroft died, she left me a costume design of herself as Imogen which Lila had given her in 1957. I keep it in memory of an actress of genius; and of a designer who taught me a great deal. Her stage was an enchanted place of extreme light and shade. But the figures that walked in it had the homespun texture of life. She would go regularly to the flea market in Paris to buy old materials to use for her costumes. I learnt from her that however impressionistic the background of the

113

stage, the foreground must have a texture as honest as the actors' own skins.

The Christmas after we were married, Leslie and I went to New York – my first trip to America. I had been asked to direct *The Rope Dancers* by Morton Wishengrad on Broadway the following autumn, an interesting if rather melodramatic story of an emigrant family at the turn of the century. I was going to the States to cast and prepare it.

Flying the Atlantic in 1956 was still something of an adventure. Heathrow was a series of temporary huts, and the journey took twenty hours or more with stops at Shannon and Goose Bay. This was the pre-jet age, and we slept comfortably in bunks, wearing pyjamas, while the four engines throbbed through the long night on either side of us. It was much less tiring than modern air travel and, although it took longer, there was more space.

We got off the plane just before dawn, drove into the city and then down Broadway into Times Square as the light was brightening. I had an extraordinary feeling of having been there before – I suspect because of all the American movies I had grown up with. Films are great colonisers. Hollywood has helped America take over the world, and has made the way straight for McDonald's and Coca-Cola. It is strange that politicians and businessmen do not realise the colonising power of art. It is a certain way to create a market.

Leslie and I finished our ghostly tour round Times Square and checked into the Algonquin Hotel. Sleep by then was essential. Two hours later, Leslie woke with an excruciating pain in her stomach. She was six months pregnant, so we were both very alarmed. Soon we were speeding down Fifth Avenue in an ambulance while I held her hand tightly; she was in agony. When we arrived at the hospital I had some difficulty proving we had the necessary money for whatever treatment was needed. Only when Leslie was recognised as the famous movie star did all financial problems fade.

The doctor was an hysteric, and, pending tests, warned us that an immediate abortion might be necessary. We insisted on a second opinion. In time, another specialist came and diagnosed a large stone in the gall bladder. In a few days, Leslie was completely recovered and Christopher was saved.

New York in the Fifties was clean and bright and hard-edged. Except for the Bowery – a horrific area of extreme poverty and garbage, most of it human – prosperity and newness seemed everywhere. The city had not yet achieved its current state of cracked and dirty senility which makes a visitor fear it is about to fall to the ground. There were operas and concerts at the beautiful old Metropolitan Opera – now, disgracefully, pulled down. And there were plays and plays and yet more plays. It is hardly possible in the Nineties to think of New York as a mecca for playgoers; but that's what it was in the Fifties. Tennessee Williams and Arthur Miller were bursting with creative energy; Elia Kazan was directing; Harold Clurman reviewed in the *Nation*; and Boris Aronson and Jo Mielziner were designing. There was something to see every night – and it usually asserted that the theatre was a place of imagination, colour, light and metaphor. Turgid naturalism was increasingly left to television and the cinema; the theatre was liberated. It was returning to its imaginative roots.

Roger Stevens, the producer of *The Rope Dancers*, was always introduced as the man who had once bought and sold the Empire State Building. Producers, in my experience, are a very complex breed. They have the power to hire and fire; and theirs is the choice of the creative team, which is what matters. But if they make a mistake there is very little they can do about it except remove their choice. To attempt to alter an artist when he is at work is rather like trying to reform your partner in a marriage; it never succeeds.

Producers understandably tend to resent the fact that they have to raise all the money, and then watch others spend it. Though they select the artists, they have to stand on the sidelines while the artists have the fun. If they interfere, they become a writer or director or actor manqué. Roger Stevens had none of these insecurities. He was a truly great producer whose manner was that of an old-style patron. He picked the people and then let them get on with it. I did several plays for him in New York, and in London, and he was never anything but a support.

My newly-acquired New York agent was Audrey Wood. She was a power in the mighty Music Corporation of America, and had nurtured the talents of Tennessee Williams, Bill Inge and many others. She referred to me as 'young man', with a reproving air, as if she suspected I was just about to do something reprehensible. But I think she was proud of me, and I was certainly proud of her. She was under five feet, precise, and extremely well-read. She was always immaculately turned out, her head crowned with a tiny hat and her hands clad in a crisp pair of gloves. Her husband and former business partner, Bill Liebling, was equally diminutive. His mocking friendly smile was overhung by a large black Homburg hat; he appeared to be straight out of Damon Runyon. They were an incongruous couple: an Edith Wharton wit on the arm of a wise-cracker from Broadway.

It is, I'm sure, difficult to be an agent, and certainly I have known several better at acquiring clients than promoting them. It is a job where it is easy to talk big and then do nothing. In a profession riddled with insecurity, an actor can often believe that his fortunes would improve if he had the right agent. But no agent can make jobs where none exist. An agent is a bit like a pimp – always protecting the whore and constantly telling her (when custom declines) that her looks are not as bad as

116

she thinks. Part of the job, certainly, is to reassure. But the measure of achievement is of course to strike the biggest deal. Agents can therefore easily become totally fixated by success. A few keep their integrity and rarely put the dollar before the development of talent. Audrey Wood and Sam Cohn, the current big wheel of ICM in New York, achieved this. I am lucky to have worked with both of them.

I gathered an amazing cast for *The Rope Dancers*: Siobhan McKenna, Art Carney, Joan Blondell and Theodore Bikel. Best of all, Boris Aronson, a superb artist with a wily understanding of Broadway, agreed to be the designer. He was an immigrant Jew from Russia whose expressionistic work created poetry out of ordinariness. He made haunted landscapes of New York, so that I looked at the city with new eyes. I learnt avidly from him. Three years later, I brought him to Stratford to design *Coriolanus*.

I designed my own lighting for *The Rope Dancers* – a difficult and time-consuming job. I had learnt the technique from experience; having always done my own lighting as a matter of course. Since Peter Brook started the fashion, it had become almost a badge of a director's virility. Boris sat with me during all the long hours in which I focused and set the lights. He was watching over the look of his set no doubt, but he was also getting the best out of me. He encouraged me to be confident about colour and shape and shadow. He was friend and taskmaster.

It took me many years to realise that to spend forty-eight hours without going to bed (as I did once as a production reached the lighting stage) is not a good use of a director's energies. He should be nursing his actors rather than playing with the lamps. But I am glad I had ten years of lighting my own productions; it helped me understand space in the theatre.

After a couple of weeks in New York, Leslie and I flew

to Key West to stay with Tennessee Williams. I was going to direct *Camino Real* in London and I jumped at the chance to spend some time with him.

Tennessee had a house in New Orleans in which he lived fitfully; but Key West was home to him. He loved the climate, the swimming and, most of all, I suspect, the rather run-down unfashionable air. It was a place for outsiders, and already a colony for homosexuals. This was never even mentioned, because nobody then would think of being that up-front. But there was an atmosphere of covert naughtiness – as if a wicked party was just about to begin. Both Leslie and I found it very congenial. Nonetheless, as a young married couple expecting a baby, we felt like visitors from another world.

After an early start, Tennessee tapped away through each morning on his faithful old typewriter, no matter what. He wrote every day of his life. Then, before lunch, he swam up and down his pool, a porpoise with a serious purpose. After that, he felt free to indulge in drink and fun and friends for the rest of the day. Or he might suddenly disappear. He was always on the move, taking a plane here or there, sometimes to the most outlandish places. He believed that a moving target was less likely to be hit. Whenever he was in London, he would leave me word to phone him at Claridge's or the Savoy or Brown's; but by the time I called back he was usually gone – to Tokyo or Rome or Mexico. The last time I tried to return his call was only a few years ago. He was already back in New York, lying dead in a hotel room, asphyxiated by a bottle cap.

Tennessee was a shrewd and generous man, with an anarchic sense of humour. He could be silent for long periods, with no unease. He might be busy thinking about something; or he might be watching, carefully listening. Then, suddenly, he would decide to take part and the wit would flow and the laughter spurt out of him. He often found things very funny which others found only mildly amusing. He saw comedy in the blackest things.

He laughed his way through Maggie Smith's first night of *Hedda Gabler* at the National, and though this thoroughly disconcerted the actors and the audience I think Ibsen would have approved.

I tried hard, but didn't get much out of him about *Camino Real*. He didn't like talking about his plays – not in theory. He was a practical man, and he could only be illuminating about them once they were on the stage. So Leslie and I rested and sunned ourselves and got to know his companion, Frank Merlo, a Sicilian from New York. He was the love of Tennessee's life, and cared for him until Frank's tragic death in the early Sixties. I don't think Tennessee ever fully recovered from the loss. He called him the Little Horse because he always flashed an infectious toothy grin. Loving Frank was the inspiration behind Tennessee's comic masterpiece, *The Rose Tattoo*. It is his only play with a happy ending.

Leslie and I sailed sedately back to England on one of the great old liners, the *America*. It was like being locked up for five days in a not very good hotel that smelled of oil and the sea. I didn't care for it. You could never get away from the people; nor from the enforced camaraderie of the Captain's table. Leslie suffered as the movie star who was always watched and always whispered about. It was a curse to be perpetually on show. She often longed to be nobody.

Christopher was born between the technical rehearsal and the first dress rehearsal of *Camino Real*. Eighteen months later, Jennifer joined him. We showed off our children to the Caron family on frequent trips to Paris.

I did more and more productions: Peggy Ashcroft in *Cymbeline*; Kim Stanley in *Cat on a Hot Tin Roof*; Dorothy Tutin and Geraldine McEwan in *Twelfth Night*. Leslie continued her spectacular progress as an MGM star. She made *Gigi* as a musical, and with all this work came new acquaintances.

One of them, Cecil Beaton, who designed *Gigi*, I

loved for his constantly surprising taste and equally surprising tongue. Some years later I tried to get him to design a production, a Shakespeare comedy. But it was almost impossible to collaborate with him; the ability to change simply wasn't there; you had to accept what he did. He wanted a series of pictorial sets that would have taken for ever to change and would have ruined the rhythm of the play. I wanted a set that allowed scene to follow scene in quick contrasting articulation. He wouldn't bend; neither would I.

Despite this, we remained friends. He was not friends with everybody though. I remember one night working on the model with him at my house when the doorbell rang. I told him it was Peter Brook and his wife, Natasha, come for dinner. Without a word, Cecil rushed down into the basement and hid under the stairs. He waved at me to let the Brooks in. But once they were in the drawing room he made a secret, speedy exit out into the night. He explained later that he was not talking to Peter Brook . . .

Gigi's first day of shooting was in Paris, in the Bois de Boulogne. Maurice Chevalier and Hermione Gingold were out for a carriage ride among the spreading trees. I leant against one of the trees to watch. It gave under my weight because it was false. The Bois had been replanted here and there so that the trees could be adequately 'dressed' to camera. The pictorial sense of *Gigi*'s director, Vincent Minelli, moved trees as well as actors.

He was a man I immediately liked and a director whose political acumen I learnt to respect. His reputation was as a great designer of images. But to survive in the dream factory of Hollywood as he did, while passing some highly individual work through its sausage machine, takes a very shrewd operator.

Leslie and I went to Hollywood. It was completely unlike the place I had imagined. There was a stink of exhaust fumes and the endless prospect of a geometric wasteland, the houses and architecture often less realistic than the back lot of the nearby movie studio. There was no indigenous style. It seemed you could have whatever kind of house you wanted: French château, Elizabethan Tudor, Mexican ranch, Swiss chalet, even Japanese. They were all built of concrete and then faced with the required decor.

Leslie hired a black, open-topped Thunderbird and we drove from Sunset Strip all the way to the ocean. I enjoyed the sky, the light, the sun, the sunsets. I enjoyed, too, my first encounter with Japanese and South Sea Island food. But I couldn't stand the prodigal use of land, the wasted space and the endless parking lots. The motor car was more important than the person, nobody walked and there was no street life. Hardly anything man-made was beautiful; nothing was old. Nostalgia is a dangerous drug; society must renew itself, and art is born out of change. But our heritage needs to be preserved as a counterbalance to our ruthless pursuit of the new. Very little would be lost if most of Los Angeles were dismantled. Indeed, it might be good to start again. I dreamt, on that first visit, of what it must have been like when the early settlers arrived – a miraculous valley by the sea. Or when those pioneer movie-makers set up their tripods for the first time in the everlasting sun.

Whenever Leslie's film work took her to Hollywood in the late Fifties, which was quite often, I joined her between plays. Our lives proceeded, marked by a series of agonising separations. We both felt guilty and defensive about the work that kept us away from each other. The emotional and sexual agonies were almost too much to bear. Our two beautiful children played on, looked after by their French nanny.

In Hollywood, we generally stayed at the Château Marmont on Sunset Strip. It was a large tumbledown building, and the fashionable place in those days for cool people from the east coast and Europe. There was always a gathering of disaffected actors and writers who complained edgily while lounging by the pool. The whole place was tacky and tawdry. Outside, down the drive, an enormous Thirties bathing belle in gleaming plaster held a ball above her head while she revolved round and round, day and night. I think she was advertising laxatives. One of Christopher's first pleasures as a baby was to gaze up entranced at this slowly turning monster. Perhaps she was as potent to him as the Ovaltine lady had been to me.

While Leslie was filming, I was made much of, as the husband of a famous movie star, and as a young director known to have earned his spurs in London. One day I was given lunch in MGM's executive restaurant by Arthur Freed, the producer of many immortal Hollywood musicals, among them *An American in Paris*, *Gigi* and *Singing in the Rain*. He had started life as a lyricist in Tin Pan Alley and having written the lyrics for the song *Singing in the Rain* had used it to great effect in no fewer than three Hollywood musicals.

Arthur was a man of awesome silences. I never heard him express an opinion which helped me understand how he had created such wonderfully exhilarating and popular movies. Keeping silent at a meal clearly gave him no embarrassment, no feeling he should be making social chat. Everybody else talked and talked in compensation. Arthur sat in silence while their voices became shrill.

Before lunch, and before we entered the MGM sanctum, Arthur warned me not to mention last night's or indeed any other night's television. I said I wouldn't; I had not been watching television. He showed relief at this. Few people in the movie business in America at that time admitted that TV existed, it was the secret spectre stalking the great studios. Canute-like, the executives tried to outface the tide.

I met many Hollywood legends with Leslie. Fred Astaire was charming, yet his charm was clearly a protective mask that allowed him to be secret and detached. Gene Kelly was exuberant and noisy but, like many veterans in show business, only really warmed up when the subject was himself. By the side of Vincent Minelli's swimming pool I made friends with a scrawny eleven-year-old with enormous teeth-braces: Liza. I did not meet her mother, Judy Garland, until my later New York days.

Any student of drama should, I think, study how Garland sings. She could turn a banal lyric into a little one-act drama that expressed a truth about human emotions. She also had beautiful diction, a model for all singers. She and Frank Sinatra leave a body of work in their songs which is without falseness or striving for effect, and which contains some of the truest acting of the twentieth century.

Stan Laurel was eager for visitors. He was living in a modest little flat by the ocean, crammed with pictures and cuttings and awards. He was old and felt he had been forgotten. We tried to reassure him; a sad and anxious little Englishman.

We spent several evenings with Alfred Hitchcock and found him almost as silent as Arthur Freed and slightly more inscrutable. He seemed not to approve of anything or anybody.

I have known two really great film directors – men who made something out of nothing, true creators who wrote with the camera: Orson Welles and Jean Renoir. Welles I met on a few uproarious occasions and was always entranced by his performance (for performance it was) as a roguish mountebank. But I did not know him well. Jean Renoir became a friend. Leslie had acted in a play for him in Paris in the early Fifties, and he was clearly besotted with her, mainly, I think, because she looked so astonishingly like the children in many of his father's paintings.

When I met Jean, he was a vigorous man in his sixties with the sly, marmoset face of a French peasant. To be with him was like an expedition to the French countryside for a very good lunch. There were roars of laughter at unexpected jokes; then sudden changes into seriousness. He talked often and lovingly of 'mon père' and this blew my mind as surely as many years later hearing Wolfgang Wagner talk about 'mein Grossvater'.

Jean and his wife came to stay with us when Leslie and I were living in Stratford. We suggested he might like to see a play. He shied like a startled horse. Many directors don't much enjoy going to the theatre or seeing other people's movies. Orson Welles always said that he never saw other people's work because he wanted to preserve his innocence. Jean, I think, preferred living and talking, drinking and doing, to watching the fantasies of others. Nevertheless, I persuaded him into the car and slipped him into the theatre to stand – just for a moment – at the back of the stalls. On stage was a girl like a rush of sunlight. After a short time I took his arm to show him the way out, but he resisted and stayed, his eyes alight. He was watching the twenty-four-year-old Vanessa Redgrave play Rosalind, her first unqualified triumph.

During the years before his death, Jean lived mainly in Hollywood. His son was a cameraman there, and Jean's sense of family was at the centre of his being. He was still desperate to make films and always bubbling with new ideas. But he had gone out of fashion, and in the eyes of Hollywood was no longer 'hot'. There is of course an endless string of geniuses that the movie capital undervalued, the refugees from Germany – Thomas Mann, Heinrich Mann, Arnold Schoenberg and Bertolt Brecht – among them. Jean Renoir was a master of the town's very own medium: film. But it still ignored him. It can be a shameful place, and its spectacular wins should not blind people to the fact that it gambles and wastes talent as if it were money in the fruit machines of Las Vegas.

I met Buster Keaton briefly. I admire him above all the stars of the silent cinema, both as director and actor. His comedy deals honestly with pain and danger, whereas Chaplin's is often manipulative and sentimental. It is curious that Chaplin was for a time the most famous man in the world and became a myth, while Keaton, the complex and contradictory artist, never reached the same level of popularity. When I saw Keaton he was a dried-out drunk. He was also hard-up, because he had not been as clever with his money as Chaplin. I wished I hadn't met him. There was almost nothing to meet.

I had the same disillusionment once in the fine old Savoy Grill, now ruinously modernised. I was lunching with Laurence Olivier; he wanted to talk about the coming of the National Theatre. He suddenly waved at a figure finishing his lunch alone across the room: 'It's Charlie.' 'Charlie who?' I asked. 'Charlie Chaplin. Do you know him?' enquired Larry. I said I didn't. So I found myself in my late twenties sitting at a table having after-lunch drinks with two of the legends of my lifetime. I looked from one to the other with awe and admiration. They then proceeded to out-boast each other about their possessions, lifestyles, houses, coming projects and conquests. They were like a couple of competitive schoolboys.

Talent is often richer and more interesting than the people who possess it. 'Never trust the artist, trust the tale' said D. H. Lawrence. It's difficult, in any case, if you are by nature a hero-worshipper, to know how to come face to face with your hero. You should perhaps always keep your distance and worship from afar. Otherwise, what happens? To ask penetrating questions, or difficult questions, is pretentious and presumptuous. So you stare and make small talk. Embarrassed by the unnaturalness of the situation, the hero, on his part, often defends himself by trying to live up to his reputation and over-acting. Or he says nothing and is disappointing.

Edward Gordon Craig is a special hero of mine. His book *On the Art of the Theatre* has had a lasting effect on the way I have tried to go about my work. In old age, he lived in the South of France, to all intents and purposes a recluse. But Peter Brook used to visit him and, in the early Sixties, said that Craig, who kept up with the theatre by reading all the latest newspapers and magazines, would like to meet me. I agonised, then made an excuse. I was frightened to meet another legend. I wish now I had taken the risk.

My longest period in Hollywood was for some eight weeks when Leslie was making *The Man Who Understood Women* with Henry Fonda. While there, I prepared productions of *A Midsummer Night's Dream* and *Coriolanus* which I was to stage in 1959 for Stratford's 100th season, Glen Byam Shaw's last as the theatre's director.

This Hollywood visit was twice blessed. It gave me time to work on the texts of the two plays; it also gave me an opportunity to talk to my two stars. Charles Laughton was to play Bottom, and Laurence Olivier was to play Coriolanus – and both actors were at Universal Studios filming *Spartacus*.

Laughton lived up on the Hollywood hills in an elegant mansion. Around his swimming pool was a large collection of pre-Columbian statuary – bulbous stones with vast faces all looking rather like their proud owner. He had just turned sixty, and was an unhealthy hulk of a man, quick of speech and of eye. His mind worked at a furious speed, only barely hiding the anxieties below the surface. He had been away from the English classical theatre since the mid Thirties. His performances as Angelo and as Macbeth at the Old Vic had received the kind of enraged comments that critics reserve for actors who, like the young Olivier, Burton or David Warner, remake the classical mould.

Laughton constantly justified Hollywood to me. He said that it had brought entertainment and drama to a whole new world of people, and I believed him. But he also maintained that had Shakespeare been alive today

Shakespeare would have been working in Hollywood. Of that I wasn't so sure.

He was obsessed by Olivier, at that time the un-questioned monarch of the British theatre. His feeling had added resonance because Charlie was of course an international film star and Larry, despite all his cha-risma and the legend that glowed around him, was not – not quite. Charlie couldn't help thinking of the coming Stratford season as his return to his rightful place at the head of the English classical theatre. He thought this particularly since he was leading the company alongside Olivier, playing King Lear as well as Bottom.

His other great obsession (never spoken about) was his homosexuality. I have an idea he left England in the Thir-ties partly because of the persecution of homosexuals. When we met, he was still married to Elsa Lanchester and they seemed to have an affectionate friendship. But the marriage was of course a cover-up, common at the time. The wife gave respectability and endorsed the appearance of heterosexuality. Underneath, though, and hidden, Charlie's life was a succession of valets, companions and chauffeurs. Yet he made jeering anti-homosexual remarks to me whenever the opportunity arose. Did he do it to affirm that he wasn't gay? I can hardly believe it. Was he trying to provoke me into some homophobic response? But – and this I think baffled him – I tried to be as tolerant, understanding and uncensorious as I felt. I wished that circumstances – and his own anxieties – could have given him a little peace.

For twenty-five years up in the hills of Hollywood he had read and dreamed of Shakespeare. This passion had shored up a great deal of his waking life. He knew Shakespeare backwards, as a faithful curate knows his Bible. He had a passion, too, for the imaginative potency of the theatre – the fact that it is a game of make-believe with the audience; that if the audience is won over they will believe anything. In his study he demonstrated to me how he saw the storm scene in *Lear*; it was not created by a collection of noisy drums and thunder sheets. He spoke the words quietly and distantly, muted by an enormous sense of strain, drowned by an unheard wind. The eyes bulged, the voice was hoarse, and I seemed to hear the winds cracking their cheeks. I *imagined* the storm because I could hear every word. But it could only have been done in his study.

I have often thought that at another time, and if he had acted the part in an intimate space, he might have been one of the great Lears. As it was, his achievement was uncertain. The pathos and the ribaldry of his unhinged mind were certainly extraordinary. But in the storm he became, on the huge stage of the Stratford theatre, an aging actor whose voice had weakened, and who no longer had the equipment to do what was needed. He had been away too long. Playing Shakespeare is like athletics; you have to keep in training.

Charlie had caught on to a quirky theory from a fashionable scholar. He maintained that in the Folio and Quarto editions of the plays, the erratic use of capital initial letters for certain words indicated that the actor should emphasise them. I argued that the placing of capitals was now known to be the personal and idiosyncratic choice of the Elizabethan printer. But he wouldn't be swayed, and when *Lear* was being rehearsed, its director, Glen Byam Shaw, asked me to try and persuade Charlie that what he was doing was dangerous nonsense. I failed to convince him and he stuck to it doggedly, producing many strange stresses which made nonsense of the rhythm and certainly didn't help the sense.

Nonetheless, I learnt from Charlie a reaffirmation of what I had been brought up to believe: trust the text. If it is written by a master, it works like yeast on the audience's imagination. And although he quarrelled with me over the verse, he taught me a lot about the structure of Shakespeare's prose: how it is

128

built on antithetical phrases that balance each other; above all, how the alliterative words mark the stresses, the words the actor should point. This was no scholarly fashion. In performance, it held the attention of the audience and obtained the laughs. Even now, I can hear Charlie's relish as he said, 'When my cue comes call me and I will answer . . .' gleefully accentuating each hard *c*.

Leslie shot her film, and *Spartacus* proceeded on its epic and dilatory way. Charlie had many days off. I sat with him and wondered at this unhappy genius while we talked Shakespeare and read Shakespeare together. Later, at Stratford, I loved rehearsing with him. But when the *Dream* was played, his very presence was almost unfair to the other actors. His huge moon of a face appeared to be much larger than anybody else's. The audience would watch only him, even if he modestly retired downstage. After the *Dream*, he agreed to return in a couple of years to play Falstaff for me. It seemed to me casting made in heaven. He died suddenly, of cancer, before the time came.

I also had talks in Hollywood with Olivier about *Coriolanus*. They were not at all like my free-ranging meetings with Laughton. Larry had a deep suspicion of intellectuals. He liked to bring things down to basics – to the hard sweat of rehearsal or the simple appeal to the audience. He had played Coriolanus before at the Old Vic in the Thirties. The critics had then found him heroic, but rather neutral, and surprisingly lacking in character.

He started off our meetings by amazing me; he announced that all the lines that express Coriolanus's modesty should be cut. For instance, there is a moment when he is lauded by his General before the whole army for his prowess in battle. He finds this unbearable because he is a man so proud, so self-contained, that praise implies a kind of ownership of him. He is too proud to be loved.

129

He says:

> *I will go wash and when my wounds are cold*
> *You shall perceive whether I blush or no . . .*

and exits. Larry insisted that this be cut. He said it was a mock modesty fashionable with aristocratic Elizabethans, but modern audiences would find it tedious and improbable.

I said that if we took away Coriolanus's pride – which is mainly expressed by his conceited modesty – we would have little more than a simplified Henry V. We were still arguing at three in the morning. Finally, the thick Olivier eyebrows came down in a frown. 'I'll do what you say because you feel so strongly,' he said. 'But you are wrong.'

So we used a fairly full text, and Larry's performance was praised as one of his finest, the crown of the Stratford season. I was especially delighted that he was commended for his overweening pride.

By the time I directed these two giant actors, it had already been announced that from January 1960 I was to be the new director at Stratford. The two productions were a great gift to me by Glen Byam Shaw, whose place I was taking. He generously wanted to see me launched with the best.

In that same 1959 season, as well as Olivier and Laughton, I directed Edith Evans, Vanessa Redgrave, Albert Finney, Harry Andrews, Mary Ure and a group of marvellous young actors – Ian Holm among them – who were to be my future. I also began planning to create the Royal Shakespeare Company. I did this with my heart in my mouth. I now had to justify my ambitions and do the job. At the same time I knew that the great Stratford adventure would almost certainly spell the end of my marriage to Leslie.

The talk of MGM offering me a job in Hollywood was heard again. I had to choose between Hollywood and Leslie, or Stratford; and I chose Stratford. Our separations began to get longer, the sadnesses between us greater. Leslie tried to help by cutting down her commitments in films. I tried by working with her in the theatre. Within five years it was all over. At the time, it felt like the price of making the Royal Shakespeare Company. No wonder my marvellous marriage failed. I never gave it time to succeed.

– 19 –

I have a strange gap in my memory: I simply cannot recall my first-ever visit to Stratford-upon-Avon, even though from my adolescence the place had taken such a hold on my imagination. Now it was to be my home for ten years. I think I first went there in a school party. But the play I saw is a complete blank, and we may well have just toured the town. A little later, though, Peter Brook's beautiful Watteau-like *Love's Labour's Lost* marked my memory indelibly. Its central image I remember to this day: consumptive ladies and languid courtiers listening to white pierrots playing mandolins in haunted groves.

I made many visits to Stratford as schoolboy, RAF conscript and undergraduate. I not only grew to know the theatre, but the town and its surroundings. I spent hours in the public library, in visits to the little cinema, or in the art gallery. This last was not today's jolly collection of T-shirts, postcards, RSC programmes and tourist souvenirs, but a deserted Gothic-revival gallery, with a musty museum smell and many rather dreary Victorian paintings. It was all that remained of the old theatre, a late nineteenth-century half-timbered fantasy which would have looked well in Disneyland. When it burnt down in 1926 Bernard Shaw sent a postcard to the governors congratulating them on its loss. But its replacement – the present theatre – seemed to me, as I stood at the back or perched in the gallery, equally chilling to the spirit: a Thirties world of chromium and veneered woods, harsh and clinical and full of straight lines. There was nothing soft or mysterious, nothing warm or reassuring or curving; the imagination felt unwelcome in such an environment. The acting area was thrust way back behind the proscenium arch, and the acoustics were as hollow as a bathroom. The whole building was like a well-designed movie palace. When the curtain went up I expected the beam from a projector suddenly to thrust its way towards the screen.

The Stratford theatre has gone through many remodellings since, and is now a happier place for artists and audiences. But before these compromises, its Art Deco purity froze generations of performers into anonymity. It was not a theatre for subtlety. Nor was it a theatre that suited Shakespeare. The only really successful pre-war productions there were by the great Russian director, Komisarjevsky. I would guess that his energy defeated the clinical atmosphere by turning the stage into a carnival.

The repertoire in those days consisted of up to eight or nine plays put on with terrifying rapidity after the briefest of rehearsals. First performances are inevitably tentative, and at that time, to make matters worse, previews hadn't been invented, so the production opened 'cold' to the critics, unseen until then by any audiences. For the actors, this was like entering a room full of strangers, not sure if you are welcome at the party. If actors feel indifference, they tense up, try too hard, or become reserved and cautious. It is therefore not surprising that throughout the Forties and Fifties, the critics' response to a Stratford first night was a variation of: 'The new Shakespeare festival began yesterday and the cold wind blowing off the Avon seemed to have invaded the auditorium, paralysing actors and audience alike . . .' If critics ever revisited any of the productions later in the season, they were always amazed by the warmth and energy that had developed.

At the end of the war, the festival had been run by a splendidly robust actor of great panache, Robert Atkins. But after two years, apparently in some dudgeon, he handed in his resignation to the chairman, one of the Flowers, the famous local brewing family who had started the festival in 1876. Atkins was not a man to mince words. When he was being seen off with formal ceremony at Stratford station, he leant from the train as it drew away and thundered in his rich actor's voice to the assembled dignitaries: 'And what's more, Flower's ale is piss . . .'

Stratford itself, to my East Anglian schoolboy's eyes, was initially very foreign – a strangeness emphasised by all that Midlands red brick. I liked the church and the town hall and the half-timbered houses. I also liked the practicality of the place. A large busy timber store stood near the theatre, and there was a weekly invasion by farmers and merchants and livestock. It was a market town. It appeared respectable, even prim, and it neither liked nor approved of the actors. There were very few people about, except in the evenings when the playgoers arrived. More trains ran in those days – indeed you could still catch the train out of Stratford after the play was over. But the town and the theatre stood apart from each other, going their separate ways.

I travelled to work in the summer by boat, speeding down the deserted river. In the winter, I walked for miles through the infinitely varied countryside, sensing all the time how much the fields and villages around Stratford are quintessentially Shakespeare. It was impossible not to feel, as season followed season, that this was the landscape that made his images – the trees, the skies, the birds, the light, the river; all part of a Warwickshire that inspired him 400 years ago.

When I saw Brook's *Love's Labour's Lost*, the theatre was run by Atkins' successor – and his polar opposite

– Sir Barry Jackson: dilettante, scholar, rich man and impresario of the Birmingham Repertory Theatre. For thirty years, he had shown an amazing ability for picking young talent, from Richardson and Ashcroft and Olivier to Paul Scofield and Peter Brook. Jackson made Stratford fashionable. It began to glitter. He also developed an organisation of workshops and facilities which allowed all of us who came after him to do the job. The first beneficiary, in 1948, was Anthony Quayle, a considerable actor and a man whose superb talents as a leader obviously appealed to the new chairman, Sir Fordham Flower. I can't imagine that Fordie was ever very comfortable with the rather effete, mandarin-like Barry Jackson. Quayle's bluff 'man among men' approach, bred of a good war and a keen mind, was far more his style.

Quayle – joined in a few years by Glen Byam Shaw, who later took over alone – built on what Jackson had started. The stars began to come. By the great History Cycle of 1951, the annual Shakespeare seasons at Stratford had moved to the centre of the theatre world. Young actors, directors and designers were developing there alongside the great contemporary talents – Gielgud, Olivier, Wynyard, Ashcroft, Scofield, Vivien Leigh, Michael Redgrave, Richard Burton, Alan Badel.

I first worked at Stratford in 1956, directing *Love's Labour's Lost*. It wasn't a smart choice, since Brook's beautiful production was still remembered. But it was a play I knew and loved from Cambridge. I moved more into my stride over the next two seasons, first with *Cymbeline*, in which Peggy Ashcroft was a sublime Imogen, and next with *Twelfth Night*.

Twelfth Night, like all the comedies, is about growing up. I wanted to get back to its youth and to its comic heart, so I chose a young cast – Dorothy Tutin, Geraldine McEwan, Richard Johnson, Patrick Wymark, Ian Holm, and many others who were soon to become part of my life and work. The production is remembered as a definitive *Twelfth Night*; but at the time it was extremely controversial, even provoking outrage. This was largely because I had rethought the interpretation of Olivia, a part beautifully played by the twenty-six-year-old Geraldine McEwan. Traditionally, the character had always been portrayed as rather straight-laced and matronly. But the play is, among other things, about Olivia's tribulations in growing up. Geraldine's Olivia was vain, a little ditsy, not to say silly. But she was nonetheless heartbreaking – a young girl suddenly thrust into being mistress of a big household. She needed her Malvolio as much as the young Queen Victoria needed her Melbourne. I have to say that it did not occur to me that I was being revolutionary. I was simply responding to the text.

One night towards the end of the run I was in the audience checking on the health of the production. As the interval ended, the man next to me turned and said sadly: 'What *has* he done to Olivia!' I debated with myself for a tortured second. Should I take him on? Or should I not bother? I looked at him for a long moment, shook my head, and uttered a knowing, conciliatory sigh of agreement. 'A-a-a-ah . . .' I said. It was one of my last experiences of anonymity in the auditorium of a theatre.

PART TWO

A Little Bit Famous

– 1 –

I never found out whose idea it was that I should take over at Stratford, whether it was Glen Byam Shaw's – which I suspect – or Fordham Flower's.

I was devoted to Glen. He was cultivated and elegant, like a gentlemanly schoolmaster, yet possessing a sudden and surprising ability to descend to earth and call a spade a spade, usually in robust and scatalogical terms. He was a director who was often under-praised, for he was a great craftsman. He almost always worked with Margaret Harris – called Percy – of the legendary team of designers, the Motleys, who started out in the Thirties. The team, as well as Percy, consisted of her sister Sophie and Elizabeth Montgomery. They did wonderful work, but by the Fifties, though revolutionaries of twenty years before, they had become somewhat predictable. Even so, Glen and Percy staged vigorous, honest and lucid Shakespeare that allowed great acting to flare into genius, as in the superb Redgrave/Ashcroft *Antony and Cleopatra*.

Glen was foxy. Everyone who runs a theatre has to keep their own counsel, and sometimes this is seen as duplicity. Perhaps it comes with the territory. You can't tell everybody everything all the time, particularly when you're dealing with the insecurities and vanities of talent. You try to avoid lying, but you sometimes have to withhold the truth, or some of it. Glen was a master of theatre diplomacy. He loved actors – his wife was the marvellous Angela Baddeley – and understood very well that because they did a difficult job they needed to be selfish to protect themselves. This explained, he said, why they could sometimes behave like terrible children, likely to break up the nursery.

Fordie Flower, though clearly urbane, well-read and a rather aristocratic businessman, seemed, when I first met him, very much the ex-World War Two senior officer – a fine straight-forward professional soldier. He was now back as a partner in the prosperous family brewing business. But he had another side to him which was visionary and mystic. He sometimes seemed to disappear – to go into long reveries with himself. I think he knew about demons. As a chairman, he could be maddening on small matters, because he simply couldn't be bothered with them. But he was always wide awake on large issues. He was also brilliant at strategic thinking – and that was my good fortune.

Following a sounding-out talk with Glen about my taking over, I had several conversations with Fordie to discuss the job in more detail. He was not exactly evasive, but the conversations could not be called conclusive. Fordie was a master at waiting. He listened and said as little as possible. I was full of plans, but he seemed neither to accept nor to reject my torrent of ideas.

I remember hearing my appointment as the next director at Stratford formally announced on the radio one night in the autumn of 1958. I was driving through Warwickshire on my way from London. The next morning I was to re-rehearse *Twelfth Night* for the Stratford company's visit to Russia that winter. As I listened, I felt sick with apprehension. Now I had what I'd longed for. But could I do it? Would Fordie and the Board *let* me do it? I had been appointed, but the fundamental changes that I wanted to make had not yet been agreed. They were merely hazy ideas floating in the air. Could I insist on what I wanted? Had I the muscle? Did Fordie's vagueness mean support or uncertainty?

Even a month or two later, when we all boarded the chartered Aeroflot plane bound for Russia, I was still uncertain of where I stood.

Peter Brook's *Hamlet* with Paul Scofield had ventured to the USSR two years earlier – the first theatre company to breach the Iron Curtain. But we were the first since the Revolution to go with a full repertoire. As well as *Twelfth Night*, we took *Hamlet* with Michael Redgrave and Coral Browne, and *Romeo and Juliet* with Dorothy Tutin and Richard Johnson. Leslie wasn't with me. There were two babies to be cared for at home; and wives, unless they were members of the company, were not encouraged to come.

Over the three weeks we were there our eleven performances in Leningrad and our fifteen at the Moscow Art Theatre were greeted with almost hysterical enthusiasm. Audiences were not just applauding our work, but the opportunity, long lost, to communicate with another society, another culture. The desperate eagerness of their response was very moving.

The contrast between the beauty of Leningrad itself and the depressed and broken spirit of the people was distressing. Everyone was cautious and inhibited because everyone was frightened. They wouldn't say what they actually thought.

The cold burnt the cheeks, the river Neva was frozen solid and the snow on the streets (perpetually cleared by hefty figures who looked like bulging sacks but were in fact women of a certain age) muffled the sound of what little traffic there was.

Krushchev had just decreed that the Russians drank too much, so alcohol was almost impossible to find. The actors in their desperate search for drink discovered an illegal dive where rough vodka was sold. It looked like a setting for the *Lower Depths*, but was filled with the sound of accordions and laughter. The hotel had no vodka, only a disgusting root beer; the meals were equally disgusting, worse than school dinners. Bad eggs were regularly cracked open at breakfast. The only time I really enjoyed eating was travelling from Leningrad to Moscow on the old Red Arrow Express, all brass and leather and red-shaded lights. At the end of each carriage, caviar was served with coarse bread and tea, provided by a lady with a samovar.

Our Leningrad hotel was splendid but run-down. It was all very Edwardian. A large woman policed each floor, sitting immoveably at a table in the corridor, checking our comings and goings. It wasn't until I had returned to London and was able to walk around unprogrammed that I realised fully the chill horror of this obsessive supervision. Every minute of our lives was organised. We were not allowed to go anywhere or meet anyone without a minder or an interpreter. We were shepherded like a dangerous flock, even to and from our own performances.

I wanted to see a lot of theatre, but my request caused official consternation. I was allowed to go to the ballet because they were proud of that: it was fantasy and nothing to do with reality. But they weren't too sure about anything else. I began to see why. The plays were either classics embalmed in the style of 1900, or cheerful modern dramas, mindless in their propaganda. Theatre was not allowed to mean anything; if it did it might challenge the existing order. I was sent to a jolly musical which took place in a Black Sea holiday camp. The juvenile leads were played by extremely old actors and actresses heavily made up.

I talked to the director of the Gorky Theatre and, with my head full of the ensemble I hoped to make at Stratford, asked him about the contract of employment among his actors. He told me they had ample pensions, wonderful conditions and a job for life. What happened,

142

I asked, if any of them should feel they were being miscast? He answered (this was all through the ameliorating medium of the interpreter) that, as far as he was aware, miscasting did not occur in his theatre. I suggested that actors often felt they were either miscast or undercast, it was in the nature of the job; to aspire to parts that might be beyond their range was surely a healthy sign? 'But,' he said, 'if any actors are unhappy with us, they can resign and leave within two weeks.' 'Then what?' I asked. 'Do they apply to another theatre?' 'No,' came the reply. 'They cease to be actors.'

I mused on this conversation. I was already sensing that an ensemble such as I dreamed of could not be permanent – that it would have to change with circumstances and with the development of the individual actors. But how could one keep them together without the sanctions of a police state? The old romantic idea that an actor could play Hamlet one night and the butler the next has an in-built flaw: there are many butlers needed in the repertory, but only one Hamlet.

Soon after my visit to Russia, I had a conversation with Helene Weigel, Brecht's widow and leader of the fabled Berliner Ensemble. Every British theatre person I knew was in awe of the talent of the Ensemble, and particularly of the weight and richness of the middle-aged actors playing the small parts. Weigel startled me by attacking their spoilt, lazy-cat ways. She said that all they ever wanted to do was to appear in plays on television for vast amounts of money. Indeed, only by letting them do television could she keep them happy. Pride in the Ensemble and in playing a small part in a big play came very low in their priorities.

In Russia, our actors had endless meetings with representatives of the actors' union, the writers' union, the artists' union. Toasts were drunk to better understanding and to cultural exchange. But there was, alas, little understanding and no exchange was possible, only an emotional yearning between the two nationalities; a sad recognition of what might have been if we had been meeting in freedom. We could only see what they wanted us to see. They could only say what they were permitted to say.

Coral Browne was playing Gertrude. Guy Burgess, the spy who had absconded, sought her out and some of us met him. He was drunk and shy yet belligerent. Years later, Alan Bennett's brilliant television play *An Englishman Abroad*, beautifully directed by John Schlesinger, took for its theme the meeting between Coral and Burgess, and uncannily conveyed the off-beat, rather nightmarish nature of our whole visit.

I had known something of what to expect. Peter Daubeny had earlier brought the Moscow Art Theatre to London and we had seen magnificent players working in productions that certainly cast a spell but were so old they seemed fixed in amber. Without question, these had a compelling and historic fascination. But I couldn't escape the thought that in the frightened, atrophied Soviet Union there was no possibility of thinking freshly, no possibility of original theatre work, because nothing radical or challenging was allowed.

I asked people what they thought of Meyerhold, the great Soviet director whose expressionistic techniques still inspire the theatres of the West. My question was met with bewilderment or terror. At that time, Meyerhold was a non-person: he didn't exist. In 1939, at a Soviet drama conference, he had made a powerful speech affirming that the theatre must be free to challenge society. He must have known that he was signing his own death warrant. A few days later, he disappeared. Even in the Fifties, it was a mystery what had happened to him. We now know that he was murdered by Stalin's thugs. Soon afterwards, his wife was murdered too.

I had been commissioned to write two articles on the Russian theatre for the *Observer*, and foolishly dictated the first (which was only mildly critical) by telephone from my hotel room. Our phones were of course tapped and next day the official attitude to me was distinctly more frigid. An odd, perhaps related, episode at the end of my stay is worth telling. I was scheduled to leave Moscow ahead of the company with our press office chief John Goodwin, who was writing about the visit for the *Daily Telegraph*, and Roger Wood, the photographer. But on the morning we were due to go, two uniformed guards woke us at dawn to say our departure was delayed by twenty-four hours. The same thing happened on the two subsequent mornings. Both times we were told that there was fog at the airport; yet outside the sun blazed down from a cold blue sky. After these three unexplained postponements, we were suspicious as well as exasperated. We collected our baggage together, left the hotel, miraculously found a taxi, and drove to the British Embassy to tell our story. Within hours, they had whisked us to the airport and on to a plane for Stockholm. Soviet records probably show that we still haven't left. Was all this bureaucratic revenge? I certainly thought so at the time.

– 2 –

The most important event of the Russian tour for me took place at the hotel in Leningrad. Fordie Flower and his wife Hersey were with us and I had a drink with them both in their suite after one of the performances. We fell to discussing future plans – the plans Fordie had conscientiously evaded in the past. After a while, Hersey went off to bed, but Fordie and I, in that big dusty over-decorated room, a setting fit for Diaghilev, continued talking through the night. The policy of the as yet unformed and unnamed Royal Shakespeare Company, its aims and ideals, were defined and finally accepted that night. They are still much the same today. But it was in Leningrad, in late 1958, that they took shape.

Stratford had never tried to have an ensemble – a group of actors bonded together over a length of time. A few, like the young Paul Scofield, had come up through the ranks and achieved stardom by doing two or three consecutive seasons. But usually each season was cast from scratch, and everything depended on who could be engaged to play leading roles each year. I urged upon Fordie the virtues of a company who knew each other; who supported and depended on each other; who knew whom they disliked as well as whom they admired. I explained that I didn't mean only actors. Directors and designers, composers and writers should also be encouraged to make Stratford their creative home. I proposed that we should offer a three-year contract – though if people wished it, they could opt out for short periods to do other work. They would only stay by being allowed to go away.

I then came to the crucial part of my plan. I believed intensely that the kind of classical company I wanted to form must be not only highly trained in Shakespeare and the speaking of his verse but also in modern drama – open to the present as well as expert in the past. Only thus could we develop the kind of protean actors, alive to the issues of the day, that Shakespeare deserved and that would give his plays contemporary life. To do this, I said, we would need a second theatre, a London home, where – in addition to transfers from Stratford of the previous season's Shakespeares – we could stage other classics and modern drama.

These were new ideas in Britain, and in that sense they were revolutionary. But they were old ideas too. My reading of Stanislavsky; my obsession with Jean Vilar's TNP (Théâtre National Populaire) and the Barrault/Renaud Company; my talks with Michel St Denis; my study of the Berliner Ensemble – these influences had formed my thinking. Above all, I was convinced that Shakespeare demanded, as well as technical dedication, contemporary awareness if he was to continue to speak forcefully to the second half of the century.

Fordie didn't comment very much. I think he appreciated the strength of my beliefs, but they were hardly new to him. He had heard them from me before, though not so comprehensively, nor so urgently. My passion had been increased, I think, by the appalling deadness of the Russian theatre.

I tried to put my plans in historical perspective. I reminded him of what he knew well: that a national theatre, after over a hundred years of government procrastination, was finally on the horizon; Olivier would make it happen. It would be with us, I thought, within five years. Once it was working, it could well deal a death blow to Stratford if Stratford remained as it was. Without anything like the same resources, we would be unable to compete, and might quickly wither into no more than a short summer festival for tourists. All the heavyweight actors and directors would go to the National where conditions and pay were bound to be much better.

Fordie wondered whether in fact there would be room for two national theatres, although we both knew that in France the competition between the Comédie Française and the TNP had done only good. But the point was that Stratford had to be turned into a national organisation that could compete on even terms. I was as worried as Fordie at the thought of one well-subsidised State institution, the National Theatre, being at the top of the pile.

Stratford at that time had no subsidy. It kept going by paying its actors pitiably low wages and demanding only a small proportion of their time. The top salary was sixty pounds a week – even for Laurence Olivier. Little wonder that he could give only a few months to playing in Warwickshire, with several years between his visits. Times, however, were changing. The late Fifties were the start of the great days of the Arts Council. They were not, as later, trying to *plan* art into existence.

They were watching to see where creativity happened and were then encouraging it with extra funds. I believed the Council would support Stratford if we showed them what we could do.

The governors had about £175,000 in the bank, husbanded carefully, as an emergency fund. This was a substantial sum in 1958. It had been earned over the years from successful foreign tours and from donations by patrons and well-wishers. I knew we would never get any form of state grant whilst this fund existed. I suggested to Fordie that the money could be well spent on launching us in London. He blinked.

At the same time, I told him that I hated the name of our enterprise: the Shakespeare Memorial Theatre. It sounded like a gravestone. I wanted, since the Queen was our patron, to rename the building the Royal Shakespeare Theatre and have the company known as the Royal Shakespeare Company; I thought 'RSC' could become as easy on the tongue as my beloved 'TNP'. Years later, when we were well established, my old friend Bill Gaskill, who was running the Royal Court, praised me waspishly for the invention. He said the title had everything in it except God.

Much of what Fordie and I discussed that night in Leningrad was speculative; much of it instinctive. But I knew where I was going and was sure of the problems that Stratford would be facing in the future. I felt that there was a fusion of aesthetic and political need which had to be taken seriously. Fordie played his cards with care. Sometimes he seemed practically asleep. Sometimes he counselled caution and wondered whether the Board would ever wear such extreme and risky schemes. Sometimes he worried whether they would benefit Shakespeare – which was after all what the theatre was there for. Perhaps he was a bit suspicious that I just wanted to use up the resources of Stratford in order to do modern plays?

As the night was coming to an end, I believed I'd

lost. It is my usual experience, at the end of dress rehearsals, of first nights, of lectures, of broadcasts, or of writing an article, to believe that I have lost. I thought I had talked too much. Perhaps – always a fault of mine – I had been too revealing about my own doubts and insecurities. It was true that if the plan was adopted and went wrong, the theatre would be broke. I admitted as much. I also had another anxiety at the back of my mind: I was wondering whether I had the strength of will to resign from Stratford before I even began if I was told my dream couldn't be attempted. I *knew* my proposals were right – right for the theatre, right for me. Whether they could happen, much less whether they could succeed, were unanswered questions which scared me. One thing was certain: I was not going to run an annual Shakespeare season at Stratford with an ad hoc collection of actors and directors.

Fordie gave himself another drink. Then, full of doubts, but nonetheless convinced of the inevitability of what he was doing, he said: 'I think you're absolutely mad, but it's very exciting. Let's talk to the governors and get it moving. I'll back you to the hilt.' It was four in the morning.

Throughout the next eight years, until his death from cancer in 1966, Fordie never wavered in his support for me and for my Leningrad ideas. He was always encouraging, and completely and utterly steady through some very difficult and wobbly times. People in the theatre and among the public are naturally inclined to think now that the RSC has always been there. But it was a revolution that made it happen, and what we were trying to do frequently met with opposition, even derision. Fordie, as chairman, stood to lose everything if we had failed. I loved him and admired him, and owe him more than I can say.

– 3 –

The 100th season at Stratford-upon-Avon in 1959 was carefully devised by Glen Byam Shaw as a star-studded occasion: Edith Evans as Volumnia and the Countess in *All's Well*; Paul Robeson as Othello; Charles Laughton as Bottom and Lear; Laurence Olivier as Coriolanus. As this was the year before I succeeded Glen – in addition to directing the *Dream* and *Coriolanus* – I had to begin work on my new plans. And, amazingly, I could because, with incredible ease, Fordie had secured the Board's sanction, skilfully preparing the ground and then having me talk to them. I was allowed to spend the savings.

I was interviewed about my aims and aspirations, and began to experience for the first time the sceptical nature of the British media. Scepticism is of course a necessary and healthy response to a world more and more run by hype and public relations. But it has the danger of withering enterprise and stifling creativity. I was quite shocked by my inability to raise enthusiasm for my ideas. There was a good deal of 'Who does this young man think he is?'; and plentiful reminders that I had made my reputation in modern drama: why did I think I could set myself up as an expert on Shakespeare? I also noticed that actors treated me in a different way. It was part reverence, because I was the anointed leader of their future, and part suspicion, because I had yet to prove that I could do it. I rushed on, telling myself that my luck would hold.

The first important step was to speak to Peggy Ashcroft. I took her out to dinner and talked and talked of my hopes for the new company, the RSC. She was enthusiastic, though cautious. We were like two people contemplating a love affair; but by the end of the meal, I still hadn't mustered the courage to pop the direct question. Coffee came and went and my courage still failed me. I couldn't bear to be refused. I drove Peggy back to her home in Hampstead, and, when time was running out and we were more than half-way there, gulped and asked her if she would lead the company – be the first three-year contract artist. 'Yes, of course,' she said, without a moment's hesitation. She didn't quite say she thought I would never ask.

Throughout her life, Peggy was always part of any serious new movement in the theatre. She was with John Gielgud and Michel St Denis in the Thirties; with Gielgud at the Haymarket in the war; with Tony Quayle and Glen Byam Shaw at Stratford in the Forties; with George Devine at the Royal Court in the Fifties. And she joined me in the Sixties. The RSC would never have happened so quickly without her. Where she led, others followed. And, like Fordie Flower, she never wavered.

In all the years I worked with her, we only had one real quarrel. In the early Seventies, I was asked to direct the National Theatre. Peggy's initial reaction was violent. She said that if I did it would be like crossing the floor of the House, spurning my background and joining the Tories. We argued for months. Finally, she relented and became one of those who were with me through the hell of the South Bank opening. Characteristically, she did her best for the National as she had always done for anything new: she cared about the theatre as a whole.

But she remained fiercely loyal to the RSC – the 'Co' as she called it. To the end of her days, she saw everything the RSC presented, commented on everything, helped young talent and attacked the vagaries of directors who arrogantly ignored Shakespeare's text. By nature she fervently espoused causes, and the theatre owes much to her convictions. Throughout my career, her belief in me gave me strength. It was never more important than in 1959, at the start of the RSC.

*

The all-powerful West End impresario Binkie Beaumont was on the Board of the Stratford theatre. I think he had been persuaded to serve by Tony Quayle, who knew well that where Binkie approved, the stars would follow. He completely controlled the West End. Very few plays were produced outside his management. He was clever and charming, secret as a lizard, and at the centre of an elegant and predominantly homosexual circle that included Noel Coward and Terence Rattigan. In the Fifties, you had to be truly original to be taken into that circle – though being of the right sexual persuasion helped. It was a continually threatened world of innuendo and covert glances, of gossip and the unsaid. It was also very talented.

At Binkie's parties, I always felt as if I had ten thumbs and straw in my hair; I was the outsider. I didn't resent his influence: he had infallible taste; was a brilliant manager with none of the usual envy of the creative; and, unlike many producers, he loved and respected actors. They loved him in return, however much he manipulated and conned them. There is a famous story of Binkie thinking out a way to explain a disastrous mistake to John Gielgud, a close friend and confidant over many years. 'Well,' said Binkie, 'if the worst comes to the worst, I suppose we can always tell him the truth.'

His philosophy was not unlike Glen's – that performers need care and understanding because to stand on the stage emotionally naked and face the merciless judgement of an audience requires immense courage. Bouts of selfishness, childishness and vanity must therefore be forgiven. I don't altogether agree with this judgement: it is a touch patronising. There are as many kinds of actors as there are kinds of people. Actors are certainly vulnerable, yet the best of them are tough-minded craftsmen, frequently inspired, who have a passion for what they do and a dedication and discipline in doing it which puts many other professions to shame.

I worked for Binkie in 1958 directing the first English production of Tennessee Williams's *Cat on a Hot Tin Roof* in which Kim Stanley was brilliant as the sex-starved wife. The play was banned by the Lord Chamberlain. In order to stage it – together with Arthur Miller's *A View from the Bridge* and Bill Inge's *Tea and Sympathy* – it was necessary to convert a London theatre (in this case the Comedy) into a club. Only then could these 'undesirable' plays, which dared to mention that homosexuality was a human condition that clearly existed, escape the Lord Chamberlain. Throughout the season, Binkie's concern for detail, his enthusiasm and tireless devotion to his actors and his directors, were a lesson to me. He spent the early part of every morning ringing round his key artists: just keeping in touch, even if there was nothing much to say except 'How are you?' in his silken tones.

As the leading West End impresario and a Stratford governor he had, however, a lot to say about my plans for the RSC. He believed that if I expanded Stratford into London and succeeded in running a year-round repertory there, I would ruin the West End theatre. Actors, he thought, would be seduced away from him. With the RSC, they would only have to perform two or three times a week in a range of plays, instead of eight times a week in one play. I pointed out that they would earn much less money. He was also worried that new plays would come to me. The repertory system gave a safer opportunity for writers to find their audience, since the play could be nursed. He added to these objections a dire warning. If I failed, he said, I would bankrupt Stratford and destroy a thriving institution. In his most charming tones, he told me he was implacably opposed to what I was trying to do, would resign from the Board if they continued to back my plans and would do his very best to persuade any theatre owner from leasing me a London home. He was frighteningly honest and forthright. And true to his word. Once I had had the go-ahead, he did indeed resign from the Board. But he was careful to go quietly. It is possible he thought publicity would not serve his turn. On the other hand, he always went out of his way to remain an enigma, to be secret and anonymous. In those days it was still possible. Today, such Greta Garbo behaviour would attract wide attention.

Again true to his word, he made it very difficult for me to find a suitable London theatre. 'No chance as far as I'm concerned,' said Prince Littler, head of the giant Stoll Moss empire, who freely confessed not only that he didn't think I could run a successful repertory system in the West End, but that he was worried by Binkie's unrelenting opposition. So I went next to Emile Littler, his brother and head of another group of theatres. They were sworn enemies and, according to report, never spoke. Emile was the pantomime king but, it was said, longed to be culturally respectable. I told him Prince had turned down my request for a theatre. Could he suggest anything? He looked pensive, then offered me the Cambridge, in those days a not-very-successful house on the fringe of the West End. I thanked him and asked for time to think.

I went back to see Prince and said that the attempt to stop the RSC moving into the West End was doomed: Emile had offered me the Cambridge. But I added that it was a theatre which didn't excite me. Surely Prince could now help? He did. Within a short time we had negotiated a three-year lease on the Aldwych. We arranged to open there at the end of 1960, after my first year's season at Stratford.

– 4 –

It seemed to me that a new Shakespeare company should begin at the beginning. So I started with Shakespeare's comedies, presenting in my first Stratford season six productions which traced the development of his comedy from the very earliest through to the later plays. Shakespeare's actors had developed with him, and as time went on simple early verse became a complex medium in the mouths of virtuosi. Perhaps over the first years, my company could develop in the same way.

Penelope Gilliatt wrote of the company that it included 'a number of actors better known to audiences at the Royal Court and the Arts and Theatre Workshop'. She was welcoming new talent to Shakespeare. Among the younger ones, some of them then hardly known, were Dorothy Tutin, Ian Holm, Ian Richardson, Patrick Wymark, Eric Porter, Dinsdale Landen, Francis Cuka, Derek Godfrey and Jack McGowran. The established was balanced with the new by Peggy Ashcroft being cast as the Shrew and Paulina in *The Winter's Tale*, both for the first time, and Max Adrian as Pandarus in *Troilus and Cressida* and as Feste.

Bumps and disasters lay ahead though. Paul Scofield had agreed to three parts: Shylock, Petruchio and Thersites. But a few weeks before rehearsals started he sent me one of those letters all impresarios dread. It was reasonable, well argued -- and devastating. He said he knew he was committed to Stratford to lead my first season, knew the contract was agreed, but now found he just couldn't face it. Something deep

155

inside was telling him that it wasn't right. He had to be released.

I had a moment of great anger, even of a desire for revenge. Then I calmed down. If actors change their minds, there is nothing you can do about it. For better or worse, their selfishness is the root of their talent. They have to do what they have to do and, when the crunch comes, nothing else matters. They are what they play, and if it doesn't feel right – for whatever reason – it won't *be* right. Of course I tried to persuade Paul to change his mind. But I failed. I had to accept his decision with a good grace, hoping he would join me many times in the future – which I'm glad to say he did. All this explains the impresario's shriek of rage: 'I will never work with you again – until I need you.'

Meantime, I was left with the urgent need to find a new male star to lead the company alongside Peggy. The previous year, I had been to Bristol and seen an electrifying young actor called Peter O'Toole burn up the stage as Hamlet. His performance was rough and crude; but it had an animal magnetism and danger which proclaimed the real thing. He made Hamlet unendurably exciting. He was a tall gangling figure with an enormous hooter of a nose, and looked witty, intelligent and very sexy. I asked him if he would take over Paul's roles. He said yes, and became the sensation of the season.

At the beginning of rehearsals, I had been slightly dismayed to meet an unrecognisable O'Toole at the stage door. His marvellous hooter had been transformed into a delicate, almost retroussé nose. It seemed hardly the ideal preparation for Shylock. I asked him what he had done. 'I'm going to be a movie star,' he quipped. I didn't take the remark seriously at the time . . .

O'Toole was, in truth, too young for Shylock, which he performed as the first of his three parts. But in the event he was mesmeric. With brilliant power, he found both the anarchic humour and the pathos of the man.

156

On the first night of *The Merchant of Venice*, in Michael Langham's lucid production, it was clear that a new star had arrived.

Many old friends supported me in this first season, among them Lila de Nobili; the conductor and composer, Raymond Leppard; Peter Wood and John Barton. Not everything went well. My opening production of *The Two Gentlemen of Verona* was judged a complete disaster and was rather a dim affair. But there was work which planted seeds for the future. The production of *Troilus and Cressida*, in which the characters thrashed out their physical and mental conflicts in a big sandpit designed by Leslie Hurry, started me on a journey through Shakespeare's political ironies which led to *The Wars of the Roses* and David Warner's *Hamlet*.

It is strange to think now of the controversy that the sandpit *Troilus* provoked. It was as if that degree of reality was an affront to the drama – as if I had brought the distraction of a real dog or a real child on to the stage. But the sandpit was a wonderful image: Mediterranean, a cockpit for hand-to-hand combat, an arena for political debate. It slowed down movement, represented heat and intensified sexuality.

Leslie Hurry and I reached it by chance. We had a hexagonal-shaped arena as the floor of our model setting, and I kept asking him to make it look more and more like sand. I wanted it to be yellow – a colour his palette for the play did not readily encompass. Finally he rolled his grey eyes to heaven and said, 'Why don't you just have real sand?' To, I think, his surprise I jumped at the suggestion. And though we had to endure the jokes of the cast turning up for rehearsal clad in large sunglasses, and the scoffing of critics who thought real sand ridiculous, the texture and movement of it made the production sing.

I worked on *Troilus* with my old friend John Barton. I had persuaded him to give up his life as a don at Cambridge and join me at Stratford. He was to direct plays and help me train the company in verse speaking.

In 1960, there was still a gulf of suspicion between theatre people and academics. The theatre was pragmatic; the academic world absolute – or so it was thought. I think both sides have now learnt to appreciate the virtues of each other. When John arrived, however, it was a gulf which I didn't sufficiently appreciate. I had found no difficulty myself in going from Cambridge into the professional theatre, and couldn't see why anybody else should. John, initially, had problems. Shortly before the opening of *The Taming of the Shrew*, which he was directing, there was a company revolt led by Peggy Ashcroft and Peter O'Toole. They were happy with the concept of the production, but were getting insufficient help on the detail. There was too much theory and not enough practice. I had to take over the final rehearsals and edit the proceedings. It was devastating for John.

Scholastic absolutes terrify actors. They have to be led to discover for themselves. In time, John became more flexible; and actors, for their part, saw more and more the strength of his vision and integrity. In season after season, he proved his extraordinary qualities as a director. In 1960, it was a jibe that going to the RSC was like going back to university. Within five years, the jibe had become affectionate.

Throughout this first season I worked non-stop. Apart from directing four of the six productions and planning the opening of the Aldwych, I lobbied the Palace for permission to change the Shakespeare Memorial Theatre's name; remodelled its stage so that the action was brought closer to the audience; and signed up a rich group of actors, directors and designers for the three-year adventure I had outlined to Fordie.

Meanwhile, Leslie was in the South of France filming the Hollywood version of *Fanny*. I tried to see her and the children as much as I could, and flew nearly every weekend to Nice and then drove the hundred miles into Marcel Pagnol country to spend a few precious hours in their company. But our absurdly pressured

158

life was taking its toll; the separations were chipping away at our marriage. If you don't have time to share the ordinary details of life, the large issues start to get neglected too.

Early on, I had a sense that in starting the RSC I had created something that had a vitality and a will to grow which was unstoppable. It was clearly the right idea at the right time. Ashcroft's Shrew and Paulina, O'Toole's Shylock, Tutin's Cressida and Viola, the *Troilus and Cressida*, Peter Wood's *Winter's Tale* and my revival of *Twelfth Night* made the box office hum. We became hot and fashionable. Reams were written about the new company – whether it should have happened or whether it shouldn't; whether we should move to London or whether we shouldn't; whether we had a new style of presenting Shakespeare or were still in search of it. There was plenty of controversy and plenty of comment. We were news.

By then, though, it was clear that I had brought into being something that was much too big for one man to handle. The responsibilities of a large theatre company whose theatres were a hundred miles apart were too complex and far-reaching to be borne alone. I have always believed that the clever way to run anything is to have around you people you think are better than yourself, and who will challenge and provoke. Running a theatre is a lonely job, and it is no help to be surrounded by a team of yes men.

Peter Brook had been a friend since 1954. He, and soon afterwards Michel St Denis, agreed to join the RSC as co-directors. I couldn't believe my luck. We were a strong triumvirate of which I was the day-to-day chairman and manager. We aimed to create an innovative Shakespeare company with techniques that were unmatched anywhere else. Michel founded a studio for research and training; Peter, over the next few years, directed a series of historic productions which led us into new territories; and they both provided me personally with a store of wisdom and stimulation that I have drawn on ever since.

The years with Michel taught me to remember what is owed to the public if you are in charge of a theatre. If you invite an audience to surrender two or three hours of their lives to you, you must do all you possibly can to offer them something very special in return; and it is far, far better to fail in that attempt than to repeat an empty pattern. He felt, too, that all of us in the theatre should not just display whatever talents we may have to their best advantage, but also be at our best as people. For him, the two qualities were one: they were indistinguishable. Talent did not excuse unbalanced or selfish behaviour and could only be diminished by it. His favourite question about a colleague with whom he was about to work was: 'Is he in a good state?'

Michel was very careful of people. Everything he did in the theatre was based on cherishing the quality of the human being – indeed his career is a testament to his own quality, his own integrity. He was the sworn enemy of dead convention. For him, the truth was something which changes as our lives change; thus the search for truth was never ending. It is not a comfortable philosophy; but it is alive.

He was an intellectual who was instinctive; a peasant who was an aristocrat; a radical who was careful to conserve the past; a man of control who fought sometimes recklessly for his beliefs. He was sceptical and responsible, ironic and dedicated. I can hear him laugh approvingly at my inability to categorise him. But the contradictions in his character were signs of his own renewal and continuing growth.

He was as French as one of my other great heroes, Jean Renoir. Yet Michel's influence on the British theatre directly touched and changed several generations, and, indirectly, the generations to come. Four major theatres – the Royal Court, the National Theatre, the English National Opera, and the Royal Shakespeare Company – all owe part of their way of working and part of their aesthetic to his ideas.

What he gave to the Royal Shakespeare Company and to me, its young founder, is incalculable. The company was callow, messy, bustling, adventurous, all over the place – and he, a man of great wisdom, decided to join the adventure. He gave me ballast and direction when it was critically needed. He spoke to a new ensemble of young actors about the European heritage, about Stanislavsky, Copeau and Brecht. He had actually known these men and worked with them. But he did not give us cold theory. Michel hated dogma. He had a deep-rooted suspicion of any method, old or new; of anything which inhibited challenge and change. He knew well how quickly yesterday's belief becomes today's comfortable conformity, imitated unthinkingly and without effect.

He was a superb teacher who loved the young. For him, they were instinctive and giving – 'open', a favourite word of his. But was this same 'openness', which contributed to the English admiration for amateurs and dislike of theory, often an excuse for avoiding craft? It was a danger which Michel never failed to point out. He believed, of course, in craft, in technique, but only as a *means*. Acting was not a trick to be learnt and then performed as a mechanical repetition; it was not imitation, but rather revelation of the whole human personality. An actor had to use acting not to hide himself, but to reveal himself.

He once sat with me at a dress rehearsal at the Aldwych, and afterwards listened to the director giving notes to the cast. He was advising the actors to go much slower, to give themselves time to think. This was disastrous advice. No actors, as they meet an audience for the first time, are thinking as quickly as the audience. It normally takes several previews to get the speed of acting up to the speed of the audience's thought. Michel whispered to me that I would have to do something – take over, or at least help the director. I said I couldn't do that. Michel reminded me that I had to, or else I had no right to be running a theatre. I followed his advice.

As my first Stratford season neared its end, I was struck with two considerable crises. The first concerned Harold Hobson, the drama critic of the *Sunday Times*. Throughout the season he had included a paragraph in every notice expressing his hostility to the projected expansion of the RSC to London, even when he was reporting favourably on what he had seen. He wrote roundly that Stratford was for Stratford and should stay there. I suffered all this for a while and then, in some anger, I wrote to the editor of the *Sunday Times* enclosing the notices and saying that although I respected his critic's absolute right to like or dislike our productions, Hobson's avowed prejudices against something that was not as yet even started might well spoil our first year at the Aldwych. I added that the whole formation of the RSC was being done without subsidy and was a considerable gamble. I asked the editor if he would in future send his second drama critic, Jack Lambert, to the Aldwych and to Stratford so that there was no danger of us being badly damaged by Hobson's prejudices.

I must have been crazy. I have learnt the hard way that taking on the British press is a high-risk indulgence. As for arguing with critics, they always have the last word and tend to be very thin-skinned, so it is best to keep your mouth shut.

Today, I believe my action would produce editorial frenzy and righteous indignation for days on end. It is not the policy of most newspapers to admit that they are ever wrong. Then, however, attitudes must have been more gentlemanly and urbane, for my letter produced a courteous invitation from Harold Hobson to lunch at Pruniers. Over excellent fish, he said it had all been a misunderstanding; he simply enjoyed tweaking my tail. I was so serious about the move to London that a little mockery seemed in order. But if this expansion was so important, he would delay making final judgement until after December when we were due to open at the Aldwych.

I hadn't exaggerated my anxiety to the *Sunday Times* editor. With no subsidy, and under-written with just the £175,000 savings, only immediate outright success at the Aldwych would enable the scheme to survive, let alone win support from the Arts Council. The gamble was nerve-wracking. Preparations went on apace. Along with three Shakespeares from Stratford and *The Duchess of Malfi* with Peggy, I had arranged to present a play from my Francophile past, Giraudoux's *Ondine*, with Leslie in the lead, and the superb new epic that John Whiting had made from Aldous Huxley's book *The Devils of Loudun*. But we needed something with real commercial power.

Anouilh's new play, *Becket*, was currently a sensation in Paris. In those days, he was as big a name as Tennessee Williams or Arthur Miller. I knew him quite well having already directed his *Waltz of the Toreadors* and *Traveller Without Luggage*. In the teeth of competition from Binkie Beaumont, I begged Anouilh to let me have his new play. I said I would cast Eric Porter as Becket and Peter O'Toole as Henry II. My plea was successful. Anouilh was wryness personified. I think he was amused by my audacity.

Then the second crisis hit. Sam Spiegel and David Lean decided they wanted Peter O'Toole for the film of *Lawrence of Arabia*. Peter admitted he had an agreement with the RSC, but said that now he couldn't possibly do *Becket*, or appear in *The Merchant* and *The Shrew* when they moved to London. He merely repeated that he was going to be a movie star. This time I took the remark very seriously indeed.

Suddenly, two of our biggest hits at Stratford could not go to the Aldwych. Even worse, I was not sure I could keep *Becket* out of the clutches of Binkie if I couldn't find a star comparable to O'Toole. I tried to work a compromise – a short London run of the two plays Peter was already in, and a delay of the film. Of course, it was impossible. Mega movies, with millions of dollars riding on their every movement, are not remotely concerned with the financial and artistic problems of the Royal Shakespeare Company. I learnt, too, a hard lesson. The law is not usually about right or wrong, but about having sufficient resources at the right time. Sam Spiegel invited the RSC to sue him over O'Toole's broken contract, but we decided that we couldn't risk the cost of a probably lengthy case. Also there was little point. If an actor doesn't want to act for you, there's nothing in the world you can do to make him.

After many desperate weeks, the situation was saved. Christopher Plummer, the fine Canadian actor, said he would play the King in *Becket* and combine it with Benedick and Richard III in the next Stratford season. I was relieved beyond measure.

– 5 –

My home at Stratford was Avoncliffe, a beautiful Regency house made of soft Bath stone, built in 1818. It stood by the banks of the Avon and had a large garden which Leslie planted with roses and set with gravel paths and bay trees in tubs in the French manner. The garden sloped down to the river and there were views over the water to the fields on the other side. The house had once been a very minor stately home – in fact it was rumoured to be connected with the family of Lady Hamilton. But in this century it had fallen on hard times.

During the Thirties, it had been used as some kind of drama school, and had also provided dormitories for actors at the theatre. Then, after the war, it was lent as accommodation to the star of each season. In the years immediately before we moved in, it had been occupied in turn by Tony Quayle and his wife Dot Hyson, Laurence Olivier and Vivien Leigh, Charles Laughton, and Peggy Ashcroft. When Leslie and I lived there, Avoncliffe was companionable as well as beautiful, for the kitchen areas and the stables attached to the main building had been converted into comfortable flats for some of the company.

We decorated the house in a confusion of Gallic and English styles – Cecil Beaton meets French provincial. And I was more prosperous than before or since. My salary of £5,000 a year was worth a great deal in those days, and the house and the Spanish couple, who did the garden and looked after us, were provided free.

I had a lovely collection of adult toys. I would go to work in the summer in my little power boat. I owned, as well, an open Jaguar XK150 in British racing green with tan upholstery in which I ran up and down to London at least once a week. One night in Stratford, I found an identical car parked next to mine. It belonged to John Osborne. And I have a notion that his intense public dislike of me – though he is always extremely cordial in private – sprang from this encounter. There was also the vintage Rolls-Royce which Leslie had given me on my thirtieth birthday. I drove round Warwickshire in it, sitting high, seeing over the hedges. I adored it.

I am told that I gave out at this time an aura of calm, even arrogant, confidence. In truth, I was scared to death at what I had started. The RSC grew almost daily in amazing headline-catching style. In its first five years the company developed fast and frighteningly, helped along by work which galvanised attention – the epic *Wars of the Roses*; Peter Brook's *Lear* with Paul Scofield; Clifford Williams's *Comedy of Errors* and *The Representative* (Rolf Hochhuth's play claiming that Pius XII failed to intervene at the slaughter of Jews in the Holocaust); my collaboration with John Barton on *Troilus and Cressida*; Vanessa Redgrave's Rosalind; David Warner's Hamlet; Peter Brook's Theatre of Cruelty and his staging of Peter Weiss's *The Marat/Sade*; and Harold Pinter's *The Collection* and *The Homecoming*. These two productions were the start of my long friendship with him and of our fruitful work together on all his new plays over the next twenty years.

For a time, the RSC even had two London theatres – the Arts as well as the Aldwych. We took the smaller house so we could have a showcase for new talent. It was a rich harvest. David Rudkin and Henry Livings emerged as new writers; Nicol Williamson as a leading actor; Sally Jacobs as a designer; and Tony Page and David Jones as directors.

We were a ferment of activity, and despite the inevitable failures I always felt we were running with the tide. This confidence enabled me to get through nightmares like the Zeffirelli production of *Othello* with Gielgud, Ashcroft, Tutin and Ian Bannen. Franco had designed realistic Italian sets, more suited to Verdi than to Shakespeare, which took for ever to change. I sat with him in the auditorium one morning at 5.30, still trying unsuccessfully to get him to cut some of the scenery. We were opening that evening, and it was clear that if things were left as they were the interval was going to last some forty minutes. Franco was of the opinion that audiences wouldn't mind the wait if what they saw finally was beautiful. I told him that nothing could be that beautiful. Also, I was desperately worried that the full sexuality Gielgud had found in previous years, in his tortured Angelo in *Measure*, his jealous Leontes and his questing Hamlet, were eluding him as he came to the simple naiveté of Othello. He was unhappy and uncertain, and appeared swamped in the enormous misplaced splendour of the production.

The setting was dark. Indeed, against it Gielgud's dark face all but disappeared. On the first night, monumental stone-like pillars swayed when he leant against them. And Ian Bannen as Iago, uncertain of his lines, pluckily improvised, but to disastrous effect. It was a nightmare evening with everything going wrong – a famous catastrophe, as much talked about as our great successes.

I felt very responsible for John's failure in the part. After all, I had listened when he and Franco had said they wanted to do the play. It had seemed to me, given the extraordinary sweetness and innocence of one side of Gielgud's personality, that he could create the trusting Moor. But he was never the soldier: the poetry was extraordinary and the naiveté was honest; but the animal wasn't there.

Though famous for his capacity to drop bricks and his love of gossip, I know no-one kinder, and no-one more loyal and tender. After *Othello*, he picked himself up and gave a beautiful performance as Gaev in Michel St Denis's *Cherry Orchard*.

Some great actors have the capacity of defining a part for ever. I cannot think of Hamlet or Angelo or Leontes or Gaev, or Spooner in Pinter's *No Man's Land*, without thinking of John. In rehearsal, he is as quick as a thoroughbred horse, speeding this way, then suddenly changing direction and speeding the other. He improvises, takes risks, lives dangerously and, as he proved in the Pinter, is perfectly prepared to play a seedy, unsympathetic character. He has the quality of mercury, and his instincts and his diction are so incredibly swift that I am sure it is this, together with his timing, wit and infallible sense of rhythm, that breeds such excitement in an audience. He seems to live several points faster than ordinary human beings.

Is he easy to direct? Yes. He demands help, demands stimulation, and he leaves you exhausted. But he also leaves you feeling slightly cleverer than you know you are.

– 6 –

By nature I am a night person, somebody who works well late at night or, indeed, can go on working right through it. But I found I could not combine that nature with running a large organisation and directing plays. So in the early Sixties I turned myself into an early-morning person, establishing at the RSC a routine which I have continued ever since.

At a quarter to six I get up and do some exercises. Then, for the first two hours of the day, I deal with the problems of yesterday – taping replies to all letters and messages. Anybody I need to speak to I can usually get easily on the phone between eight and nine. I can also cope better with crises early in the morning, and have a rule that I am not given bad news at night unless it is absolutely vital. During the rest of the morning and in the afternoon I rehearse, with only a short lunch – normally a light working meal shared with someone. And for those five or six hours of rehearsal I insist that I am not disturbed. This uninterrupted concentration on a production keeps me fresh and ready when I return to the entirely different tangles of administration. Evenings are given over to meeting people, or seeing previews, dress rehearsals or performances.

At the RSC – as later at the National Theatre – it amounted to a particularly packed day, even if I wasn't directing (which I mostly was). Time had to be found, too, for reading scripts, searching for fresh talent by seeing the work of other theatres and other actors, and dealing with sudden shocks and alarms. The greatest need was, of course, planning for the future; ironically, this tended to be neglected because of the demands of the day, crisis management and the unexpected emergencies.

There were, as well, the Board meetings. I have always loved the politics of committees – the ebb and flow of chat, and the fact that it is possible to persuade a group to reverse completely its initial position if you put your case well at precisely the right moment. I must have spent many weeks of my life at governors' meetings of the RSC and the NT, and on the Arts Council and its committees, and seldom found them anything but fascinating. Such gatherings are a basic form of theatre. Everybody is playing a part, and most people are saying less than they mean.

It was a hectic life. But I was happy, sometimes dangerously exhausted and often close to the edge. No-one had run a theatre company the size of the RSC before and directed plays at the same time, so I was more or less making it up as I went along. Certainly, the idea that I am power-mad has pursued me ever since. The notion stemmed from the fact that I once, in the Sixties, foolishly declared that I loved power. I said it to Peter Lewis who was writing a piece for the archetypal Sixties magazine *Nova*. I said it suddenly and mischievously because the question was one I was growing tired of denying. It passed into the cutting libraries and has been a ready-reference for all future interviewers.

I hope I wouldn't be so ridiculously unguarded now. I know that I am not power-mad. I do, however, enjoy making things happen; giving a focus to a group of people and creating the conditions in which good theatre work can grow and flourish. I don't think I am interested in power for its own sake. If I was, I would have gone into politics.

– 7 –

We got through the first year at the Aldwych without breaking the bank, though it took us until October 1962 to win our first small subsidy from the Arts Council. Our great gamble had paid off – grant-aided existence had begun. But in establishing ourselves, unasked, in London we had made many quiet enemies in high places. Hostility to the RSC in London was to continue from time to time for the next thirty years.

It was not clear in 1962 how the RSC would be affected by the next big change in the theatrical landscape: the coming of the National Theatre in 1963 in its temporary home at the Old Vic, under Olivier. I thought that two national companies in Britain, one based on Shakespeare and one based on a world repertoire drawn from Aeschylus to the present day, were exactly what was needed for the country's theatrical health. But it was evident that the powers that be, and certainly Larry himself, were not thinking of two equal organisations at all.

Just before I became director of the RSC, Larry had asked me whether I would like to join him if he succeeded in getting the NT started. From the heights of certainty which being twenty-eight allows, I thanked him, but said I was committed to Stratford. Some months later, Arnold Goodman, acting for the National Theatre Board, called on Fordie and myself to propose an amalgamation with the National. We listened and sent him away empty-handed. He says his humiliation was so great he ought to have travelled back to London disguised as a washerwoman, like Mr Toad.

There seemed to Fordie and me, at that time, no

benefit to Stratford in the idea. Indeed, it looked as if we would simply be destroying a great tradition. Much later on, when it appeared it might be of benefit to both organisations, we did try to flesh out a way of making the scheme work, but it came to nothing.

Now, in spite of rebuffs and misunderstandings, relations with Olivier continued to be personally cordial. But there was a sense that both our theatres were competing for the future, and this was much played on by the media. My passion was Shakespeare, and the RSC was where I belonged. My aim was for the RSC to be recognised and properly funded so as to be equal in resources with the NT. Larry wanted the National to be pre-eminent – to pay more, spend more and mean more. And his views were shared by many in the Establishment.

– 8 –

Through all the furious activity of the early Sixties, one thing constantly disturbed me: the extent to which my hectic pace was affecting my life at home.

When I met Leslie in 1956, I was the fashionable young director of *Waiting for Godot*. She was recently divorced and, on one of her periodic rejections of Hollywood, eager to develop herself as a stage actress in Europe. We were very attracted to each other – and we were very proud of each other. There was a delight between us that seemed unquenchable. We raced around the world listening to music, looking at pictures, seeing films, going to the theatre. At the beginning, and for several years, our marriage was an enchantment. To the outsider, it must have looked like a fairy story. We were young, successful, madly in love, and quickly had our two beautiful children, Christopher and Jenny.

But, as Leslie had foreseen, Stratford changed all that. It revealed terrible flaws in our relationship. I became a man possessed, working so hard that I had little to offer her. The RSC came before everything else. Leslie, for her part, may have been extraordinarily famous but, like many actors, she was very insecure. Only sporadically did she believe in herself, and was repeatedly torn, wondering whether her career lay in the movies or in the theatre. Or whether the happiest kind of life for her was being a wife and mother.

Her French father, a wise and witty pharmacist, was from the Parisian haute bourgeoisie. A grandfather had been Mayor of Paris. Her American mother, who had the charm and eccentricity of a Tennessee Williams character about to disintegrate, took to her bed the day the Germans invaded Paris and stayed there until the war ended.

She had been a dancer, a talent her daughter inherited. At fifteen Leslie was already in the Champs Élysées Ballet, learning from Jean Cocteau, Jean Babilée, Roland Petit and Zizi Jeanmaire. Although Leslie's education was patchy because she spent all her formative years exercising at the barre, she learnt much from the extraordinary eruption of post-war talent in the Parisian theatre and ballet. She was still only a teenager when Gene Kelly took her from the ballet company and groomed her for stardom in Hollywood. There she made *An American in Paris* and *Lili* in quick succession.

I was captivated by *Lili* some years before we actually met. I saw the film on a wet afternoon in Exeter where I was on tour with the Elizabethan Theatre Company's *Twelfth Night*. Tony Church claims that after the film my comment was: 'Imagine that lovely girl being married to Spam.' Leslie was then the wife of George Hormell, heir to the pressed-meat millions.

At heart she despised much of Hollywood. She had

the discipline and dedication of the ballet dancer – always wanting to learn, always wanting to improve herself. Understandably, she felt she needed to maintain her position as an international film star. So one week she would decide to go back to the States and do whatever the studio said; the next she would affirm that she was a European and decide to make a career there, giving up Hollywood altogether. It was a place that bred insecurity – indeed thrived upon it – using its contract actors as expendable commodities that were only promoted if their last picture did well. They were forgotten if it did badly. For a short period, Leslie tried to live in Stratford and be just Mrs Hall. But she could not deny her talent nor her ambition. Why should she?

Her French accent was an added difficulty, because it limited what she could do in British theatre. After Giraudoux's *Ondine* at the Aldwych, in the RSC's first year there, she had wanted to play Titania. But I, perhaps mistakenly, was against it.

My tiredness, her anxieties and our perpetual separations chipped the marriage away. We both had affairs. By 1962, there wasn't much left but resentment – made worse because we remembered how wonderfully it had all started. My mother observed the tensions from a distance and sniffed. She had always suspected it would end in tears. I should, she said, have thought of that before.

In 1963, in the midst of this worst unhappiness of my life, I began work on *The Wars of the Roses*. It was the most ambitious and difficult project of my career. It was also the beginning of an even bigger plan: to perform all Shakespeare's histories in 1964, the quartercentenary of his birth. Ever since I had been appointed to Stratford, people had been asking me what I was going to do for the 400th birthday. For some time I had replied that I would leave on the 399th.

The Wars of the Roses was the overall name that I gave to a trilogy of plays adapted from Shakespeare's three parts of *Henry VI* and his *Richard III*. The four plays became three because I felt (wrongly I think now) that the action of the three *Henry VI* plays was too protracted. I had longed to present them as an epic sequence ever since I had realised their narrative muscularity when Douglas Seale produced them at Birmingham in the Fifties.

My first choice as director was Peter Brook, sticking to my principle that you should always aim higher than yourself. He said that they were not for him; they would take him three years, and their content was too nakedly political to interest him at the moment. He said I should do them myself. For once, I was relieved that his answer was no.

So John Barton and I set to work to prepare a text, compressing and shaping the four plays into three. We had some ten months to achieve the whole thing before rehearsals started. We cut and patched and clarified with a will. We quickly found, however, that we needed some linking passages to keep the story in focus. Most of them came from Edward Hall's chronicles – a Tudor history which had been Shakespeare's main source book. But a few we wrote ourselves. John became brilliant at composing Shakespearean pastiche, and I tried my hand as well. Indeed, we discovered an aptitude for writing early Shakespearean blank verse that grew wildly overexuberant; and in our zeal to show clearly what Shakespeare meant, we put many new words into his text. One speech was considered so central to the production's meaning by the programme editor, John Goodwin, that he printed it in full. It was a speech John Barton and I had written. It was hastily removed.

I blush at our frenzy of adaptation in the light of the present fashion for authenticity: for the earliest, purest texts, for performances on original instruments, for editions from original manuscripts. When our final version of *The Wars of the Roses* was published, we confessed what we had done. Was it as reprehensible as Nahum Tate's happy ending to *King Lear* or Dr Bowdler's cleaned-up Shakespeare? I think it was, even though, before rehearsal, I removed a lot more of our rewrites. They had helped us understand and clarify, but I felt they had to be few and far between, especially under the watchful eye of Peggy Ashcroft.

Interpreters of Shakespeare have a tendency to feel they are giving him a helping hand to meet their audience. For instance, the texts of Olivier's films were, in my view, dreadfully insensitive. They patronised Shakespeare in the hope of speaking to the cinema public of the Forties. Garrick and Irving were also keen adaptors of the Bard in order to engage their audience.

Another reason for tampering with the words was the star consciousness of the actor-manager. Irving's Hamlet ended with Horatio saying:

> *Good night, sweet prince,*
> *And flights of angels sing thee to thy rest!*
> *Whilst I behind remain to tell a tale*
> *Which shall hereafter make the hearers pale.*

At this point the curtain descended. Irving was not going to be upstaged by Fortinbras. It is not recorded who wrote the last two lines.

The Wars of the Roses was bred of its time. John Barton and I aimed for a lean, quick rendering that concentrated on the story. We wanted to reveal the political ironies which are at the heart of any power struggle at any time. Hypocrisy and cant were as common on the lips of politicians in Tudor England as they are on television during modern British elections. Nonetheless, our adaptation, though well-intentioned, was indeed wrong-headed. It is true that in the end most of our work amounted to cuts rather than rewrites; but these were so heavy they amounted to rewrites. Once you start monkeying with original texts, either as a translator or an adaptor, you start to put on the creative cloak yourself. And it soon becomes easy to believe that you have a right to 'improve' Shakespeare, reorchestrate Mozart, or cut

Wagner. You haven't. Most of the cutting and editing and rewriting of the classics occurs because we don't understand what the original is doing or – even more likely – are incapable of realising it. As a young man I didn't know it is better to work a little harder and a little longer than to cut; that the author often doesn't need help.

Finally, of course, whatever is done to the great masterpieces only makes the adaptors look silly. We are not, after all, defacing the 'Mona Lisa' for all time. The original is still there, mocking our inability to realise it as it stands.

We began working with the actors on *The Wars of the Roses* and everything seemed set for the creation of something special. I journeyed down to Stratford by train on the morning of our first rehearsal having been the previous night at the opening of an Aldwych production. It was a fine spring day and I was avidly reading Jan Kott's book, *Shakespeare Our Contemporary*. His thesis was simple: that Shakespeare is the mirror of our own age as he has been the mirror for every other; but we have to make sure we are alert to the new images that can express him. Among other matters, Kott was writing about the power politics of Shakespeare's history plays and how they illuminated the world of the Iron Curtain and totalitarian communism. It was fascinating.

But since it was afterwards sometimes reported that *The Wars of the Roses* was actually born out of the influence of the book, I think I should record that by the time I read it the production, in its intentions, political thrust and design, was already established. All Kott said was in the air then; it was the very stuff of the Sixties.

John Bury had designed a massive arena of steel in which these clashing abrasive plays could come to life. Not only did it look ominous and magnificent, it *sounded* right. In the great battle scenes, the swords rang as they were scraped across the metal floor. In *Richard III*, the tyrant's soldiers wore steel soles on their boots so that the inhuman tramp of authority was heard throughout the theatre.

Peggy Ashcroft was to be Margaret of Anjou, at that time one of the great undiscovered parts in classic drama: at the start, a beautiful young French princess of seventeen and by the end of the trilogy a mad old crone in her late seventies. A miraculous new young actor, David Warner, was cast as Henry VI (when we opened his reception by the audience was as thunderous as O'Toole's Shylock). Other brilliant new talents in the plays, all soon to be stars of the RSC, were Ian Holm as Richard Crookback, Janet Suzman as Joan of Arc, and Roy Dotrice as King Edward. The more mature section of the company included Donald Sinden as York and Brewster Mason as Warwick, both of them, in the event, superb.

The three plays had to be staged in three months. It looked possible but was an enormous task. And we all knew what a target we would be if we failed.

Two weeks into rehearsal I broke down. My body was host to every passing psychosomatic disease: upset stomach, roaring sinuses, terrible headaches and, above all, an overwhelming tiredness. I had fits of weeping. Once more, I thought of suicide. I lay in bed in a darkened room, clearly in the grip of a serious breakdown. I was told not to work for at least six months, and that if I didn't improve, a little electric shock treatment might be prescribed – an alarming suggestion that I rejected right away.

What was actually wrong with me? Part of it, I am sure, was fear. I felt as frightened as a child, sometimes to the point of panic. Our second Stratford season had been rather shaky, especially at the start. Money worries were threatening the future of the company. The disintegration of my marriage was wrenching me apart – I was in a turmoil not knowing whether I wanted it

177

to end or not, though I knew in my heart of hearts that it was past. Physically, mentally and emotionally, I had reached my lowest ebb. I was not ready to meet the greatest challenge of my professional life. Like a child who doesn't want to take the exam because he fears he will fail, I collapsed.

For some days I lay in bed at Avoncliffe in despair. At the theatre, John Barton was staunch, rehearsing the scenes over and over, attempting to keep a sense of purpose alive. Leslie, at home, tried to make me think positively. Then Peter Brook flew over from Paris. He told me to get back to work. This was against the doctor's advice. Leslie and Peggy supported Peter; they said that if I didn't, I might lose my nerve for ever. My three friends probably saved my career; they certainly saved my immediate sanity. Two weeks later, side by side with John, I began the mighty task again. Dr Theatre is very potent.

It was, however, an uphill struggle all the way. I have never been so miserable in my life as when we were creating *The Wars of the Roses*. I continued to have every minor ailment known to man and often felt wretched. But if I had not gone back, I don't think I would have directed again.

As it was, the production turned into an astonishing success. The RSC was crowned. *The Wars of the Roses* established, as nothing else had, the style and purpose of the company. Suddenly, we had done all that we had aimed to do – and more. We were told that by stressing the ironies of politics, the realities of power and the ordinary fallibility of kings, and by moving away from abstractions and generalities, we were truly post-Brechtian. Certainly, we were very much a company of the Sixties – asking questions rather than expecting answers.

What we did came out of the most rigorous scrutiny (the Leavis word) of each scene. What was it for? What did it mean? And how could it be expressed to a modern audience? With this came ferocious study not just of the meaning of the text but of its form and how it should be spoken. Our concentration on text throughout the early years of the RSC went virtually unnoticed. But we had captured the public imagination, and our triumph flared all over the press. The *Sunday Times* went most satisfyingly over the top with an ecstatic article headed 'The Greatest Theatrical Feat of the Century'.

The trilogy moved to the Aldwych and was televised. On a few days at Stratford, and later at the Aldwych, we played all three parts in one day: epic playgoing new to our audiences. The ancient Greek example was reborn.

In 1964 – the 400th anniversary of Shakespeare's birth – we revived *The Wars of the Roses* at Stratford and added to them *Richard II*, the two *Henry IV* plays and *Henry V*. Given all together, these revealed a great chronological sweep of bloodstained English history, from Bolingbroke's usurpation of the throne to Richard III's death at Bosworth Field. The plays had never been done as a sequence. And I would never have come through the effort of putting them on without the help of committed colleagues – principally John Barton, but also Peter Wood and Clifford Williams. The company of actors, led by Peggy Ashcroft and Ian Holm, had made something live that had never lived before.

I learnt several lessons from *The Wars of the Roses*. One was that there is never a good time to do your best or most demanding work. You don't have to be happy; you don't even have to feel well. You just have to do it to your limit and hope for the best. I also learnt that, whatever the challenge, it is vital to recognise where that limit is – to know when you're getting too close to the edge. My refusal to admit that I was so near disaster was the principle reason for my collapse. Once I recognised it, I was able to go on.

My debt to Peter Brook is enormous. He is the best

friend in the world if you are in trouble – but it has to be disastrous trouble. Then he will drop everything to help. I would never go to him because of a small crisis: he would not be bothered with it.

He doesn't see everything in the theatre but he has an extraordinary instinct for what is important; he has always been ahead, finding new ways with work of extreme intensity and clarity.

In the immediate post-war years he made magic, returning the theatre to a place of fantasy and delight after the drabness of the war. In those years, Oliver Messel designed for him stages of delicate beauty. Later, his productions of *Measure for Measure* and *The Winter's Tale* illuminated Gielgud's romantic soul with pain and passion. And as a piece of astonishing total theatre – Peter not only directed but designed the set and composed the music – the *Titus Andronicus* he did at Stratford, with Olivier in the name part, brought the harshness of Seneca into a Shakespeare rarity. His great productions for me at the RSC – especially of *King Lear* and *The Marat/Sade* – set paths for the future.

At his Paris centre, his vision of a multiracial theatre has been wonderfully realised. But why, oh why, couldn't it have been in Britain? Two of the greatest directors of my time, he and Joan Littlewood, have both left the British theatre and gone abroad – Joan to retire and Peter to start again. Peter should have been given a theatre in this country to work out his genius. Alas, the British never subsidise people: they subsidise institutions. They suspect the artist.

– 9 –

In the early Sixties, I could not have been more successful professionally. At home, everything was in tatters. My marriage to Leslie had reached its lowest ebb. And on

19. Avoncliffe, our Stratford home. The back half of the house was divided into flats for the company and staff.

20. With John Barton, rehearsing *The War of the Roses*.

21. *above left* Peggy Ashcroft as Margaret in the trilogy *The Wars of the Roses* (RSC). She played the Queen as a young girl, as a middle-aged warrior – here – and at the end as a half-crazed old harridan.

22. *above right* Peter O'Toole as Shylock: Michael Langham directed the production (RSC)

23. *below* David Warner as Hamlet (RSC). His performance defined the play for a decade. With Michael Williams as Rosencrantz.

24. *above* Paul Scofield as Lear in Peter Brook's production (RSC).

25. *below left* Dorothy Tutin as Cressida in *Troilus and Cressida* (RSC); with her is Clive Swift. The production was staged in a sandpit.

26. *below right* Vanessa Redgrave as Rosalind, her first unqualified success. This *As You Like It* was directed by Michael Elliott (RSC). Max Adrian is Jaques.

27. *The Homecoming* (RSC). From left: John Normington, Paul Rogers, Terence Rigby, Ian Holm, Michael Jayston.

28. *The Government Inspector* (RSC): Paul Scofield is the drunken inspector.

29. A theatre cricket match. Peggy Ashcroft plays a captain's innings. Janet Suzman, left, and Susan Engel are behind the wicket.

30. With Jacky, Lucy and Edward in our Barbican flat at the top of the Cromwell Tower. The Barbican Arts Centre is being built below.

 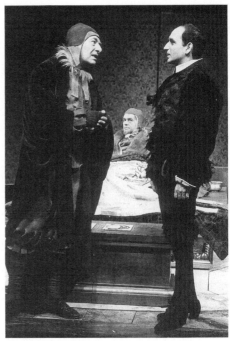

31. With Edward. **32.** Paul Rogers, Paul Scofield, Ben Kingsley: *Volpone* (NT).

33. Ralph Richardson and John Gielgud: *No Man's Land* (NT).

34. Rehearsing the orgy round the Golden Calf in *Moses and Aaron* (Covent Garden). The cast included strippers from Soho.

35. *Figaro* (Glyndebourne). Ileana Cotrubas and Frederica von Stade as Susanna and Cherubino.

36. Technical rehearsal of *Ulisse* (Glyndebourne). Foreground, Ray Leppard. Aloft, Ian Caley and Anne Howells.

37. *Così fan tutte* (Glyndebourne). From left: Hakan Hagegard, Maria Ewing, Nan Christie, Stafford Dean. It was while directing this production in 1978 that I met Maria.

her return from filming in Los Angeles, we went on a brief holiday to Morocco in a last desperate effort to try and repair some of the damage done by our constant separations. It did the opposite. There was clearly a huge gulf between us. After a couple of days, Leslie told me she was in love with Warren Beatty and had decided to leave me and go back to Hollywood. She didn't, however, wish to disrupt the lives of the children and suggested that they live with me in Stratford with their nanny and Jay, our Scottish housekeeper, and come to her for holidays. I was devastated – but chiefly for Christopher and Jenny who trusted and loved us. I didn't blame Leslie; I didn't even blame Warren Beatty. He was just the catalyst for a split that had long been inevitable.

Leslie left for Hollywood immediately and the situation rapidly became front-page news. It was my first experience of being 'door-stepped', which meant seeing a posse of bored and frozen journalists permanently stationed outside the house waiting for statements I was not prepared to give. I went on with my work at the theatre and gave thanks that I was so busy.

After six or seven weeks, I had a phone call from Leslie telling me she was flying to England in two days to pick up the children. She had decided it was wrong for them to be away from their mother, and would therefore bring them up in Los Angeles. I said I didn't want that.

I knew this wasn't going to work for Leslie. Quite apart from the dubious stability of her relationship with Warren Beatty, I did not believe she would make a permanent new life in Hollywood. It was a place, as I well knew, that she both admired and loathed. She was a fierce European. The oscillations would be certain to continue: she would go on moving constantly between the two continents and the children would be caught up in these hectic changes.

Who could I go to for advice? John Roberts, the RSC's general manager at the Aldwych, always knew the best professional advisers – whether they were lawyers, dentists or chiropodists. He recommended a top solicitor with an awesome record of victories in difficult divorce cases. This was a person whose extravagant personality would not have been out of place in Dickens or Gogol. He wore full make-up even in broad daylight, very skilfully applied. He was brilliant and had amazing clarity of thought; he was also, I felt, ruthless and cynical. I didn't like him.

He asked me what I wanted for my children. I said I would like them to be Europeans and educated in England or France. I stressed that I hated the idea of them being dragged from country to country, from film set to film set, and that, most of all, I didn't want them brought up in Los Angeles, a place as foreign to me as anywhere I have ever been.

He told me that if Leslie took Jenny and Christopher to America, no court there would ever be likely to allow them out of their mother's control, particularly if the father was living thousands of miles away. Then came his main point: unless he served a notice on Leslie as she stepped off the plane, making the children wards of court, I had no chance whatsoever of influencing any aspect of their future. I said I didn't want to go to such lengths. He emphasised that Leslie could bring them up in America and educate them how and where she liked; that it was up to me to decide, but if I decided not to take his advice, I needn't ask him for help later on.

I had until next day to make up my mind, and I spent a sleepless night frantically worrying what to do. I despise revenge. Was I taking this stand against Leslie to pay her back for loving Warren Beatty? I thought I wasn't – but I needed to be absolutely sure of my motives. By the morning, I believed I knew what was best, and told the solicitor to go ahead. As Leslie arrived she was presented with papers under which Christopher and Jenny could not leave the country without the courts' permission.

The legal battle dragged on as legal battles always do. I hate the law. Victory depends on who can play the game in the quickest and most cool-handed way.

After more than a year, I was given custody – an amazing verdict at that time. Fathers were not generally so favoured. There was no feeling of triumph in the victory; I was just relieved that the children could grow up and go to school in England. They lived primarily with me, spending their holidays with Leslie, wherever she might be in the world. They early became much-travelled, international children. But at least they had stability in their education. What happened certainly affected their lives adversely, but how far they have been damaged is difficult to say. They were surrounded by love and care from both of us, and they had a good education at Bedales, both ending up at Cambridge with Exhibitions.

Leslie's affair with Warren Beatty was short-lived. But the fact that I had taken legal action to keep the children, whom she adored, and had succeeded in my attempt, was something she found very hard to forgive. Only many years later did we become friends again. We now remember the good times and not the bad times. Three grandchildren have put our quarrels into perspective.

The break-up had its comic side. My alarming solicitor had warned me that Leslie would be advised to fight with every weapon. In the eyes of the law, therefore, my own conduct had to be discreet, not to say blameless. He told me to keep a weather eye on the rear-view mirror of my car; and when walking always to take note of who was behind me. He predicted that I would be watched and followed. I thought he was letting his professional fantasies go to his head. He wasn't. These were the days when the law insisted that there had to be a good party and a bad in any divorce; the conflict was black and white. So Leslie was constrained to hire a team of private detectives in order to prove that I was an undesirable and unsuitable father. My solicitor countered by talking about her as if he was judging her by Old Testament principles: she was a scarlet woman.

Leslie's detectives proved less than efficient, however. By mistake, they sent detailed reports of my doings to me instead of to her. The reports were full of innuendo and smouldering, scarcely concealed, outrage. To be well-dressed or to go to an expensive restaurant was, by implication, the beginning of a moral collapse. One report delighted me. It recorded my behaviour on a Sunday evening. Everything I did was an insult to the Sabbath. I left my 'large Stratford house' driving an 'open British racing-green Jaguar sports car', proceeded to the theatre, parked and went inside. There were many lights on in the building. 'Sounds of music, chatter and laughter were audible, and several young women, some of them in a state of undress' were hanging out of various windows. The watcher speculated that some kind of party appeared to be in progress. He recorded that I stayed until nearly midnight. The 'party' I had been attending was the dress rehearsal of *Richard III*.

Our divorce finally came through in 1965. I was sad that a magical relationship had ended, but I could not be sad that we had met. As young people, we developed and challenged each other in many ways. I became more European, and had my eyes opened to the visual world. I also became less snobbishly certain that British art, particularly British theatre, was the best. As an outsider, I had always had a reluctance, if not an inability, to spend time enjoying myself if it had no purpose, partly, perhaps, because I am an East Anglian puritan. Leslie tempered that, and I became a little better at living.

For her part, Leslie eagerly absorbed British traditions, gardens, furniture, British irony and humour. I admired her sophistication, her Frenchness and her beauty. Above all, I admired her courage. For she had – indeed she still has – an indomitable will. In 1991, at the age of nearly sixty, she appeared in the American musical *Grand Hotel* on the Berlin stage. Not only did she have to go back to dancing at a time when most dancers have long retired; she also learnt German, acted in it *and* sang in public for the first time. She did all this, I am sure, because she won't be beaten. She always loved a challenge.

I haven't much of a memory for pain or unhappiness. I sometimes, indeed, neglect to remember who my enemies are. In spite of all the strain and the hurry, I am content to recall the good things of the Fifties and Sixties: the miracle of being completely in love; the miracle of two beautiful children. For a short time, then, both privately and publicly, I had the joy of complete achievement.

– 10 –

In 1965 I directed the David Warner *Hamlet* at Stratford; *Moses and Aaron* at Covent Garden; and Pinter's *The Homecoming* and Gogol's *The Government Inspector*, with Paul Scofield in the name part, at the Aldwych. It was one of my best years of work. Professionally I was riding high.

In my personal life, I began again. Through the anguish of the break-up, I had been sustained by a love affair with Jacqueline Taylor, an attractive and funny girl who had worked at Stratford since the late Fifties. She was first a secretary in the production department, then moved to the press office, and finally ran my life as my assistant. She was intelligent, but she had no pretensions to being an intellectual. I liked her practicality, her down-to-earth approach to life, her strong likes and good instincts.

She loved the theatre, and because she knew what I did and why and how I did it, she understood and supported my obsessive work rate. I thought at the time that this would always be so.

In the year that my divorce from Leslie came through, Jacky and I married. It seemed a new start. There was no rival career to cram into our over-full life, for Jacky left her job and left it gladly. No siren Hollywood voices called her away on long agonising separations. She loved children and initially was quite wonderful with Christopher and Jennifer. She went out of her way to help them; she knew how important it was for them to have security.

Yet before long, the very things that had been the strengths of our marriage became the weaknesses. I hadn't realised that Jacky was not as strong as she gave out, that in fact she worried far more than I knew about the daily ebb and flow of disaster and crisis which is the basis of all theatre life. You cannot come home from a day running a theatre and report a predominance of good news. Success is transitory and difficulty the norm. Tales of broken contracts, changed minds, sudden feuds and unexpected failures are much more likely than the warm glow of success that show business likes to project to the public.

Jacky took this constant hurly-burly very personally, and I was too preoccupied to recognise that it caused her genuine distress. During a decade of anxiously suffering my hectic existence, she became gradually more aloof. By the mid Seventies, her imperviousness seemed complete. And by that time I had become a singularly unpopular figure, much attacked. The young lion of the Sixties, who could do no wrong, was long forgotten. I had succeeded a great figure, Laurence Olivier, as director of the National Theatre, and had the task of moving the company from the modest Old Vic to its vast new home on the South Bank. It was a hugely expensive building relative to the Old Vic, and it was opened to the public right in the middle of an appalling economic slump. I was the focus for some venomous criticism.

Jacky remained apparently strong. But the silence between us grew like a dreadful weed. She appeared not to know what was being written about me or what I was going through. She made no comment as I tried to cope with a very public purgatory. My resentment increased. I thought she didn't care; worse, I thought she was ashamed of me. In fact, she didn't want to hurt me or herself and thought it better to ignore my distress. I had no idea at the time. It became an agony to live with her.

We had two lovely children, Edward born in 1967 and Lucy who arrived two years later. They adored their half-brother and -sister, and a family group, with all its fun and security, developed. But this also, like the happiness I had found with Jacky, seemed inevitably to breed its own unhappiness. Jenny and Christopher lived part of their lives as the children of a famous film star travelling round the world at holiday times. The rest of the time they had a more down-to-earth existence with us. We were not very affluent – I never have been. I have worked at what I liked rather than what would make money, so we by no means had the standards of the jet set. Inevitably, Jacky became increasingly protective of her own son and daughter and what the future might hold for them. Her concern for Jenny and Christopher became noticeably less and less. I thought she was jealous of them.

The problems multiplied and in a few years a relationship that had been full of hope was dead. The life I led wrought terrible changes in Jacky. Finally, it must have been healthy for her to have no more of me.

– 11 –

David Warner had ambled on to the Aldwych stage to give an audition way back in 1962. I was sure even then that he would make a Hamlet. He had that authentic quality stars always possess – they are completely watchable. You need to hang on to their every word, understand their every thought, note their merest gesture.

David's mesmeric stage presence was confirmed by his Henry VI in *The Wars of the Roses*. When we came to *Hamlet* in 1965, he was the very embodiment of the Sixties student – tall, blond, gangling. He was passive, yet had an anarchic wit. His performance, I believe, defined the play for a decade. It completely expressed the spirit of the young of that period, gentle but dangerous. Student unrest was becoming more and more part of our daily lives as the new generation questioned and challenged the old; we were part of the culture that was marching inexorably towards 1968, the year of student revolution.

I don't much like records of stage performances – photographs, designs or even videotapes. Theatre is ephemeral; it should burst like a bubble once it has ceased to live before its audience. But there are times when I find myself wishing that I could re-experience performances of the past. David's Hamlet is one of them. It lives for many people as the moment when they realised that Hamlet is always our contemporary.

I did not try to make this happen. I had no overall theory of the play to take into the rehearsal room. I worked with the company to find the meaning of each scene and to express it as best we could. Out of that scrutiny – as it always will if honestly pursued – came a concept. And we found ourselves speaking straight to our audience. We did not, however, speak to the critics. Apart from Ronald Bryden in the *New Statesman*, nearly all of them were unimpressed, not to say hostile. *Hamlet* is always a big target, particularly if the leading actor is in his early twenties. But the public rushed to see David Warner as if his was the performance they had been waiting for.

Something else marked the Sixties for me. A parcel arrived from Harold Pinter. Inside was a beautifully typed manuscript accompanied by a characteristically terse letter. It read: 'This is it.' 'It' was *The Homecoming*; and directing the play sealed a friendship with the author which, except for one serious but short-lived break, has lasted ever since.

The production had a clarity I had long been trying to achieve. I wanted my work to be hard-edged and unsentimental – and to demonstrate that in the theatre 'less is more'; it seemed to me that economy and selection intensified drama and made it more vivid. John Bury's set was inspired by Magritte, and in the huge, bleached, antiseptic room which he designed, the green apples on the sideboard were the only splash of colour. Nothing was on stage unless it had a specific meaning.

My friendship with Harold began when, after seeing *Waiting for Godot*, he sent me *The Birthday Party*. I couldn't do it; nor could I do his next play, *The Caretaker*. So we didn't actually work together until his one-acter, *The Collection*, was staged at the Aldwych in 1962. And as time went by we discovered a remarkable similarity of taste and thought.

The Homecoming is a big and terrifying play about survival in the jungle of the family. But rehearsing it was a joy; the rhythmic certainties which I found in Shakespeare and Beckett I found in quite a different way in Pinter. A director cannot question this writer's form, he can only endorse it; he has to work backwards, discovering a feeling which will support that form. It is exactly like a singer learning the notes and *then* creating a feeling which will match those notes.

I was as rigorous with the actors over Pinter's punctuation as I was with them over Shakespeare's line endings. I even held a 'dot-and-pause' rehearsal. Pinter marks his texts with three different notations. The longest break is marked *silence*: the character comes out of it in a different state to when he or she began it; the next is marked *pause*, which is a crisis point, filled with the unsaid; and the shortest is marked with three dots, which is a plain hesitation. The actors had to understand why there were these differences. They chafed a little, but finally accepted that what was not said often spoke as forcefully as the words themselves. The breaks represented a journey in the actor's emotions, sometimes a surprising transition.

I learnt something else from *The Homecoming* which helped me through the eleven Pinter premieres that I subsequently directed. The words are weapons that the characters use to discomfort or destroy each other; and, in defence, to conceal feelings. Pinter is always a cockney, albeit sometimes a very well-bred one. The essence of his work is 'taking the piss': deriding an antagonist while treating him with extreme friendliness and charm. Ideally, the person whose piss is being taken should be entirely unaware of the fact. London taxi drivers are experts at the technique.

Pinter's words are used to hide the emotions (because to show them in this jungle is to be weak). But the actors have to be aware of the ebb and flow of violence that lies *below* the words. Otherwise, the surface of the play will seem bland and pretentious. And the pauses will mean nothing. Actors in Pinter have to feel every moment intensely, but then disguise it. I have sometimes held rehearsals in which these sub-text feelings are deliberately brought to the surface and the naked aggression of the characters is demonstrated. The actors then know what they are covering up. It is alarming and melodramatic. There is nonetheless lyricism, even nostalgia, in Pinter's work, heard most eloquently at the end of *Landscape* and in *A Kind of Alaska*.

The Homecoming proved my belief that the textual discipline of the classics could and should be applied to modern drama. Ian Holm's superb Lenny was all the better for playing Richard Crookback throughout *The Wars of the Roses*.

The first ever performance of *The Homecoming* was in Cardiff. Some of the audience walked out, furious, when it was suggested in the play that Ruth, the central female character – a wonderfully sexy and mysterious performance by Vivien Merchant – could only stay with the family if she 'went on the game'. There was the same reaction the following week in Brighton. Audiences were not, initially, prepared to accept the anarchy of these people; and by the time we reached London, the public were still shocked by the horror, and found it difficult to laugh. From then on, though, the energy of the play became unstoppable. After running for eighteen months it went to America. But in Boston, as in Cardiff and Brighton, many walked out. Alexander Cohen, the producer, asked Harold to 'fix the second act'. He didn't know his man. Harold took his glasses off, his eyes glinting. 'What exactly did you have in mind?' he said. It was one of the few times I have seen a Broadway producer at a loss for words. Cohen never returned to the subject.

The New York first night was miraculous. The cast acted with arrogance and clarity and the play consequently exerted a terrible grip. But Walter Kerr, the *New York Times* critic (and the only one that mattered), didn't like it; or not enough anyway. Alexander Cohen warned me next morning that it would probably be off by the end of the week. Did he really mean that? I asked. Because if so, I was just setting up the next Stratford season and would be only too pleased to have *The Homecoming* actors in the Stratford company – particularly Ian Holm and Paul Rogers. Cohen was furious. 'You have no right to talk about future plans,' he shouted. 'You have just had a flop on Broadway.'

We hadn't. *The Homecoming* was the one that bucked the system. It became a cult success, was garlanded with Tony Awards, and we subsequently made a film of it.

With some trepidation, I did the play again many years later, in London in 1990. I considered a new set. But the more I thought about it, the more indispensable the original John Bury designs seemed. Finally, I felt it would be perverse and self-conscious to try to alter them; it would be change for the sake of change. We had different actors, of course, with one extraordinary exception: the superb John Normington, now almost the right age for Uncle Sam, playing the part he had created twenty-five years earlier.

This revival showed beyond doubt that *The Homecoming* and its production were still living entities; and the laughter was readier than it had been in the Sixties. There are many plays that use the family as an image of society, but none I know that are as honest or savage. The play will endure, but not, of course, my staging of it; that was the product of its time. Strong productions can last for a couple of decades, as did *The Homecoming*. But after that, they become curiosities – period pieces that represent the past.

The Homecoming nearly wasn't staged by the RSC. At a meeting in Avoncliffe, held beneath the ceiling of rioting plaster cupids and flowers which Leslie had Frenchified by painting them every colour of the rainbow, the directors of the RSC gravely considered their responsibilities. Peter Brook thought the play too small for the large spaces of the Aldwych. So did John Barton. Michel St Denis felt that it was not poetic enough. Clifford Williams and Trevor Nunn were less specific, but neither said anything to stop the strong tide of objection.

None of them wanted to direct the play. On the other hand, I did, passionately, and said as much. I thought it would be overpowering in the Aldwych with actors who, trained in Shakespeare, were uniquely able to perform a modern poetic text. Peter Brook then said that I was at the RSC to express my own tastes and prejudices; the directors had joined me because they respected these, even if they didn't agree with all of them; and I should therefore have everyone's backing to do what I wanted: it was my prerogative.

The meeting perfectly illustrated why the running

of a theatre cannot ultimately be democratic. But it has to treasure people's individual obsessions even if they arouse contrary opinions: the strength of them is what makes a theatre thrive.

Pinter is a poet whose theatre is funny, violent and lyrical. It can, as well, produce unforgettable images from its actors. I can still see the bull-like strength of Paul Rogers's shoulders in the original *Homecoming*, and Vivien Merchant's shapely legs; Warren Mitchell's predatory eyes under the butcher's cap in the revival; John Gielgud's Spooner with socks peeping through his sandals in *No Man's Land* and Ralph Richardson's fall as Hirst, collapsing with the unexpectedness of a tree; the sexiness of Dorothy Tutin as she surveyed the world from her sofa in *Old Times*; and Penny Wilton in *Betrayal*, Peggy Ashcroft in *Landscape* and Judi Dench in *A Kind of Alaska*, all strongly feminine in a masculine and abrasive world.

I have had as much joy from working with Pinter as I have had from staging Mozart and Shakespeare. Harold is a meticulous man, and a warm friend with a sharp sense of humour – though this does not, it has to be said, readily extend to himself. He has an enormous understanding of his own position. But this is not conceit. He *is* very special and knows it.

In his early years, he was committed to being uncommitted. I remember that *Encounter* ran a symposium in the Sixties to decide whether or not we should join the Common Market. A few of us in the arts were asked to contribute a thousand words each giving our opinions. I dutifully sent in mine. Harold sent one sentence, which announced that he did not care one way or the other. That 'not caring' has completely reversed itself in recent years to caring very much about world events and world politics. His engagement is now intense and I respect him for it; I was shocked by his indifference when he was young. He has grown into political responsibility, while many colleagues of his generation have backed away.

High passion lurks under his urbane, controlled exterior. It is difficult to connect some artists with their work; not Harold. His love of poetry, his precision with words, his accuracy about appointments, his fastidiousness in dress, and the threat of violence just under his charm, are inescapably the man who made the plays.

– 12 –

I woke up one morning in the summer of 1964 to discover that I was once more a centre of newspaper attention. One of the RSC governors, Emile Littler, had attacked me and Fordie Flower for 'presenting, harbouring and promoting' a season of dirty plays at the Aldwych. He said that we were ruining the Royal Shakespeare Company and the theatre in general. The great 'dirty plays' row had begun.

It was the middle of the silly season and there wasn't much other news. The combination of sex and subsidy, theatre and reputation, was irresistible. The press fell on it like starving wolves, and for some three weeks the controversy howled on.

Much of the RSC's work in London at that time was disturbing and radical, but I would hardly have called any of it obscene. The repertory at the Aldwych contained Peter Weiss's *Marat/Sade*; David Rudkin's *Afore Night Come* (which contained a violent ritual murder); a French surrealist farce called *Victor* with a central character with uncontrollable wind (the farts provided by a musician on a tuba in the wings); and, for good measure, Pinter's *The Birthday Party* and Beckett's *Endgame* (these last two writers were mildly surprised, I think, to find themselves the authors of dirty plays).

The basis of the row may well have been political. Did Emile Littler want to get rid of Fordie and of me? Possibly he had his eye on the chairmanship; certainly he was worried about the effect on the West End of the growing power of the subsidised theatre.

Happily, no damage came from this puritan fit. Fordie and I emerged much strengthened by it, and plays and their content became, for once, front-page news. The RSC was widely seen as progressive and daring – and the box office boomed.

Most important of all, the debate about the very existence of the Lord Chamberlain hotted up. It began to look more and more absurd that the theatre was gagged by an official of the Court (a practice 200 years old) and that playwrights did not have the same freedoms as novelists, journalists or broadcasters whose only curb was, rightly, the law of the land.

I prepared an anthology of verse for one of our special poetry evenings at the Aldwych. It included a poem by e. e. cummings which had the word 'shit' in the last line. The Lord Chamberlain promptly banned it. So we printed it in the programme (which was not against the law). At the performance, the house-lights were raised when the poem should have been spoken, and the audience were asked to read it silently to themselves. The RSC made front-page news again.

Meanwhile, Emile Littler had presented a rather salacious play about the Dilke case, a famous nineteenth-century sex-and-politics scandal. This prompted BBC television, in a show called *Not So Much a Programme – More a Way of Life*, to include an item in which an actor, made up as Littler, sang a ditty about not liking other people's dirty plays, only his own. Incandescent with rage, Littler sued the BBC in a long and costly case which he eventually won.

At the trial, I had been in the witness box, sub-poenaed for the defence. I became so overexcited about the perniciousness of stage censorship that I began arguing with the judge. 'Mr Hall,' said he, 'when both of us are talking at once, you must be silent.'

All this was part of the silly Sixties. But like much of the craziness of that decade, there were serious issues at stake. The cause of free speech and an open society was being advanced. Also, the excitements did not stop with the 'dirty plays' flare-up and the scandals of the orgy scene in *Moses and Aaron* at Covent Garden. For while sex in the theatre was one thing, being politically provocative on the stage was quite another.

In 1966 Peter Brook developed for the RSC a show fiercely critical of American involvement in Vietnam, when such views were well ahead of their time. He gave it the punning title, *US*. There was nothing in it that the Lord Chamberlain, Lord Cobald, could directly censor but he was unhappy about the enterprise. I was invited for an after-hours drink at St James's Palace: sherry and a chat. Lord Cobald asked me whether I thought it right for a major theatre company in receipt of public money to present something which was critical of a great ally with whom we had a special relationship. I said that if the writers, the directors and other artists involved sincerely believed what they were saying, and had reached their judgements responsibly, the short answer had to be yes. To my mind, I said, the theatre had every right to be as polemical as the press and, if need be, as prejudiced. I didn't forget to mention freedom of speech . . .

The Lord Chamberlain pondered. He was clearly not pleased. He then warned me that he would be having a word with my chairman, and that the purpose of this would be to advise the cancellation of the show. He also reminded me that the president of the RSC was Anthony Eden, well known for his fervent support of American intervention in Vietnam. I thanked him for his frankness and left.

Once more, I had reason to be grateful for the wisdom

and strength of Fordie. He was outraged at this unofficial interference, told me to go ahead with the production and discussed the whole problem with the Board, getting their full backing. He then went further. Anthony Eden was due to retire as our president in about six months. To prevent him being in an embarrassing position when we did the show, Fordie explained the situation to him, and gently hastened his retirement.

Shaping events by just 'having a word' in private is still the habit of the Establishment. Fortunately, we now have a more disrespectful press to publicise these contortions.

I wish I could write that *US* was a triumph, but that wouldn't be true. It succeeded in its aim of stirring up feeling about an escalating war which, as yet, had not registered with the British public. The play angered, embarrassed and impressed people in fairly equal measure. The text by Adrian Mitchell, Denis Cannan and Michael Kustow was a tough mixture of documentary material, accusatory lyrics and conventional playwriting. Peter's production had strong images and moments of extraordinary beauty. It was a savage, ferocious piece. But it contained several eccentricities.

At the end, the cast covered their heads with brown paper bags and moved as if blinded, some descending from the stage to wander among the puzzled and irritated audience. The actors annoyed the audience still further by silencing any applause. On the first night, the long, uneasy moment that followed was only broken when Peter Cook bawled from the circle, 'Are you waiting for us, or are we waiting for you?'

Peter Brook showed a typically Machiavellian streak the day the notices appeared. Much was made in them of the last few minutes, in which a member of the cast, Michael Williams, stepped to the front of the stage and released a box full of butterflies into the auditorium. He then picked up a butterfly and set fire to it with a cigarette lighter. It was an action precisely calculated to horrify the British.

Within hours of the press reports, the RSPCA telephoned John Goodwin at the Aldwych demanding that the episode be cut; hundreds of their members were complaining. Peter was told and looked thoughtful. 'I will tell you a secret only the actor and I know,' he said to John. 'The butterfly he burns is actually made of paper. Why not explain that to the RSPCA? But add that if they give our secret away to anyone at all, it is bound to become public. And if that happens, from then on we *will* burn a live butterfly.'

The blackmail worked. There was not another word from the RSPCA and people went on believing what they were meant to believe.

Peter Brook's contribution to those RSC years was amazing. His *King Lear* with Paul Scofield's definitive performance re-evaluated a great masterpiece. For the first time, audiences were persuaded that Goneril and Regan had a reasonable case against their difficult and wilful father.

Peter's whole approach was innovative, and the simplicity of the physical staging added immeasurably to the effect. His first design had been for a beautiful but harsh Renaissance world. The set was elaborate and the Stratford workshops had started to make it. Then Brook suddenly arrived in my office with a new model that was austere, spare, and hung with sheets of rusted iron. This was the set he used, and during the storm the huge iron sheets vibrated to make the thunder. The play became all the more powerful because it was not illustrated literally.

Peter constantly fed European thought into the RSC. The *Lear* had been much influenced by the Polish scholar Jan Kott, who asserted the timeless politics of Shakespeare. Brook's *Theatre of Cruelty* season followed. It was inspired by the French director Antonin Artaud, whose vision of theatre stressed violent images and formal ritual more than words. From this experimental season (done in a studio space outside the Lord Chamberlain's censorship) developed Peter's brilliant Aldwych production of Peter Weiss's play *The Persecution and Murder of Marat as Performed by the Inmates of the Asylum of Charenton under the Direction of the Marquis de Sade* – quickly shortened to *The Marat/Sade*. It overwhelmed audiences in London and New York. Startling images, especially of Glenda Jackson, stay with me: in *The Theatre of Cruelty*, naked in a bath while excerpts from the Keeler trial were spoken; whipping de Sade with her hair in *The Marat/Sade*. These thrilled many and disgusted some. Our theatre was responding to its times.

Peter went on exploring. He brought to London the Polish director Jan Grotowski who was interested in 'what happens to the psyche of the actor beyond the threshold of pain'. Grotowski used difficult physical exercises in order to examine his ideas and test the endurance of the actors. I spent a long evening on the telephone trying to explain to the husband of an actress why an afternoon rehearsal had seriously dislocated her back.

Much of this seems pretentious now. But the Sixties had the energy to challenge because they dared to be foolish. They opened minds and swept away dead convention. It was good to be head of a theatre at that time.

Founding the RSC pitchforked me into politics and I cannot pretend that I minded. Politics, and particularly politicians, have always fascinated me. Their capacity to deceive themselves, to sanction their actions as being in the public interest when they are often only to satisfy their personal ambition, seems infinite. I had seen it on stage in the conniving barons of Shakespeare's histories; I saw it again off stage in politicians and government departments during ten years at the RSC and fifteen years running the National. Even before then, I was a member of the committee that advised the Arts Council on drama policy, learning at first hand how such gatherings went about their business. And once the RSC started, I was continually lobbying, attending meetings, writing articles, doing broadcasts. I was passionate for the cause of subsidised, ensemble theatre.

In the early Sixties, I managed to persuade James Callaghan, then Shadow Chancellor, to issue a statement from the Opposition that Labour supported the RSC and would fund us properly when they came to power. In the polarised Thatcher years, this would have been a disaster, like breaking bread with the enemy. But in those more democratic times it was very helpful. I conclude that both political parties are generous about the arts when they are in Opposition, but once they are in power they tend to forget their promises.

More and more, as I mixed with politicians, I became intrigued by their world. Indeed in the mid Sixties, following a hint from Jennie Lee, the ebullient and revolutionary arts minister, I thought of putting myself forward as a Labour candidate. Again, Peter Brook saved me. He said that however ephemeral and however frivolous our theatre work might be, we actually *made* something, and that it existed in complete terms which could undoubtedly influence people. The compromises of politics were essentially shady and, at the lower levels, had no such influence. What on earth would I do with my energy, sitting on the back benches for years? I abandoned the idea.

I also became slowly disillusioned with government departments; surprisingly, their word was rarely their bond. Trust was always the problem with the Arts Council. The RSC was a success very quickly, but there was an immediate undertow of anxiety. From the moment we expanded into London in December 1960, all our problems were related to the possible arrival, before too long, of the National Theatre. And that, of course, reflected directly on our claim for subsidy. A heated, often bitter, debate about whether the two companies could, or even should, coexist caused the RSC's political crises during my time with them. The details are complicated but have the fascination of all Byzantine negotiations.

In 1957, Laurence Olivier became a Trustee of the National Theatre and began to lobby strenuously for its creation. In 1958, I was offered the directorship at Stratford and put forward the policy of an ensemble company trained in the classics, but expert in modern drama, and with a London base. My thinking was certainly influenced by the possible arrival of the National Theatre; but that had been coming for nearly 150 years, and although now probable was by no means certain.

In 1959, some time after my plans had been announced, informal talks began between the National Theatre campaigners – Olivier and the prospective chairman, Lord Chandos – and Fordham Flower and myself, about a possible amalgamation. I have read in various histories that I wanted the RSC to be the National Theatre. That is not true. I was in love with Shakespeare. Fordie and I were simply anxious to protect the Stratford tradition, and not to be crippled by a National Theatre that was likely to have disproportionately larger resources and so attract all the talent. Besides, I had always believed that the country should have *two* national theatres: artistic competition means better work.

Though when these talks took place the National Theatre was still not much more than an unrealised dream, nonetheless, what most of those who were campaigning for it thought, but didn't say, was that when and if the RSC arrived in London, it might be an embarrassing competitor, both artistically and for funds.

It was at this time, in 1959, while I was directing Olivier in *Coriolanus* at Stratford, that he invited me to be his number two at the National Theatre. I was flattered but said that I would sooner be my own number one. Larry told me he didn't think the government would subsidise *two* national theatres. I said I thought it should and could. And so matters were left.

By 1960, it was clear that the National Theatre was at last going to happen. That was also the year when the RSC began performing under its new title and working in London as well as in Stratford. And in the same year a committee was set up to prepare the National Theatre's proposals for the government. Fordie and I were invited to join, which we gladly did; and a series of complicated meetings began.

By the end of 1960, a memorandum had gone to the Chancellor of the Exchequer proposing an amalgamation. The National would be made up of a company of 150 actors, divided into three groups: one would appear at the National to be built on the South Bank; one at Stratford; and one would tour. The Old Vic would be used for a young company, or for experimental work. Meanwhile, the existing Old Vic Company and the RSC would receive subsidy to build up a team of suitable actors.

It is almost unbelievable to remember it now, but Fordie and I had actually agreed that for the sake of the theatre as a whole a gradual amalgamation was a correct and wise decision.

Then, in March 1961, the government announced that there would be no National Theatre after all. Instead, it intended to subsidise the Old Vic, Stratford and a group of regional repertory companies; and Lord Cottesloe, the chairman of the Arts Council, wrote asking us to submit figures for a three-year grant. But the lobbying for the National Theatre continued unabated; and the whole scheme was suddenly resuscitated when the London County Council, under the leadership of Isaac Hayward, offered funding. It was a sufficiently large sum to make Selwyn Lloyd, the Chancellor of the Exchequer, change his mind about the entire National Theatre idea. It was on again.

This was the age when big was beautiful: small

firms amalgamating to make a vast firm, such as British Leyland, was considered admirable. The new plan, blessed by the chancellor, embraced not only the amalgamation of the Old Vic, Stratford and the coming National Theatre, but threw in for good measure a huge new opera house as well. It was to be administered artistically by three directors – one from Stratford, one from the Old Vic and one from Sadler's Wells – and they would all report to a general director, who was to be Laurence Olivier. The South Bank, thanks to the munificence of the LCC, would boast a new theatre *and* a new opera house.

By now the full cost of running the RSC as an ensemble (even one that did very good business) was becoming evident; our savings were running out. However, we made plans for the second part of 1961 and for 1962 based on the subsidy we had been told we were going to get. We were therefore appalled to receive in July 1961 a letter from the chairman of the Arts Council, saying that everything was changed because of the chancellor's new plans. The RSC would not now receive any grant until the whole new scheme had been finally agreed by all the parties concerned, plus the government and the LCC. This process, Lord Cottesloe wrote, 'may of course take some considerable time to complete'.

Fordie and I were dumbfounded. First of all it looked as if we were being blackmailed by the withholding of the grant; as if we had either to agree to the 'British Leyland' solution, or to become a small regional festival. Also, we had, increasingly, no taste for this new grandiose scheme – the arrival of the opera house had been the last straw. We became more and more sure that the new conglomerate would produce work without particularity and character. Fordie, because of the betrayal over the grant and the blackmail it implied, finally revolted. He said to me, 'Let's get out. Stratford cannot be governed by remote control.' I thought he was absolutely right. I believed the new plan to be a mad compromise which would result in a huge departmental store of drama, designed to please all parties, but which would in fact diminish them all.

We pulled out. And there is no doubt that the RSC's money troubles with the government and the Arts Council for the next thirty years all stemmed from this very risky decision. The company has never had an easy time financially. But it has existed, whereas it might have been stillborn. And it has created a triumphant procession of productions.

In 1962 and 1963 the RSC hit wonderful artistic form in Stratford and at the Aldwych. This greatly aggravated the anxieties of the National Theatre lobby. The prospect of competition increasingly scared many of them, including Olivier and Lord Chandos, and they clearly wanted us out of London. Our attempts to gain subsidy were frustrated at every turn. The times were dangerous.

In the spring of 1962, John Goodwin urged me to give an exclusive interview to Ronald Hastings, theatre correspondent of the *Daily Telegraph*, in order to make public that unless we received a grant we would have to leave the Aldwych and retreat to Stratford. The story was given a great deal of space, and as soon as it appeared John suggested that I sent copies to leading drama critics, saying that our situation was indeed desperate. The result was extraordinary, including a letter to the *Telegraph* from eleven senior critics calling on the government to keep us in London. Newspaper comment drawing attention to our case continued to blaze away all through that summer. Questions were asked in the House.

Finally, T. C. Worsley, in the *Financial Times*, let the cat out of the bag. He wrote, 'Perhaps it is time to be blunt. There are ugly rumours about that some of those who negotiated the National Theatre scheme would not be sorry (to put it no lower) to see Peter Hall's RSC out of London.' I was greatly heartened by such support from the media, though it has to be said that unless the work we were doing had justified it, it would not have happened.

By the end of 1962, Fordie and I could at least draw breath. We were free of the grandiose National Theatre muddle and we had been given a subsidy. It was a small one of £47,000, but a beginning. It came, however, with a Treasury qualification warning us that though the RSC might decide to operate on a national theatre level, this would not guarantee us a future subsidy consistent with such a level. This minute has been quoted at the RSC for the last thirty years.

We had saved the Aldwych, but in doing so had made enemies. The National Theatre, with a subsidy five times the size of ours, opened at the Old Vic in the autumn of 1963, and immediately the pressure to get us out of London, this time by squeezing our grant, hotted up. If the 'dirty plays' row had come before our great run of productions in '62 and '63 rather than after, I doubt whether we could have withstood the onslaught. It would have given too much ammunition to our opponents. *The Wars of the Roses* and Brook's *King Lear* were crucial to our future. They had received the kind of acclaim that cannot be argued with; and success breeds success. More and more talent came to the RSC: it was a magnet which attracted young actors, designers and writers – Glenda Jackson, Nicol Williamson, Sally Jacobs, David Rudkin. Also, I signed up, within a few months of each other, two young directors who were to lead the company over the next twenty-five years, Trevor Nunn and Terry Hands.

I don't believe that theatre is made by buildings; theatre is made by people and the work they create. But governments are reassured by buildings, as they are by institutions, and if one is there then something has to be put into it. I was aware that we were very vulnerable on that score because if we lost the Aldwych and couldn't find another suitable London home, the whole idea of the

RSC could collapse. This was long before Trevor Nunn's invention of the Swan and the Other Place as additions to the main theatre at Stratford, thus establishing there the most comprehensive theatrical plant in the country.

I thought that if we could achieve a purpose-built theatre in London which was ours, and born out of the RSC aesthetic, our future would be that much surer. The first idea was to rebuild the Mercury Theatre in Ladbroke Grove, but the site was not adequate for a decent stage. So, after many fits and starts, the RSC signed an agreement with the City of London to become tenants of the new Barbican Theatre. John Bury and I set to work to design it and found in Joe Chamberlain an architect with what was, to us, a rare advantage. He believed in listening to the theatre people and allowed them to dictate the needs of the auditorium.

I love the Barbican Theatre because it is created from ideas shared by John and myself. I do not, however, love the Barbican Arts Centre. In the long hours we spent working on the auditorium and stage, we had little idea that an inhuman environment like a second-rate airport was going to surround us.

Meanwhile, Olivier, offering an olive branch, had asked Michel St Denis, Peter Brook and myself to join the National Theatre Building Committee, which was chaired by Lord Cottesloe. Michel, Peter, George Devine and I wanted only two auditoria – a large open-stage and a flexible studio theatre. But Olivier and Tynan, supported by John Dexter, insisted that there must be a proscenium theatre too. There was a good deal of axe-grinding, and some vague talk that such an auditorium was necessary for revivals of eighteenth- and nineteenth-century plays. Tynan declared that if a proscenium theatre was good enough for Brecht, it should be good enough for the National Theatre. Olivier wondered whether, without a proscenium theatre, the Comédie Française would play at the NT when invited to London. So the Lyttelton Theatre became part of the overall design without any strong aesthetic need. Nobody was desperately for it, and I think this is revealed, now that it exists, by its largely impersonal character. The Olivier and Cottesloe are triumphantly original; but the Lyttelton is merely large and acceptable.

– 13 –

In 1966, after two years of severely pinched subsidies, the crisis came: money was running out. I quote from an interview I gave in the late Sixties to David Addenbrooke for his book on the RSC: 'Looking back on his Stratford years, Peter Hall saw 1966 as the year of his biggest mistake: "In 1966, the Arts Council and Lord Goodman said: 'There's no more money – you can't have an increase.' And we did a season of revivals . . . in order to try and mark time. You *can't* mark time in the theatre. That was my biggest mistake . . . I just saw it as a never-ending battle for subsidy. I thought it would go on for ever . . . And I made the mistake of compromising when I should *not* have compromised. I should have announced a season of new productions." '

Arnold Goodman had by now succeeded Lord Cottesloe as Arts Council chairman. He genuinely felt that London could not support two national theatres, and that things would be better all round if we returned to Warwickshire. We managed to stay at the Aldwych, but the season of revivals at Stratford was a humiliation and some of the life went out of the actors. I wondered what I had to do in order to convince the government and the Arts Council that we were worthwhile.

Then, as now, Arnold Goodman was known as The Great Mr Fixit: ace settler of quarrels; solicitor and advisor to prime ministers. He was apolitical and yet all-political in that he could seemingly arrange anything. For many years he was the man in the background, but when he ran the Arts Council with Jennie Lee as his Arts Minister he became a public figure and transformed the arts. He did not, however, help the RSC.

In the summer of 1966, and in the middle of these fights, Fordie, who had been seriously ill for some months, died of cancer. I was desolated. And things changed. The new chairman, George Farmer, was a precise accountant, and no gambler; I think I always worried him. Also, not long after Fordie's death, news came that the Barbican, scheduled to open in 1970, would be delayed. (It was in fact another ten years before it was finished.) Then in 1967 I directed one of my most disastrous productions: a *Macbeth* with Paul Scofield and Vivien Merchant. Throughout rehearsals I had shingles. Run-down and depressed, I found myself disillusioned, tired and daunted by the thought of a future spent chiefly fighting for money – now without Fordie – against a National Theatre that would always be better placed to get it. In 1968, I decided to leave the RSC, and proposed Trevor Nunn as my successor. Within six weeks I had gone.

Something else contributed to my need to go. I felt restless artistically. Shakespeare wrote thirty-seven plays – a rich number; but many of them come round with monotonous regularity in the Stratford season, which needs five or six every year. Already, I was seeing new productions that were less good than interpretations of some eight or ten years earlier. I also wanted to direct more films; I had recently made two, one of them with my old friend Michael Birkett producing. I wanted to do more opera. Above all, I suppose, I wanted to stretch my wings.

I think now, from my own point of view, that it was a mistake to leave the RSC. I could have asked for a year's sabbatical and then gone back. But I felt burnt out. And I seemed to be in a situation that had no solution except departure. I also knew that fate had given me a brilliant successor in the young Trevor Nunn. Passing on the RSC to Trevor and, much later, the National to Richard Eyre are, I believe, among the best things I have done.

I intended to go on working for the RSC from time to time, so Jacky and I and the children moved from Avoncliffe to Wallingford, a place chosen because it was half-way between London and Stratford. It was a very modern-looking house, built in the Fifties. The garden had a lake where Christopher and I fished for trout which Jacky cooked. I began to make another paradise, only this time it was aggressively contemporary, with a Peter Logan sculpture in the garden, a Wendy Taylor gazebo by the lake and a Joe Tilson hanging in the hall – all extremely Sixties. I was embracing my time. And looking forward to a fresh start.

I quickly had a surprising phone call from Lord Goodman asking me to join the Arts Council. I agreed eagerly, and the friendship that as a result grew between us is one of the most valued of my life. An attractive quality in Arnold which the public do not see is that it is in his nature always to champion the underdog and fight for lost causes (he clearly regarded the RSC as neither!). He represents the law, but is suspicious of it. More than anything else, he respects humanity and common sense. He is generous with his time and on several occasions has helped me out of troubles without any benefit to himself.

It is a paradox that my two bogies of the Sixties, the men who, as successive chairmen of the Arts Council, virtually drove me from the RSC, Lord Goodman and Lord Cottesloe, both became close friends. Cottesloe, in committee, plays Polonius. He appears to be a buffer, but underneath is a very shrewd operator. Working with him on the National Theatre Building Committee, I began to admire his political acumen; soon I treasured him as companion and colleague.

In a sense, ever since I left the RSC, I have felt

that I lacked a true home. I certainly don't regret going later to the National Theatre, but only in my last seven or eight years there did it offer me anything like the creative security that Stratford gave me from the start. But if I had had that year's sabbatical from the RSC and then gone back, I would not have had the great adventure of the National; nor perhaps the fulfilment of working at Glyndebourne.

PART THREE

Prima La Musica

– 1 –

When I was twenty-four, I applied to be Carl Ebert's assistant. I felt that this great opera director, heir to the European tradition of Reinhardt, would have much to teach me. He interviewed me in a taxi, as he rode, frantic, from the Ritz to Victoria Station on his way to Glyndebourne.

Even in the cramped confines of a taxi, Ebert seemed an ebullient, charming personality. He had a handsome actor's face, a ready smile, a warm manner and abundant white hair that cascaded in all directions. An interview when there isn't much time concentrates the mind. I talked rapidly and far too much – a fault I always have at interviews. He wasn't, I thought, much impressed by my inadequate German and patchy Italian. Victoria was reached and he rushed off to catch the train for Lewes. I wandered back to the Arts Theatre thinking I would hear no more.

To tell the truth, I was ambivalent about the great man. His command of the language of theatre – the lights, the design, the grouping of the characters on stage – was extremely impressive. But he had an irritating habit, common then in Europe, of illustrating the music; by which I mean drilling the singers for hours to walk and gesture precisely to the time and pulse of the score. This had a tendency to make everybody act like Mickey Mouse. At its best it could give vigour to comedy; but it trivialised operas such as *Così fan tutte*, and made it hard for Rossini to lift above the facetious. It was, however, the style of the day and Ebert was the master of it. His work was wonderfully specific. He didn't leave the singers attitudinising with generalised emotions.

Two weeks later, I received an offer of the job. But in that two weeks my life had changed. I had been asked to take over from John Fernald as director of the Arts. Regretfully, I declined Ebert's offer, thus delaying by twenty years the time I first worked at Glyndebourne.

I continued to go every year, however, and Glyndebourne finally, for me, was like a marriage. I fell in love there; knew great joy and great sorrow there; and, at the end, great pain and bitterness. It was like the experience of a whole lifetime and always extraordinarily vivid. The little opera house hidden in the Sussex Downs has been as important to me as Stratford-upon-Avon.

Michael Birkett introduced me to this enchanted place when we were both students at Cambridge. His father, Norman Birkett, the eminent QC and judge, had a friend who bought tickets for every performance. He must have been a rich man; he was certainly a kind one. He gave Michael two of his tickets and Michael invited me.

Michael was already in Sussex, but it was necessary for me to get myself there from Cambridgeshire. I had one of my father's free railway passes to London, but no funds to get further. There was also the problem of dress. It was obligatory – it still is – to wear dinner jackets at Glyndebourne. As luck would have it, however, my father had splashed out on a ready-made one a couple of years before so that he could attend Rotary Club dinners. I borrowed this treasured jacket, packed it in a battered cardboard suitcase, and early in the morning set off by train to Liverpool Street and thence by bus to South London. It was a route familiar to me from my visits to my aunt in Lewisham. Once on the A23, I began to hitch-hike and was given five or six lifts, mostly by lorries. Embarrassed by my cardboard suitcase, and the thought of the dinner jacket inside that would gain me admission to one of the most élite places in the world, I only told one driver where I was going and what I was doing. He clearly thought I was as barmy as the man who had built an opera house in his garden. After that I kept quiet. At Lewes, two friendly members of the audience let me share their taxi.

Glyndebourne's charm at that time was its homely, improvised quality. My first impression was of huge trees, sheep, and buildings which had a half-used, half-finished country air as if they were occupied only in good weather. I felt out of place in my sports jacket and flannels. True, the dressed-up people wandering in the gardens were not particularly elegant: that was not possible in the early Fifties because of clothes rationing. Also, many supporters of Glyndebourne then were still 'the county', not lovers of music, but lovers of the occasion. The evening dresses of the ladies looked as if they were made from tweeds.

I dived into the gents loo with my cardboard suitcase, changed into a dinner jacket that was far too big, met Michael and our benefactor, and the magic of Glyndebourne, which was to last for the next forty years, began.

But my memory plays the same trick as it does with Stratford. I cannot recall the first production I saw there. The journey and the arrival is clear in my mind, but what was the opera? It has turned into an amalgamation of all those early performances that I saw: the John Piper *Don Giovanni*; the British premiere of Stravinsky's *The Rake's Progress*; Oliver Messel's sets for Mozart; the singing of Sena Jurinac; the fizz and delight of Rossini conducted by Vittorio Gui; the excitement of hearing *La Cenerentola*, *Idomeneo* and *Le Comte Ory* for the first time. Memory is a blur of intense pleasure with no rain (which, I am sure, was regular) as the sun sets warmly over the Sussex downs and we wander to Nether

215

Wallop – a barn turned into a restaurant – for dinner and chilled white wine.

I met John Christie, the founder of Glyndebourne, and looked at him with awe. He was one of those eccentric Englishmen who achieve the impossible because it never occurs to them for a moment that it *is* impossible. He was upset in the Thirties when the government brought in legislation requiring cars to halt when approaching a major road. He wrote to *The Times* complaining that this was a slur on the skill of British drivers and calculated to bring the whole country to a stop. What was more in the national interest, he explained, was to accelerate when approaching a major road; it could then be crossed as quickly as possible. This was the mind that created Glyndebourne.

How and why did he do it? A rich man marries an opera singer, Audrey Mildmay, in the 1920s. Being a lover of music and of the Salzburg Festival, he decides to build an opera house in the garden of his Sussex estate. 'If you're going to do it, for God's sake do it properly, John,' says his wife. By chance he goes to a chamber concert in Eastbourne given by the Busch Quartet. He is introduced to its leader who advises him to contact his brother and a colleague, both of whom are thinking of leaving Germany because of the threat of Hitler. They are the conductor Fritz Busch, and Carl Ebert. John Christie has never heard of either of them. He has chanced on the leading German Mozartian and the leading German opera director. They come to Glyndebourne, the theatre is built, the festival starts. And Mozart's operas are at last performed in England to their proper scale and in a way that reveals them fully.

The auditorium of the theatre intrigued me. Small, homely and unpretentious with a lot of wood, it seated only, I suppose, 600 to 700 people in those days. Moran Caplat, the great general administrator of the festival and architect of its post-war glories, would play a game each winter of trying to pack in another seat or two.

They brought in money. He reached over 800 by the end of his tenure. The surprise, however, was the stage, for this was of a size I had seen before only on the continent: it had enormous depth – so much so that when the curtains opened it took on a dimension which seemed far greater than the auditorium. This is, I think, an important factor in its design. Opening the curtains on a small stage can often contract the experience; but if the stage has the magnificent depth of Glyndebourne, the spirits of the audience expand.

John Christie was very proud of his stage. He was equally proud of the international nature of the productions it offered, insisting that the programme printed the nationality of every artist. He didn't much like modern music. I think he found Stravinsky's *The Rake's Progress* unbearable. And I remember him pointedly staying out of a performance of Henze's *Elegy for Young Lovers*. He said that, like the Glyndebourne cows, he was keeping at a safe distance from the noise. According to him, the cows came near only for Mozart.

In time, his son, George, succeeded him as chairman. George has the same ability as his father to pick talent, but is much more enterprising in his choice of repertory. He has also done wonders for the finances of the festival through sponsorship. As I write, he is bulldozing his father's lovely old opera house and building a new, bigger one in its place. It is not a change I welcome. But George has a shrewd sense of the future. In the Sixties he helped me get seed money from the Gulbenkian Foundation in order to start the Royal Shakespeare Company.

Considerable men such as John Christie and his son have one disadvantage: they encourage the English to believe in the amateur. But they themselves are not amateur; they only pretend to be. They have both been ruthlessly professional. And Glyndebourne itself is amateur only in the sense that everyone who works there is completely in love with opera. That, and its huge public success, make the place uniquely arrogant. Like a great public school, it thinks it is the best, even on the occasions when it isn't. And if, as sometimes happens, an artist doesn't quite fit in with its country house atmosphere, he or she is disdainfully labelled as 'not Glyndebourne'.

On the other hand, the care in preparation and the time given to the work are exceptional in opera; as indeed are the standards of drama. Nowhere else are the needs of the stage given as much importance as the needs of the music. The conductor and the director are an equal partnership – a tradition which has continued for sixty years and which has given Glyndebourne a history of opera performances unmatched anywhere.

From those very first seasons that I went to with Michael Birkett, I believed I had a date to work there one day.

– 2 –

My first opera production was at Sadler's Wells in 1958. It was the premiere of John Gardner's *The Moon and Sixpence*, based on Maugham's novel. The whole experience immediately fascinated me. Here were entirely new disciplines. For a start, singers arrived having already learnt their words and music. They did this not out of consideration for the director or the conductor but because they simply would not have time to get the notes into their heads during the short four weeks of rehearsal.

Stanislavsky has harmed the theatre by spreading the doctrine that words should be learnt during rehearsals. His argument, it seems, is that you damage your instincts by learning before you know exactly what the words mean emotionally, or what the physical situation will be on the stage when they are spoken. I doubt this is true. It is of course much harder to learn the words (or the notes) out of context, but I still think it helps to be prepared. In a play, there is usually about a week of rehearsal wasted while the actors thrash around trying to remember their lines. And during that week they are inclined to take out their frustration and tension on any-thing – the play, the writer, the director, their partner – rather than their own faulty memory.

Happily, there is none of this in the opera world. If the piece is a standard part of the repertory, the role is known backwards anyway. And if it is a new piece, the fear of not knowing the words and notes means that they are thoroughly drilled-in long before the first rehearsals.

Received opinion is that the diva goes her own way and will do nothing on the stage which she has not done before. I disagree. Singers are not hard to direct. They are indeed so used to doing what the man with the baton tells them, that they are equally obedient to the director. They will do precisely what he asks. The trouble is that they rarely do anything more – unless they are actors as well as musicians. The magic of working with a good actor is that he takes the suggestion of his director and transmutes it into something complex, subtle and human. The bad actor, or the average opera singer, does just what the director has said; nothing more and nothing less. The suggestion remains inert, simple and dead.

Great actors make a director's suggestions seem better than they are. Great opera stars such as Janet Baker and Maria Ewing can do the same – simply because they are superb actors as well as superb singers. Average singers are like circus performers – concerned with their physical selves rather than emotional truth. They want to sing and sing well; it doesn't need to mean anything.

If actors do not preserve the tempo, give the cue, maintain the pace, create the atmosphere, it is impossible for the play to work. More to the point, it is impossible for each of the individual performances to work: actors depend entirely on each other. Singers need not. In opera, I discovered, it is all too possible to ignore everyone else on stage with you. As long as you are watching the conductor and keeping 'in' with the orchestra, you need never look at your colleagues. Eye contact, which is the very stuff of an actor's being, is something foreign to singers, for it tends to place them in a bad position so that the voice goes into the wings. It also takes their attention away from the conductor.

I insisted from my very first opera production that the singers, like actors, played off each other. Paradoxically, their singing became better, the drama more alive and the communication with the audience more eloquent.

It soon became plain to me that I loved working with singers. I observed that a phrase of music could be made to convey almost any emotion. You could play against it or with it; you could even treat it ironically. The emotional support of the music meant that singers could communicate the most complex things if only they could be persuaded to do very little.

Doing less to convey more was the constant problem with *The Moon and Sixpence*. Sadler's Wells Opera in the Fifties was filled with a rumbustious crew of Welsh ex-miners and raucous cockney girls. Very few of them were actors. Why should they be? They were there because they had been born with a voice. They all thought that acting was a matter of grandiloquent gestures and emotional moves. They were terrified of standing still. Whenever there was a pause from the business of singing, they would fill-in. After building up to a huge climax, instead of letting it rest and have its effect, they would feel the need to strut downstage a couple of paces or wave their arms in the air.

I also noticed that the act of singing produces the most incredible tension in the body. All that air being forced through a tiny pipe creates muscular constrictions and forces the singer into unnatural postures. Relaxation is the essence of communication in any live performance.

220

Even if a performer is playing a tense man, he must not be tense himself. This is the most difficult challenge. The tension of singing must allow the rest of the body to be relaxed, so that the audience can be let in and be able to associate with the singer's emotions and understand his or her thoughts.

I encouraged the astonished singers in *The Moon and Sixpence* to gesticulate and move as little as possible. Relaxed, still figures, with the music apparently welling up out of them created by their emotions, was my ideal. And the production, when it opened, did seem to work. John Hargreaves, for instance, a redoubtable Sadler's Wells baritone, much given to throwing himself round the stage, turned in a restrained and haunted portrait of the Gauguin figure. His colleagues and his public were amazed. I am not making undue claims for myself. His talent was his and remained his. But he had accepted how delicate operatic acting could be and he had successfully expressed it.

I took away from this first experience two overriding disciplines which have guided me ever since: that economy of movement and complete relaxation can transform acting in opera; and that you always have to work first from the music, not from the words. The tempo, the tone, the atmosphere, even the timing, are all given by the music. The task in rehearsal is to find the emotion which can make the music the end result – and the inescapable expression of that emotion. The words are secondary.

– 3 –

In 1958 I saw at Covent Garden the Visconti production of *Don Carlos*, conducted by Giulini, with a cast that included Tito Gobbi, Gre Brouwenstijn, John Vickers and

Boris Christoff. It was the greatest operatic experience of my life. From the time of this terrific production, David Webster began to succeed in his attempts to make Covent Garden an international opera house. I hoped I would be part of it.

In the early Sixties, Georg Solti, who had recently been appointed music director, asked me to do a production there with him. With infinite sadness, I had to refuse: the demands of the RSC in those years were all-embracing. Solti yelled at me with his engaging mixture of Hungarian charm and hysteria. He said it was my responsibility, no, my *duty*, to work at Covent Garden. I was flattered, and also captivated by the sheer exuberance of the man. He spoke of music as if he was eating it.

In 1965, I was able to do Schoenberg's *Moses and Aaron* with him. This began a new chapter in my life, for since then I have done over forty operas around the world, eight of them in collaboration with Solti.

He is a man of formidable energy and concentration; and his determination to get the best out of the people working with him creates an electricity, a tension, which can have the most extraordinary results. It is hard to be indifferent to a Solti performance. Even at its worst, when it is tight and overemphatic, it produces a tingling anxiety. At its best, it is genius.

Like most other conductors, he is obsessed with making the singers look at him rather than at each other as he exhorts them from the podium. Consequently, a Solti production can easily become a circle of performers disposed round the stage staring like frightened rabbits at the maestro. Given this, it is surprising that he is such a great collaborator. But he need only be reminded that true acting depends on human contact between the protagonists and he defers immediately to the director.

I suppose *Moses* was my most exhilarating experience with him. But we did a thrilling *Tristan und Isolde*, and he taught me something I shall never forget: an understanding of Wagner's time. It is not like the time of other mortals. Everything in Wagner's world takes longer because it is more intense. His music exists in a hallucinatory, slowed-up tempo – the kind that comes upon us when we are in acute crisis, as when the car moves with dreadful inevitability towards the crash. In *The Ring* there are long, long scenes in slow motion; then, in two minutes flat, the world turns upside down. The feelings are eternal; but the action when it comes is quick and apocalyptic.

Moses and Aaron was my debut at Covent Garden. It was so fearsomely difficult that we had seven weeks of rehearsal, a vastly long time for an opera house. Philosophically, the piece is one of the key works of the twentieth century. Its theme, the debate between the inspired, dogmatic prophet and the pragmatic politician who does what is possible rather than what is right, raises profound questions. The score is unfinished, yet has a strange completeness of its own, matching the irresolution of the dilemma.

The libretto, Schoenberg's own, had been newly translated into English by David Rudkin. It seemed very contemporary. The strength of an ideal set against the ability of the propagandist to sell it. Will the public accept the truth if it is not palatable? As well as being philosophically rich, musically the opera is extraordinary. Despite all its twelve-tone disciplines, its sounds are sensual and lurid, a post-Wagnerian miracle. And in the demands that it makes on stage, perhaps the grandest grand opera ever written.

The production was certainly the largest I have ever done. Over 300 people thronged the stage: dancers, singers, a double chorus, acrobats, actors. There was a menagerie of animals: goats, sheep, horses, Highland cattle. At the dress rehearsal a camel teetered down the precipitously raked stage, causing the whole of the Royal Opera House orchestra to flee the pit in consternation. The creature then shat copiously. He had to be cut.

I did ask myself, once or twice, where in all this was my belief that less meant more? But we were, after all, presenting an opera about excess and the danger of excess. It was essential to conjure that up on stage. In one notorious scene, we had to create an orgy of blood and lust around the Golden Calf which finally led to the virtual insanity of the tribe. Large ornamental penises, painted garishly and decked out with muffs of goat-hair, were designed to be strapped to the performers' middles. I kept asking for these in rehearsal; they did not appear. In the end I discovered the designs were under lock and key in, of all places, the desk of the director of Covent Garden. David Webster, ever an English gentleman, had hoped somehow that the penises would go away. He asked me sadly whether I really wanted them. I said I did. Reluctantly, but without argument, he unlocked his desk.

I have always felt that nakedness in the theatre is a basic truth: like earth, air, fire or water. It should therefore be used responsibly and for a purpose. The ungoverned lust of the orgy round the Golden Calf could be expressed only, it seemed to me, by some degree of nudity. The Lord Chamberlain still functioned, so we had to be careful.

Covent Garden allowed me to hire for the scene half a dozen strippers from Soho who found it a highly diverting change from their normal work. In those days, if you were naked on the stage you had to stand still, the theory being, I suppose, that this was less likely to inflame the audience. Our strippers, therefore, were permitted to move only if they wore pads of false pubic hair, and Elastoplast patches over their nipples. The effect was to give the girls the most noticeable breasts in Old Testament history.

Some of the staider members of the women's chorus were so shocked that they refused to come on stage while this scene was enacted, and insisted on contributing their atonal wails and cries of lust while they knitted in the wings.

At the first dress rehearsal, Forbes Robinson as Moses and Richard Lewis as Aaron found themselves singing their final metaphysical debate over an altar on which lay a naked girl covered in blood. Neither of them stopped nor made any observation about this additional prop. They merely said to me afterwards, somewhat drily, that I might have warned them about it beforehand. Any actor would certainly have stopped, not in moral indignation but amazement. For singers, the dress rehearsal has to go on . . .

Reports of the orgies on stage leaked out, and the indignation of the popular press, days before the production opened, was wonderful to behold. Should public money be wasted on this filth? Had Covent Garden, of all places, joined the unseemly ranks of those being swept along in the tide of Sixties immorality? Schoenberg, as a result, became box office, and advance ticket sales soared, which astounded the management. The pages of titillating comment in the newspapers also aroused the claque who regularly sat in the Royal Opera House gallery on first nights. They sent word that they were going to boo me loudly at the final curtain for depraving the Royal Opera House. It was, I thought, decent of them to warn me.

It was one of the most frightening first nights of my life.

But a vivid performance was given by both the cast and the orchestra, and we received not the bird but an ovation. The notices were enthusiastic and I began to be asked to work in other European opera houses.

The Lord Chamberlain was satisfied too, which rather surprised me. I once discussed with an ex-naval officer on his staff a delicate passage in a play which he suspected was hinting at sexual intercourse between two men. He was actually wrong, but he had a nose for prurience which could not easily be deflected. 'Oh, come on, Hall,' he expostulated, 'we all know what that means: "up periscopes!" ' 'What?' I asked. 'Buggery, Hall, buggery,' he shouted.

At the time of *Moses and Aaron,* Madame Furtseva was on an official visit to London. She was the Soviet Minister of Culture – a diehard Stalinist who had survived many a purge. Some bright spark at the Foreign Office had thought it might be interesting, perhaps provocative, for her to witness a modern opera at Covent Garden. She and her entourage sat stony-faced. At the end, by courtesy of an embarrassed interpreter, she harangued me soundly. She said she thought it was completely wrong for the country to grant me public money so that I could create such an erotic and reprehensible spectacle; I was pandering to decadent tastes. I asked if she liked the music. She said she found that decadent too; Covent Garden had clearly done the opera only in order to attract huge audiences. Schoenberg was at that time a difficult and rarely heard composer, and the thought of staging him as a crowd-pleaser was something to treasure.

The production is full of memories: the sheer excitement of moving hundreds of people around the stage; the letter signed 'God', postmarked St John's Wood, that threatened me with unspeakable sexual diseases if I continued this depraved activity; and the eight gallons of stage-blood prepared for each performance and poured over the cast during the Golden Calf scene. A gutter ran along the front of the stage to collect this, but it sprang a leak in early rehearsals and blood dripped down into the orchestra pit. I was not surprised when the indignant fiddle section angrily waved their violins at me.

The production became an icon of the mid Sixties, and offers of opera work poured in. I was tempted to enter the opera circuit, travelling round the main international houses. It is a career that looks glamorous, and the money is much better than in the theatre. But it is a switchback with little continuity. Productions are only a director's own for the first three or four performances. After that a new cast is rehearsed by various assistants and the work consequently sung by people the director will never even have met. The production no longer represents his work. I knew that I had to be in one place, one house.

– 4 –

Lord Drogheda was an old-style tycoon with many new-style habits. As well as being chairman of the *Financial Times*, he was chairman of Covent Garden and an influential figure in the arts. He was wealthy, cultivated and enthusiastic. And he had the gift, beloved by all artists, of being a fan. His charm made any ballerina or prima donna feel unique. He was dazzled by stars.

I began to know Garrett Drogheda and his wife during the Sixties. They came down to Stratford to see my RSC work. And our friendship was sealed when I went to the Royal Opera House to do *Moses* and, a year later, *The Magic Flute*.

Soon after I left the RSC, when I was deep in films and also in discussions about an annual contract at Glyndebourne, Jacky and I had dinner at the Droghedas' house in Lord North Street. The next music director at Covent Garden, succeeding Georg Solti, was there with his wife. I had met Colin Davis before, but had never until now had the chance of talking with him at any length. We were of the same generation – both young lions of the new artistic establishment, both impatient of formality and what we saw as the old, stuffy British way of doing things. We found an identical enthusiasm about what opera should be, how it should be created and how the audience for it should be broadened. We both wanted to bring the theatre back into opera. I felt the same excitement, the same sense of going with the current of the times, that I had felt when I dreamt up the RSC. Our wives and the Droghedas stared at us dumbfounded.

We talked on and on. It was a magical evening, as important to me as my night in Leningrad with Fordie Flower.

Within a week Colin Davis had done an extraordinary thing: he had offered me half his crown. He wanted me to share his directorship of the Royal Opera. This was an act of immense generosity. It was also absolute proof of his feeling that music and drama should be equal partners.

I accepted with alacrity and excused myself to Glyndebourne who were understanding and agreed that I could still do occasional productions for them.

Opera has a long lead-time. Plans are made two, if not three, years in advance. So before I was due to join Colin there was a long period of preparation in which I did three productions at the Royal Opera House: *Eugene Onegin* as well as *Tristan* with Solti, and the premiere of Michael Tippett's *The Knot Garden* with Colin.

Working with Tippett – humanist, mystic and humorist – was like working with all the Englishness of my past. He was steeped in Shakespeare and Eliot and Blake; he loved Purcell and Samuel Palmer. *The Knot Garden* was born of an amalgamation of *The Tempest* and *Heartbreak House*. Colin and I thrived in a frenzy of discovery, and found we had a real rapport in the rehearsal room. We also laid schemes for the future. During the eighteen months before I took up my post, much went well.

We planned to reach new audiences and to develop new singers. I remember an audition Colin and I gave to a young soprano fresh from the Opera Centre. We immediately cast her as the Countess in our forthcoming *Figaro*. Some thought it a great risk. Her name was Kiri Te Kanawa. I also remember Colin's excitement when he encountered another young voice – a personality more lyric than dramatic, and so more likely to inspire him than me. Colin recognised a talent not only beautiful but already capable of conveying subtle shades of meaning. He was talking of Jessye Norman.

228

38. With my friend, Ralph.

39. A straw-hatted Albert Finney as Tamburlaine, when excerpts of the play were given free on the NT terraces as part of the work on the production.

40. A strike by backstage staff in 1976 closed the NT for four days. With NATTKE's general secretary John Wilson (in spectacles) as the dispute ends are, from left, Michael Birkett, Peter Stevens, John Goodwin and Simon Relph. Two more strikes were to follow – in 1977 and 1979.

41. Michael Gough and Joan Hickson in *Bedroom Farce* (NT).

42. Rehearsing Peggy Ashcroft in *Happy Days* (NT).

43. With John Bury and Harold Pinter, looking at the minicab used in Pinter's *Other Places*, comprising three short plays (NT).

44. *above The Romans in Britain* (NT). Its director, Michael Bogdanov, was sued for obscenity by Mary Whitehouse: the case went to the Old Bailey but was withdrawn.

45. *below left* Judi Dench as Lady Bracknell in *The Importance of Being Earnest* (NT).

46. *below right* A rehearsal of *Amadeus* (NT). Paul Scofield, who played Salieri, is centre; Peter Shaffer is on his right.

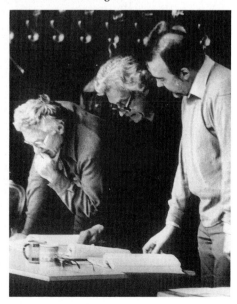

47. Working on *Jean Seberg* (NT) with its composer, Marvin Hamlisch (in spectacles), and author, Julian Barry (facing camera).

48. *Animal Farm* (NT): Barrie Rutter as Napoleon. It opened in the Cottesloe, playing later in the Lyttelton and the Olivier. It also toured abroad and all over Britain.

49. A rehearsal of *The Oresteia* at Epidaurus in 1982. The NT were the first British company to perform a Greek play there.

50. In the amphitheatre at Athens with Ian McKellen when he played Coriolanus there in my 1984 NT production.

51. Moran Caplat by the lake at Glyndebourne. To him I owe twenty years of happy work.

52. Ileana Cotrubas and James Bowman as Tytania and Oberon in Britten's *A Midsummer Night's Dream* (Glyndebourne).

53. *above left* Rehearsing Janet Baker as Orfeo (Glyndebourne).

54. *above right* The death of Carmen: Maria Ewing, with Barry McCauley as Don Jose (Glyndebourne).

55. *The Ring*, Bayreuth, 1983/4/5 (*Das Rheingold*). Alberich (Hermann Becht) clambers for the gold, teased by the Rhinemaidens. They 'sang, swam, and looked beautiful in their nakedness.' Flosshilde (Birgitta Svendén), Woglinde (Agnes Habereder), Wellgunde (Diana Montague).

"Nice to see Sir Peter taking an active interest again."

56. A cartoon by David Langdon that appeared when I returned to the NT from my sabbatical spent directing *The Ring* at Bayreuth.

57. *below left* With Rebecca, Maria and Lucy at the opening of the Torville and Dean ice show.

58. *below right* Anthony Hopkins and Judi Dench in *Antony and Cleopatra* (NT).

With the Board of Covent Garden and with Garrett Drogheda, however, all was not so well. The Royal Opera longed for the kind of new thinking that had swept through the theatre in the Sixties. Colin and I were to be new brooms; and David Webster, after a distinguished period as general director, was soon to be succeeded by John Tooley. Yet it quickly became plain that the Board were prepared only to go on exactly as before.

I also discovered that Garrett Drogheda, whom I continued to like, was one thing as a friend and quite another as a boss. He bombarded me with memoranda – an anxious hands-on chairman who tended to pick up and magnify every passing anxiety.

Colin and I had hoped to gather an ensemble of young singers, and to create a distinctive style of doing opera. Brilliant young talent existed: Frederica von Stade, Ileana Cotrubas, Kiri Te Kanawa, Janet Baker, Thomas Allen, Luis Lima. We thought we could persuade them to give us three or four months of each year so that we could build up a company. We planned to create new productions with these young, keen singers; then to revive these productions in repertory, when the great stars of the operatic circuit could arrive and take over the roles after their usual cursory rehearsals lasting a few days. We felt that this two-tier system (which would be reflected in the ticket prices) provided a central artistic policy while at the same time giving the public the big names, and maintaining Covent Garden's position as an international opera house.

The initial response of the Board was good. It was when we proposed that the first run of performances of our new *Figaro* should be in English, and the second in Italian, that feathers began to get ruffled. Both Colin and I were dedicated to making opera communicate its meaning. We believed translation would help that; and remember, this was in 1969, long before the days of surtitles. For me, now, surtitles have made the vexed question of translating opera irrelevant; I much prefer to hear the words the composer heard when he composed the music.

I grew more and more unhappy the nearer I came to taking up my appointment. Any attempt to alter the established policy was greeted with alarm. Garrett encouraged the members of the Board to think they were musical experts when they were not. They were amateurs. Our plans got nowhere. They were not exactly blocked – they just didn't happen. The great British habit of diplomatically doing nothing hung like a pall over our future.

I realised as time went by that I had made a terrible mistake. I had dreamed to do for opera what I had done for Shakespeare at Stratford, and in Colin Davis I thought I had found the ideal partner. In this I was right. What we both wanted to do was also right. But we were trying to do it in the wrong place at the wrong time. We would have been better off down the road at the English National Opera.

I now behaved badly. I left Colin Davis and John Tooley in the lurch. Just before I officially became co-director of the Royal Opera, I handed in my resignation. I have continued to feel guilty towards Colin and John who were wonderfully magnanimous in the face of my change of heart. And I have often felt since that a big chance was missed.

Glyndebourne was the operatic haven where I recovered from my disappointment over Covent Garden. It brought me Baroque opera; and joyful collaborations with Bernard Haitink and Raymond Leppard. It brought me Britten, Verdi, Bizet; and Janet Baker and Maria Ewing. Above all, it brought me Mozart and the opportunity to work on the Da Ponte operas year in, year out – refining, developing, and all the time understanding a little more.

– 5 –

I lost my conventional faith in my late teens. Shakespeare and Mozart were my gods long before then. Mozart preceded even Shakespeare in my love. When I was nine, I had a book of Mozart piano sonatas which seemed to me extraordinarily easy to play. It took me many years to realise that, though the notes might be easy, to express them was one of the hardest things on earth.

For my tenth birthday present, I had asked to be taken to King's College Chapel to hear Mozart's *Requiem*. This was, I am sure, a romantic request. I had read about his death in poverty, the unfinished *Requiem* ordered by a mysterious stranger, and the marking-up of the percussion part as he was actually dying. All this had captured my imagination. Composers – Schubert, Beethoven, Mozart – seemed to die young, usually penniless or mad. Genius, I thought, was near to madness and very romantic.

Mozart was not fashionable in the 1940s. I was brought up by my teachers to revere Beethoven and to think of him as the Titan, 'the storm that ended music'. Then, Mozart was still considered a small Rococo genius, a charming entertainer rather than a creative innovator.

I am not claiming prescience or maintaining that I understood Mozart before the fashion changed. I just remember always loving his music. It was partly that I could play it, however inadequately; partly that I was enchanted by the wit and the evocation of a more elegant age. I certainly didn't understand the pain in Mozart until my late adolescence. There was a popular piece of dance-band music in the early Forties, *In an Eighteenth-century Drawing-Room*. It took the first theme of a Mozart C major piano sonata and tricked it out with musical box tinkles and supporting saxophones: Glenn Miller meets Mozart. I hated it, but it expressed a perception of Mozart at that time: powdered wigs, crystal chandeliers and gentle minuets.

Perhaps that is why when I saw my first *Figaro* (also in my tenth birthday week) it seemed slightly soppy. But as I learnt the piece and saw it again, I became more and more aware of its sexiness; all those people yearning for love, weeping for love. I was already mightily intrigued by the power of lust. Love was clearly not a soppy thing at all. And Mozart knew it.

As I grew older I listened to a great deal of Mozart on the radio. I heard the important Mozart and Haydn symphonies performed in the Cambridge Guild Hall by the Jacques Orchestra. I heard *Così fan tutte* sung at the Arts Theatre Cambridge by the students of the Guildhall School of Music. I saw *Don Giovanni* at Sadler's Wells, and then at Glyndebourne directed by Carl Ebert and designed more apocalyptically by John Piper. I seem never to have been away from Mozart. I have listened to him avidly for more than fifty years, and for twenty-five of these I have tried to direct his operas.

Mozart and Shakespeare have this in common: they were blessed in their historical moment. They both inhabited a language of art which was ordered, formed and disciplined; and they were both able to break that form, often in order to express pain, complication and ambiguity. Shakespeare inherited the regular iambic verse-line of five beats, a line which is a pretty accurate representation of a phrase in conversation. Mozart inherited the traditions of eighteenth-century Baroque music with its rules and cadences; he had a lingua franca of defined shapes which his father, Leopold (the music master par excellence), had instilled in him.

Thus, Mozart and Shakespeare inherited forms which supported them and which they could observe as second nature. But by breaking those forms they were able to make them more human and expressive. This anarchy is at the centre of their art. Shakespeare constantly heightens emotion by creating unexpected irregularities in the verse. He writes against the verse, yet always preserves it. It is about to break and never quite does – like the counterpoint in the phrasing of a great jazz musician which never quite loses the beat. Out of these breathtaking irregularities, the actor can express extreme feeling. Lear's last agony is a pentameter of one repeated word; what is more, it reverses the normal iambic rhythm: 'Never, never, never, never, never.'

Don Giovanni starts with a formal overture. Yet within seconds, Mozart has wandered into unknown worlds of eerie chromaticism, creating the shifting, painful uncertainties that lie at the heart of this opera. Technically, what he is doing announces the beginning of nineteenth-century music.

Both Shakespeare's theatre and Mozart's theatre were based on direct audience address – the ancient storyteller's convention which allowed the actor to tell the audience exactly what he is thinking and feeling. Hamlet does not wonder to himself whether he should be or should not be: he argues it out directly with his audience. It is a public speech requiring confirmation or contradiction. In the same way, the basis of opera from Monteverdi until Wagner is that in a solo aria the character unpacks his emotions and shares his or her thoughts with the spectators. The aria is not for private musing; that is a naturalistic concept. It is a sharing, and it is always truthful.

I learnt at Glyndebourne that naturalist conventions, by destroying the kind of theatre that preceded them, had done as much damage to opera as they had to Shakespeare. The nineteenth century developed naturalism as a revolutionary force. For the first time, rooms were presented with four walls, though one of them was of course removed so that the audience could peep in. Doors and windows were no longer painted on backcloths – they were real, with catches and locks and knobs. This theatre reached its climax with Ibsen and Chekhov. Time became 'real', acting tried to be natural behaviour and dialogue pretended to be real speech. The audience, like privileged voyeurs, watched a simulation of life. The vigorous public story-telling of the Greeks or the Elizabethans, where a character is formalised and indeed shows he is aware that an audience is watching him, was challenged. Long, unreal 'speeches' or arias had to be disguised. Theatre turned into a representation of reality rather than a game of make-believe where the audience was asked to use its imagination.

This revolution was embarrassing for opera because, like the old theatre, it had been based from its beginnings on the conventions of public story-telling. In Monteverdi or in Cavalli or even in the *opera seria* of the eighteenth century, the singers of solo arias, by opening their hearts to the spectators, telling them the truth, are involving them in their predicaments. They only dissimulate or tell lies to the other characters on stage.

This public demonstration of the heart is even greater when we come to the ensembles – those unique glories of Mozart operas; a musical blend of six, sometimes seven, voices where balance, rhythmic precision and unity are paramount. Musically they are one; dramatically, though, they are not unified but utterly disparate. The characters frequently sing the same words, but the irony is that, with a different inflection, they can have a different meaning. This device is unique to opera: no other medium can convey contradictory thoughts from several people at one and the same time. If several actors speak at once in a play, the result is incoherent. But in Mozart's operas we can look at each one of the characters for a split second and then move on to the next, comparing their different attitudes, contrasting their different emotions. We listen to what is often the same text from each of them, but we understand the irony because their emotions differ. It is a moment of chaos and contradiction – made clear by the music.

I discovered all this at Glyndebourne because the nature of the stage and auditorium made me understand that the whole of Mozart's drama is based on the performer's freedom to communicate straight to the audience. I have directed Mozart at Covent Garden, in Chicago, in Los Angeles, in Geneva. But only at Glyndebourne was the scale of the theatre absolutely right for releasing these complex riches.

But Mozart is not only infinitely subtle, he is also lewd and scatalogical. I sometimes think that the sly obscenities and double entendres in the libretti were slipped in by Da Ponte to make Mozart giggle as he composed. We can see from his letters that he enjoyed a bit of smut.

Peter Shaffer recorded this provocatively in his play *Amadeus* which I directed at the National Theatre. At one performance, Mozart got me into a good deal of trouble. Margaret Thatcher came to see the play, and by the end of the evening she was clearly displeased. She berated me like a headmistress who has caught one of her pupils behaving badly. She couldn't think it right, she declared, that the National Theatre of Great Britain should put on a play in which Mozart uttered disgusting four-letter words. I murmured that Mozart's letters are exuberantly peppered with such words; he delighted, I said, in a bit of bawdry. The Prime Minister told me I was wrong – it was inconceivable that a genius who had written such elegant music would have used such inelegant language. She was quite cross with me for contradicting her. I said that I would send a copy of Mozart's letters round to No. 10 the next morning, which I duly did, drawing attention in my covering note to one or two of the ruder passages. The reply thanking me, from the Prime Minister's private secretary, avoided mentioning Mozart's scatology. I think Mrs Thatcher would have sorted out Mozart with the same despatch as the Archbishop of Salzburg.

In the spring of 1970, I was directing Cavalli's *La Calisto* at Glyndebourne, with Janet Baker as Diana – the first time I had worked with this magnificent artist – and using Raymond Leppard's edition of the score.

Ray, an old friend from Cambridge and early Stratford days, was the first to bring the Baroque Venetian repertory back to mainstream opera. His editions of Monteverdi as well as of Cavalli, and the productions at Glyndebourne, made the pieces popular again after being long out of fashion.

John Bury came with me to design *Calisto* and brought to the production the same revolutionary honesty he had shown in the theatre. Glyndebourne then was still thinking in terms of the designs of twenty years earlier – painted trompe-l'oeil fantasies of illusion, colour and light. But even a decade before 1970, theatre was changing all that. A gauze was no longer painted to look like an old, sun-drenched brick wall. Instead, there would be an actual wall of old bricks on the stage, splashed with strong sunlight. We revelled in the power and brilliance of our new lights and the beauty of texture that they could reveal.

With *La Calisto*, and two years later with Monteverdi's *Il Ritorno d'Ulisse in Patria* in which Janet Baker was a lovely Penelope, John Bury and I set ourselves the task of making the Baroque stage live again – but with modern materials.

In *Ulisse*, some twenty people – stage management, stage hands, prop-makers and two of Glyndebourne's gardeners – gave cues, unseen of course by the house, which enabled Jupiter to fly towards the audience on his eagle and Neptune to rise from the deep while the seas parted and clouds filled the sky, covering the setting sun. All this was done with the utmost precision and grace. And it gave to the spectacle the metaphorical weight of the Baroque world, where the Gods live above in the

flys; men walk on a stage which is the earth; and underneath, with access by trapdoor, are darkness and devils
and the supernatural.

Both *Calisto* and *Ulisse* were very ambitious technically. Because Glyndebourne is now unionised, it would
not be possible to present them there today in the same
way. Too many people would be involved. Today the
technical work would be done by computer. But I would
far rather have a man's hand on a rope (and a man's
brain which is able to take account of the human vari-
ations below him) than use an automatic flying system
which does no more – if you are lucky – than start
precisely when it starts and stop precisely when it
stops.

The machinery used in our two productions gave us
worrying moments. For example, at a dress rehearsal
of *Ulisse*, the singer performing Human Destiny dropped
suddenly from the clouds towards the stage. There was
a safety device on the flying equipment, so she fell only
four feet before an automatic brake was applied. She
hung in the air, dangling like a trussed-up chicken,
while below her the rehearsal continued, with singers
performing busily as Ray Leppard conducted the London
Philharmonic Orchestra. I froze in panic. At my elbow
I heard the voice of Geoffrey Gilbertson, the unflappable
stage director. 'I don't know whether you've noticed,'
he said, 'but Human Destiny has fainted. We'll just
get to the end of the scene and then I'll quietly ask
everyone to take a coffee break while we cut her down.'
Meanwhile the orchestra went on playing. An orchestra
is never stopped at an opera dress rehearsal: the time is
too precious and the bill too expensive.

The best Baroque theatre I know, where spectacle can
work perfectly and have a meaning beyond decoration,
is at Dröttningholm just outside Stockholm. This is an
original eighteenth-century private theatre built for the
entertainment of the King during his summer holidays.
It is a Sleeping Beauty theatre: the door was shut on it

in the early nineteenth century – much like a family who lock up an attic that is no longer useful – and not opened again for more than a hundred years. All the Baroque machinery is still there and much of the Baroque scenery.

Dröttningholm is a theatre created out of the technology of sailing ships. By a miracle of pulleys and hemp lines, each moving piece is connected to a central capstan under the stage. When the capstan is turned the cloths go up, the sliding scenery slides, periactoids turn, the gods descend. The miracle is that everything not only moves silently, but starts and stops at precisely the same moment. Yet it all has a human rhythm, varied only by those who push. I love change and I love new ways of doing things. But we have lost something here.

La Calisto deals with Jove's passion for Calisto, one of the virgin attendants on Diana, goddess of chastity. He comes down to earth and, thinking it the craftiest disguise, transforms himself into Diana. Thus changed, he proceeds to seduce Calisto. Originally, Ray Leppard and I thought that the bass who played Jove would also be able to play the pretend Diana, singing falsetto, a register which many bass voices have no trouble achieving.

After a week's rehearsal I asked for something that is not usual in opera: a very rough run-through. I always work crudely (and speedily) in the first stages, leaving the detail for later. But it is useful to have a quick look early on to see how the whole show is shaping.

This run-through was a particular blessing. It revealed that while the bass singing of Ugo Trama as Jove was splendid, his falsetto singing as Diana was absurd; nor, good actor though he was, could he have convinced Calisto that he was the real Diana. He looked and – more to the point – sounded nothing like Janet Baker.

What was to be done? I had an inspiration. Why not, I said to Ray, ask Janet if she would sing Jove disguised as Diana as well as Diana herself? It would provide her with a wonderful double. Diana was chaste and Jove/Diana was lustful. One was spiritual, the other full of raunchy humour. The two Dianas could be costumed entirely the same, as befitted a credible transformation, but Jove as Diana should always sport a silver-headed walking stick, to give the signal the audience needed.

Janet agreed and put herself through three weeks of extremely hard learning and rehearsing. In performance she was triumphantly funny and heartbreaking in both roles. And the opera, a shrewd analysis of the anguish of lust, was seen generally as an important rediscovery.

We had strong support from Moran Caplat. A man of the theatre and at heart an actor who loved opera, he understood singers, and was always insistent that opera should never forget that it was theatre: otherwise it might as well be done at a concert. He was a keen yachtsman, and ran his theatre like the captain of a ship. The twinkle in his eye always betrayed the buccaneer, and he was a quick politician. I was devoted to him. Moran gave me room to expand and work my way in opera. He suggested one production after another. He led me into doing the Mozart/Da Ponte operas, starting with *Figaro* and going on to *Don Giovanni* and *Così fan tutte*. He persuaded me to do Britten's *Dream* and *Albert Herring*, Gluck's *Orfeo*, and Bizet's *Carmen*. I owe him twenty years of happy work.

– 6 –

Glyndebourne is where I met my third wife, Maria Ewing. She sang Dorabella in the *Così fan tutte* which I directed there in 1978. She was immediately noticeable in the cast: American, wide-eyed and with the absolute beauty that can come of mixed race.

She was then twenty-seven years old, a rising opera star and the youngest of four daughters of a lower middle-class Detroit family. Her mother was Dutch. Her father,

239

an engineer and much older than her mother, was dead. It seems he had African as well as Indian blood; indeed an aunt who was especially dark-skinned was not allowed to visit the girls in daylight. Maria had no hang-ups herself about any of this. She was proud of the racial cocktail that had produced her. But she had grown up with a deep anxiety about it in the family.

She is a product of the appalling American public education system, but her brilliance has surmounted it. I remember her telling me that her set-book for senior English was *Rosemary's Baby*. But she is one of those rare people to whom formal education is irrelevant; she taught herself. She has an astonishing ability to learn, and a photographic memory.

She had been a good pianist as a girl, but did not discover she had a voice until her late teens. She then went to New York, trained, and started an operatic career. When she was in her early twenties, she was taken to Salzburg to sing Cherubino, and everything else followed.

I thought her delightful, provocative and very, very attractive; formidable too, but wonderfully funny. We played piano duets and found that we both hated the dead conventions, the laziness and the silliness of much opera production.

Truth in performance – dramatic truth – was overwhelmingly important to her; she had an actor's instinct but was fiercely musical. I later watched her in admiration as she learnt a major operatic role in forty-eight hours by going without sleep and using her extraordinary memory.

We worked together easily on *Così*, as if rehearsals with her had always been happening. She was reticent yet opinionated – a cat who walked very much alone. We had an early argument in a coffee break about the merits of New York. I said it was falling apart, violent and depressing. She championed it. She lived, apparently, thirty floors up in the Lincoln Plaza, overlooking Manhattan from her little eyrie, strengthened by her music

and her solitude. I discovered that she shared my love
of jazz. She could, she said, listen compulsively to jazz
records all through the night.

We became friendly at Glyndebourne. The intimacy
forced on performers during a rehearsal period is always
slightly unreal. It seemed likely that we would see each
other again, because we would be bound to work together
in the future. At first, it was no more than that.

At the end of the run of *Così*, I shared a carriage
with Maria on the train from Lewes to Waterloo. She
was travelling with all her possessions crammed into one
huge suitcase. It needed a helpful male like me to negotiate it to London. We talked opera and theatre all the
way. She told me she planned to do *Carmen* within the
next few years. I said that if she wanted me to direct it,
I would love to.

Many months afterwards, I was in New York and rang
her. Improbably for a girl who was always whizzing
round the world, an international opera singer, she was
at home. We met for a drink. We went to the Met and
saw a perfectly awful production of *Don Pasquale* which
we hated so much we slipped away in the interval for
dinner.

We were together for ten years. They were years
of passion, of highs and lows, excitements and despair.
They also brought, in Rebecca, a beloved and talented
daughter.

I remain full of admiration for Maria. Many singers
just sing the notes, squarely and accurately, and work
from scores at their concerts. They do not give much of
themselves. Maria learns even her concert programmes
by heart, including extremely difficult modern pieces
by Berg and Messiaen. She learns because she feels she
has to recreate the piece in order to communicate it.
Her whole being is about performing; and truthful performing. She can only work with complete commitment
and honesty.

If this sounds fearsome, it is. Her blazing integrity

and refusal to compromise do not make her an easy person to live with. But her performances are incandescent. Even if you don't like them you cannot ignore them.

It follows that she is much criticised. Some people cannot take her highly personal approach; they say she pulls the music about, remaking it in her own image. This is not true; she is a meticulous musician. But her need to *express* leads her to emphasise and inflect outside the well-bred norm. She is a disturbing performer, a star, with so much temperament she can become terribly depressed. The mixture of our two volatile natures and our two careers – I was running the National Theatre; she was singing all over the world – made for a turbulent life, sometimes gloriously happy, sometimes acutely miserable.

The richest times were when we were working together. The creations of *Carmen*, *L'Incoronazione di Poppea* and, above all, *Salome* were as vivid working experiences as I have had in my life. It has saddened me that I missed a long-planned production of *Tosca* with her, a part she was born to play. When it was due, though, we were in the middle of an ugly divorce. But I have a date with Maria and Puccini in the future, I hope.

We are friends again, and have worked together since the split. She is not a well-mannered artist and does not live her life calmly. I love her for that.

– 7 –

Georg Solti rang up one day in 1980 and asked if he could see me at once in my office at the National Theatre. It was urgent, he said – and very confidential. In this atmosphere of secrecy he arrived and rattled off his message. He had been asked to conduct the next

production of *The Ring* at Bayreuth in 1983. The Jewish
Hungarian outcast had at last been summoned to the
holy of holies. Would I join him and direct Wagner's
marathon?

My stomach turned over. I felt sick. Of course, I was
flattered to be asked; of course I wanted to do *The Ring*
and said so. What opera director worthy of his salt would
not? Yet the sheer impossibility of the task appalled me.
First of all, I was not a complete Wagnerian, and I knew
it. True, no-one who loves music can fail to be overcome
by his revolutionary talent, his massive architectural
sense and his ability to create amazingy erotic effects
in what was one of the most stifled and puritanical
centuries in history. But, at the same time, he drives me
mad. He is long-winded and almost totally without
humour.

His politics and philosophy are often alarmingly
self-serving and suspect, and though we cannot blame
Wagner that Hitler adopted him as the official composer
of the Third Reich, it would be hard to deny that there
are definite Fascist tendencies in his work. And, great
genius though he is, he was clearly one of the most odious
individuals in the history of art.

Solti and I tried to persuade Wolfgang Wagner –
Wagner's grandson, the director at Bayreuth – that the
best course would be to stage in the first year of the
festival only two of the cycle of four operas, with the
other two in the following year. Wolfgang would not
hear of it. His face, a disturbing blend of his grandfather
and Liszt, was adamant, despite all the auguries. In 1876,
when Wagner finished putting on the entire *Ring* himself
for the first time, he said to Cosima, 'I wish I were dead.'
Ever since, the historical progress of each production
had been the same, with hardly any exceptions: it is
a failure in its first year; accepted in its second; a
success in its third; a definitive statement in its fourth;
and mythologised in its fifth – when lamentations break
out wondering why the production is to be replaced.

We – Solti and I – had no wish to be part of this pattern. We knew that to try and put on four huge operas in one year was madness. There was a deadlock with Wolfgang. Then, foolishly, we gave way to him, believing it would be better to fail than not to do it at all. We failed. But there was much to reward, fascinate and amuse us on the way.

The superb Hildegard Behrens as Brunnehilde did with a will whatever we asked of her. At one point, after the Immolation scene, she had to hang upside down for fifteen minutes, some thirty feet in the air, strapped to the centre of a vast platform as it turned through 360 degrees. Wolfgang was most resistant to this, as he was to practically everything else we wanted to do. He first of all demanded that I myself take out a special insurance to cover Behrens: the festival would not be responsible. When I said no, and while Behrens went on urging him that she did not at all mind doing it, he had a mock-up constructed in the workshop so that we could have a full test. Hildegard was wired up and a doctor and attendant nurse monitored her blood pressure, heart rate and general well-being during the fifteen minutes of the 360-degree turn. To Wolfgang's disappointment, there was not a flutter on the electro-cardiogram.

This episode was typical of many absurdities. We were known in the Festspielhaus as the makers of the British *Ring*, which was fairly ridiculous as we were led by a Hungarian. Dislike of us was evident from the beginning. Our designer was William Dudley, a brilliant and cheerful cockney who was not about to be pushed around. When the difficulties and animosity became unbearable, I had to warn him against muttering under his breath, 'We won, y'know.'

Bill had a wonderful idea for the Rhinemaidens: they floated in a big, shallow pool on stage, and their image was reflected to the audience by means of a huge mirror standing at a forty-five-degree angle. The device worked brilliantly: the only Rhinemaidens I have ever seen who looked as if they were truly swimming – because they were. Their appearance, their sound, and the whole nature of the scene exactly matched the music: it shimmered. To achieve this was monumentally difficult. First Wolfgang told us we couldn't put that amount of water on the stage because it wouldn't bear the weight; then that the water would be too cold for the singers and to heat it would cost too much; and then that no Rhinemaidens could sing and swim at the same time. But the biggest problem was my wish that they should be naked.

Asking *singers* to be naked at Bayreuth was unheard of. It was suggested, instead, that the Rhinemaidens should have doubles: three strong girls from the Bayreuth Swimming Club. No Bayreuth young lady, however, would appear at the Festspielhaus unclothed. So it went on . . . and on . . . But in the end our Rhinemaidens sang, swam, and looked beautiful in their nakedness, like Cranachs come to life, only a little more fleshly. Well before this happy outcome, though, a hearty Teutonic joke had been played upon us. We returned from supper to a technical rehearsal to discover a nude female figure bobbing up and down in the Rhine with her legs in the air. She turned out to be a life-size inflatable doll from the Bayreuth sex shop.

Doing *The Ring* was an endurance test. Rehearsals began at the end of April for this near fifteen-hour epic, which was due to open at the end of July. There wasn't time to do more than shape each scene and return to it perhaps twice more. My usual method of working is to ask questions, not only of myself but of the cast, and so try to worry the text into yielding its secrets. This was just not possible. I had to have ready answers; there was no time for questions.

Ironically, the weeks allowed for rehearsal added up to less for each *Ring* opera than a director would have for an isolated, normal length opera. Also, three of the four are incredibly long. And Wagnerian singers are scarce, which means they are able to stipulate how much rehearsal time they are prepared to give – and it was never enough.

I did my best, and tried not to be daunted as each vast scene was rehearsed and the next one reared its massive head over the horizon. Before we came to Bayreuth I had made desperate attempts to brush up my German, and for a year had early-morning lessons in my office at the National. But I never had time to concentrate on the homework. I also failed to break through my everlasting difficulty with languages. The Germans thought my stumbling attempts to speak their tongue were odd, and I don't blame them. I would have thought it strange to find a German director who spoke little English doing *Henry V* at Stratford.

By the time I directed *The Ring* I had been running the National for nearly ten years, so the Board agreed I could have time off to go to Bayreuth as a sabbatical three months; and while I was away Christopher Morahan took charge on the South Bank. He was an extremely able second-in-command, but I seemed to spend a good deal of my Bavarian summer on the phone to London explaining to puzzled dramatists and directors why I was not there. Soon, the British press began to write about the absentee director of the National Theatre.

Another situation was also not too happy. Maria had originally agreed to sing Gutrune in *The Ring* – not a very big part, but one that can be marvellously effective, and has to be very sexy. At the last moment she pulled out and spent the summer with our small daughter Rebecca, just over a year old, in a hideous little house outside Bayreuth. Domestically, life was hardly blissful, though Rebecca was an enchantment.

Meanwhile, all my energies were concentrated on trying to present a *Ring* which looked like the music: which returned the piece to nature, to the flicker of light on water and the sway of leaves in the forest. I wanted to do a romantic *Ring* which took the myth back to its fairy-tale origins.

Bill Dudley helped me wonderfully in this. His designs were lush and naive while being very advanced technically, and the movement of the vast circular platform on which most of the action took place often achieved a poetry which supported Wagner's extraordinary score. Siegfried's Death March was one of the profoundest visual moments I have seen in the theatre. He was borne away by his captains through huge trees. The stage tracked into the distance, growing ever higher and higher until the funeral party and forest vanished among the clouds.

However, we makers of the British *Ring* got heartily booed for our pains as we stepped on to the stage after the opening. This didn't bother me too much; booing at Bayreuth is an essential part of the blood sport of going to the opera. But many of the notices were terrible, especially in the German papers – though the English contingent were generally enthusiastic, particularly Bernard Levin and John Higgins. I do not want to excuse the shortcomings that were seen in my production. It is a fact, nonetheless, and an interesting one, that I had done it at a time when most German offerings of this great work were heavily politicised; when a director was expected to have a social concept – an unswerving theory of the piece – and force everything to that end. For example, Chéreau's *Ring* – which preceded mine at Bayreuth – seemed to me to be based on a simple reading of Bernard Shaw. I enjoyed it. But I think of *The Ring* as being more complex than that. And if Wagner had seen the Rhinemaidens as sequinned tarts in a hydro-electric power station, as Chéreau did, he would surely have written very different music.

I was clear about my concept. It was to try to reveal the corruption of power and of wealth, and the purity of regeneration, with natural forces as the important corrective to human faults. But this was considered altogether too contradictory and ambiguous. What did

I *mean?* the critics cried. But the public, I'm happy to say, increasingly responded to what we had done. The production was revived in 1984 and 1985 and, by its last appearance, had become a considerable success. And my sore feelings were salved by a big mail from supporters.

I would certainly like to do *The Ring* again. Having spent so long learning it, and having experienced it on the pulse, I reckon I am ready to have another go. But it will never happen, for no opera house could give me the sort of rehearsal time that I would want.

The wonder of Bayreuth is the theatre itself. During the nineteenth century orchestras became larger and louder, and the sheer volume of sound unleashed by Wagner was enough to swamp most human voices. So he invented a miraculous opera house where the singer, not the orchestra, is in the foreground and where the sound of his or her voice is paramount. Famously, he did this by placing the orchestra under the stage, where it is invisible. It still sounds full blooded and resonant, yet slightly, very slightly, distant. This is aurally magnificent. Visually it works wonderfully too because there is no distraction to the audience from the orchestra, or from the conductor waving his arms. They can be seen only by the singers.

Bayreuth is unquestionably the best opera house in the world. It has the finest acoustics; the most sensitive relationship between auditorium and stage. Why has it never been copied in any of the hundreds of opera houses built since? I suspect this is due to conductors: they don't like being invisible.

– 8 –

During the Seventies and early Eighties, I received more praise for my opera work at Glyndebourne than I did for my theatre work at the National. This was partly because the paradox of the situation made good copy: the theatre director only did good work when he turned to opera on his summer holidays. I exaggerate, but the feeling was there. The truth is also that my opera productions then were to an extent revolutionary. I was trying to do with them what I had done with Shakespeare at the RSC in the Sixties: to discover the world the characters lived in and the underlying reasons for their actions. And just as there used to be a tradition for actors to declaim Shakespeare, so in opera many singers merely stood and sang. I tried to get the Susannas and the Fiordiligis to reveal their humanity, to become real girls whose hearts were both longing and sad.

I worked with Bernard Haitink at Glyndebourne on some nine productions, and these were the most subtle and intricate collaborations I have experienced with a conductor. He is a man of great charm and warmth, yet of infinite shyness. He seems only to find himself in music. In life he is hesitant, diffident and, if off-colour, suspicious. But he is always generous and benevolent, with much humour behind the reserve. There are black shadows inside him, I am sure, otherwise he couldn't express so sensitively such an extraordinary range of music. What a production looks like and the way the characters behave fundamentally affects his music-making. For a theatre director, he is the ideal partner.

My original production of *Don Giovanni* was with John Pritchard, and his music was very elegant and ambiguous. But when Bernard took it over for its revival, he reacted intensely to the production, and the music expressed the ferocious passions and the darkness of the Don, as he stands there challenging the very existence of God. This rare aptitude of Bernard's was an inspiration to me through many productions, from the broad humanity of *Falstaff* to the subtle, poker-faced absurdity of *Albert Herring*.

In 1984 I became artistic director of Glyndebourne

with Bernard as music director. For three years it was a wonderful partnership. But then he moved to the same position at Covent Garden. I think he knew it could turn out to be a poisoned chalice, but felt that it was a risk he had to take: it gave him the opportunity to conduct Wagner.

Much else was changing on the Sussex downs. Brian Dickie, who in 1981 had taken over from Moran, left to run the Toronto Opera. And George Christie became more and more the chief executive as well as the chairman.

George's prowess with sponsors has led the way in Britain. True, there is a ready market among company directors, their wives and guests, for a stylish summer evening in a beautiful country house setting with a little music thrown in. But it is George who has revitalised Glyndebourne's sponsorship from business – and it is huge. The finances of the opera house are also enormously helped by the comparatively low fees paid to the artists. It is a tradition that you work at Glyndebourne because you want to, not to earn money – leading singers getting a tenth of their normal fee. They go there because the working conditions are superb and it is a good place for a young artist to develop or for a mature artist to learn a new role. But they pay for it. Glyndebourne has always been subsidised by its casts.

This may change with the new, bigger opera house: George Christie's dream come true. What was planned looked at first fairly modest – extending the existing building, modernising it, and improving the acoustics which were badly in need of attention. But gradually the ideas became more and more radical. Now, a theatre that for sixty years has enchanted its audience is no more, without a peep from the guardians of our heritage.

I am all for change, particularly in the arts where there is a tendency to stay with what works rather than risk something new. But I am very torn over the new Glyndebourne. I look forward to it, while at the same time being desperately sad that an historic opera house, born so much of its time, and out of the obsessions of John Christie, should be totally destroyed.

– 9 –

Few pleasures are greater than directing the same opera again and again if it is a masterpiece. There are new emphases because there are new performers; and different circumstances and audiences make a different communication necessary. The journey of discovery is never over – especially with Mozart. I have done *Figaro* in Glyndebourne, Chicago, Geneva and Los Angeles; *Così* in Glyndebourne, Chicago and Los Angeles; and *The Magic Flute* in Los Angeles. Each time I worked with fresh delight and excitement.

Opera has taken me round the world – not always so happily. At the Metropolitan Opera I directed a production of Verdi's *Macbeth* and attempted to take it back to nineteenth-century melodrama which, rather more than Shakespeare, is at its heart. An engraving of Macready in the play, wearing a kilt with a feathered tam-o'-shanter on his head, has more than a touch of Walter Scott in it, and I think that is a good image for Verdi's opera. It is an early work, and though he has a very modern psychological fascination with the woman's domination of the man, the piece seems to me close to the world of the Gothic novel.

This was not the view of many New Yorkers. Met audiences had become accustomed to a very heavily cut and Shakespeareanised version of the opera, deliberately short on fantasy. So what we presented, which included warlocks, sprites, goblins, flying witches and a full ballet – all the romantic vocabulary – affronted them. They thought we were mocking Verdi. At the first night, there were not only catcalls; fights broke out in the audience between those who approved and those who did not. Peter Shaffer got thumped on the head with somebody's programme when he loudly voiced his enthusiasm.

The Metropolitan Opera is an amazingly impersonal place. When I arrived in New York to do *Macbeth*, I found a rehearsal call awaiting me at the hotel: I was to report to level C at ten-thirty on Monday morning. I happened to know where level C was because I had collected Maria from the rehearsal room there the previous year.

I duly reported at the time mentioned and was introduced to the stage management and cast. The only person I knew was my assistant. I asked if the conductor, James Levine, was coming and was told that this morning he had a dress rehearsal of tomorrow night's opera. We would not be seeing him for some days. I showed the model of the designs in scene one to the singers and began staging it. An hour later we took a coffee break. As we came into the canteen, a voice rang out from a man sitting at a table – 'Peter! What are you doing here? I didn't know you were in New York . . .' It was the general administrator of the Metropolitan Opera, Anthony Bliss.

Later, again at the Met, I re-directed Maria's *Carmen*. This had only a limited success, despite her spellbinding performance. Perhaps the use of the full dialogue and the attempt to create a genuine *opera comique* style, which had worked so well at Glyndebourne and on video, could not function in the elephantine interior of the New York house.

I first directed Maria in *Salome* in America – and, with this, success was immediate. The production, which started in Los Angeles, was also seen in Washington, Chicago and San Francisco, given twice at Covent Garden, and on television and video. John Bury was the designer and we staged the piece as a Klimt-inspired nightmare, with sumptuous projections. John seldom does what is expected, and here he produced something far outside his usual style. I intended to take the decadence of the opera to its limits. Maria, at the end of the dance before Herod, was totally naked. Salome sings to the head of John the Baptist, 'The mystery of love is greater than the mystery of death . . .' Oscar Wilde created extraordinary, sick tenderness, and Strauss responded.

In Houston I did the premiere of Michael Tippett's opera *New Year*. Some years before, Tippett had called on me at the National Theatre and shared his worries about this piece. He wasn't sure whether it was opera or drama. And he wasn't sure what he could ask of actors or of singers. He wanted a set which changed its scale – sometimes vast and threatening, sometimes small and claustrophobic. Above all, he wanted dance. He wondered what was possible. He talked and talked and I watched, fascinated. Here was a musical genius of our age wrestling once again with the age-old problem of opera. Words first? Music first? How important is the acting if they can sing? How important is the dancing if they can act?

I made the only comment interpreters can offer to creators. I advised him to follow his imagination. It was up to people like me to realise his fantasies; there should be no prior constraints.

When we eventually came to the premiere, Alison Chitty's designs succeeded in making all Tippett's eclectic imaginings coherent. The dancers, too, vividly expressed the diversity of modern city life, chiefly because Bill T. Jones, the choreographer, is in love with the individuality of people and wants their quirkiness rather than trained uniformity. His group contained tall dancers, small dancers, thin dancers and alarmingly fat dancers. Throughout the rehearsals Tippett had been a model of grace and charm. His advice was always clear and precise. Though old in wisdom, he has the clarity and energy of someone whose eyes are just opening on the world.

New Year had been technically difficult to get on

the stage. None of us had energy left for the Houston opening, which turned out to be a heavy business in itself: long dresses, dinner jackets, charm for our sponsors, and a great deal of jewellery – more trappings even than at Glyndebourne, where the production was later revived. Michael walked through all the Texan nobs apparently oblivious, though cannily picking up every absurdity. They were slightly nonplussed by his appearance: he wore a green and white striped blazer, a bow tie and large, new pink sneakers. He looked like a naughty adolescent, rather than the Grand Old Man of English music.

A couple of years before I left the National Theatre, I went with Brian Dickie, then still Glyndebourne's general administrator, to the Queen Elizabeth Hall to hear a concert performance of *Idomeneo*. Simon Rattle was conducting the Orchestra of the Age of Enlightenment, and it was his first use of original instruments in a Mozart opera. The result was a revelation. The clear sound, the brisk muscular tempi and, above all, the perfect balance between singer and orchestra made a completely new experience. The words were totally audible, and the singers could inflect them subtly because the orchestra was not too loud. Yet because the actual instruments were quieter, they were played without inhibition. There was no holding back so as not to drown the singers. The drama in Mozart is always in the orchestra, and this liberated playing was amazingly intense.

I was already set to direct a second cycle of the Da Ponte/Mozart operas at Glyndebourne. It seemed to me and to Brian that we simply had to persuade Simon and this orchestra to do the performances. Glyndebourne was the perfect – indeed the only – opera house in England of the right size for such an undertaking. After a great deal of debate and rearrangement, this was agreed, with the wholehearted endorsement of George Christie and

Bernard Haitink.

Figaro, in a production designed by John Gunter, opened during the summer of 1989. There was some uneasiness on the first night. Doing something new brought problems of balance and ensemble. And the singers' throats seemed to close up even more than is usual at first performances. I sometimes wonder if music critics realise that they spend their professional lives hearing voices which, because of first-night nerves, are reduced by twenty to thirty per cent. With a play, the adrenalin released by the occasion is often helpful; it concentrates and clarifies. In opera, it inhibits; a purely physical reaction.

By the ninth or tenth performance this production was the best all-round *Figaro* I have ever seen. I looked forward eagerly to doing *Così fan tutte* and *Don Giovanni*.

I had settled with George Christie that – after my return to these three operas, and before the time of the rebuilding – I would give up my artistic directorship. I thought it was the right moment for Glyndebourne to have a change and for me to move on. It was all very amicable. But there is much to be said for the American doctrine that if you are going you should go at once.

Peter Sellars, the startlingly original young American director, had been asked to do *The Magic Flute*. I supported the idea strongly. To hold the balance in this opera between the serious and the funny is very difficult and I believed Peter might well achieve it. When I went to the first night, however, I found that every word of the dialogue had been cut. I was appalled. *The Magic Flute* is constructed with extreme cunning. After a section of dialogue the emotions become so intense that the character has to move again into music. Once the emotions are released, the character returns to dialogue again. What I was witnessing was not *The Magic Flute* at all but a deconstructed version of it. Peter Sellars had of course a perfect right to try this experiment, though I would certainly have advised him that in my view it would fail – that is, if I had known about it. What upset me was that, despite the fact that I was Glyndebourne's artistic director, nobody had told me what Peter was doing. And he had done it at a very late stage of rehearsal.

Since I have often declared publicly my passion for trying to honour a writer's text and a composer's score, I was not surprised to get a huge mail asking me where my principles had gone.

I would have liked from Glyndebourne a sensible explanation and an apology. I received neither; I was told that neither was 'appropriate'.

Though I had only a year to go before I gave up my post as artistic director, it was clear that in Glyndebourne's eyes I had left the job already. So I resigned; a twenty-year association finished in acrimony. Perhaps I was angry and precipitate. But I couldn't stand my most central beliefs being treated so casually. The management warned me that if I said anything to the press it might well get very ugly. I said nothing, but very ugly it became. Many unattributed stories surfaced: that the job of artistic director was not terribly important – it was only a courtesy title; that I hadn't had very much influence; that I had been 'deficient in my attendance'.

Glyndebourne and my friendship with George and Mary Christie was for a long time a very important and very happy part of my life. I owe George a great deal. I had done fourteen productions and there were a great many revivals of those productions.

I had to realise now that I was at the end of that particular journey.

PART FOUR

The War That Had To Be Won

– 1 –

Being the director of the National Theatre is much like the predicament of Nelson on top of his column. You inevitably attract the attention of the pigeons. Nevertheless, I consider myself a very lucky man to have had the job.

The Royal Shakespeare Company was a straight line: I never doubted what I wanted, though I often doubted my ability to do it. The National Theatre was entirely different: it was a public task and quickly turned into a war that had to be won.

My time was so packed with action and effort that the details of board meetings, the cravenness of the Arts Council and the regular betrayals of Whitehall seem to me now like the stale gossip of many years ago. Nonetheless, certain events, certain productions and people, are exciting to remember.

I started the job with much enthusiasm. But the building in the recession-hit mid-Seventies looked lavishly expensive (which it wasn't). It also opened ludicrously late. And I, who had hitherto been spoilt by the media, was suddenly turned into a target of some derision. The newspapers wallowed in unhelpful nostalgia for 'Larry and the dear Old Vic'. And a small number of people, led by Ken Tynan, Jonathan Miller and Michael Blakemore, chattered obsessively, both on the record and off, about my weaknesses.

Then there were the dreadful strikes: silly to look back on, yet almost unendurably painful at the time.

Censorship rows continued: Michael Bogdanov was threatened with prison for directing Howard Brenton's *The Romans in Britain.*

I saw the Arts Council turn from an independent champion of the arts into an instrument of government, gradually reducing its support all round, and progressively weakening the idea of what a National Theatre could and should be. I had a vision which was perhaps naive.

I wanted the National Theatre to be truly national; to be available to regional theatre companies and to exchange productions with them. I believed that it should be more than a company of actors doing plays; it should be a centre available to the whole of the country's theatre. But the Arts Council refused to view it like that, and so threw away the greatest opportunity in its history.

I saw the Trojan horse of commercial sponsorship wheeled into the subsidised arts. In a mixed economy, this seemed at first unarguable. Moreover, we were told the money thus raised was intended for new enterprises; we were promised it would never be set against the central grant. That promise was broken. Commercial sponsorship had clearly been designed to reduce the government's commitment; and it succeeded.

I saw the Thatcher government dismantle the performing arts, spoil our education system and partially destroy our great tradition of public service broadcasting. I protested vehemently and publicly, and lived, rather like a politician, in a constant dialogue with the media.

On the other hand there was much to relish. New plays predominated in our programme at the National. A generation of younger writers brought their work to us – Hare, Hampton, Poliakoff, Bond, Edgar, Tony Harrison, Mamet, Shephard – to join the generation of Pinter,

Shaffer, Stoppard, Simon Gray and Ayckbourn.

I relished, too, the productions that only a National Theatre can create because they need extra time and special resources: Bill Bryden's overwhelming *Mysteries*, which reclaimed medieval theatre for our age; *The Oresteia*, a massive undertaking achieved after six months of research and rehearsal; the luxury of three months given to staging the Judi Dench/Anthony Hopkins *Antony and Cleopatra*; and mounting the two parts of *Tamburlaine* on the same evening as a mighty diptych.

– 2 –

To begin at the beginning, in the summer of 1971 I ran into Lord Goodman at Glyndebourne. I told him that I was about to resign from the Royal Opera. He greeted the news with delight; he said he always thought I had made a mistake in going to Covent Garden: it was possible it needed me, but he was sure I didn't need it. He invited me to lunch in a few days' time.

There I met Max Rayne, who had just become the new NT chairman. They asked me if I was interested in succeeding Larry at the National. The idea horrified yet also attracted me. In many ways, I did not want the job, but had a sickening feeling I would have to do it. Trevor Nunn, some years later, put my dilemma exactly: 'If you are asked to run a national theatre, it is difficult to say no. It is as though destiny is working in your life . . . Peter was genuinely unable to decide.' I was also worried about Larry. The NT had been housed at the Old Vic for eight years – a long occupation of a temporary home. Now he believed that he and his team would at last be moving, for their new, permanent home on the South Bank was due to be ready in 1973. But they had just had a bad season and Larry, after two ghastly illnesses, was far from strong. It was questioned whether he could manage, or indeed would want, to stay on for the opening of the new building. He himself was havering: first he was going, then he was not.

His uncertainty, therefore, was very worrying to me, as was the thought of taking over the job of a man I revered, the giant of the theatre, who had created the National. I had no wish to be cast in the role of the usurper. It was vital, I believed, that he should head the company when they moved. It would also be his just reward.

I said I was interested, but would only talk further if Larry were present and if he were definitely resigning. And that is how things were left.

Meanwhile, I talked privately to my RSC colleagues: Peggy, Trevor, John Barton, Peter Brook. Only Peter was for it: a new challenge, he said.

Eventually, after an endless nine months, Olivier was told by Max Rayne that the Board felt it necessary to appoint a successor, that I was favoured, but that they wanted him to stay on for the move. Larry responded by sending me a generous telegram, saying in elaborate prose that he was delighted at the prospect. Yet within three weeks, he had provoked a huge ferment, indicating to a full meeting of the National Theatre Company that he hadn't been consulted. He also, I gather, gave the impression, though without directly saying so, that he didn't wish me as a successor. I was from the opposition; the man from the RSC. In all this he was encouraged by Ken Tynan with whom he had a curious love–hate relationship, and who was a power behind the throne.

But despite such contradictions and alarms, and after many fevered talks to and fro, my appointment was confirmed, and I took up the job at the beginning of 1973, initially working alongside Larry. I still hoped he would lead the company into the South Bank.

It was not a happy time. Larry blew hot and cold

in his enthusiasm for endorsing the new theatre and the new regime; and his love of intrigue intensified the confused loyalties of the actors and staff.

It was now five years since my resignation from the RSC, but I had remained an associate director. Also, my colleagues in the company were my closest friends. I continued to have emotional meetings with them. At one point we were all so anxious to safeguard the aesthetic that we had built and cherished, so reluctant to break with the past, that the idea of some sort of amalgamation, based on a sharing of buildings, came up. It gathered head when it was seen by the guardians of public funds as a possible way to save money. Animated discussions went on. But it never really made sense, and after some months came to nothing. To Olivier, it was an attempt to make one vast organisation with me at the head and Trevor as my deputy; he felt the RSC was simply taking over the National. To George Farmer, it was clearly a takeover by the National of the RSC. I wrote in my *Diaries*, that it was 'one of the silliest ideas I've ever been seduced by'.

Finally, we all settled down. I continued to regret leaving the RSC, and indeed regretted it more as the years passed. The old friendships held, though there were the occasional rows between the two organisations when we clashed over plays or casting, both sides behaving in a proprietorial this-one-belongs-to-me manner. Now, of course, the notion that there is such a being as an RSC actor or a National actor on an exclusive basis seems odd, even unhealthy – which means, sadly I think, that neither is a clearly defined company. By the mid Eighties, actors, directors and designers were moving freely from one to the other.

− 3 −

Through the early Seventies it seemed to me that there were two kinds of time – real time and builders' time. Successive delays in the construction of the NT caused frustration and distress to those of us who were trying to open the place, not helped by the fact that whenever I had to announce another hold-up I was threatened with legal action by the builders if I made any critical public comment. The worst delay was in March 1974 when, at the last moment, they admitted that their latest promise, which had guaranteed an opening in the spring of 1975, could not be kept.

I was staging a whole collection of productions at the Old Vic ready for transferring on that date. Ralph Richardson said they were like aircraft circling the airfield waiting to come in when the runway was clear. But because it was now revealed that the runway wasn't even built, plans had to be aborted and actors laid off. Delay costs mounted alarmingly. And it was not a good moment in the arts to have financial difficulties: the country was dipping into recession; inflation was going up and up. The boom of the 1960s, which had made the dream of a national theatre a reality, was well and truly over.

The troubled times made everybody fretful, and contributed to the envy much of the profession increasingly displayed towards the new National. They looked at it with suspicion and resentment. To them, it was a fat cat likely to weaken the rest of the theatre by gobbling up talent and funds. I was deeply upset by a letter forcibly expressing this which was printed in *The Times* in October 1974 and drawn up by Oscar Lewenstein of the Royal Court, who had persuaded thirteen other directors of subsidised theatres – among them, ironically, my successor at the NT, Richard Eyre – to sign it with him. Their fears, though understandable, were not justified. Time has shown this very clearly.

The British are a conservative people who would prefer not to have anything new; or, at best, are distinctly wary of it. New institutions, it seems, have to be tempered on the anvil of hostility. So it was perhaps not surprising that as the new National lurched towards its opening, both the Left and Right seemed united in decrying it. Shaw and Granville-Barker must have whirled in their graves. There were also fierce attacks in the press, including a memorably vicious leading article in the *New Statesman*: 'As cumbersome as a dreadnought . . . dubiously relevant to the twentieth century . . . naive if not actually damaging to the cause of good theatre'. I sent a spirited reply.

As much as nine years later, Stewart Trotter, the director, reviewing my *Diaries*, wrote: 'The villain is not Lord Olivier, not the strikers, not the building, but the entire concept of the National Theatre itself as realised after the war.' How dated this looks now. At the time, however, arguments in favour of a national theatre needed putting all over again. I seemed to live on the public stage, writing, arguing, making the case.

'Change', I wrote, 'is of the essence of the theatre, of any dialogue with the public. But one thing is constant for me: a belief that the theatre is a living element of our community, altering its nature according to the responses it receives and modifying those responses by its work . . . you almost always disturb people when your theatre is alive, because art always challenges preconceptions.'

Such statements, which had fallen on willing ears in the Sixties, were, in the miserable Seventies, greeted coolly. This was helped along by those who were uneasy about my taking over the National. They saw in the

RSC already one company of my making; British fair play considered it wrong there should be another.

I thought, and still think, that it was a failure on Olivier's part that he had not chosen and developed his own successor. As the man from the opposition, I found it difficult to persuade those who had loved and admired his regime at the Vic to respond with equal enthusiasm to a new theatre that was so radically different, not only architecturally but in the style of its management.

Larry was rightly worshipped by the profession. He returned that love by flirting with his company, sometimes giving favours, sometimes withdrawing them. He was an old-style monarch who could be inspiring but also awesome and wilful.

When I joined the National, the offices were little more than cupboards, opening off a central corridor running the length of temporary huts in Aquinas Street. They were infested by rats and had holes in the roof. When it rained, buckets were placed on the floor to collect the drips. Larry progressed up and down this corridor every morning, putting his head in here and there, greeting, cajoling, flattering. He was a fascinator, and most of those working for him would have gone to the South Pole and back if he'd asked them to.

He headed a tight-knit little court, and who was in and who was out was always the main news of the day. Ken Tynan, who loved politics (but wasn't good at them, mainly because his manoeuvres were transparent), thrived in this hothouse atmosphere.

But it couldn't be like that any more. For one thing, the organisation I had to run was more than three times the size of the Vic, and we had to do many more productions. For another, I hadn't the great actor's extraordinary magic, which was so much a part of Larry's personality. I hoped, however, that my style was more democratic; it was certainly more open. You cannot, of course, run a theatre without taking responsibility for all that happens, and without seeing that you have the final decision on everything that matters. Even so, healthy discussion and argument are necessary to check and challenge ultimate power. It can, however, bruise egos.

I still remember even Jonathan Miller's confidence faltering as he tried to convince some unimpressed NT directors that it would be revealing to do *The Importance of Being Earnest* with an all-male cast. Harold Pinter asked him beadily what he was trying to prove. Was it, he enquired, that Wilde had actually wished that he could write a homosexual play about the pairing off of men?

I have always tried to make room for projects that my colleagues had a real fervour to do. But this idea seemed to me, and to all those present, a touch mad. It was firmly squashed.

I think these open discussions were one of the reasons why Jonathan Miller resigned – as he was to do, much to my relief, a year before we opened on the South Bank. He and Michael Blakemore, and to a lesser degree Ken Tynan, seemed to me to be enemies within. Ken had gone, by mutual agreement, soon after I was appointed. But I had kept on Michael and Jonathan in an attempt at continuity. It was very stupid of me. Like Ken, they appeared to regard me as an unwanted interloper from the RSC. They also disliked my way of working and the chemistry between us was bad. Fortunately for me, Michael was to resign a year or so after Jonathan. Once they had departed, however, they both, for years, seemed to me to lose no chance of knocking me publicly.

I did some other unwise things at this time. Thinking that to achieve a high profile would help me sell the cause of the National, I began presenting the weekly arts programme *Aquarius* on LWT. Though it took only a day of my seven-day week, eyebrows at once shot up. It was even questioned in the House of Lords, by Ted Willis, whether it was right that the director of the National

267

Theatre, with all his responsibilities, should do such a job. I smile wrily now when I see Jeremy Isaacs, the general director of the Royal Opera House, presenting the television programme *Face to Face*, without (quite rightly in my view) a mutter of disapproval.

I also agreed to feature in a Sanderson's wallpaper advert; harmless enough, I thought. Many actors had done the same, and though the money was not much, Sanderson's completely redecorated a room in my house at Wallingford, so that they could take the photograph they wanted. A colour picture of me sitting at my piano duly appeared in many magazines, the room glowing in the background, with the words, 'Very Peter Hall, Very Sanderson's' blazoned across it. I was much sent up as a result and, given the climate then, was foolish to have done it.

– 4 –

The National Theatre, though poised to move to the South Bank as soon as possible, played at the Old Vic during the whole of my first two years with the company. The initial repertory was patchy in quality. Jonathan Miller provided two damp squibs in *Figaro* and *The Freeway*, and Michael Blakemore added another with *Grand Manoeuvres*. I directed *The Tempest* with John Gielgud which didn't come off either. I had tried to interpret the play as a masque, using my experience of Baroque theatre at Glyndebourne. But the play's complexities sank under the heavy effects.

However, Bill Bryden joined the company and did a fine production of *Spring Awakening*. And then, in 1975, we hit form. John Schlesinger had a big success with *Heartbreak House*, and I added to the repertory *Happy*

Days with Peggy Ashcroft (who had crossed the river from the RSC to help me), the premiere of Pinter's *No Man's Land* with Ralph Richardson and John Gielgud, and *John Gabriel Borkman* with Ashcroft, Richardson and Wendy Hiller. I directed, as well, Albert Finney's *Hamlet*, received half-heartedly by the critics but enthusiastically by the public. The theatre buzzed with people and we began to play to full houses.

My relationship with Max Rayne and the NT Board was also settling down by this time. Rayne had started from nothing after the war and was now one of the richest people in Britain. He was, as Goodman had remarked to me, self-made, like both of us. He had, apparently, everything. An immensely successful property developer and businessman, he had married into the royal family, and he loved helping the arts and bringing his commercial skills to bear on cultural institutions. Anxious and suspicious, his temperament teetering on the brink of paranoia, he was, as Goodman said, driven in a way that he and I were not. This anxiety gave Rayne his edge and his ability always to keep six jumps ahead. He had brilliant foresight.

Most of my difficulties with Rayne related to how much I said in public about the National Theatre's position. John Goodwin and I talked freely to journalists. We spoke about how the new building was progressing or not progressing; we gave the facts about our finances; we answered our detractors. We both tried to be as informative at the National as we had been at the RSC. But this openness did not always please Max. In particular, he had been infuriated at a big article by Stephen Fay in the *Sunday Times* which went into some detail about the appalling disruptions to our plans caused by the building delays. The information Fay used was not confidential, but it was comprehensive. For the first time, Rayne sang what was to become a familiar song: 'In future nothing can appear without the consent of the Board'. I confronted him on this, saying the director of the National was a public figure who obviously had to be sensitive to the Board's feelings and desires, but could not be like a ventriloquist's doll. Our clash of views about the press rumbled on for the next fifteen years, with neither of us giving an inch.

In the spring of 1987 Mrs Thatcher was in Moscow where she revealed a sudden and surprising enthusiasm for culture when promoting an 'artswop' deal between Britain and the Soviets. I sent a letter to *The Times* pointing out that while the Prime Minister was boasting abroad about the achievements of our arts, she was busy cutting their subsidies at home. I copied the letter to Max. He replied that to publish would be counter-productive to the interests of the National, and that if I did he might have to disassociate himself from it.

When my letter was printed, that is what he did. He wrote to *The Times* stating how deeply deplorable it would be if my letter detracted from Mrs Thatcher's fine achievements in Russia.

This caused the *Evening Standard* mockingly to wonder whether 'the National Theatre might become as good as gold when its insubordinate director leaves next spring'. Meanwhile, the British Council surprised us by setting aside £100,000 for the NT to go to Russia. This was (for then) generosity on an unprecedented scale. Thelma Holt, in charge of the visit, told Max it was 'one hundred per cent due to Peter's sabre-rattling'.

Max did not think so. Our relationship over the whole of my directorship, despite being amazingly productive and loyal on both sides, never had the same candour and warmth as I had with Fordie Flower at the RSC. Max and I, though in the event we managed very well, were not natural collaborators. Private and elusive, his way was to seek a word in the corridors of power. Rightly or wrongly, I was rumbustious and outspoken. I believed that a national theatre company in receipt of public funds was a political organisation and needed to be publicly discussed. Indeed, it was our only weapon when the government was so obviously out of sympathy with us and the performing arts generally.

An incident similar to my *Times* letter gave me the opportunity to put on paper to Rayne exactly why I responded to our problems as I did. I wrote: 'Of course I am sorry that you think I am damaging the National Theatre by discussing the lowering of subsidy levels to the arts, in public. If I thought that myself, I wouldn't do it. I believe that to stay quiet when you see something that you believe is fundamentally important to the whole country being dismantled is morally not right, and tactically ridiculous. We live in a democracy. Free discussion is the only way to highlight problems. If I wanted to be pompous, I would quote a hero of mine, Edmund Burke: "All that is necessary for the triumph of evil is that good men do nothing".'

Now it is different. Richard Eyre, my successor, has shown brilliantly that he can run the National and keep his head well down. On the other hand, I like to think that the toughest battles have been fought. He inherited a thriving organisation, and so far has not needed to harangue the government. I hope he never will.

– 5 –

It was obvious in 1975 that, while work on the Olivier and the Cottesloe was way behind schedule, the Lyttelton was more advanced. Why not plan to be playing there in the spring of the following year, and open the other two theatres as they were completed? It was a tussle to get this agreed. Architects and contractors don't like handing over buildings until they are finished, and government departments are always unhappy to support what could be seen in the end as a rash idea. However, backed by Max Rayne, I had my way. And this 'foot-in-the-door' policy got us started – with Peggy Ashcroft in Beckett's *Happy Days* opening the Lyttelton one March afternoon in 1976.

Thus Peggy and Sam Beckett, two people I loved dearly, inaugurated the whole building. In the same week we added four more productions from the Old Vic: Ben Travers's *Plunder*, superbly directed by Michael Blakemore, *John Gabriel Borkman*, *Hamlet*, and Osborne's new play *Watch it Come Down*. We were launched at last. *No Man's Land* followed successfully in April; *The Playboy of the Western World* in June.

It was, however, the hectic opening week in March that gave us the springboard we needed. I wrote in my *Diaries* that it had been a 'bit of a triumph'. The Lyttelton was packed.

A few days later the associate directors had an evening meeting. We were in a celebratory mood. Then Michael Blakemore asked if he could have our attention and, after a short preamble, eyes staring and in a strained voice, read out a paper he had prepared. It was a half-hour indictment of me and the way I ran the National. He said the associate directors had no power, but merely rubber-stamped my decisions, often without being consulted. He brought up the fact that I went on to commercial rates when NT productions I had directed transferred to the West End, despite this being established practice (sanctified by the Arts Council) for all directors in the subsidised theatre, including of course Michael himself. He predicted that there was a revolution breeding in the company; that the technial staff were unregarded and unappreciated; and that there was a series of press attacks on the way. Harold Pinter asked him to be more specific. 'I cannot name names,' he said.

I was very angry, but did my best to stay calm while trying to deal with his criticisms, particularly his main one: did the associates have less power than they

272

wanted? There was a discussion and it was generally felt that this was not true. Michael maintained that the associates should be called an advisory body. I said advice was easy to obtain; I wanted responsibility, commitment and, if necessary, agreement to disagree. I was trying to practise cabinet government.

The meeting was inconclusive. Blakemore had not aroused support. At the end, he asked those there to take his paper away to study. He had handed it out before he read it. But as we broke up, John Schlesinger passed his copy back and everyone followed suit. Their gesture clearly marked a refusal to consider the matter any further. By May, Michael had resigned.

A few weeks after the Blakemore thunderclap, there was the expected aftermath. Gaia Servadio went for me in the *Evening Standard*, replaying Michael's accusations, adding I was taking on too much, and warning of my downfall. This was followed later by (incredibly) three further big attacks in the same paper by Max Hastings, developing similar themes along with a new one – our supposed extravagance. The *Standard* had A Cause. They were dedicated, I thought, to getting me out of the job. Some other newspapers took up the story. I became, so they said, 'beleaguered'. Tom Stoppard and Arnold Goodman, however, defended me vigorously in print from many of these blows; so did Michael Billington in the *Guardian*; and Stephen Fay in the *Sunday Times* wrote that the NT was 'the target of an increasingly spiteful and envious campaign'.

Meanwhile, though the profession were still frightened of the new power of the National, the public had taken Denys Lasdun's building to its heart. Many, it is true, disliked the outside appearance, but the inside spaces were an unqualified success. We did fantastic business, despite the hottest summer for years. I wrote in July: 'Crowds of people milling around the theatre this lunch-time. A kite-flying festival by the river, a Dixieland

273

band playing on the terraces, hordes of children watching a puppet show near the main entrance, a full house for the *Hamlet* matinée. Wine is flowing freely in the bars. It's the way this building has to be – a place for a party.'

The fun was soon interrupted. In August our first strike closed the building for four days. I was about to start technical rehearsals for *Tamburlaine* in the Olivier – which the play was due to open – when some sixty stage staff walked out, refusing to work that theatre while also working the Lyttelton. This was in the middle of negotiations for a new backstage agreement. The real problem, though, was not the issue but the ringleaders. We had some troublemakers who saw the vast new building as a great opportunity for political unrest and material gain. We reckoned even then that by not sacking them, we were storing up trouble for the future.

I resisted such an extreme step at this stage. I thought that direct confrontation might close us down for months just when we had begun, and I didn't believe we could survive that.

Three of the many talented people who worked with me through the first years on the South Bank were Peter Stevens, who was general administrator; my old friend Michael Birkett, who was my deputy; and Simon Relph who had the hardest job of all, looking after the workshops and the stage staff. Peter and Simon thought we should have risked a big strike. I, however, backed by the Board, went for a compromise solution. This decision nearly split the management apart. But the men returned to work.

We had been in an ugly situation. Most of the Old Vic stage crew had come to the South Bank with us. They were a volatile and greedy combination of militant Marxists backed by members of the South London heavy mob who were extreme Tories to a man. They had been attracted to the Vic during Olivier's time because of the huge sums they could earn working a major repertory of plays in a cramped Victorian theatre. Every night they stayed on into the small hours, changing the sets for the next day's performance. The overtime money gushed.

It is not enough to finish building a new theatre: there has to be time to make it function properly. I thought the architecture magnificent, but very little worked at the National during that first improbable year. The doors stuck, the hinges screamed hideously when late-comers were admitted, and the stage-lighting switch-boards regularly plunged us into darkness. The address system calling the actors bled through from the dressing rooms into the auditoriums and startled the public. The ventilation system overheated the air in the hot summer and froze it as the autumn chill arrived. Everybody – actors, staff and audience – lost their way: Denys Lasdun's direction signs were so tasteful as to be in-visible. An actor in *Plunder* who, true to Ben Travers, spent an entire act in pyjamas, found himself in the foyer rather than in the wings and couldn't navigate his way back to the stage. 'Teething troubles' said the builders philosophically, as yet another set of snags presented themselves.

I am obsessed with the need for silence in the theatre. Without it, audiences and actors cannot concentrate. Before the Olivier opened, I was anxious that its air conditioning should be soundless, and was taken in to hear it by Denys and Peter Softley, his partner. The plant was turned on. It was like the thunder of an ocean-going liner. I said it would be impossible to act against the noise. Peter Softley told me it was silent. I asked him to listen again. He repeated that it was silent. He then explained that the Olivier acoustics were of such an exceptionally high standard they picked up noise where ordinary acoustics would not.

We lived in this Alice-in-Wonderland atmosphere for eighteen months as we gradually opened more and

more of the building. Quite a lot of the time we laughed.
Occasionally I had to cry.

– 6 –

During our four-day strike the troublemakers were
led by a romantic-looking shop-steward, Kon Fredericks.
I remember him saying that our computerised and
supposedly very advanced stage machinery was unwork-
able. As it was designed partly to cut manning levels,
he was hardly unbiased. But he had a point: the
installations couldn't be trusted to operate on cue,
and the automatic flying systems often, and with many
a twitch, went up when they should have gone down, and
down when they should have gone up.

The famous drum revolve in the Olivier was especially
elaborate and complicated. Conceived to sink one
entire set into the basement while, at the same
time, corkscrewing another up on to the stage, it
remained unfinished and virtually unusable throughout
the first five years of its existence. Now it works and
has featured in a number of plays, including a lavish
Pygmalion, almost obscured by its twirling sets, and
the spectacular *Wind in the Willows*. But it is still
not entirely dependable. Jane Asher tells me that she
came up on its revolving stage recently, making her
first entrance in *The School for Scandal*, and found
herself facing not the audience but the back wall of
the Olivier.

I don't, on the whole, like machinery in the theatre.
Yet at Glyndebourne, at Bayreuth, and at theatres all
over the world, I have allowed myself to be captured by its
lure. Hour after hour of precious rehearsal time has been
spent waiting in darkened auditoriums while technical

boffins explain why something which was intended to work with amazing efficiency is not working at all. Even so, I have to say that Bill Dudley's vision of Brunnehilde fading through the mists at Bayreuth, or John Bury's recreation of Baroque opera at Glyndebourne, are images I shall never forget.

In the Nineties, extremely elaborate design has become fashionable in the theatre. No doubt this is partly the influence of special-effect movies (which I love) and video games; partly the new opportunities offered by high-tech stage machinery; and partly a response to the fast-growing popularity of opera and its visually more opulent world. Spectacle can indeed be a potent aspect of play production. But the theatre is about imagination, not actuality. My ideal theatre would use machinery to make the changeovers in repertory from one play to another easier and cheaper, more than as an outright encouragement of spectacle.

– 7 –

The Lyttelton had got off to a splendid start with *Happy Days* and *Plunder*, though the first-ever tickets for the National carried the misprint 'Blunder'. I sometimes wondered whether my foot-in-the-door policy was just that.

Because the completion of the Olivier was repeatedly postponed, I rehearsed the play that was to open it, *Tamburlaine*, on and off for six months. In that hot summer of 1976, in despair as to whether we would ever be able to stage the production and urgently needing to contact an audience with our work, we performed some scenes outside on the river terraces while the traffic roared by on Waterloo Bridge. The spectators were those who happened to be passing. Many stopped and watched, fascinated by the central figure of Albert Finney in the name part, rakishly wearing a beribboned straw hat against the beating sun.

To our surprise and delight, this rough venture in the open air helped us to define the style of the play. It was public advocacy, each character asking the approval of the audience for his or her actions. And when *Tamburlaine* finally inaugurated the Olivier in early October, Albert, surviving severe bronchitis, was magnificent. The drama took the stage and sang. We had successfully launched the second and largest and, in my view, most exciting of our three theatres.

Three weeks later, however, we had to negotiate another big occasion: the official opening of the new building in the presence of the Queen and an auditorium packed with assorted grandees. Because of the constant building delays, my plans had kept changing, and all I could salvage which seemed suitable was a light, short, seemingly amusing comedy by Goldoni, *Il Campiello*. Bill Bryden directed it in the Olivier for half of the official audience, while the other half watched Tom Stoppard's *Jumpers* in the Lyttelton. They arrived in torrential rain, a dismal start which foreshadowed a nightmare evening. Its only bright spot was at the very beginning when Larry spoke movingly from the stage named after him; he was never, alas, well enough to appear on it again.

The Goldoni was a disaster. So was the special fanfare version of *God Save the Queen* which Harry Birtwistle had commissioned from Howarth Davies. Harry and I had thought it sounded well, if somewhat progressive, when rehearsed. But on the night it was horrible. The Queen visibly shuddered as if she had sipped lemon juice. The band had been augmented at the last moment by trumpeters of the Household Cavalry who provided many shrill and nervous mistakes, heightening, if anything, the modernity of the arrangement. The royal opening had made a piece of history by being about as big a flop as could be imagined.

Although we were by now in the late autumn of 1976, the Cottesloe was still unfinished. Not until the following spring, in March, were we able to use it. It began life with Ken Campbell's and Chris Langham's *Illuminatus*, an eight-hour epic by the Science Fiction Theatre of Liverpool. This was original, anarchic and funny, and I was delighted to have something at the National which represented the Fringe.

As time passed, the Cottesloe proved to be the most flexible and, to many, the most interesting of our three theatres. It is a space where new work can be done at not too high a risk, and without it we would have cut ourselves off from new writing. A new play put on in the Olivier or the Lyttelton has to be not only fully achieved but of a certain size.

Unbelievably, the Arts Council early on had tried their best to remove the Cottesloe from the architect's designs: they believed the Fringe and the Royal Court provided sufficient studio-type auditoriums. But Denys Lasdun knew something which nobody else did, and made sure that the area set aside for the Cottesloe, deep in the bowels of the building, was kept. It was (appropriately) part of the foundations.

So by the spring of 1977, I thought I had completed my obstacle course. I had got through it: the National was open, and working, and full. But Jacky told a friend that I often woke in the middle of the night, shouting.

There were great compensations, however. In the year the Cottesloe opened I collaborated for the first time with Alan Ayckbourn. I had invited him and a number of other leading dramatists to write new plays for our start on the South Bank. Harold Pinter, Robert Bolt, John Osborne, David Hare, Stephen Poliakoff and Howard Brenton had all delivered; Alan's contribution was *Bedroom Farce* which we directed together.

Its announcement caused a severe attack of pious

indignation in the press. Was it right, they sniffed, for the National Theatre to stage such a commercial writer? I was furious. I had long believed that Alan was one of our major dramatists. To social historians in the twenty-first century his plays will be essential reading if they are to understand what it was like to live in Britain in the Seventies and Eighties. I found it imposs- ible to accept the argument of the press. A subsidised theatre does not exist to do only those plays that are so difficult (and possibly so boring) that nobody else will put them on. It is there to cherish excellence in every form.

Staging *Bedroom Farce* alongside Alan allowed me to appreciate his extraordinary skill as a director. At that time he had not directed in London – only at his small theatre in Scarborough. But during the next fifteen years, his work at the National established him as a consummate director of other people's plays as well as his own. He also emerged over those NT years as a great dramatist, and was increasingly recognised as such.

Alan's working methods are by now well charted. Before he even begins to write a play he has to know what he will call it, the cast, and when rehearsals start. He also has to know that the date of the first night has been announced and that tickets are on sale. Deadlines galvanise him into action: he recognises that he can best write within a set period and when there is no escape from the task.

I count Alan as a friend both in work and in life. He has helped me through several severe personal crises. And unlike many great writers of comedy, he is not only genuinely witty, but compassionate. He is very shy, as are many theatre people, and sometimes I am sure the black dogs of melancholy attack his spirit – though this is always well-hidden. An acute under- standing of the bleakness of life is underneath all the laughter in his plays; and loneliness, embarrassment and the intrinsic absurdity of sex are his themes.

He is a complex man of the theatre, and his plays have a profound sense of what works, born of an experience comparable to Molière's or Goldoni's. All these men tested their work on a live audience. Alan's great strength is that he never stays still: his plays go on developing, offering a deeper and often darker vision.

His dialogue is meticulous in word and punctuation. It sounds naturalistic, but it has a rhythm and choice of vocabulary which are entirely his. This precise text both supports the actors and limits them. What an Ayckbourn character must do is very clearly prescribed, and the actor cannot move out of this without spoiling the rhythm of the play and the truth of the comedy. Thus, inexpert actors are made better by the clarity and precision of his writing, whereas imaginative actors can find playing him a little restricting, once they have succeeded in fulfilling his considerable demands. This ability to define his characters within exact limits is something that Alan shares with all the masters. We are a fortunate age to have had our own Molière.

– 8 –

Granville-Barker is Britain's unsung dramatist. He was clearly our first great director, and his *Prefaces to Shakespeare* remain the most practical guide among all the countless books on that over-scrutinised subject. Without Granville-Barker's inspiration, there probably would not be a National Theatre. He articulated what it could do and campaigned for its existence throughout his life. So one of the joys of my early period at the NT was getting Bill Gaskill to stage *The Madras House*. The production was beautiful, the text full of rich paradox, and Bill sustained the wit with a perfect sense of early twentieth-century society.

Another joy was my friend Maximilian Schell's production of *Tales from the Vienna Woods* by Ödon von Horvath – a major European dramatist being performed in England for the first time.

It is unlikely that either of these productions could have happened without the existence of a national theatre. The same is certainly true of a major reclamation begun by Bill Bryden around this time. On a bright, cold Easter Saturday in 1977 (it even snowed a little) he directed *The Crucifixion* outside the theatre on its river terraces. This was the start of a project that was to grow into an epic trilogy, brilliantly adapted by Tony Harrison from the ancient English Mystery Plays. The designs were by Bill Dudley, and the Albion Band provided the music.

It brought medieval drama back to life, and was developed by Bill over eight years into the three-play cycle known as *The Mysteries*, which moved from *The Creation* to *Doomsday*. It was performed as a promenade production in the Cottesloe with audiences mingling among the performers and creating natural playing spaces for the action. But it all began that cold Easter Saturday on the terraces when the absorbed crowds visibly flinched as Jesus was nailed to the Cross.

It was an astonishing afternoon that made me glad I had been able to resist the Board members who had urged me not only to fire Bill after the disaster of *Il Campiello* at our Royal opening, but were proposing themselves as a play-reading committee to safeguard the National against future flops.

I had admired Bill's talents since seeing, some years earlier, a production in Scotland of a play he had written himself called *Willie Rough*. He is a director who needs particular conditions. For him, work in the theatre has to be work among friends; he has to feel himself to be the genial captain of the team in order to give of his best. Many thought that when rehearsing he did more good work on the play in the Green Room bar than in the rehearsal room. His Cottesloe company was matey, boozy and extremely male.

Bill's strengths are his obsessions: he is totally loyal to his friends and to his ideas. And he did wonderful productions in the Cottesloe – from Mamet to O'Neill and from *Lark Rise* to *The Mysteries*. When occasionally he moved into the larger spaces of the Lyttelton or the Olivier, the impact was less powerful.

I have always been bad at knowing what will shock people in the theatre – I suppose because I am not shocked myself by anything that is honest to the meaning of a piece. In 1977, Tony Harrison and Harrison Birtwistle collaborated on *Bow Down*. The play contained strong language and disturbing situations, but seemed to me to have integrity. Princess Margaret did not take the same view. She saw it on a semi-official visit, and despatched a message to Max Rayne forcefully expressing her extreme displeasure. He was greatly perturbed. My belief that living theatre should provoke, and Max's fear that provocative theatre might not win or keep us our necessary friends, now and again came between him and me. Max was broadminded himself; but he was continually anxious because he well understood that others might not be. The *Bow Down* trouble blew over, but the royal disapproval was often referred to as a cautionary tale.

However, even I was worried (though enchanted) when I saw the preview of a Cottesloe pantomime based on *The Hunchback of Notre Dame*. It was deliberately rude, crude, and high-spirited. Michael Bogdanov directed it with exuberance, and it had in David Rappaport an extraordinary dwarf performer who at one point made a human missile of himelf, hurling his tiny body at a series of vast locked doors. There was community singing when the audience joined in the lyric, 'Bums and tits, bums and tits – having it away'. At a later performance this was objected to by a lady as chauvinism; she led the audience in an alternative version, 'bums and pricks'. I sat at the preview in some trepidation. Christ, I thought, this is the National's family Christmas show! But the packed house of children, my own among them, were helpless with giggles and adored it. Indeed Edward and Lucy sang 'bums and tits' for some time regularly at breakfast. It was obviously a children's dream-come-true to sing rude words in public at the National Theatre; and to see adults being as rude as themselves. I wondered who would write to the chairman about it. Surprisingly, no-one did.

– 9 –

I was trying at this time to do something I attempted more than once over the years. It wasn't enough, I thought, to seek the best actors, the best plays and the best directors. By doing that I was well on the way to turning the building into a high-class cultural department store. What I wanted was to provide the place with an identifiable aesthetic. I knew from my RSC years that a cohesive company of actors, concentrating mainly on one dramatist, could forge a recognisable style. But that was an impossible objective for the National. Its brief was to stage plays from Aeschylus to Brenton; moreover, we had three theatres that were entirely different, with nothing in common architecturally. They shared only one characteristic: a need to be filled with audiences at every performance.

It seemed to me from the beginning that a division, either into separate companies within each theatre, or into separate companies that moved around our three stages, was the only way to achieve particularity. Our actors numbered over a hundred – too many to develop an ensemble feeling. I was very aware that our best productions at the RSC had been done by a group of some thirty or forty people, the absolute maximum if the actors are to know each other and thus work well together.

But in order to divide up our large company into smaller groups, I needed impresario talent. Only a few first-class directors of plays are also impresarios, or indeed want to be. I asked Stuart Burge to join me. At first he said yes, but then backed out. He had suddenly been asked to run the Royal Court which was in serious trouble. Then I asked Terry Hands, who had indicated he was ready to leave the RSC. My idea was that Terry and I should each head a crack Olivier ensemble, while Christopher Morahan ran the Lyttelton, and Bill Bryden the Cottesloe. Terry said yes, while making it clear that he wanted to be my number two. I had reservations about this. Finally, Trevor Nunn persuaded Terry to co-direct the RSC with him and this was clearly a better job.

These early frustrations were compounded by Paul Scofield. He had given a magnificent performance in the production I did of *Volpone* and he was also very fine in Bill Gaskill's *Madras House*. I asked Paul if he would head my Olivier group, and initially he was very enthusiastic. 'How exciting, how marvellous,' he said. Then came the inevitable letter saying no. Paul combines a generous instinct for the new and exciting with a deep natural caution. There is often an aftermath.

Eventually, I found the solution to realising the National's full potential: three or four separate directors each heading a company and each company giving three plays in repertory – one in the Olivier, one in the Lyttelton and one in the Cottesloe. Out of this came some superlative productions from Ayckbourn's company, and also from the one led by Ian McKellen and Edward Petherbridge. The work was individual and special to each group. It provided a rich amount of roles for the actors, and thus opportunity for growth; also three very different stages on which to perform. The scheme was set up late in my time at the National and, though expensive, because it used more actors, it was beginning to flourish as I prepared to leave. I am sad that it did not continue.

– 10 –

In May 1977 we had another strike. This time the cause was absurd. Ralph Cooper, a plumber and shop steward who had been repeatedly warned about the quality of his work, was sacked for not fixing two wash basins. The resulting walkout closed the theatre for four days and thirteen performances were lost. Cooper was reinstated pending arbitration and then kept on because of a technicality. Seven months later he was again dismissed for inefficiency, this time successfully.

My chief memory of those lost performances is the helplessness of well-intentioned liberals like Chris Morahan, Michael Bryant and myself in the face of expert extremists. At this time, union power was sanctified and absolute, and it was genuinely difficult for managers to manage. The plumber's strike, however, had one advantage. It prepared us for what lay ahead. We began to develop the know-how that was to help us through the disruptions by the stage staff in the coming year, led by Kon Fredericks, and the terrible strike of 1979. But well before these crises hit us, we had troubles of another kind.

The National Theatre was created by Act of Parliament, and the building was paid for by the government and by the Greater London Council. But in typical British fashion, these begetters of the dream had never settled who was to foot the bills for the upkeep of the building once it was there. Nor were its running costs ever evaluated. I suspect that those who should have worked out these figures had kept diplomatically quiet; they feared the whole enterprise would be doomed if the true running costs were known. By the autumn of 1977, the National was in appalling financial straits despite the fact that we were hugely successful with the public and our box office was booming. The trouble was caused partly by the building delays, partly by the strikes of that year and the year before, but mainly because it was only now becoming apparent that the place was hideously expensive to run before even a single play was performed.

At last, a special government grant rescued us; but we could no longer afford visiting companies: there just wasn't the money. This was a bitter blow. I had wanted the National to welcome great foreign companies regularly. The RSC, in my time, had put on Peter Daubeny's twelve illuminating World Theatre Seasons at the Aldwych. So I knew at first hand how renewing to the British theatre such work was. In the National's first eighteen months on the South Bank, we had been able to present the TNP from Lyon in productions by Roger Planchon and Patrice Chéreau (*Tartuffe* and *La Dispute* respectively); the Schaubühne from West Berlin in Gorky's *Summerfolk*, which staggered audiences and was Peter Stein's London debut; and the astonishing Spanish actress and director Nuria Espert in *Divinas Palabras*.

Now all this had to end. We were caught in a bureaucratic absurdity. The British Council exists to promote British arts abroad; the Arts Council exists to promote British arts at home; but nobody exists to promote foreign art in Britain. Peter Daubeny, with fervent tenacity, had regularly blackmailed the governments of the foreign companies into paying themselves for the chance of appearing in London. Unfortunately, those days – and, sadly, Peter – had gone. Why, asked the French and the Germans, weren't we, as the National Theatre, able to get additional funds from the British government towards the cost of presenting productions from abroad? Their own governments did, the other way round.

I tried to rehearse *The Country Wife* during the height of the financial crisis. To make matters worse, this was my first (and only) attempt at a Restoration comedy, so I was dealing with an unfamiliar world. Although there were pleasures along the way – among them a cast including Albert Finney, Susan Littler and Richard Johnson – the production was a failure. The energy I draw from rehearsals and can then reapply to administration just wasn't there. Normally, I find few things more satisfying than the concentration of the rehearsal room after the hurly-burly of the office. But at this time, the task was too daunting in both departments and my work as a director unquestionably suffered.

I was also disappointed by my production of *The Cherry Orchard* at the start of 1978. It had a dazzling cast: Albert Finney, Dorothy Tutin, Robert Stephens, Susan Fleetwood, Ben Kingsley and – crowning it – Ralph Richardson as Firs. Rehearsals were exhilarating. And, though it was over twenty-five years since *Uncle Vanya* at Cambridge, my last attempt at Chekhov, I found my belief that his comedy is about the complete and painful disregard that one character has for another still valid. But once we moved from the rehearsal room into the great spaces of the Olivier, the play simply vanished. All the interplay between the actors seemed to disappear. The Olivier is a theatre for dialectical discussion and big epic statements. Irony, ambiguity, delicacy and the eloquence of the unsaid are very difficult to convey in it.

I followed *The Cherry Orchard* with Albert Finney and Dorothy Tutin in *Macbeth*. I didn't want to do

Macbeth again, but had promised Albert I would. It proved to me once more that a most crucial decision for any director is whether he or she really *wants* to do the play. It is most unlikely to succeed unless an intense appetite for the job is there. The strength of that feeling has to carry you through many weeks of stressful rehearsals. I have done rigorous intellectual tasks and I have done hard physical labour as a farm worker, but nothing I have done is anything like as hard, physically or emotionally, as directing a play. Ninagawa, the great Japanese director, has said: 'Since I became a director, there hasn't been a time when I didn't have a pain in my stomach.'

My *Macbeth* was honest, plain – and dull. John Bury and I tried to set an example by doing it economically. We ended up doing it boringly. The notices for me and for Albert were terrible. I was very upset for Albert. Without him, I know I would not have succeeded in getting the building open. He was staunch through all our difficulties. But after the set-back of *Macbeth* his attitude towards the National and towards me changed. His agent, Laurie Evans, told me that Albert felt he had been exploited. Failure always brings unhappiness, and I was saddened to realise that I had lost not only a collaborator but a friend.

There were other antagonisms in the air that were less rational. I was riding down the Strand in a taxi after a lunch appointment when I saw placards for the *Evening News* plastered with a chilling announcement: A NATIONAL DISASTER. Was it Aintree or us?

When I reached the theatre, I was handed the paper. The whole of its front page was given over to this 'disaster', under the headline THEATRE CHIEF PETER HALL ACCUSED. Of what? A book on the National Theatre by John Elsom was about to be published in which he made it clear that his idea of how the place should be run was very different from mine.

It was evident that the source of the *Evening News* story was the material in this book, suitably hotted up. And the book itself, when it appeared, made me feel very raw-skinned, with its reiteration of extravagance and mismanagement. But it received little further attention. Harold Hobson in a review wrote that 'the author has allowed himself to be run away with by prejudice and personal feeling'. I felt better, picked myself up and went on.

Work kept me going, and I was supported by my friends in the profession. At home it was lonely. Jacky never mentioned the shock of the *Evening News*. We shielded ourselves from each other and there was a cold silence. It was an encouragement when the Board extended my contract by three years, giving me a total of another five. I felt I now had the time to sweat out the battle.

It pleased me that, in 1978, the National was putting on more and more new plays: indeed, they began to be the most popular part of our repertory. We presented David Mamet's *American Buffalo*, Edward Bond's *The Woman*, and David Hare's *Plenty*. I had admired David's work ever since *Knuckle*. He developed into a major writer during my time at the NT, and his distinctive voice began to be heard by large audiences. *Plenty* was a crucial part of this, and demonstrated the strength of repertory. The notices were not good, and in the West End the play would have been lucky to last a fortnight. But I believed in it and was able to keep it on, nursing it carefully by giving it only a few performances, and those towards the end of each week. Within three months, it was drawing full houses. The public had decided they liked the play, and if it had not achieved this success on the South Bank it would never have been done in America, nor become a film.

Plenty was introduced to me when David appeared in my office sporting what I'm sure was a deliberately torn sweater. He told me that if I would commit to doing the play, he might be prepared to let me read it, and placed it on my desk.

He is one of the warmest and most generous men I know, but he carefully hides these qualities under an icy and prickly manner that is sardonic and flip by turns. As a writer he is fastidious in his use of words, and the same goes for his productions. The total effect is sometimes chilly, but he can be a formidable director. When I was starting at the National, he did a touring production of Trevor Griffiths's *The Party*. I took him out to lunch and asked him what he would like to direct next. *'King Lear,'* he replied without hesitation. It was the only classic play that interested him and he was not prepared to waste time, as he saw it, on doing any others. Much later, in 1986, he staged it in the Olivier, not very successfully I'm afraid, with Anthony Hopkins as Lear. The production was a combination of amazing insights and inexpertness. I was to blame: it is not a play to begin on, even if you are as talented as David.

He is naturally paranoid, nervous and edgy. In the early days, I felt he was suspicious, wanting to cast me as the cigar-smoking producer who was waiting to stamp on his darlings. But gradually, I think, he learned to trust me.

Edward Bond is even more touchy. There is no question about his status as a dramatist; there is also no question that his defensiveness has cut him off from the mainstream of the theatre. Yet it needs him as much as he needs it. Over the last years, he has become a proud misanthropist, distrusting most actors, and disliking most productions and all directors. He is much like John Osborne: they are both exuberantly abusive on paper, but charming and very human face to face.

Edward can elevate class prejudice until it becomes almost racist. He didn't want to have Sebastian Graham-Jones as his assistant director when he discovered that

Sebastian had been at Harrow.

In Glyndebourne that summer of 1978, I found yet
again that a month working in Sussex, if possible on
Mozart, was far better for me than a holiday at the
seaside. It seemed I could still do no wrong in opera and
this particular time was golden. I was adding *Così fan
tutte*, the last and most difficult of the three Da Ponte
operas, to *Figaro* and *Don Giovanni* – and I met Maria
Ewing.

I knew that my marriage to Jacky was dead and that
nothing would resuscitate it. I worried about Edward
and Lucy and could see no course of action that would
solve the situation without pain. So I did nothing and
became neurotic.

But within less than a year of meeting Maria, the
passion unleashed was so violent that I ceased to be
anxious about either my family or public pressures.

– 11 –

I had always dreamed of a theatre at the centre of
society. I now had my wish: the new National was
certainly that. Its high profile made it very political: it
was used as an argument by both parties to grind their
own axes. The extreme Left suspected it of being elitist
and not community-based; the Right believed it to be a
hotbed of Left-wing playwrights, and the resort of actors
and directors living on subsidy.

Throughout 1978, the fight went on to establish the
National as a theatre that could justifiably claim the
finance to do the job that was expected of it. In this
we were greatly strengthened by the enthusiasm of the
public, who by this time would have been vociferous had
the NT closed.

Putting on a play is always a social act. The choice of audience, time and place make it unavoidably a political act as well. The National with all its troubles became at this time an emblem, and a potent one, of the country itself. The ugly atmosphere of union confrontation, so unpleasant at the NT, increasingly paralysed the whole of Britain.

The grants for the following year were announced in the autumn and the National was given £130,000 less than the very tight budget we had submitted. More worrying still, there was a condition attached to the grant: we had to keep all wage offers within the government's five per cent pay policy. Our backstage staff did not accept this. Indeed, earlier they had asked for a thirty-five per cent raise. In November, they flexed their muscles with two token walkouts that caused a few cancelled performances. With the encouragement of the Board, the management sought the advice of a firm of industrial trouble-shooters. They advised that unless we could get the government's permission to break the pay code, we might as well close.

In the middle of this unease, I was trying to direct the premiere of Harold Pinter's *Betrayal*. Although rehearsals kept me sane and balanced, I was constantly concerned about whether I was giving the play the concentration it deserved, especially when there were growing threats that the opening might be halted by unofficial strike action. The climax came on the morning of the first night when the stage staff told us all, including the actors, that we would have to 'wait and see' if we would get through the performance. This did not help the actors' nerves, stretched already; and Harold Pinter and I sat in the audience wondering whether each cue for the small revolving stage to move – the production depended on it – would be the last.

In the event, nothing happened. And I reckoned that *Betrayal* was one of my best pieces of work at the National for some time. But it was not an apt moment for a play of this kind. Michael Billington dismissed it in the *Guardian* as 'the amatory exploits of upper middle-class intellectuals'. Time has shown it to be much more than that.

A fragile peace was negotiated with the stage staff towards the end of the year. But I was convinced that chaos would soon return. Union confrontation was everywhere; it seemed a civil war in all but name was about to start. Who ran the country? Its elected representatives, or its self-perpetuating union leaders? On the day *Betrayal* opened, *The Times* printed its last copy for almost twelve months. Many thought it might be the last copy ever.

The strike that nearly broke the National, the really big one, started on 16 March 1979. On that day about seventy backstage workers walked out, beginning an unofficial strike over work shifts and pay that lasted ten weeks. It cost us – apart from the horrible expense of spirit – about £250,000 and initially closed all three theatres. But by the time it petered out in late May, few actual performances had been lost. Rather than not perform, we presented the plays in limited decor, or in the wrong sets (the staff who should have changed them were outside the building); sometimes in the wrong theatre. The actors had refused to support the strikers, so we were able to keep partial faith with the public, though audiences, even at the reduced prices, were often small.

After three weeks of negotiation, the strikers were dismissed. All were offered reinstatement if they signed a guarantee to take no more unofficial action, and eventually some did sign. But outside the theatre, over the next painful month and more, there was a permanent picket, complete with the full impedimenta of industrial action – including huts and braziers. It was a sight that was becoming a nightly cliché on television news.

The absurdity was that the union had declared the

picket official, yet lacked the courage to declare the same about the strike.

I hated it all: the naked hostility between the factions; the breaking up of friendships and of decencies; the sheer hypocrisy of some of the strikers and the cowardice of their union in not disciplining them and upholding agreements. Trust disappeared and with it any respect for the truth. I loathed seeing my father's progressive ideals perverted into blatant self-interest.

A vote was taken in the end to make the strike official; it was heavily defeated. The air, apparently, was thick with cries of 'betrayal' from the extremists, and with fragments of torn up NATTKE union cards. Following this, Len Murray, then general secretary of the TUC, intervened and ruled that the huts outside the theatre should go. Soon after, the strike suddenly and mysteriously collapsed. The management was branded by some as right-wing and union-bashing. But there was general praise for the stand the National had made. To sustain the sacking of seventy men at this particular point in the country's social history was fairly astounding. Alone at that time we had withstood unofficial industrial anarchy.

Our own crisis was of course just one outcome of the Winter of Discontent. In January, Denis Healey had warned on the radio that Britain was on the brink of ruin. Even those on whom we relied for our lives – the ambulance, water and sewage workers – even those who buried the dead, were striking. After decades of abuse, the workers, having at last gained some power and the capability of protecting themselves, were, in turn, abusing that power. It was understandable; but they were led by a new cast of trade union barons whose chief aim seemed to be chaos.

During all this turbulence, I had slept little and talked much: life was a perpetual stormy meeting. I was depressed and exhausted and had to keep reminding myself that we had achieved something at the National.

For, in truth, we couldn't say we were the out-and-out winners. Indeed, can such a claim ever be made by either side at the end of a violent disruption such as ours?

There were comical moments, however. Soon after the strike folded some of the sacked men halted a performance of *The Double Dealer* by climbing on the stage shouting abuse at the management. The audience were appalled; and among them was my friend, the playwright Simon Gray, who stood up and coolly challenged the accusations. His wife went further: she stepped up to the stage to argue a point, was pushed aside by a demonstrator, and hit him hard round the face. The audience applauded and the demonstrator threatened legal action for grievous bodily harm.

The press coverage of the strike was dramatic and, on the whole, fair. One piece, though, did not please me very much. The *Evening News* yet again devoted an entire front page to the NT under a blaring headline, A NATIONAL DISGRACE. The strikers had supplied the paper with a score of wild allegations about the management's 'extravagances'. An example was Ralph Richardson's boots in *John Gabriel Borkman*, which, as an experiment, I had tried to amplify by placing small contact microphones in the heels so that his footsteps rang out ominously as he paced his vast salon. But on the wooden stage the sound had no edge, and I abandoned the idea. The *Evening News* claimed that this experiment (it sounded sensationally stupid in the reading) had wasted many hundreds of pounds. It hadn't.

Later the paper published our detailed refutation of everything we were accused of, but only, as always in these matters, tucked away on an inside page. Our complaint to the Press Council about this was upheld, though it, too, received remarkably little space.

I love reading newspapers, but sometimes wonder why. If they are printing a story that, because I have lived through it, I know well, nine times out of ten it is factually wrong, even allowing for the political or emotional bias of the paper. We expect, indeed encourage, our newspapers to be prejudiced. But we don't seem to mind if the need to make news and comment dramatic is often at the expense of the truth.

The crisis of the strike had bonded us all – directors, actors, management – together, and during it much good work had been done by the general administrator, Michael Elliott. This unity marked the end of the beginning of the new building, and although it had been tough going we emerged from it healthy and trim to start a very good period of work. The same did not happen to the country. Britain went into the long deception of Margaret Thatcher, putting off for longer the recognition of who we were and what we meant in a contracting world.

At the general election that May the country thudded to the Right. I too voted Tory – something I have never done before and have certainly not done since. Like many others, I believed the Conservatives to be the only party with the courage and the strength to sort out the unions. My father brought me up as a radical, believing in change as part of life, but he also taught me that all governments and institutions tend in time to become corrupt. The unions had become corrupt. They were now a threat to democracy.

Thatcher of course did sort out the unions; it is her abiding achievement. But I think few people realised in 1979 that she was going to change the face of the Tory Party as well. In the name of free-market dogma she devastated our education system, our broadcasting system and our performing arts. It is also now evident that her economic miracle was a sham founded on dismantling our manufacturing base while riding on the luck of North Sea oil and the international profitability of the City. We are paying in the Nineties for the excesses of the Eighties when, for the first time in our history, greed was turned into a shining virtue.

During the Thatcher years, I campaigned vigorously

for the arts and was not, as a consequence, popular with either the Arts Council or Downing Street. There was a story going round at the time which may well be true. One morning the prime minister heard me on the *Today* programme attacking the government's short-sighted policy on subsidy. Afterwards she greeted Richard Luce, the arts minister, with the question, 'When are we going to be able to stop giving money to awful people like Peter Hall?'

I have had several argumentative meetings with Mrs Thatcher, public and private. It was like talking to a suspicious headmistress who feared that artiness among the boys and girls might lead to softness and possible left-wing tendencies; they should all aim to get a proper job instead. On one occasion, taking me to task for complaining in public about the state of the British theatre, she pointed out that the British theatre was famous the world over. 'Look at Andrew Lloyd Webber,' she said. That comment can't, I'm sure, have had anything to do with the fact that Lloyd Webber is the richest composer in the history of music . . .

I can understand even now why I voted Tory. I very much wish that I hadn't had to.

– 12 –

In the spring of 1979 Ayckbourn's *Bedroom Farce*, which had been a big success on the South Bank, opened on Broadway with its original British cast. I could not remember a new play on Broadway (and certainly not a comedy) receiving such superlative notices. We thought we had an incontrovertible hit. But American Equity had ruled that our actors could only stay for ten weeks, so I went to New York and replaced them, when those weeks were up, with a very good American cast.

The play had been doing excellent business; but now this stopped with the suddenness of a tap being turned off. The British hit without British actors was, in the most supremely fashion-conscious town in the world, unfashionable overnight. Nobody came. American Equity had turned a big success into a failure.

Throughout my career, I have been angered by the prejudiced behaviour of both British and American Equity. I have never met an actor who did not lament the awfulness of the situation. The two unions seem content merely to run protection societies. Yet our countries share a common language and we certainly benefit by understanding each other's culture. It would enormously advantage our theatres if British plays could be done by British actors on Broadway and American plays by Americans in London. Instead, both unions are obstructionist and practise an unpleasant discrimination which allows 'stars' into either country without question, but which prevents lesser actors, however talented, from performing. This particularly hurts the young, and seems to me inequable in the extreme. It is as if British publishers refused to publish American books on the grounds that we have enough of our own books already. The only hope is government action on both sides of the Atlantic to insist on freedom and equality of opportunity.

That summer, at Glyndebourne, I directed *Fidelio*, Beethoven's great hymn to freedom, honesty and love. Elizabeth Söderstrom created a Leonora full of strength and beauty, yet devoid of sentimentality; and Bernard Haitink paced the opera so that it grew from a small domestic *singspiel* to the high epic aspirations of its finale. I had done a good piece of work. Nonetheless, Glyndebourne seemed an empty place without Maria. We had made a commitment to each other during this eventful year of strikes, tensions and overwork. I was trying to plan a way of disentangling myself from my marriage. There was no way forward without many hurts. I was tormented by the thought of facing my family with another break-up.

At the National, my fellow directors – Christopher Morahan, Harold Pinter, Peter Wood, Michael Rudman and Bill Bryden – were making the theatre healthy again after the long sickness of the strike. Peter's elegant production of Schnitzler's *Undiscovered Country* brought another unfamiliar play to the Olivier. And Michael's *Death of a Salesman* began the English canonisation of Arthur Miller. This also had a performance by Warren Mitchell as Willy Loman that remains with me as one of the half-dozen or so great pieces of character-acting I have seen. The personality of Loman was totally assimilated into the actor and the audience seemed to know everything about him. I would place Wilfrid Lawson in *The Father*, Peggy Ashcroft in *The Deep Blue Sea*, Ralph Richardson's Falstaff, Judi Dench's Cleopatra, Paul Scofield in *The Government Inspector* and Dustin Hoffman's final, New York version of Shylock in that same pantheon. They were all, in a sense, *imitations*, in that the actors concerned were not immediately like the characters portrayed. Yet in each case they had developed and emphasised the qualities in themselves that were in the role, until they became the whole person.

In November, Peter Shaffer's *Amadeus* opened in the Olivier. Although Shaffer had been a friend of mine for years (and I had done one play of his, *The Battle of Shrivings*, not very successfully in the West End), John Dexter was clearly Shaffer's director, having staged, dazzlingly, two of his biggest successes, *The Royal Hunt of the Sun* and *Equus*.

Shaffer has a questioning and vigorous spirit. His plays, in their first drafts, are sometimes slapdash and excessive, like vast oil sketches. There is often fine detail, but more that is approximate. They never, though, lack boldness, ambition and energy; and that energy sustains the essential refining that follows.

Some authors (Harold Pinter is a prime example) seldom change a word. They consider every comma before delivering their script to the director. Shaffer says he likes to 'carve' his text in rehearsal; there is constant cutting, shaping and altering. It is exhilarating for all concerned. But he needs actors and a director who are open to such a process and stimulated by working in that way. In the early stages the director is as much script-editor as the man who brings the play to life in the theatre.

Dexter had done all this on *Equus*, but when it came to *Amadeus* he said he was only prepared to do the same again if he was rewarded with an unusually large percentage of the play's world earnings. This was not only a precedent for directors in the future, it looked unreasonable. There was a quarrel between Shaffer and Dexter which I tried very hard to heal for most of the summer. I spent hours in the phone box at Glyndebourne on hot summer evenings speaking to one or the other. What I could not say was that from the moment I had read *Amadeus* I had wanted to direct it myself. The play fascinated me. It was about a composer I worshipped, and also dealt with one of the strangest of paradoxes to anybody who works among artists: that talent is randomly given and need not, indeed often does not, inhabit a decent person.

I did all I could to keep Dexter and Shaffer together, but in the end they split with simply no chance of reconciliation. After an interval, Peter asked me if I would direct the play, and I gladly agreed. Happily, John Dexter and I remained friends. He continued to work at the National and I worked for him a couple of times at the Metropolitan Opera, where for five years he was director of productions.

In August, Peter Shaffer and I took a quick trip to Vienna and to Salzburg in order to seal our partnership, talk through the play, and refresh ourselves about Mozart. There was, as well, a personal reason why I wanted to be in Salzburg. Maria was singing Cherubino there. It would be possible to see her and discuss our problems. As Peter and I drank Viennese white wine like lemonade, I explained the painful intricacies of my private life. He didn't judge; he listened. It was all a friend could do; and it was a help.

A month or so later I found myself immersed in rehearsals of *Amadeus*, with a cast which included Paul Scofield as Salieri, Felicity Kendal as Constanza, and Simon Callow as Mozart. Shaffer worked with his usual exuberance and creativity, but I think we all sensed that we were on a dangerous enterprise. Some of my colleagues had not been too keen on the play (one of them wrote it off as a dramatised sleeve-note for a record). We were also very conscious of the traps immortalised by Hollywood bio-pics: 'Good morning, Beethoven. Have you seen Haydn today?' How *do* you deal with historical giants without ludicrous name-dropping? How does a man called Mozart even make his first entrance? Peter Shaffer hit upon an idea. Unannounced, a small, pallid, large-eyed man in a showy wig and a showy set of clothes runs on and freezes. He is pretending to be a cat and stands immobile waiting for a mouse. He is playing a childish game, and Constanza is the mouse. Mozart was on stage.

Another big problem was the music itself. If we once let Mozart's music into the play, its potency would make it the overriding experience of the evening. Yet the music clearly had to be there to demonstrate his genius as against the ordinary talent of Salieri. Harrison Birtwistle had an original and subtle solution. He took pieces of Mozart, treated them electronically, and they became a delicate remembrance of the C minor Mass, rather than the C minor Mass itself. The public heard no distortion – only a distancing.

The first time a new play meets an audience is its greatest test. However anxious the circumstances, however rough the work, there is in that couple of hours an immediate awareness of whether the piece is speaking to the public and whether – however provoking its subject matter – it attracts them. The first preview of *Amadeus* left us in no doubt. Although we continued to work on the play for the next year and a half, making quite substantial changes right up to its opening on Broadway, we knew from that very first evening that the public adored it.

As a writer, Peter has a remarkably popular gift. Again and again, he takes an intricate metaphysical argument and, by bold speeches and strong emblems, makes it appeal to vast numbers of people. His dialogue is sinewy, antithetical and energetic. Clause tumbles on clause, qualifying and redefining. His characters speak as he speaks – in a torrent of words and with a delight in complexity. Shaffer has to be played fast. Then what is being said emerges clearly from the abundance of qualifications; then the scene 'holds' – like a plate spinning on top of a rod. To change the image, his plays are like movies that *must* be run at the right speed. If they go slowly, they jerk incoherently from one thought to another and can seem pretentious and contradictory. At the right speed, they offer the joy of actually discovering a thought.

I have had two more experiences of Shaffer plays. One I staged while still at the National, *Yonadab*, which did not achieve its promise. Neither Shaffer nor I developed our work on it enough. Peter then rewrote it brilliantly and it was scheduled for production on Broadway by the Shuberts. But it never happened: I imagine it was thought too risky in Broadway's current fearfulness. Then, in 1992, I directed *The Gift of the Gorgon* for the RSC. I found this a challenging play for any author to have created – certainly in his mid-sixties. Its subject is the very nature of revenge. We praise Greek tragedy for its terrible catharsis, when blood must have blood. Yet we think it inhuman to execute modern terrorists. As the IRA bombs continue to kill men, women and children indiscriminately, Shaffer's finger is still on the pulse of our society, making the theatre once again a place to debate its moral dilemmas.

1979 was a watershed year for the National. Relative peace and creativity marked my remaining nine years there. Early in 1980 Maria came to London with everything she possessed in the world packed into her suitcases. We found a little early nineteenth-century house in Bramerton Street and started to make our life together. I felt there was great hope for the future after the raw experiences of the past twelve months. There had been the guilt and the misery of telling Edward and Lucy; the anguish I caused to Jacky, even though she must have felt relief at no longer having to live a sham. But changes in life seem inevitably to bring pain: I can only say that I have suffered it as well as provoked it. I made my children very uneasy, if not unhappy, at this time. I could not settle for a miserable marriage. Our divorce finally came through at the end of 1981.

Soon after Maria had arrived in London she went off to Geneva to sing in *The Barber of Seville*. I took a long weekend to be with her and found myself, as I had with Leslie, quite happy to be the companion of the star. From now on, I often spent weekends in some European capital where Maria was singing. I once even flew to Chicago on a Friday night and returned on the Sunday so that I could be at an important first night of hers. When the spring came, we went to Eden Roc in the South of France for a few days of luxury. Holidays had never been part of my way of life; I was beginning to relax a little.

In January, Trevor Nunn had taken Peter Brook and me to see the progress that had been made on the Barbican Theatre – now, unbelievably, ten years late. What John Bury and I had conceived all those years ago looked,

I thought, good; and, to my mind, it has proved to be the best theatre in London for large-scale Shakespeare. Sadly, though, I have never worked there. Trevor wanted me to do one of the productions at its opening in 1982 (he even proposed *Peter Pan*), but the NT Board, in one of its rare moments of pig-headedness, refused me permission on the grounds that the differences between the two companies would become blurred. I thought this was short-sighted.

In my early years at the National, when I was still with Jacky, we lived at the Barbican, thirty-nine floors up on top of the Cromwell Tower. Way beneath us we could see the whole sweep of the river and the dome of St Paul's. Though our real home was at Wallingford, the Barbican apartment was very convenient for the South Bank; and from our vantage point we could watch the Arts Centre being built below us. But as it grew I became increasingly disenchanted with the place. Along with the silence and the sense of exhilaration that went with living so high was the added benefit that I couldn't see the brutal architecture of the Centre unless I looked down.

Larry Olivier lived at the top of a similar, sky-scraping block in Victoria. One night he phoned me and, competitive as always, wondered who was higher, he or I. He told me he would flash his lights on and off, and I was to tell him if I could see them. I couldn't . . .

The 1981 *Evening Standard* drama awards were held in the Olivier. I was given a special trophy for 'Twenty-Five Years of Service to the Theatre'. The press were no longer dubbing me as beleaguered. I wrote in my *Diaries*: 'Two years ago the *Standard* was crucifying me, so I hope the presentation statue has a little blood on it.'

The last forty years have seen a proliferation of awards, for achievements ranging from poetry to bee-keeping. Awards are like school prizes, very gratifying to collect yet finally meaningless. There is clearly no 'best' anything, and the whole business has now become merely a marketing tool. Awards have had the thoroughly bad effect of concentrating the market; in making one a winner, they brand all the rest as losers.

I was pleased to get my *Evening Standard* statue for twenty-five years' service. But this was partly because I knew beforehand that I was going to get it. The hyped, competitive drama of the Oscars, Tonys and Oliviers was avoided. When I was given a Tony for best director on Broadway for *Amadeus*, I had no idea whether I had won it or not. My fellow competitors and I sat at the ceremony with carefully composed faces, knowing that the TV cameras were trained on us while the results were read out. We were all primed to act generosity in defeat.

– 13 –

At the National in the summer of 1980, *Galileo*, with Michael Gambon in the name part, was the first Brecht play to become a big popular success in this country. Michael had a role he was born for. He was unsentimental, dangerous and immensely powerful. Ralph Richardson had seen what was in him, dubbing him from the first 'The Great Gambon'. Yet four major directors whom I asked to stage the play had turned me down: they did not think Michael was a starry enough choice. Convinced they were wrong, I stuck to the actor and went on looking. My fifth choice, John Dexter, accepted, and Gambon became an immediate star, not least with his fellow actors. The dressing rooms at the National look on to a four-sided courtyard, and after the first night all the windows contained actors in various states of undress leaning out and applauding him – a unique tribute.

The War That Had To Be Won

*

The notorious event of the year was *The Romans in Britain* which I had commissioned from Howard Brenton and liked because it was a strong indictment of imperialism that touched a contemporary nerve. It also clearly needed the epic spaces of the Olivier stage. Michael Bogdanov took on the play as director and, when the time came, delivered a clear, tough account of it.

I warned the NT Board, as I had done in similar situations in the past, that the play was politically as well as sexually contentious. And after seeing the first preview (I had also seen some late rehearsals) I told Howard and Michael that if the crucial scene of homosexual rape were to take place not front stage, as was happening, but out of sight, the play stood more chance of being reviewed as a serious piece of work. My worry was that little would be written about *except* the rape, and much else that was interesting would be ignored. But I didn't press the point because they persuaded me that they had good reasons for presenting the scene as they did – it was shocking; but then it was meant to be. Next day, I had to leave for New York where I was due to put on *Amadeus*.

At a later preview of *The Romans*, Horace Cutler, the leader of the Greater London Council (which partially subsidised the National), walked out angrily with his chief whip Geoffrey Seaton, and sent me a strong letter of protest, releasing it to the press. Their action made front-page news and the story rumbled on for days, especially as the letter contained GLC threats (never realised) to suspend the NT's grant. There were some memorable headlines: 'Take off this nude shocker', 'Hard times for the Celts', 'Psst . . . wanna see a show?' 'Nude show fills stalls'.

Meanwhile, our perpetual guardian of the nation's morals, Mary Whitehouse, laid a complaint with Scotland Yard. But the police, after watching some performances,

307

decided that a prosecution was not justified. Unlike the police, Mrs Whitehouse never saw the play; she did not, she said, wish to run the risk of sullying her mind. She sent her solicitor instead.

From New York, I defended *The Romans* vigorously in every part of the media that would give me space, while the Arts Council muttered about my lack of wisdom in providing ammunition for the National's enemies at Westminster.

On the whole the notices had been cool – though Harold Hobson was impressed in the *Sunday Times* (so, many months later, was Bernard Levin in a big feature in *The Times*). Among the avalanche of letters printed in the newspapers, both of support and condemnation, was a defence of the play from Edward Bond, and another from the head of Eyre Methuen, Geoffrey Strachan: 'It is part of the business of theatre to dramatise painful subjects,' he wrote, '. . . a theatre that is afraid of great failures will see no great successes.'

Well into the run, controversy was still buzzing. One night a small group of hecklers in the audience threw fireworks and bags of flour at the actors, shouting, 'Get poofs off the stage.'

Then, at Christmas, Michael Bogdanov had a summons served on him at the stage door by Mary Whitehouse's solicitor. Having failed to get any action from the police, she was bringing a private prosecution against Michael under the sexual offences act, accusing him of 'procuring an act of gross indecency' in staging the rape scene. This summons was a curious interpretation of the law because the act had been designed to deal with pimping, not theatre performances.

In the agonising fifteen months before the case came to court at the Old Bailey in March 1982, the misery inflicted on Michael and his family was enormous. He was a man marked by the press, his children were tormented at school, and he had several packets of excreta pushed through his letter box. All this was borne by him and his wife Patsy with extraordinary strength of mind.

On the third day of the trial, however, Ian Kennedy, Mrs Whitehouse's counsel, suddenly and dramatically abandoned the prosecution. 'I cannot continue to try an honourable man,' he said. The attorney general had to invoke an obscure legal procedure, *nolle prosequi*, which means 'unwilling to proceed'. The case presented by the defence counsel, Jeremy Hutchinson, centred on the distinction between illusion and reality. Was Michael Bogdanov, as the director of the play, creating a *real* act of gross indecency, or only the illusion of one?

If Michael had been convicted he could have spent up to two years in prison. As it was, he walked out of the court free and the state paid his costs; Mary Whitehouse had to pay her own. It was a victory – of a sort.

The NT Board behaved in an exemplary way over *The Romans in Britain*. A leading theatre in any country is prone to play safe, and there is an inbuilt temptation to make sure that it ruffles nobody's sensibilities. Board members would indeed sometimes sigh when I told them of a coming controversial play and say, 'Yes, yes . . . but surely not at the National!' I always urged vehemently against this qualification. Without controversial work in the repertory, we would be evading our social responsibilities and becoming merely a fixture of the establishment, unwilling to deal with new and dissenting issues or young writers or to attract young audiences.

Richard Eyre had an anxious moment soon after succeeding me at the NT. This was caused by something as innocuous as the Queen being a principal character in Alan Bennett's *A Question of Attribution*. The Board liked the play but thought the reigning monarch should not be portrayed on the stage of the National, though apparently any other theatre would be fine. Richard talked this over with me and wondered whether it was a reason to resign. Fortunately it did not come to that; but at the time I said that such a situation must always be a reason for resigning. What plays are staged ought not to be decided by committee, or tempered by compromise. The surest way of driving away an audience is to inhibit the director's taste; that is what gives a theatre personality.

– 14 –

In 1981 I at last directed *The Oresteia*. It had been a long eight years coming, for it was in 1973 that I first determined to stage Aeschylus's masterpiece and Tony Harrison started work on the translation. The task proved slow, and there were then postponements while I wrestled with strikes.

I had learned the art of the mask from Michel St Denis. The Greek stage is in itself a mask: hideous murders and violence happen behind the scenes; the terror is imagined. In the same way, Greek tragedians, because they were masked, could deal with passions so extreme they would be intolerable if expressed naturalistically. Any actor knows that if he weeps the audience does not; but if he stifles overwhelming emotion he will win sympathy and understanding. A child trying desperately not to cry is always more moving than a child who cries. The mask allows that particular containment of exorbitant feelings.

A simple exercise is the beginning of all mask work. A variety of masks are placed on a table. Each actor is asked to choose one that appeals. The actor looks at the mask very carefully. Then he looks at his own face and the mask side by side in a full-length mirror. He drops his head and puts on the mask. Now comes the traumatic moment. The actor slowly looks up into the full-length mirror and confronts his new character. He sees a person totally unlike himself and he must use this moment to *become* what he sees. He looks for a few seconds – no more. Then he accepts the changed person in front of him and follows its characteristics, allowing it to affect the way he talks, walks, thinks and feels.

There is only one proviso. Every actor has the ability to recognise acutely what it feels like to be untrue, to be acting badly. If the mask provokes him to this dishonesty, however briefly, he must immediately take it off.

Normally the image he sees liberates him; it can occasionally make him comprehend a whole new world. By the use of the mask, the actor can change his age, his bearing, his physique – even his sexuality. He can reveal areas of his personality he did not know existed. But they are parts of him; otherwise he is pretending and therefore being false. True acting is a revelation of self, not an imitation of somebody else, and the mask enormously helps the process.

The mask properly used does not obscure but reveal. In tragedy, it makes possible the expression of hysterical emotions which would be disturbing and unacceptable with the naked face. And in comedy, it releases an anarchic energy – alarming, bawdy and frequently child-like – which expresses the absurdities of human be-haviour as vividly as a good caricature.

In a sense, any demanding *form* in the theatre is a mask: a precise and balanced Mozart aria; the discipline of Shakespeare's iambic pentameters. Hamlet's advice to the Players tells us that even in the greatest passion the actor must 'beget a smoothness'. And that smoothness is obtained by endorsing the form – the mask.

The Greeks brought a sophisticated cunning into the architecture of their theatres as well as into their drama. When Denys Lasdun and I visited Epidaurus in the early Seventies for a television programme about the National, he pointed out the secret wonders of the place. Although the vast auditorium, cut into the side of a hill, appears to be a regular fan-shape, bisected by the straight lines of the aisles, none of it is, in fact, geometrically perfect. The design of the human body is never precisely symmetrical, and neither is the design of Epidaurus (or, for that matter, the Parthenon). It seems as if the Greeks deliberately bent the form, so that geometry was humanised. The Romans scorned such artifice. For example, the Herodias Atticus in Athens, where I staged my 1984 NT production of *Coriolanus*, is of an absolutely pure geometric design; and there is no doubt that the Greek auditorium is the richer experience.

Epidaurus still feels what it was originally – a holy place, a place of healing. The audience look from their stone benches down on to the stage and beyond it to the riches of the Greek landscape. This vision of the country is part of the theatre.

Epidaurus also possesses mythical acoustics. When I took *The Oresteia* there in 1982, and *The Tempest*, *The Winter's Tale*, and *Cymbeline* six years later, every word of these difficult texts was heard by some 15,000 people at each performance. There was no amplification, yet no need to shout. Providing the ends of the lines were sustained and the consonants kept distinct, the sound was crystal clear.

The production of *The Oresteia* was partly based on an understanding of how Epidaurus had influenced Denys Lasdun in designing the Olivier. It seems to me now that while the Olivier is a great theatre, it bears as much relation to Epidaurus as St Pancras Station does to Venice. But inspiration has to have a beginning. Lasdun had a vision of a fine modern theatre after he saw those great stone benches at Epidaurus, sweeping round in a half circle.

The Oresteia took us six months. We started from the very beginning and investigated how we could do classical drama in the twentieth century and still respect its form. We discovered a great deal. I soon realised that, for me, Greek plays are impossible without the mask. Because of its primitive origins, we are now inclined to patronise the mask in the theatre. But I found that its

312

very mystery solved not only the problem of expressing unbearable feeling, but also how to make the unending laments of the Greek Chorus understandable to a modern audience.

We decided that the Chorus would not, as is usual, all speak together. More than two voices speaking at the same time is incomprehensible unless they are mechanically drilled, and the effect then is inhuman and generalised. The fifteen actors comprising our Chorus wore copies of the same full mask of an old man. If one actor spoke a line while the rest of the Chorus acted it, it seemed as if the whole group had spoken. One voice was easy to understand. The thought was then taken up, qualified and expanded by other single voices. It worked.

The same fifteen male actors who made up the Chorus also played all the roles, men and women. When terrible tragedy struck the chief protagonists – Orestes, Clytemnestra, or Agamemnon – they could wail in the most primal anguish because their emotions were contained by the form and discipline of the full mask.

During the first days of wearing their masks – which were created individually for each actor by the designer of the production, Jocelyn Herbert – the cast found it difficult to speak. Like infants learning to talk, the actors began with grunts and gibberish and progressed until they used words. We had to rehearse the text independently, without the mask. After weeks of improvisation, it was possible to bring the two together, to persuade the characters to speak the text without disruption while masked.

The cast was all male; but this was not an attempt at historical accuracy. The three plays that make up *The Oresteia* are very much a man's view of woman as seen at a moment when matriarchy had given way to a male-dominated society. Tony Harrison and I felt that the sexuality of the plays needed abstracting in order to be fully understood. In the primitive world that Aeschylus portrayed, a masked man dressed as Clytemnestra is paradoxically more womanly than a woman.

Each day we worked on a dozen lines of Tony's strong, alliterative translation. We improvised to release the feeling, and then returned to the text to find the pulse, the tempo, that would express the emotions and support the verbal rhythms. Then Harrison Birtwistle took our findings home that night and composed around them, thus completing a further small chunk of the enterprise.

Harry Birtwistle had been the National's head of music from the beginning of my time there; and apart from his great work in that position, his contribution to the associate directors' meetings was unique. He would sit for long periods without saying a word and then suddenly offer a solution to a problem with the conviction of a man who seldom has any doubt. The NT gave Harry security over the ten years he developed into a great composer. But what he gave us, not only by writing scores but by his vision, was far more valuable than anything he was ever paid.

The four-and-a-half hours of *The Oresteia* ends with the lighting of a flame. This is both actual and metaphoric; it is the resolution of the trilogy, as light is brought into the darkness. The GLC, however, banned this enlightenment; they saw it as a fire risk: a naked flame on the stage could only be used for a specific purpose in a story, like the burning of incriminating evidence. They suggested an electric torch. I appealed, and the case was taken to the magistrate's court at Horseferry Road. To my delight, we were allowed our flame. The magistrate had studied *The Oresteia* at school and fondly quoted the relevant Greek passage.

The production opened in the late autumn of 1981. The critics, though fascinated, were divided. A few of them couldn't get past the masks. But I knew we had made something live which in my lifetime had been dead; that the fusion of text and music, mask and movement, had created an experience both primitive and tragic. And audiences were genuinely affected.

Immediately after the first night I telephoned John Goodwin from Geneva – I was there for the weekend to hear Maria sing. John mentioned he'd heard that James Fenton of the *Sunday Times* had loved it and was going again. So emotional was I about *The Oresteia* that I distinctly remember replying that I'd hate James Fenton to like my work. Fenton is a considerable poet; but he was at that time a bogeyman among the critics. He seemed to enjoy acting the terrorist, and had conducted a single-handed campaign against *Amadeus* – which, among the critics, he was virtually alone in disliking – by printing a thumbnail attack on it in the *Sunday Times* theatre listings every week of its run for a year. He didn't affect the box office. But he did give Shaffer a weekly upset.

The Oresteia vindicated itself. The scheduled twenty performances were extended to sixty-five, all of which packed; and Channel 4 filmed the production for television. It became the first Greek drama ever played in English at Epidaurus; and, I am told, has had a lasting effect on the way the Greeks recreate their plays. For me, it united my passion for form and music and mask. I am still exploring what it taught me.

– 15 –

Before *The Oresteia* opened, the National's 1981 repertory had included, among much else, the complete four-and-a-half hours of *Man and Superman*, including the Don Juan in Hell scene, which is nearly always cut. The production was directed by Christopher Morahan, and proved that Shaw's theatre of rational debate went well in the public space of the Olivier.

In the same year, Edward Albee's *Who's Afraid of Virginia Woolf?* was staged by Nancy Meckler. This marked the first time a woman director had worked at the NT on the South Bank, thus providing much chatter among the new feminists. I was accused of running a male-dominated theatre – an accusation which was simply not true. I belong to a profession which, with its administration, stage management, designers and performers, has shown for hundreds of years less male prejudice than almost any other. It is true that, until recently, not many women were encouraged to be directors or decided to try; but then not many women were encouraged or decided to be conductors either. Things have changed in the last twenty years, though. And I rank Joan Littlewood, Buzz Goodbody and Deborah Warner among the finest directors I have known.

Joan Plowright was cast as Martha in *Virginia Woolf*. She appeared in it on tour in Bath, and also in previews in the Lyttelton. Then she suddenly left, officially because of a throat infection. Soon a wicked rumour was going the rounds that Larry had contrived a black joke by sending her a petition for divorce, enclosing a note saying: 'No wife of mine will appear at Peter Hall's National Theatre.' True or not, Joan left. The play was delayed for a month until Margaret Tyzack successfully took over. Joan, alas, didn't come to the National for another four years.

The National's first ever production of a musical, *Guys and Dolls*, opened in the Olivier in the early spring of 1982, with Julia McKenzie, Bob Hoskins, Ian Charleson and Julie Covington. Directed by Richard Eyre, it won a huge number of awards, transferred to the West End, and gave 750 performances. So enormous was its popularity at the box office that we were able to withstand some unpleasant cuts in real terms to our grant.

When we announced the production, there was immediate alarm in the press. Was the National Theatre funded in order to present American musicals? Could

English actors deliver performances that would work? Should something so obviously commercial be staged at the National? I took the view that *Guys and Dolls* was a masterpiece of its form – possibly the finest musical ever written – and said so. It makes me smile that the NT, as I write this, is giving a six-month run of *Carousel* – and not in repertory (as was *Guys and Dolls*), and also with the financial help of the most successful commercial impresario of our time, Cameron Mackintosh. How well our commentators have been Thatcherised.

In the summer, Richard had another big success, this time with *The Beggar's Opera* in the Cottesloe. His work, as always, was meticulous; also I loved the strong, shy integrity of his personality. I began to think of him as a possible successor. Although he liked to be liked, as most of us do, I suspected that were he in charge he could be ruthless when necessary. Over the next years, I watched him with special interest.

Judi Dench came back to the National in 1982 to appear in two productions of mine: *The Importance of Being Earnest* and the premiere of Pinter's *A Kind of Alaska*. In the Pinter, playing a woman who awakens from a sleep of many years, a sleeping 'sickness', she gave a performance which haunts the memories of those who saw it. In *The Importance* she played Lady Bracknell, and it was a revelation to bring that overblown character back to her proper age, and also to consider the true nature of the play – a satire on the upper-class marriage market. This market was a reality: if young upper-class girls did not marry well, they would have little identity and no full life. Wilde is showing their desperation – and Lady Bracknell's.

The Importance was my first attempt at Wilde. I'd always been worried by his epigrams, actors standing on opposite sides of the stage, competing in wit. But the discovery was that the epigrams are not produced by the author's desire to be clever, but because they are satirising the tradition of the English stiff upper-lip.

The more intensely a character feels and the greater his passions the more outrageous the epigrams become in an attempt to control and mask those passions. The characters are not simply trying to see who can be funniest.

Years later, with Bill Kenwright backing my own company in the West End, I staged a production of *An Ideal Husband* which developed this discovery. I believe that Wilde is popular with audiences not just because he is amusing. He was the most good-hearted and tender of men, and this quality shines through his writing. He understands love, and pain, in all their forms.

A bizarre event of this summer was a Falklands Victory Show, televised on a Sunday night with contributions from the whole of show business. Officially, it was to raise money for Falklands widows. Actually, it was to raise applause for Thatcher's somewhat dubious finest hour. The NT was asked to do its bit and provide a number by the Hot Box Girls from *Guys and Dolls*. Bravely, they flatly refused to hoof it for Thatcher. Nothing could persuade them to change their mind. And because it was extra to their contracts, the management couldn't make them; nor did we want to. In the end Frank Finlay, who was now playing Salieri in *Amadeus*, helped us out by making a token appearance on behalf of the National.

In 1982 we started an original experiment. A generous anonymous donor had made it possible for us to give one Bargain Night for each play in the repertory. All tickets were only two pounds. Crowds for our first offering, *Guys and Dolls*, had begun to gather outside the National twenty-four hours before the performance. By next morning, when the box office opened, coffee and jumble stalls had been set up, there were TV cameras, and many thousands of people stretched in queues along the South Bank as far as the eye could see. Months later,

318

when every production had been given its single Bargain Night, it was clear that the whole series had been a revealing success.

It is a dangerous cliché that people only value what they pay for. I believe that if good art were cheap – really cheap – the need for it would grow enormously. At the end of the war, the idea of subsidy embraced the intention to make the arts available to as many people as possible, especially those who could not otherwise afford it. That idea has been lost. Now the Arts Council tells its clients that they must get the market rate – without apparently realising that the market rate often keeps out the very people who are longing to come in. I think it obscene that today Covent Garden charges £120 and more for a good ticket. The Royal Opera House should have a subsidy that enables it to charge dramatically lower prices. Then its audience would be drawn from the whole population. At the moment, every taxpayer is subsidising opera goers who are already wealthy.

Early in the year, Maria and I were married in New York, and in May our daughter, Rebecca, was born. I found being a parent in my fifties a pleasure even more intense than when I had been younger. All my children rallied round and shared our joy at the arrival of a new baby. Also, I did more of the actual looking after than I had ever done before.

Although there were depressing lows in my roller-coaster life with Maria, there were dazzling heights – and I thought I was beginning to understand her and her talent. I realised that she was not in the least interested in fame. What she cared about was, and still is, perfection. If she did not get it, she felt ill. It was a difficult burden for her to bear.

– 16 –

The most notorious flop of my career, *Jean Seberg*, happened in the winter of 1983. The year before, the American composer Marvin Hamlish had invited me to direct it on Broadway. 'Get me the *Amadeus* guy,' he was reported as saying. However, my contract with the National allowed me to work only on theatre productions which originated there. So I suggested to Hamlish that we stage *Seberg* in the Olivier. I thought it would be rewarding for the NT to try to construct a musical from its very beginnings. It had a serious and interesting theme: a society which, because it lacked religious or royal totems, made film stars its objects of worship, sometimes with tragic consequences.

Jean Seberg was a girl from the Midwest of America turned into a star before her talent had developed and who, broken as a result, committed suicide in Paris in 1979. She had political affiliations, particularly with the Black Panther movement, and was persecuted by the FBI under J. Edgar Hoover.

I had liked Hamlish's music for *A Chorus Line*, though I hadn't liked the show itself, which seemed to me, as theatre, to reek of Broadway double standards: it castigated the star system, but ended up celebrating it. For *Seberg*, the words were by different people: Christopher Adler had written the lyrics and the book was by Julian Barry, the screenwriter.

The production was announced six months before we went into rehearsal and immediately provoked hostility after the normally open-minded Michael Billington had suggested in the *Guardian* that the subsidised National Theatre was financing the tryout of a Broadway musical with public money. This set off an avalanche of comment which, long before we opened, labelled the enterprise as a shocking misuse of public funds. I went into the attack. I asked if the NT should avoid works which looked as though they might have commercial potential. I said that if we went along with such a notion, any new play offered to us by an established and popular dramatist – be he Stoppard or Ayckbourn, Shaffer or Pinter, David Hare or Christopher Hampton – would have to be refused. But the antagonism mounted and no argument worked. I stressed that *Seberg* widened the range of our repertory and continued our demonstrable interest in new American drama; that I hoped it would bring in a new audience, as *Guys and Dolls* had done. Finally, I pointed out that because we had negotiated a stake in all later productions of the show (as we had done, for instance, with *Amadeus*) it would, if liked, make money for the National.

The hostile publicity fed on itself, and there were a number of untrue newspaper stories about rows backstage. To make matters worse, one of the leading actors, David Ryall, broke his ankle and the opening had to be delayed. By the time the first night came, only a presentation of the Second Coming would have lived down the climate of disapproval. The show opened after twenty-two packed-out previews. But it was not liked by most of the critics, and their notices made it sound rather glum. After that, public interest fell away, though we managed to nurse the production in the repertory for four months.

Paradoxically, the work we did on *Seberg* in rehearsal was an exciting experience and taught me much about musical structure and story-telling. So why did it fail? The cast was talented, and nineteen-year-old Kelly Hunter, fragile yet tough, was memorable as the young Jean.

There was something about *Seberg* that audiences rejected. They couldn't, I believe, bear the contrast

321

between Marvin's glittering, showy music and the pain of the story. I thought this contrast worked. It was also, perhaps, a mistake to tell the story with two heroines – an old Seberg and a young Seberg: the audience did not know whom to identify with.

I'm sure it was not a mistake to do the show at the National; but clearly – and this was my misjudgement – it was the wrong time to try. Once we were launched on the production, however, there could be no turning back. One thing is certain: nothing fails like the failure of a musical.

Julian Barry and I have worked together since and he has remained a friend. Marvin Hamlish has not, alas. So often in the theatre disaster separates, success binds.

Earlier in 1983, another flop had caused me great heartache. In May, Harold Pinter staged a revival of Giradoux's *The Trojan War Will Not Take Place*. Somehow he missed the ironic style of the piece, and it was badly received. Soon afterwards he resigned as an associate director of the National and, surprising in such a private man, announced publicly that 'the fundamental problem with the NT is that its artistic director spends a great deal of his time elsewhere,' and that 'he and the Board had failed to appoint a deputy to him entrusted with full artistic responsibility in Peter Hall's absence.'

Harold was speaking about my sabbatical in Bayreuth, which coincided with his rehearsals. I lost, for the time being, one of my closest friends and collaborators.

The split was made worse when my *Diaries* came out that autumn. I thought I had written about Harold with the love and care I have always felt for him. But he didn't. He did not make it up for eight years.

The publication of my *Diaries* presented me with a new experience and it was not entirely comfortable: my character was reviewed in public. 'You should have thought of that before,' said my mother.

When I left the RSC in 1968, I possessed no records at all of that period, not even notes about my own productions. And when sleuthing academics, theatre historians and friends asked me about those years I had to confess that, despite having a good memory, I had forgotten many of the details. I was determined not to make the same mistake at the NT.

Between March 1972, when I was invited to launch the National on the South Bank, and January 1980, I spent half an hour early every morning dictating the happenings of the previous day into a small tape recorder. After a while I began to enjoy this; it became an essential habit, almost a daily confessional. I never listened afterwards to the tapes, nor – although they were typed for me – read them. I wanted them to stay as they were, uncorrected, probably inconsistent in places, but a record that might some time be useful. They were never intended for publication. Then one day I mentioned their existence to John Goodwin. He was very interested, asked to read them, and came back to say he thought that if they were shortened they would tell an intriguing story. Two years later, he showed me his edited version, condensed from well over a million words. I was as startled as when I see myself on TV or hear my own voice on the radio. The man in the diaries seemed someone else, someone I only partly recognised, full of contradictions; and what I read showed a hectic, at times somewhat desperate, life – no doubt because each morning, as I dictated, the drama and the bad things had been uppermost in my mind. Not so evident were the rehearsals that had gone wonderfully well, my friendships among the people I worked with, and the satisfaction I had felt at the way we had, together, fought and won the battle to open the National.

Over the years, the *Diaries* have won me many friends. Theatre directors all over the world, from Elia Kazan to Ninagawa, have said how glad they are that

323

someone has put into print the wonder and the purgatory of running a big theatre company.

At the time, they produced every possible kind of review, from heartening approval, to zestful character assassination by John Osborne in the *Sunday Times*.

– 17 –

In the October of 1983, Ralph Richardson died. He was acting for the NT in Eduardo de Filippo's *Inner Voices* and had had a slight stroke. When told by his doctor that he would not be able to live a full life in the future, he turned over and I think decided to die. It took two days. He was eighty-one. I felt I had lost a second father. That evening, the leading actor in each of the National's three theatres asked for a minute's silence in which the audience and those on stage could remember him.

His greatness as an actor is undisputed and happily survives in innumerable films. He created characters who revealed the poetry of ordinariness. He always said he had a potato face, but underneath that face was an ardent, imaginative soul, and his audiences recognised it. That is what made him the finest of Cyranos. He understood eccentrics, perhaps because he was an eccentric himself, with his love of Bentleys, motorbikes and hamsters. He was the best Falstaff I have seen.

I adored working with him, though his inventiveness could make rehearsals an alarming experience. Most actors rehearse giving about eighty per cent, indicating what they will do in performance. Ralph created the thing itself: he could plug into the character and then instantaneously drop it, commenting on what he had just done, usually in a deprecating manner. He had the

59. Steven Mackintosh as Ariel, flying, in *The Tempest*, one of my last three productions at the NT. Together, these staged the world of Shakespeare's late plays, cruel but beautiful.

60. *Akenfield*: the harvest in 1912. From my film of Ronald Blythe's touching book about an East Anglian village.

61. With David Warner and Cilla Black while making the film *Work is a Four Letter Word*.

62. Rebecca, aged nine, with Toby Stephens in *The Camomile Lawn* (Channel 4).

63. The last time I worked with Peggy Ashcroft, seen here with Geraldine James and James Fox in *She's Been Away* (BBC TV).

64. Vanessa Redgrave in *Orpheus Descending* (PH Company). Every day of rehearsal was an adventure.

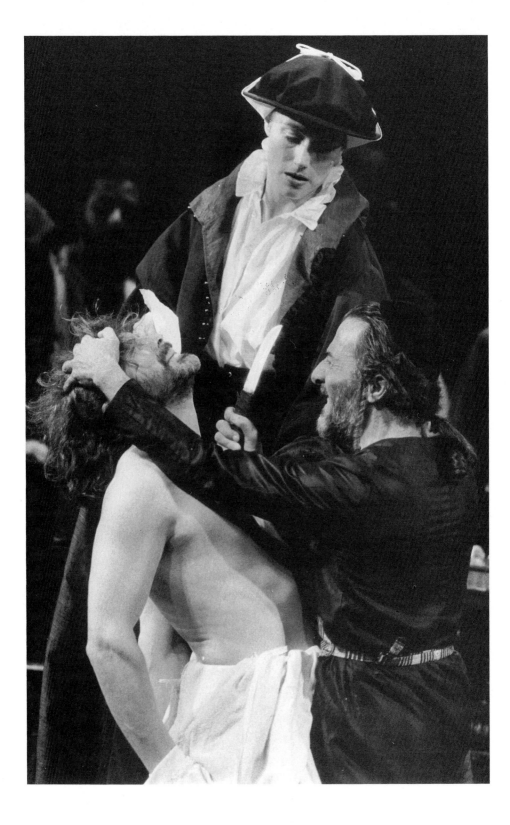

65. *left* Dustin Hoffman with Leigh Lawson and Geraldine James in *The Merchant of Venice* (PH Company). Dustin lived and breathed his work twenty-four hours a day.

66. *right* In *The Rose Tattoo* (PH Company) Julie Walters created someone utterly unlike herself.

67. *below* My second production of *The Homecoming* (PH Company), twenty-five years after the first. From left: Cherie Lunghi, Douglas McFerran, Warren Mitchell, Greg Hicks.

68. John Sessions, Jennifer Ehle and Paul Eddington in *Tartuffe* (PH Company). My first Moliere: I was lucky enough to have a cast of expert comedians.

69. Judi Dench in *The Gift of the Gorgon* (PH Company). The play included several scenes representing the Perseus and Athena myths.

70. *Born Again* (Chichester). Gerald Scarfe's huge rhinosceros, straight out of Dürer, made its entrance by descending in a lift and crashing through the glass door.

71. With John Guare, author of *Four Baboons Adoring the Sun* (Lincoln Center): the happiest and most fruitful of collaborations.

72. Nicki. We found these giraffes in a park when filming *Orpheus Descending*, on location in Jacksonville, Florida, for American TV. **73.** With Emma.

ability, in rehearsal, to associate completely with the character from the start. In my experience he shared this commitment only with Edith Evans and Vanessa Redgrave.

Ralph was a firm friend. I lunched with him every few weeks and I often think of him now. We were together a couple of months before he died. He said something like this (I will try to remember the words as I remember the voice): 'I don't think I've been a particularly bad person. I've tried to be good – as good as I can. And I've tried to have a bit of faith. But when I die and go up to the pearly gates, will St Peter come and open them and say "Hello, Richardson. Come in!"? You know, I don't think so. I don't think there'll be anyone there at all.'

– 18 –

The director's job of putting a play together so that it comes to life is an intense pleasure for me, but I find a pleasure almost as great in editing a film or adapting a book for a movie or the stage. The agents for George Orwell's estate had given me the irresistible chance of making a stage version of *Animal Farm*, one of those rare and original allegories that all ages respond to, like *Gulliver's Travels* or *Alice in Wonderland*.

I directed my adaptation in the Cottesloe in the spring of 1984. Jennifer Carey had designed fine masks for the animals; lyrics were by Adrian Mitchell and music by Richard Peaslee. The piece became an amazing success, and over the next few years was given in all three of the National's theatres, also touring widely in Britain and abroad. Everywhere houses were full. At an International Theatre Festival in Baltimore there was a wonderful row when the American organisers, under pressure from the visiting Eastern bloc countries, made it clear that they would like us to withdraw *Animal Farm* from the festival because of Orwell's anti-communist viewpoint. We refused, but not before Wole Soyinka, president of the festival, and loyally on the communists' side, had devised an ingeniously liberal defence of their attitude. Thus the production, while invited by the festival and playing at the festival, was now designated as officially outside the festival. Orwell would have been delighted.

In the winter of 1984, I had another crack at *Coriolanus*, twenty-five years after I had done it with Olivier at Stratford. Now the name part was played by Ian McKellen and I emphasised the political resonances more by using, for the first and only time in any of my Shakespeare productions, fragments of modern costume. The same thinking also led me to put the audience on to the Olivier stage – a hundred of them each night – seated at low ticket prices along the back, close to the action. Marshalled by seven or eight actors, they became the citizens of Rome at necessary points in the play. This device worked well, particularly when we went to the Herodias Atticus, the vast Roman theatre just below the Acropolis in Athens. The Greeks enjoyed taking part in the drama of politics far more than the inhibited Londoners, and were much more exuberant in their reactions.

– 19 –

By the autumn of 1984 – despite a strong repertory and high audience levels – a financial show-down was clearly on the way for the National.

An examination of our figures from 1979 (when Thatcher became prime minister) revealed that while the retail price index had risen by sixty-five per cent the NT's grant had risen by only forty-four per cent, thus failing to match inflation by a third. Unless we were given an extra £1.5 million to restore the grant and take account of inflation, we would soon have to face a major deficit.

We made our case to the Arts Council, but in December were told that our increase for 1985/6 would not be £1.5 million but £129,000. I was worried not only about the National: the whole theatre scene was under attack. The Thatcher revolution – with grants deliberately pegged well below inflation and theatres expected to make up the shortfall by private-sector sponsorship – was beginning to bite. Plans were shrinking, experiment was threatened and morale was generally very low. The government's promise, made in 1979, that private sponsorship would never be used as a means of reducing subsidy had been broken.

In January, at the *Evening Standard* drama awards in the Guildhall, I spoke out about the state of the theatre up and down the country. The Minister for the Arts, Lord Gowrie, showed his displeasure in the House of Lords with a patronising speech, making out that I just wanted another million for the NT. This angered me, and in a letter to him I pointed out that I had not mentioned the National at all, adding, 'I don't believe the Arts Council, or, if I may say so, you, realise what a wasteland is developing, peopled by demoralised directors. I am not saying, "Give me a million or you are a vandal." That would be politically naive. But I am saying, "Look out, the British theatre is disappearing."'

The public debate became very heated. Max Rayne and his deputy, Lord Mishcon, were increasingly anxious that I was damaging the NT by speaking out. Early in February, I accompanied them to a meeting with Gowrie who seemed to me far more concerned with pleasing Thatcher than with the creative potential of the arts.

He obviously loathed the new NT building and, when the subject of our high running costs came up, indicated that for us to move out and occupy some old, existing theatre such as the Lyceum or Drury Lane would be much cheaper. I couldn't believe my ears. He didn't say what would happen to our South Bank home. Gloomily, I wondered whether he was thinking of it as an ideal business conference centre.

The government was at last showing its true attitude towards the arts; and, in William Rees-Mogg, Thatcher had appointed a chairman of the Arts Council who was seemingly content to dismantle the subsidy structure of the previous twenty years and allow the Council to dwindle from an independent agency, fighting the cause of the artist, into a tool of government policy.

Faced with our huge impending deficit, I persuaded the Board to take draconian action. At a press conference held at the NT in February, I attacked the government cut-backs and set out the particular measures the National would have to take. I had to pull myself together before going into the conference because I had just finished having a terrible row on the telephone with Maria which had made me feel like a punch-drunk boxer.

It was difficult to get through the room because it was so crammed with an enormous turnout of journalists, TV crews and waving microphones. But I grabbed a coffee

328

table and climbed on to it. I knew there was no hope of holding an audience unless I could be seen and heard. I announced the closure of the Cottesloe which would save £500,000 over a year; a staff reduction of one hundred jobs, about a fifth of our total; and the end of touring. I then accused Gowrie and Rees-Mogg of betraying the artistic standards of the country.

This coffee-table speech (as the newspapers named it) was given vast media coverage, nearly all of it favourable to the arts, and caused a sensation. The rest of the theatre closed ranks around me. Forty-seven artistic directors of subsidised theatres arrived at the National to discuss our common plight. A unanimous vote of no confidence in the Arts Council was passed. And there was a general recognition, at last, that the Council had divided the theatre world by indicating to the regions that they were underfunded because of the needs of the National, while indicating to the National that it was underfunded because of the needs of the regions.

I was in politics with a vengeance, and Max Rayne and Victor Mishcon grew daily more uneasy. Clearly I had made unforgiving enemies of Gowrie and Rees-Mogg. I believe that from then on, the government's arts establishment wanted to get me out of the National. I had always known that politics could be a dirty business and one that had to be fought with no holds barred. But it was one thing to know that. Another to experience it.

There was, however, an interesting and helpful twist to the affair. I thought I was closing a theatre; I discovered I had committed a political act. Accused by the Right of shutting the Cottesloe when such a measure was not, or so they said, necessary, I was then rewarded by the Left. To enable the theatre to reopen, the GLC made us a special grant of £375,000. This munificence was one of their last acts before being abolished, and was largely seen as an anti-Thatcher gesture. Combined with a healthy box office and our biting economies –

which included what we'd saved over the five months the Cottesloe was closed – it turned our position round. A financial year that had started with a prediction of bankruptcy, fully justified by the facts at that time, ended in April 1986 with a small profit. Our hits – *Pravda*, *The Mysteries*, *Wild Honey* and *A Chorus of Disapproval* – had increased box-office takings. Apart from that, we had won no fewer than twenty awards, as well as many allies in theatres all over the country.

Typically, the government marked this astonishing achievement by giving the National no increase in grant at all for 1987, though inflation was by then running at four per cent. Once more, it was easy to demonstrate that we were being penalised for success, and thus prevented from doing all that we could have done with a subsidy only marginally higher. A little more money would have enabled us to be a lot more productive.

Even so, it had been a lucky year and I knew it. Fortunes can change quickly in the theatre. Takings for a production can drop dramatically within days – particularly if it is attracting a specialised audience which is used up. But the reasons for failure in the theatre are legion: a sudden cold snap, a heatwave, the state of the pound and its effect on tourists, or now (horrifically) a bomb scare. Leaving these aside, any theatre conducts its own very efficient market research every night of the year: if no-one comes, we know we should not have done the play, for a play without an audience is communicating nothing. And it is no help to repeat last year's formula for success in order to draw the crowds; this year it is unlikely to work. The public expect us to be innovative, to lead fashion, not to follow it.

Throughout my time at the National, my first anxious act every morning was to read the returns from the three theatres for the performances of the previous night. We had to play to an average of eighty per cent capacity; below that and we were below budget.

Though 1986 was lucky for us, concern for the whole theatre community continued. On top of the government's subsidy cuts and the punishing inflation, most of the arts were desperately worried about their money from local authorities. Four hundred arts organisations had become threatened because of rate-capping. I have kept a poem, published in the *New Statesman*, which expresses the feeling at this time. It is by Roger Woddis who subtitled it 'After "Bagpipe Music" by Louis MacNeice':

RATE CAP MUSIC

It's no go the concert-hall,
It's no go the opera,
All they want is a darkened house
And a corpse cut up by a doctor.
Their pockets are filled with lumps of lead,
Their boots are made for kicking,
Their hearts are lined with frosted glass
And their heads with metal sheeting.

It's no go the council grant,
It's no go the players,
All they want is a nation starved
And robbed of its eyes and ears.
It's no go the soaring voice,
It's no go the dancers,
Say goodbye to the living stage
And the life that art enhances.
The pound is falling hour by hour,
The pound will fall forever,
But if you break their bloody necks,
You won't destroy their ledgers.

That was a long while ago. The slow miserable decline has gone on, and the capacity of the arts for survival is still being severely tested. The Fringe remains full of vitality, though the quantity of work produced has shrunk. The National Theatre, so far, thrives against enormous odds, but the other national companies lurch from one crisis to another. Up and down the country, theatres are doing less. There is also less room for risk-taking and more room for the ordinary. The eroding of the fertile and profitable landscape, created by Maynard Keynes and tilled by Jennie Lee and Arnold Goodman and their successors, still continues. The waste is shameful when the potential is so great.

– 20 –

David Hare's and Howard Brenton's *Pravda* was a very apt satire for us to stage during the ferment of 1985/6; but before it was put on, just in case several of the protagonists seemed suspiciously like certain members of the Establishment, I took Counsel's advice. His opinion was that if anybody claimed to be one of the deliberately cartoon-like characters, he would have virtually no hope of proving this, and would anyway be considered a fool. Nonetheless, I warned the Board of possible problems ahead, and they asked to read the play. Their general view of it was chilly. It wasn't libellous, they thought, but a thin and silly piece of work, most unlikely to succeed. Plays are never easy to judge in manuscript, and in this case the Board's assessment was adrift. *Pravda* ran in the Olivier to capacity business for over a hundred performances, and was the biggest success the National ever had with a modern play. I loved it. Though often crude and deliberately over-the-top, it had vigour and the outrageousness of Ben Jonson. And it contained, at its centre, Anthony Hopkins's blazing star performance as the predatory newspaper tycoon, who seduced everyone with his dangerous Afrikaans vowels.

Soon after the first night of *Pravda*, I had another

passage of arms with John Osborne, who had often labelled me publicly as the Ghengis Khan of the South Bank. We had met – and he was predictably cordial, as always when face to face – to talk about a revival at the National of his 1957 success *The Entertainer*. Alan Bates was to play the role created by Olivier, and I suggested Joan Plowright might now be the right age to play Phoebe, the wife; she would be very good casting, and there was the added interest that she had originally created the role of the daughter. He agreed.

Just before rehearsals began, Osborne suddenly protested that he had never been consulted about the casting and would not have Joan in the production. It was a 'bizarre notion that was never put to me', he declared. The rights of the play belonged to him of course; and though terms had been agreed with his agent, John had not yet returned his signed contract. I had no alternative but to drop the project – and John achieved public humiliation of Joan, the National and me.

I suppose that this was his intention because no-one has ever been able to discover another motive. Even if the NT had confirmed every conversation in writing (and maybe it was a fault that we hadn't), I am fairly sure he would still have found some other means of upsetting the applecart. He is driven by demons which are probably hell for him. But they are also hell for anybody else who has the misfortune of getting too close.

Joan, instead, played the lead in *Mrs Warren's Profession* in the Lyttelton, and gave a brilliant performance. At last she was at the new National Theatre.

I went on accusing the Arts Council, publicly as well as privately, of feebleness right up to the end of my time at the National. In 1986 and 1987 there was again no increase at all in the NT's grant despite inflation. And in 1988, my last year, our increase was 1.3 per cent with inflation at 3.2 per cent. We still managed to balance our books – just. But, like every other theatre in the country, we were forced to become less and less productive.

Commercial sponsorship was the only answer. And in 1986, for the first time at the NT, a main house production, *The Threepenny Opera*, had been paid for by an outside firm. There is certainly a case for the use of sponsorship for experimental work (what industry would call research and development) but the National has a clear responsibility, under the government, to provide a strong, varied central repertory. It is totally wrong that this work should exist at the whim of commercial patronage. It should be fully subsidised by the state, which brought the theatre into being by Act of Parliament.

We were soon beset by absurdities. We found it impossible to raise money for the Jacobean play *'Tis Pity She's a Whore* because sponsors were fearful of being besmirched by its title. And though we had better luck with my production of *Antony and Cleopatra*, which Ladbroke's sponsored, they put up a large marquee in the foyer to give pre-performance champagne to their guests, who then came in late, loudly interrupting the crucial early scenes. They were not play goers, but party goers.

My public objections to sponsorship, and how it was being used to cut grants, exasperated the new arts minister, Richard Luce. He took my colleagues and me to task for having a 'welfare-state mentality'.

– 21 –

In the spring of 1986, the chairman of the Arts Council, William Rees-Mogg, told the chairman of the National Theatre, Max Rayne, and the chairman of the Royal Shakespeare Company, Geoffrey Cass, that there were bad rumours in the air about the way Trevor Nunn and

I were running our organisations. There was concern about the time we took off and the money we had earned on the commercial exploitation of our own productions. There were darker, unspecified allegations.

I didn't think Trevor or I should worry. We certainly made money when our own subsidised work was transferred by an independent producer into the commercial theatre. But this was only following an approved practice that existed throughout the profession, not only for directors but actors, writers, designers, fight-arrangers, lighting designers. Everyone went on to a new contract when commercial interests were making money out of their subsidised work.

At this time, a really big star could reckon on earning between five and six hundred pounds a week at the National. As the star of a huge West End success it was possible for him or her to take home £8,000 a week. I was earning £1,000 a week at the National as its director. A commercial hit on my normal percentage of box office would bring me up to £3,000 a week. Broadway earnings were even higher.

As far as Trevor and I were concerned, what transferred, what the terms were, how much money we got, everything, was set by market-forces and monitored in detail by our respective Boards as well as by the Arts Council. Time off, too, had to be approved by our Boards; indeed, Trevor had for some time wanted to leave the RSC but had been persuaded to stay on a part-time basis.

In June Trevor and I were at Glyndebourne. I was directing *Simon Boccanegra* and he was reviving his superb *Porgy and Bess*. The *Sunday Times* Insight team asked if they could do a joint interview with us early one morning before rehearsals to talk about the virtues and dangers of sponsorship. Trevor was hesitant, but I thought it would be a good idea for us to speak together on such a vexed subject.

However, the two reporters – after the photographer had taken a jolly picture of us laughing together in the garden of Glyndebourne – had next to nothing to ask about sponsorship. Instead, they surprised us with a series of charges. We had both made, they said, a lot of money out of commercial transfers, in my case *Amadeus* (in Trevor's, *Les Misérables*), claiming – wrongly – that I'd made more from the transfer than the NT had. They said that we both spent long periods away doing outside work. There was also an implication that I had been engaged in some sort of conspiracy to reduce the National's financial stake in Shaffer's *Yonadab* if it went to Broadway (which it didn't) in order to increase my own as its director. This last charge was based on their description of a meeting with the Shubert Organization (which had never happened).

The following Sunday, the jolly photograph of Trevor and me appeared in the *Sunday Times* over a massive story with the headline 'Laughing All the Way to the Bank'.

That morning, I was invited to defend myself on *The World This Weekend*, but I wanted time to think. I cooked the Sunday lunch instead. Two days later, I gave a press conference at the National to set the record straight. Soon afterwards an article of mine was printed in the *Sunday Times* answering the accusations. But there still remained the professional slur and the implications of conspiracy. Trevor and I both sued for libel amidst enormous press coverage. *Spitting Image* showed us both riding on a gravy train.

In former days – the days of Jennie Lee and Arnold Goodman or, later, of David Eccles and Patrick Gibson – the Minister of the Arts and the chairman of the Arts Council would almost certainly have rushed to the defence of Trevor and myself, pointing out that we had done nothing whatsoever out of order. On this occasion there was not a word. Hearteningly, many others had rallied round (Judi Dench wrote me a dashing postcard: 'Dear Peter, Fuck the Press, Love Judi'). But I cannot easily forgive either Richard Luce or William Rees-Mogg for their silence, or for implying by it that there was something to investigate. The overall effect of the article had certainly tended to discredit the subsidised arts, as well as Trevor and myself. But that presumably was its aim, like similar, personalised attacks on the BBC which had been going on from time to time over the previous four or five years.

Much of what the *Sunday Times* said was of the unfair, knockabout kind that inevitably comes with public life. Anonymous sources and unknown friends were liberally quoted. But I sued only to disprove the especially damaging *Yonadab* conspiracy charge. I ran, however, into an enormous snag. I could not legally confine my case to that alone. The *Sunday Times*, I was warned, were planning to use *all* their accusations as defence – and that could well spin the court proceedings out over many weeks. Even if I conducted my own case, thus saving on lawyers' fees, I had to be prepared for hundreds of thousands of pounds of costs in the event of not winning; and perhaps even if I won. In other words, to sue would be crazy unless I had half a million pounds that I could afford to lose. I had a house in Chelsea worth about £250,000. And that was all. My extended family and alimony had seen to that. Finally, I withdrew my libel action.

Trevor kept up his intention to sue for years. He was obsessive about it, as I had been for a time. At one point it was rumoured that he was setting spies on Andrew Neil, the *Sunday Times* editor, and that Neil had responded by setting spies on him. Or the other way round. It was an image that gave gleeful gossip to London chatterers. In the end, though, Trevor also withdrew. The paper, at his insistence, had printed a piece clarifying, as they put it, what they had written. It was, I suppose, the nearest the media ever get to a climb-down.

In May 1988, eight months after I had abandoned my libel action, I was interviewed on BBC Radio for the *Today* programme. Under pressure, I was unwise enough

337

to make some highly critical remarks about the *Sunday Times*. The next day, the paper threatened to sue unless they had an apology and a complete withdrawal. They said that my remarks were a slur on the integrity of a fine group of journalists. The BBC made a complete apology, and I had no alternative but to admit my remarks were intemperate. I was, however, able to stress that there had been no conspiracy over *Yonadab*.

The whole painful business proved to me beyond doubt that suing for libel is a gamble that can only be taken by wealthy organisations or by individual people who are extremely rich. What was printed in the *Sunday Times*, though I suffered no serious lasting effect from it, has stuck in the memories of some people and been, now and again, a disconcerting irritant to me. So far-flung is the power of newspaper cuttings that when I was promoting my film *She's Been Away* in Japan in 1990, the first subject brought up at a press conference was the *Sunday Times* and my earnings, so many years before, from *Amadeus*.

Amadeus was far and away the most commercial production I have been involved with, and made me the only big money I have ever earned. My royalties for the five years it played Broadway, the West End and commercial tours (including a tiny share of the producers' profits – I had nothing from the film) amounted to some £700,000. The author and the producers made, of course, much more. The NT itself has so far made over £2 million from the play and the film.

– 22 –

On 4 September 1986 I wrote a letter to Max Rayne saying that it was 'my formal and firm decision' not to continue at the National when my contract expired in just over two years; and as the contract required that I suggest a successor, I proposed Richard Eyre. I added that the matter was now urgent as planning for 1988/9 had to start in some six months' time. All this felt exactly right. By the end of 1988 I would have completed fifteen years at the NT and it was time for a change.

To my great delight, the Board endorsed my suggestion of Richard. But there were the inevitable contortions about the appointment. The Arts Council, under pressure from the government, insisted the job be advertised. I also feared considerable opposition to Richard from the Establishment: he had, perhaps, shown his left-wing sympathies too openly in anti-Thatcher films such as *The Ploughman's Lunch* and *Tumbledown*. However, reports in the press that he was my choice had, it seemed, effectively discouraged other applicants. There were only four, one mad and another a Belgian who, though he had no experience in the theatre, wrote that he'd always been interested in British drama.

Max Rayne had resisted being forced to advertise the post. But this was a time of increasing government pressure. The National's Board was becoming less and less progressive as those who had served their term were replaced. The government found acceptable as Board members only those they could call 'one of us'. The old idea of keeping a rough balance was gone. It was happening in all public institutions – a new development in British public life, and a dangerous one.

But Richard's appointment was secure, an achievement at that time. He had made only one proviso. He wanted an administrative director jointly to share the responsibility with him; specifically David Aukin, a talented producer who had run Hampstead Theatre with Michael Rudman and then made a considerable success of the Haymarket in Leicester.

Both the NT and the RSC had by now become huge organisations, desperately doing, in my view, too much in order to justify their subsidies. In consequence, the job of director appeared to need help at the highest level, an administrative wizard who would lighten the load.

I therefore asked David to join us, and he came well before Richard took over. But the truth is that I do not believe in two people running a theatre on an equal footing. Actors need to know who they are working for, who in the end has the authority; and a theatre, like a newspaper, finally has to express one person's tastes.

David's arrival was seen by many as a move towards separating the administration, under him, from the artistic direction. But it is a false division which seldom if ever works. In any case, David was more of an impresario than a nuts-and-bolts man. He left in 1990 to take charge of Channel 4's film division, and the National as a result reverted to one-man rule.

Now I knew I was going a great peace settled over me, and I spent my last two years on the South Bank working happily and well.

In January 1987, I began rehearsing *Antony and Cleopatra* and had the wonderful advantage of twelve weeks in which to bring this vast and intricate master-piece to the stage. Judi Dench honoured a pact we'd made many years before by agreeing to play the fiendishly difficult part of Cleopatra; and, with her genius for self-deprecation, warned me on the first day of rehearsal that I might have taken on more than I had bargained for. 'You have cast Cleopatra with a menopausal dwarf,' she told me cheerfully.

In the event, however, she created the greatest Cleo-patra I have seen – wilful, dangerous, feminine, and shifting in mood and movement like quicksilver.

The Antony of Tony Hopkins was, from the start, a great man in dangerous decline. Tony has a restless temperament, and this often leads him to dislike what he has just done. Within months of the play closing he was telling the press what a miserable time he'd had at the NT. He had similarly rejected Olivier's National at the Old Vic when he left it in the early Seventies for Hollywood. Then he rejected Hollywood when he came back to us for *Pravda*, Lear and Antony. Now he is having moral doubts about his Oscar-winning performance in *The Silence of the Lambs*.

Antony and Cleopatra played to capacity throughout its run and was garlanded with every kind of award. I could not have hoped for a better cast, with Tim Piggott-Smith as an icily political Octavius and Michael Bryant quite superb as Enobarbus, paradoxically making a soldier of few words live by speaking the verse impeccably.

Normally, sets have to be designed well before rehearsals start. This time, because we had the luxury of an especially long rehearsal period, Alison Chitty's work was able to evolve organically, the usually unattainable ideal. For the first three weeks Alison sat with us and sketched furiously while we discovered the physical dynamic of each scene. Only then did she design it.

With *Antony*, I had the thrilling sense of coming very close to the play. The canvas is so vast that it defies analysis. But I know nothing which reveals with richer perception the madness of love, the hypocrisy of politics, and the mystery of mortality.

I enjoyed 1987, not simply because I remember *Antony* as a particular pleasure. It was also the year when *A View from the Bridge* was a triumph for both Alan Ayckbourn as its director and Michael Gambon in the central part. And, among other good work, we managed, by dint of Thelma Holt's tenacity with fund-raising, to have visiting companies again: Peter Stein's Schaubühne from West Germany; the Royal Dramatic Theatre of Sweden in two Ingmar Bergman productions (*Hamlet* and *Miss Julie*); Ninagawa's group from Japan; the Mayakovsky from Moscow; and the Market Theatre of Johannesburg. I seemed at last to be getting back to my original dreams for the National.

In his review of my *Diaries*, in 1983 Martin Hoyle

had written: 'Though the RSC remains his glittering creation, the National Theatre may end up merely as his Frankenstein.' By now I knew it hadn't.

It is true that with the RSC I was venturing where no-one had been before, and that for a young man who loved to take risks and had very little to lose it was a glorious opportunity, infinitely exciting. But the National, too, was an extraordinary and rewarding experience. In a perverse way, the fact that it was, in the beginning at least, so crises-ridden suited me. Peter Wood once said that the moment a crisis occurred, my whole being went into a state of relaxation.

In my memory, my ten years at the RSC seem much longer than my fifteen at the National. The National was so crammed with events that it passed like lightning.

Some time after I left, Roy Strong did a detailed survey on radio about government funding for the arts. He found against the National and the RSC: 'Everybody thinks we ought to have these centres of excellence . . . but the tide is not going the way of these big old war-horses. They will be maintained, but the excitement, the push, the drive, will be with the wider cultural spread throughout the country.'

I do not believe this is remotely true. Innovation continues to be the main characteristic of our two national theatres. Also, they keep alive the repertory of the past; give opportunities to new writers; train actors, directors, designers and technicians; and carry out essential studio research. Most of all, they bring on tomorrow's audience.

I believe if we had not had the RSC and the National, London would have become much like Broadway, with plastic musicals running for decades, few new plays, and many dark theatres.

– 23 –

My last piece of work at the National was a cycle of Shakespeare's Late Plays *Cymbeline*, *The Winter's Tale*, and *The Tempest*.

I had been taught as a boy that the Late Plays were Shakespeare's return, as an ageing man, to the romantic fairy stories of his youth, with *The Tempest*, the culmination, seen as a gentle and nostalgic farewell to his art. Every age reads what it needs into Shakespeare; and if the Late Plays are cut and softened in production it is possible to end up with a sentimental view. But study of the texts cannot support it.

The Tempest is Shakespeare's Faust play; it is terrifyingly blasphemous. A man who is a politician as well as an artist has the temerity to cast himself as God. He judges and punishes those who have done wrong to him, finally engineering a cosmic act of forgiveness. He calls for heavenly music to heal his enemies; and it is provided. Any ambiguity in the play is, I am sure, the result of Shakespeare being unable to write precisely what he meant: the stringent laws against blasphemy at that time would have prevented him.

The Winter's Tale finishes with similar uncertainty. Many questions are in the air, and there is still much for the characters to discuss and understand if fragile love and trust are to be reborn.

The plays may be fairy stories, in which nightmare cruelties abound, but they do not end happily. Throughout rehearsals I found myself emphasising the degree to which they deal with extremes, especially emotional extremes. They are not works of gentle resignation but, like all archetypal stories, hard-edged, sharp and absolute. All three plays look fiercely at lust, jealousy and betrayal. In *Cymbeline*, a woman wakes by what she thinks is her husband's headless corpse.

In that production and in the programme, Imogen was called Innogen, following the new Oxford spelling. Innogen means 'innocent person' – an appropriate conceit in a play where the hero is called Posthumous. The *m* in the first printed text is clearly a misprint for double *nn*; and there is no recorded reference to the name 'Imogen' before this play.

Some of my closest colleagues helped me to realise the Late Plays: Michael Bryant, Tim Piggott-Smith and Basil Henson were among a group of actors who, I knew, could deliver what was needed. Alison Chitty was the designer, Harry Birtwistle the composer. Right at the start, however, we had a problem. Wendy Morgan, my Innogen and Miranda, had just had a baby and found working on these two big roles, plus the demands of young motherhood, too much to deal with. She asked to be released and I had to search for a replacement.

I'm not a great party goer; I greatly prefer dinner with a few people I am fond of to waving with vague goodwill at fifty people I hardly know. But at a Christmas party given by Duncan Weldon (who was going to back my productions when I left the National) I met Sarah Miles. I knew her slightly, and knew Robert Bolt, her husband, very well indeed. As we chatted, I began to wonder if Sarah could play Innogen. She had had no experience in Shakespeare, but I admired the daring honesty of her film performances. The next week I auditioned her and gave her the part.

Within days I knew I'd made a terrible mistake. Sarah learnt the meaning of Innogen's verse with aptitude, and she worked hard to breathe in the right places and to develop her voice. But she had great difficulty in delivering the words as spontaneous descriptions of her feelings. Too often she sounded false, not to say calculating, and her tempo was very slow. I realised that her strength as an actress was in conveying emotions below and beyond the words. On film you can see what she is thinking and this makes her a great asset to the camera. But Shakespeare expresses everything by what he *says*. His characters have an ability to describe and illustrate what they are feeling *as* they are feeling it. So his actors have to give the impression of creating the text while they experience the emotion. This is hard; and it has nothing to do with naturalistic acting, where feeling is always paramount, and what is actually said often masks or disguises it.

I had grown used to directors, at the end of their first week of rehearsals, asking me if they could fire this or that actor. I always refused, taking the view that if they had cast the actor, they should persevere with him or her. Only if every attempt had been made to avert failure should the actor be replaced. So I persevered with Sarah. I had known many actors break through the barrier she was up against. But as she worked harder and harder, the problem became worse and worse. The spring of the verse, the skill needed to speak trippingly on the tongue, eluded her.

Finally, I realised Sarah just couldn't do it, and I had to tell her so. It must have been a horrible experience for her. I know it was a bewildering one for Robert Bolt; I lost a friend. But fine actors can be incapable of playing Shakespeare, just as fine opera singers can embarrass when singing Cole Porter. It is not a judgement on their talent; only on their ability to achieve a particular style of expression.

Geraldine James took over Innogen at frighteningly short notice and gave a beautiful performance. She had no time to worry about the technique; she had the instinct, and simply practised the verse round the clock.

My daughter Jennifer, who had steadily made a good career for herself as an actress since she came down from Cambridge, played Miranda in *The Tempest* and had a success in the part. But she left the play before the run was over. To this day I don't quite know why. I do know she felt there was great pressure on her as my daughter; and her action caused, I'm afraid, immense bad feeling in the company.

It is hard for children when their parents are frequently in the public eye. I know that all my children have found this difficult in some measure, but for Jenny it has been a real trial, and she has tried to cure herself of the feeling by writing about it. The divorces have hurt her, too, and that, together with a good dose of the discontented Pamment blood, has caused her much unhappiness. She is immensely talented both as a writer and actress; and she is a superlative mother. But she has yet to find her place. As a child, Jenny would never take an examination unless she believed she would pass it.

– 24 –

The years around my sixtieth birthday in 1990 – those before, when I was preparing to leave the National, and those after, culminating in the birth of my sixth child, Emma – have been a period of expanding horizons in my work and, most of all, of the greatest happiness personally. I owe much of this to Nicki.

Nicki trained as a lawyer and she loved the law while it remained an intellectual puzzle in text books. But when she came to apply it to people she left the profession, for she was horrified to find she was dealing not with right and wrong, but with the quirks and oddities of a specialised game.

She has a practical attitude to each day and gets as much out of it as she can. When she had to tell her father, a devout Catholic, that she was contemplating marriage with a man who had already had three wives, she was prepared for some distress. Being a wit and a realist, she told her father that I was uxurious – someone who believed in marriage, and had therefore spent a lifetime trying to get it right.

The randomness of life alarms me. If Nicki hadn't decided against becoming a barrister we would never have met. When she gave up the law, she went to Riverside Studios as a temporary switchboard operator. She wanted to do something in the arts. But it was the time of Thatcher's cuts and the place was on the verge of bankruptcy. Many staff were leaving to find other work; indeed anyone with a mortgage was advised to go. Within three weeks, Nicki had been promoted from the switchboard to running Riverside's publicity. There she caught the eye of John Goodwin, joined his press office team at the National, and worked with me on all my productions from *Antony and Cleopatra* to the end of my time at the NT.

If none of this had happened, I suppose I would still be alone. I hate loneliness. Each of my marriages has been an attempt to share my life completely with another person; and each attempt before Nicki has, in the end, produced an agonising loneliness.

Nicki and I married in September 1990, soon after my divorce from Maria. She is thirty years younger than I am. When I was creating the RSC she was a baby. But this distance of years seems to give an increased edge and pleasure to our relationship. We know that we haven't all that amount of time left. So far, our marriage has everything I've always hoped for; I say 'so far' not because I can imagine disaster – this time the possibility never crosses my mind – but because intense love is so strong, and at the same time so fragile, it can never be taken for granted.

When our love affair started, in 1988, Nicki and I had hoped to keep it secret until the Late Shakespeares were launched and I was on my way out of the National. The result was some months of sickening duplicity. I do not like the hypocrisy of an affair, of being forced to dissemble. Some people find it exciting, even erotic. I don't.

Meanwhile, the Late Shakespeares were full of problems. The sets and costumes were behind schedule, mainly because the NT's workshop had been closed to save money and the work had been given to outside contractors. The *Salome* I had done in Los Angeles was revived at Covent Garden, so I had to fit in a few rehearsals with Maria. And, as an added complication, a television crew was filming me most of the time for a documentary programme about my work at the RSC and the National.

In the middle of all this, Michael Owen of the *Evening Standard* asked Nicki to have a drink with him in the National Theatre bar. While they were chatting, a photographer suddenly appeared and took a picture. Michael then taxed Nicki about our affair and said he was intending to do a story about it. She told him nothing and he asked to talk to me. I had a quick word with John Goodwin and he didn't hesitate. 'Deny it,' he said. It was the first time in thirty years I had heard him advocate a lie.

I lied with extreme misgivings (and felt guilty enough to try to make my peace with Michael Owen some months later). But, as John knew, Maria had yet to be told, also my children and my parents. There were enormous human problems still to be tackled.

That spring and summer of 1988 were hectic: very alive because of the promise of new beginnings; nerve-wracking because so much was at stake. The three Late Shakespeares packed during their Cottesloe season, transferred to the Olivier, and toured to Russia, Japan and Greece. They were hugely successful on tour, but in London hadn't quite lived up to the expectations aroused by such a big farewell enterprise. However, at the time the press notices were appearing, the papers were also printing massive and complimentary summaries of my work at the NT. That was nice. But I began to feel as if I were reading my own obituaries.

In Russia we presented the three plays at the Moscow Art Theatre. The city seemed very different from my first visit there in 1958 with the Stratford company. Then it was deep winter; now it was high summer. And though the food was as terrible as ever, people were starting to talk to each other. There was a feeling of change in the air, and Gorbachev and Reagan were holding their summit. Theatre people were still chary of looking you in the eye, but were beginning, I think, to tell the truth. They yearned, they said, to have a mixed economy like ours in the West. They explained that their theatres were always full because the tickets were distributed through trade unions, school organisations and party structures. It was impossible to tell whether the work was appealing to the public or not; the audience would be there anyway. Ironically, they longed for the empty seats that would tell them whether they were staging the wrong things.

We played to wildly appreciative houses, and before every performance there were mobs of people clamouring unsuccessfully to get in. It emerged that tickets had never gone on sale to the general public at all. By the time Party officials, theatre union bosses and the educational hierarchy had had their pickings there were no seats left. So Thelma Holt, the tour organiser, Nicki and I went outside the theatre each evening and gave away the NT's nightly quota of forty tickets. The result was tears in the street.

Cymbeline, the first in our three-play cycle, very nearly didn't start. It had a number of entrances through the audience, and therefore the pass doors between stage and auditorium had to be left open. But one of the doors was locked and nobody could find the key. Meetings about this went on throughout the whole day before the first night. We did not uncover the truth until 5 p.m.: the key was held by the KGB. The door opened on to a secret corridor used by Party bosses, so the area was one of very high security. The door, we were informed, was never unlocked.

I told the authorities that I understood their position, but as there were less than two hours before the play began it was impossible for me to restage the production. With great regret, I said, we would have to cancel the first night. The door was unlocked half an hour before the performance was due to begin.

From Moscow the company went on to Georgia; then to Tokyo. On the way to Georgia, however, the trucks carrying the sets and costumes broke down. Sabotage was suspected; water had certainly been introduced by somebody into the diesel oil. The plays had to be staged with whatever could be improvised or borrowed. It was apparently a memorable occasion. The actors became extraordinarily creative because the very simplicity of the productions gave the text a new power. Many critics, including Michael Billington who was in Georgia for the *Guardian*, found it unforgettable.

I wish I could have seen these performances. I had to leave the tour in Moscow in order to start rehearsing *Falstaff* at Glyndebourne – another world.

There is a small collection of masterpieces which, while looking honestly at the absurdity of human behaviour, end up celebrating it: *Twelfth Night, A Midsummer Night's Dream, She Stoops to Conquer, The Marriage of Figaro*. I would add *Falstaff* to that list. I had looked forward for a long time to directing it. It turned out to be a horrible experience. Just before rehearsals began, I trapped a nerve in my neck and had to wear one of those torturing collars designed to limit head movement. For the entire rehearsal period I was on strong painkillers and, I'm sure, somewhat hazy. If it hadn't been for Stephen Lawless, my brilliant assistant, I doubt if the show would ever have reached the stage.

Both in work and in my private life, I was pushing

myself to the edge again. I was advised that an operation was necessary to cure my neck. As a last resort I tried a course of acupuncture. In the first minute of treatment I felt the pain draining out of me. It was like silence after six weeks of excruciating noise. A few more sessions and the cure was permanent.

Once *Falstaff* had opened, Nicki and I left for France. I was in desperate need of a rest. But rest, or at any rate peace of mind, escaped me. Leaving the National, breaking with Maria, upsetting all my children yet again – particularly Rebecca who was only six – disturbing my parents, and starting another new life at my age, all seemed suddenly terrifying.

I loved Nicki deeply, but for a few horrible weeks I could not resolve all the contradictory tensions in my head. I thought of suicide again. All this made a hell for Nicki, and I will always marvel at the strength she found. She knew that I had to sort things out for myself.

As soon as we were back in England, this private turmoil was aggravated. Our affair had leaked to the press. We were suddenly on the front pages and being pursued by photographers and journalists wherever we went.

Perhaps a theatre director, who in the scheme of things rates as fairly small beer, should be flattered that his private life is of keen interest to the reading millions. But I didn't see it that way. The attentions of the tabloid press made it ten times more difficult to clear my tangled head. Nicki and I were now figures in an absurd public drama and we did not recognise ourselves.

We even split up briefly to see if separation would help me make up my mind; and she wrote me a letter full of understanding and completely devoid of any emotional blackmail. It was this letter more than anything that brought me back from the edge. It is typical of my care for the past that I have lost it.

The pain of that summer of 1988 was also mixed with farce. I was due to go to Scarborough to see Alan

Ayckbourn's new play, *Man of the Moment*. But all the exits from the National were posted with journalists waiting to waylay me. We had, however, a remarkable security officer, David Mundy, whose job was to remind us constantly that all theatres are a frightful risk to the well-being of the public. Naked flames, insecure handrails, pieces of loose carpet on the stairs haunted his dreams. I shared the problem of my escape with him and he came up with a plan.

During lunch my secretary, Mary Cooper, backed her Mini in through the enormous scene-dock doors at the rear of the building. The doors were then shut with the car inside. When it was time for me to leave I crouched in the back seat of the Mini while Mary, armed with a mobile phone, sat in the driver's seat waiting for her cue from David who was outside watching. As soon as the group of journalists wandered away for a cup of tea, he phoned her and gave the signal. The dock doors opened and we hurtled out.

As I collapsed with relief into my seat on the train, I saw to my horror that the man opposite was reading an evening paper which had a large picture of me with Maria on the front page. I buried my face in a script.

It was embarrassing the next morning to find that Alan's house in Scarborough was also surrounded by reporters. How the word had got out that I was there I simply couldn't guess. I stayed hidden while Heather Chasen, Alan's very funny and practical companion, showed her metal as an actress. 'He's not here,' I heard her say at the front door. 'He's a very busy man and always changing his plans. You never know where he is . . .'

That night, going to Alan's theatre by a roundabout route, I picked my way secretly across the flower beds and over the tiny ornate bridges of the municipal gardens. He met me in the shrubbery and we crept in through a little-used back entrance. I enjoyed the play.

Alan and Heather accepted all that was happening in

a wonderfully helpful and humorous spirit. I mentioned to them how furious my mother would be at her son's third crashed marriage. Alan said, 'I can see the *Daily Mirror* headline now: "Son Right off Rails says Railway Wife".'

The harrying by the press didn't let up. Back in London I found my house in Chelsea beseiged by journalists. So Alan, again with blessed kindness, lent Nicki and me his apartment in Docklands as a hideaway.

Abroad we were not spared. The Late Shakespeares were by now in Greece and reporters even tracked us there, sending bottles of champagne up to our hotel room in an attempt to persuade us to be interviewed. The representative of the *Sun* expressed great sorrow that he could not stay to attend the opening of *Cymbeline* at Epidaurus on behalf of his readers. We returned the champagne.

In September, I was followed around Los Angeles where, on a contract signed two years before, I was directing *Così fan tutte* with Maria singing Dorabella. A photograph of us going into rehearsal led to speculation about a reconciliation.

It was all silly-season stuff. But the three of us did not feel very silly, although I am sure we frequently looked it.

That autumn I left the National in a whirl of parties, speeches and presents. I have always loved presents, and the theatre staff gave me a wonderful one: a Hasselblad camera.

The Board had decided on a present that had to be specially made. It was a beautiful modern love-seat devised to go round a tree. But when the time came to give it to me, I had left Maria and the country house where we lived. I no longer had a tree.

I was starting again.

PART FIVE

Flash Forward,
Flash Back

– 1 –

Like all my generation, I spent a great deal of my childhood in cinemas – vast smoke-filled palaces of fantasy, a world away from the tiny boxes of today's multiplex movie houses.

I saw *Gone With the Wind*, *Wuthering Heights*, Olivier's *Henry V*, *Citizen Kane*; and then, thanks to the Cambridge Film Society, the great French films of the Thirties and Forties. I watched Raimu, Jean Gabin, *Les Enfants du Paradis*, and graduated to Cocteau and Eisenstein. I discovered new heroes in Jacques Tati and Buster Keaton. In fact, I have been so thoroughly marinated in film that I am surprised to find myself still chiefly a director of plays and operas.

We all have unrealised ambitions. Peter Brook is perhaps the stage's greatest living innovator; yet his ambition was to be a film director – an auteur like Godard or Truffaut or Louis Malle. I have stayed in the theatre because, although it is a minority art, it has, at its best, an unrivalled power to change the hearts and minds of audiences. Also, I love words, and a play communicates primarily by its text. Even a silence is shaped by the words that surround it; even a dance or a duel has to be set up verbally.

With film, it is the images that matter most, and

they alter literally with the speed of light. Twenty-four frames of celluloid flicker through an illuminated gate each second. And this montage of shot on shot, jump cut, dissolve, flash forward and flash back gives film the mobility and unexpectedness of a dream. Its images seem real but of course they are not. Our apprehension of film is literal before it is metaphorical. An actor on a bare wooden stage, if he has the right words and the right magnetism, can make a theatre audience believe he is in Ancient Rome. But a film of him on that same stage, saying the same words, remains just an actor making a speech on bare boards.

It seems to me that, as the cost of shooting has increased and the power of the controlling accountants with it, some of the art has gone out of film-making. In the early days, for example, rushes were a quickly developed record of yesterday's work that could be shown to the actors so they could learn by seeing their mistakes. That is the way Chaplin worked; rushes were part of the process of doing it again. Now they are too often just a check that the film has come out without any technical flaws; and actors are generally discouraged from watching them. Only the most blatant disaster can justify a retake. Thus a once-great creative strength of movie-making – its ability to hold a mirror up to the actor which helps him to refine what he is doing – is no more.

However, to see again some of the cinema's early masterpieces can be unsettling. While theatre doesn't last beyond tonight's performance, film is fixed and therefore dates because of the changing responses of a contemporary audience. The other day I experienced something I would never have thought possible: Garbo began to overact.

– 2 –

I love the physical world of movie-making. It is tatty and tawdry, a bit like a building site. Everything is improvised and taped together for the moment. The most elaborate and atmospheric lighting is achieved by torn bits of frosted gelatine and black cardboard strips fastened over the lamps with bulldog clips. A technician wafts smoke on to the set by waving a piece of rough-sawn plywood – and what the camera sees is a mist that steals gently over the heroine's hair and eyes. Only the tiny frame that the camera is actually pointing at – only the shot itself – is shaped and ordered; all else is the untidy chaos of the film studio.

Make-up and hair-do's, the preparations of prop men and of the lighting cameraman, are all allowed lengthy care and attention. When everything is ready, and only then, the actors are hurried to the set. There they are expected to deliver instant genius. If actors or director stop to think, or discuss their problems, the atmosphere quickly becomes tense. The minute one shot is over and safely in the can, the unit moves on to the next. Unlike in the theatre, there is no time for trying out solutions and jettisoning them. The director must come prepared, knowing exactly what he wants. He must always seem certain and god-like.

The pattern of a film director's day is different from that of a theatre director. For two-thirds of it he is liable to do nothing except pass the time, chat idly to other people who are also waiting to do their jobs, and try to avoid eating the mountains of food that are always available to bolster up the crew. But during the third of the day when he is actually shooting, his critical and creative energies are stretched to the full. It is a switchback ride; and I took a long time to get used to it. I would pace nervily around the studio, wondering why the lighting cameraman couldn't be quicker, or thinking that the unnatural calm around me came from laziness. I was wrong. I had to learn to trust the natural rhythm of the work.

I found, as well, that I had to change how I worked with the actor. I admire the great movie actor just as intensely as I admire the great stage actor. Both convey absolute truth in performance. But in the theatre, that truth has to be projected – though without coarsening or distorting it. In the cinema good actors do not project at all. This does not mean that they don't feel, but that when their feelings are almost hidden the camera is most eager to reveal them. If actors behave like reticent lovers, the camera wants more and more of them.

I also had to develop a different pace in dealing with film actors. In the theatre, five or six weeks of rehearsal allow the director to conduct stage actors on a journey they may never have contemplated before. Areas of their talent and their personality may be explored in ways quite new to them. This is an exciting and dangerous proceeding, and needs time. But time is the one thing the film director never has. If he challenges the film actor too obviously, he runs the risk of photographing the nervousness and tension that result from facing up to the problem. And he will film that, not the solution. Directing the film actor had, I found, to be more about reassurance than exploration.

Dirk Bogarde became a great friend during my early years in the theatre – I had directed him in a not very successful West End play – and during visits to see him on sets I watched avidly how a film was put together. Later, when I was married to Leslie, I saw Hollywood at work, and also learned about camera angles and editing. Since then, whenever I go to a movie I have to force myself to surrender to the film: otherwise I sit working out how many different shots have gone to make up each scene.

But it was not until I directed my first film that I understood the miracles that could be performed in the editing room. Editing allows the director to make the final choices, to juxtapose the images in different ways, and to become the creator. The scriptwriter may well have inspired these images, but he could not have known precisely how they would interact on each other. In the cutting room, the director, in a true sense, becomes the author. The dialogue can be retimed and repaused; the reactions altered; the mood changed by the addition of music and effects. And what is unsatisfactory can often be cut or obscured.

Orson Welles once said that being given the opportunity to make a film was like presenting the small boy that is in every director with the ultimate electric train set. I find it more like painstakingly putting together the thousand pieces of a jigsaw, one piece for each shot of the film, without knowing quite what picture the jigsaw will eventually make.

– 3 –

I made my first film, *Work is a Four Letter Word*, in 1967 for Universal. It was produced – with a great deal of courage in view of my inexperience – by Tommy Clyde. The script was freely adapted by Jeremy Brooks and myself from a play I had done for the RSC, *Eh?* by Henry Livings. In the film were David Warner, the young Cilla Black, and a group of RSC actors including Alan Howard, Elizabeth Spriggs and David Waller. But its strange mixture of anarchy and North Country humour did not take easily to the screen. I tried to turn David into a modern Buster Keaton at large in a surreal world. Looking back, I think the movie was not surreal enough. I was also very nervous, learning by doing it, learning above all how to know when a scene is adequately covered by the camera. In my anxiety, I did precisely what I wished to avoid: I filmed too many shots. If a director covers a scene from too many angles, he inevitably ends up using the majority of them. This made my first movie extremely restless.

I've always worshipped classical film-makers such as Billy Wilder and Jean Renoir. They contain the action in carefully composed shots which develop only with the movement of the actors, and the cut to the next shot is inevitable and unnoticeable. The film-makers I admire today for their technique are Louis Malle and Woody Allen. Allen is also the only modern director to take full advantage of film, keeping forty per cent of his budget for re-shooting once he has looked at the rough edit.

I do not much like those modern American films where an anxiety to hold the audience's attention results in constant cutting to a different shot. This produces a surface energy, but belongs to the world of the advertising commercial where the style becomes the meaning and the meaning itself is lost.

Every time I make a film, I struggle for the simplicity of style that I believe I can achieve on the stage. And I usually fail, because I will not economise with the camera: there are still far too many shots. Yet I yearn to make films. I dream of being Ingmar Bergman in his heyday, working with the same group of actors and making modest pictures on big subjects in the summer, then directing plays in the winter.

Perhaps, one day, it will be possible for a director to shoot his film with a tiny camera which he operates himself. Perhaps, one day, there will be a minimum of lights, with the sound created by intensely sensitive, invisible microphones. Then the vans and the lorries and the catering buses and the make-up caravans and the portable lavatories, and all the vast army of people who make up even the smallest film crew, will be reduced to a few basic technicians.

Though *Work is a Four Letter Word* was not a success, it was not such a failure that it stopped me making more films. After leaving the RSC in 1968, and before going to the National in 1973, I was a freelance director and shot, as well as a short film of Pinter's play *Landscape*, five full-length movies. One of the earliest was *Three Into Two Won't Go* with Rod Steiger, Claire Bloom and an Edna O'Brien script. I followed this with *Perfect Friday*, a caper movie with Stanley Baker, Ursula Andress and David Warner, produced by a partnership between Dimitri de Grunwald and myself.

Dimitri was an old-style European wheeler-dealer, with flair, acumen and great charm. He taught me that it is not enough for the script to be good and for the actors to be gifted; if a film is actually to be made, the project must in some way be 'hot'.

And this does not change. Some time ago I was asked if I would be interested in developing a book as a movie. It was a fascinating journal by Etty Hillesum about life in Amsterdam under the Nazis. I proposed Harold Pinter as the scriptwriter, but the producers said they could not attract the money they needed unless they could also include an actress's name. I suggested Emma Thompson. 'Emma who?' they said. Some eighteen months later, when Emma was nominated for an Oscar for *Howard's End*, the producers rang me and, after apologising for their long silence, enquired whether I knew Emma Thompson; did I think she would be good for the film? I said that I had suggested her at the start. They were dumbfounded: they couldn't remember this. Then they rallied. 'But,' they said, 'she wasn't Emma Thompson then.'

In the Sixties and early Seventies, because of the low cost of making movies in Britain and because we still had a film industry, many itinerant American producers passed through London. They would take people like me, those they believed to be 'bankable', out to an expensive lunch and discuss a glittering variety of ideas. I spent many weeks working on scripts or attending meetings for projects that never happened. Ironically, such aborted ventures earned me a lot of money. And though they achieved little they taught me a great deal. More than anything I wanted to direct a movie from my own screenplay – and still do. I found that I loved constructing a film script. I worked with writers on an adaptation of *Don Quixote* and on a version of Huxley's *Brave New World*. Then I was commissioned to write a screenplay myself from an H. E. Bates short story, *The Last of Summer*, which was very nearly made. In those days the tools of the trade were large scissors and pots of glue as the various scenes were arranged and rearranged. Now it is all done by the magic of the lap-top.

Among the films I made at this time, I think of Pinter's *The Homecoming* with special pride. The actors were mainly the marvellous group from my original RSC stage production. David Watkins, one of the great cameramen of the world, photographed it, mainly by shining a Second World War searchlight through the window of the set; the shadows and the depth of focus he achieved were extraordinary. So was the heat. The actors and crew rushed in, played the scene, and rushed out again before they melted.

Earlier, I had directed another movie with RSC actors: *A Midsummer Night's Dream.* The cast was a roll-call of my years with the company: Judi Dench, Ian Richardson, Ian Holm, Diana Rigg, Helen Mirren, David Warner, Paul Rogers, Barbara Jefford, Sebastian Shaw, Derek Godfrey, Michael Jayston. Made for CBS Television, the film was networked throughout America on a Sunday night and watched by millions. It also had a limited cinema release.

We shot in and around Compton Verney, a beautiful ruin of an eighteenth-century house, and waited until the autumn before starting so that we could capture for the screen the damp and misty look of the bad summer described in Titania's great speech. Then the money arrived late, so we had to film even later – well into November. It was cold and wet and difficult for the actors. We crawled about in the undergrowth using a hand-held camera which in those days was very noisy. I accepted this because I wanted to re-record every line of the text in the studio afterwards. As a consequence, it is a beautifully spoken *Dream*. The film, though, is now rather dated, the lovers particularly having a very Sixties look. In a few more years, it could perhaps work again as a period piece.

My film of *Akenfield* came about because of an amazing act of faith – some said of lunacy. Cyril Bennett, the controller of London Weekend Television, gave me £100,000. 'Come back with a film in a year's time,' he said.

There was no script. The idea was for local people to play the characters; the story was based loosely on Ronald Blythe's touching book about life in a Suffolk village. At last I had the opportunity to do something I had always wanted: to make an improvised movie; to catch the unexpected moment and to preserve its drama for ever – something that only cinema can do. All the actors were amateur; most of them were in situations which they had experienced in their work or in their lives. I gave them an objective, and they then talked. At the end of months of shooting, almost always at weekends because our players were not available during the working week, I had about forty-eight hours of Suffolk life. And out of it all came one hour and forty minutes of film which chimed at many points with my life as a small boy.

– 4 –

One of my anxieties on going to the National was that there would be no time for film-making, but I tried to keep my hand in by making videos of some of the plays and operas I had directed. My generation are the first children of the television age and my work over the years has often been taped by others. After helping with the recording of *The Wars of the Roses* in the Sixties, I resolved to try to do these adaptations myself.

Opera has become more popular because of television transmissions of stage productions. But these bear as little relation to the originals as postcard reproductions do to paintings. Live televised opera may increase appreciation, but we should not mistake it for the thing itself. However good the technicians, the camera angles are as imprecise and the lighting often as glaringly all-purpose as that for a football match. And the singers are never sure whether they are playing to the audience in the theatre or to the camera. I think I overcame these problems with three operas I shot at Glyndebourne: *Carmen*, *Albert Herring* and *L'Incoronazione di Poppea*. So that the performers could concentrate on communicating to the camera, we had no audience. The theatre was, in effect, turned into a television studio.

My video of *The Oresteia* gave me another opportunity to do something different. Because the actors were in full masks, which completely covered their mouths, it was possible to record the *sound* of the production independently and then fit the pictures to the soundtrack. We shot the video over four different public performances with four small cameras dotted about the Olivier auditorium. Three of them had a predetermined function – following certain characters, securing certain scripted shots – but each night one of the four cameramen was entirely free to improvise and to shoot what interested him. I ended up with sixteen shots of every second of *The Oresteia*, so the editing was a long, taxing job. Finally, however, the rhythm of the camera work answered the rhythm of Tony Harrison's text and the pulse of Harry Birtwistle's music.

– 5 –

In 1988, on leaving the National, I was asked by Stephen Poliakoff to direct for BBC Television his screenplay *She's Been Away*. This gave me the unexpected chance to work once more with Peggy Ashcroft. I had wanted to direct her in Brian Clarke's *The Petition* at the NT in 1986, but she felt her age by then had made her too nervous to appear on the stage. She thought she might still manage film. She did. And that a woman in her eighties could be so creative for so many long, gruelling days was astounding.

It was a happy shoot. On the first day, I had a moment of unease about where to put the camera: it was fifteen years since I had directed a film. But after a few set-ups I was loving the experience. The film turned out well. Peggy and Geraldine James had become devoted friends when they had acted together in *The Jewel in the Crown*. They inspired each other again, winning joint best actress awards at the Venice Film Festival.

She's Been Away fixed on film Peggy's last great performance. The final shot of our schedule was one of those ridiculous sequences, when a car is strapped on top of a low-loader so that it appears to be driving along the road but isn't really. At the end, Peggy erupted from the vehicle and addressed the unit in the resonant voice that had carried her through every major Shakespearean role. 'Well,' she said, 'thank you all very much. That's it. Cameo roles from now on!'

Our producer was a famous BBC name, Ken Trodd. A man of great taste and infinite gloom, he would stand on the set eating buns all day, never expressing a word of enthusiasm. I didn't mind about this; he was known for it, and I understood that, all the same, he was supportive and concerned.

When the editing was finished, and while the dub was being prepared, marrying the music, dialogue and sound effects, Nicki and I went to Greece. Almost immediately I was phoned there by Stephen Edwards, the composer of the music. He said he'd been sacked. Ken Trodd wanted to put in other music. I spent most of our short holiday in a hot cupboard under the stairs of the friend's house where we were staying, arguing on the phone with Ken and his boss, Mark Shivas.

When I returned to England, I discovered that another score had been commissioned. I was amazed. I said that if the BBC was going to break its tradition of honouring what the director wanted, and behave like Hollywood at its worst, it should at least pay like Hollywood. I was shown a section of the film with the new music. It was wallpaper stuff that had no specific intention. I protested that if they insisted on using it I would take my name off the credits. When I was warned that I had no right to do that, I said I would make public that the music was their choice, not mine, and was then reminded that under my contract I was not allowed to talk to the press about the production without the BBC's permission. I replied that I certainly would talk. It was then lightly hinted that if I did I would never work for the BBC again. I said that in that case I wasn't sure I wanted to.

All this was very silly. But I had a trump card. Stephen, although sacked, had, at my request, continued to work on the music. By the time the BBC and I had reached total impasse, he had completed enough of his intricate, electronic score for them to hear, not just an impression as before, but how it actually sounded. They found they liked it after all and peace was restored.

Many years ago, the film director Sidney Lumet gave me some good advice. You must always have the courage to walk out. Equally, you must always have enough money in the bank not to care about being paid. He called this his 'fuck you' fund. The next job, he said, was always less important than getting the present one right.

– 6 –

A few months after finishing *She's Been Away* I was in New York opening Tennessee Williams's *Orpheus Descending*. An American company asked me if I would make a television film of the play with the original theatre cast. They surprised me by saying they had to get a writer; I pointed out that they had one already: Tennessee Williams. What they wanted, of course, was a rewrite job. I am terrified of 'creative adaptations', so I said that I would do the shooting script myself, knowing that Nicki would help me and that I had the support of Maria St Just, Tennessee Williams's friend and the executor of his estate. With some rearrangements and cuts, Nicki and I, by working all day and much of each night, achieved in three weeks a tight two-hour screen version of this great sprawling play, using Tennessee's own words.

We shot at a cracking pace, finishing in twenty-six days. For the first time I was able to shoot film at a speed that maintained my adrenalin. And because the cast, including Vanessa Redgrave, Kevin Anderson, Miriam Margolyes and Anne Twomey, knew the material well, we usually got what was needed in the first or second take. Even so, I would always ask them to do one more, this time with the freedom of trying exactly what *they* wanted. That take rarely departed much from the rehearsed framework, but it was always fresher, more spontaneous and relaxed. I often used it in the final film.

Stephen Edwards did the music as he had done for the play. When the ominous rumblings of his score echoed round the dubbing studio, the associate producer asked him if he had ever composed music for a horror movie.

Orpheus Descending preserves one of Vanessa's greatest performances. And, while doing the screenplay, Nicki and I found we could collaborate. She is a clear-eyed critic and writes with economy and precision. I mainly look after the structure. Out of this, a new career for both of us has opened up. Soon after *Orpheus* we had the chance to work on an original script. I was in Houston staging Tippett's *New Year* when a long letter arrived from two women producers, followed by boxes of books, documents and pictures. They wanted me to direct and write (this last was the surprise) their projected *Life of Enrico Caruso*.

I don't like bio-pics and I had no wish to make *Mario Lanza Rides Again*, so I sent a note of thanks saying that unfortunately I was too busy.

But the ladies wouldn't be refused. In the end, Nicki and I went through the material and were mightily intrigued. Caruso had a secret life. Two young opera singers, sisters, met him when he was a young boy from the Naples slums. They were both very talented (indeed, both sang Tosca within a couple of years of its premiere) and they set about helping him. They taught him to act, to sing, to walk on the stage. It was *Pygmalion* with the genders reversed. Caruso became the first international superstar, and by 1921, when he died aged forty-eight, he had made over two million dollars from his records alone. He lived with one of the sisters and had children by her. With the other, he had an affair and they became engaged. Whereupon the first promptly eloped with the chauffeur. For thirteen years this *ménage à trois* played a Strindbergian farce, dangerous in its intensity, around the opera houses of the world. Their lives were more extreme and improbable than the plots of the operas they sang. Then the sisters woke one morning to read in the papers that Caruso had married a rich young American heiress; they had not even known of her existence.

This irresistible combination of Puccini and farce makes me hopeful that the film will happen. Also, our finished original script has led to other work. I had read a remarkable book, Barry Unsworth's *Sacred Hunger*, which clearly had possibilities for TV. The story of how, during the eighteenth century, millions of black people were exported from Africa to the West Indies to be slaves, thereby vastly enriching Liverpool, Manchester and Bristol, is an extraordinary and appalling episode in our history. It provided capital which made possible the Industrial Revolution.

I suggested an adaptation of *Sacred Hunger* to Michael Grade and Peter Ansorge of Channel 4. We found, however, that a Hollywood deal was about to be signed. I wrote to Barry saying that in my view his narrative needed the slow unfolding of a television series. To tell his tale in two hours on the big screen could wreck it. There was an interval while I waited in suspense for his verdict. Happily he said yes. Nicki and I were commissioned to develop scripts for eight episodes, working with Barry.

– 7 –

In the autumn of 1990 I was asked to have a drink with two young independent television producers, Sophy Belhetchet and Glenn Wilhide. The meeting showed them to be, as producers go, blissfully straightforward. Did I know Mary Wesley's novels? I was ashamed to say that I didn't. Did I know Ken Taylor? I certainly did, as one of the best screen-writers in the country. *The Jewel in the Crown* was his.

Sophy and Glenn said they were going to film Mary Wesley's *The Camomile Lawn* in five parts, that it had been scripted by Ken, and that it would go before the cameras the following March. They thought – largely because of *She's Been Away* – that I would be the right director. I took the vast script away and read it. It was about the early war years in London, years which I remembered from my childhood. I then read the novel and the rest of Mary Wesley's books. As her many readers know, these have a clarity so pin-bright that they can be quite shocking. I lunched with her and found her very much the author of her novels. She is in her late seventies, shrewd, witty and elegant, seeing life unblinkingly and unsentimentally with all its warts and absurdities.

There are many young characters in the story, so the cast we had was an interesting combination of the new – Jennifer Ehle, Tara Fitzgerald, Toby Stephens, Ben Walden – with the seasoned talents of Paul Eddington, Felicity Kendal, Rosemary Harris, Claire Bloom, Virginia McKenna and Richard Johnson. The thirteen weeks of shooting were a delight, despite the maddening contrariness of the weather. In Cornwall we had to create a beautiful summer out of the wettest season for years; and in Oxfordshire the sun blazed down while we filmed a long funeral sequence which was meant to be in the rain.

The opportunity to tell a complex tale over an extended period was something new to me. It is a strength of television that it can deal with a long narrative by presenting it as a series – much as big nineteenth-century novels were first published as serials in magazines.

My pleasure in the work was crowned by pride in my daughter Rebecca, then nine, who played the part of Sophie with the utmost truth. How myopic we can be about our own children. Even when she was very little, if Rebecca were asked whether she would like to play with her friends or come to a rehearsal, either mine or her mother's, she would always choose the rehearsal. Yet neither Maria nor I thought this in the least odd or significant. By the time of *Camomile Lawn*, Rebecca had watched with gravity and concentration many operas and plays in rehearsal, and films being shot. One afternoon, two years before, she had come on the set of *She's Been Away* and seen the excellent James Fox make the same telephone call for two hours for the benefit of various camera angles. Afterwards, she said to me 'Well, papa, I've watched you rehearse theatre, and I've watched you rehearse opera. But I think making a film is the most boring thing you do.'

It was not my idea that Rebecca should play Sophie. We had seen over 500 little girls and were only three days from shooting when Sophy and Glenn asked me if they could test Rebecca, whom they had met. With some trepidation, I agreed. I knew she could act because of her performances in school plays. But the surprise was how well; and that she knew precisely how to do what was asked of her. She had clearly learned a lot while looking so absorbed at all those rehearsals over the years. Her secret was out: she had always wanted to be an actress.

I was very nervous for her, but I needn't have been. Her work was brilliant, and she was responsive and professional. At the end of the first day, she talked over the problems of film-making with me. 'I suppose,' she said, 'if it feels silly to you, then it looks silly to the camera.'

Some of the scenes that Rebecca had to play were very emotional, some were quite adult. In one, she finds a dutch cap in a bathroom cupboard and speculates on its function, suggesting to a flustered grown-up that it might be a 'truss for a bosom'. I felt I couldn't ask her to do this scene without talking to her about it. But *I* was the uneasy one. Did she know what a dutch cap was, I asked?

373

'Oh yes,' she replied with no trace of embarrassment. Later I discovered that she had discussed the matter with Nicki weeks before as part of her preparation for the part.

There were several sexy sequences in *The Camomile Lawn*; these were praised by a few for their honesty and damned by more for their titillation. The truth is that I tried to shoot them with the same unemotional clarity that I had found in Mary Wesley's descriptions of them. Sex was, after all, part of life – even in the 1940s. In fact, all the scenes were either before sex or after it – never the act itself – and they were comic. My aim was to make sex as absurd as it can often be in reality.

I can't believe simulated sex in films. In life, sex is not something most people watch, but something they do. Observing the writhings of two people on a screen produces feelings which are nothing at all like the feelings of making love oneself.

The noisy scandal that surrounded aspects of *The Camomile Lawn* now seems an inevitable part of most television drama. To get attention in a crowded market, to entice people to watch the first episode, the advance advertising and hype for any major new series has to be vast. This massive publicity is very risky. It raises high expectations. A backlash when the programme is transmitted becomes almost certain. The sex scenes in *The Camomile Lawn* seemed to me natural and funny, and I never thought of them as special or particularly promotable. I personally loved the series, its actors and its script. I also felt I was getting near the way I want to make films. The shots were now organic.

– 8 –

To be interviewed on television would have appalled people of my parents' generation. My mother and father would have been speechless. Their bosses would have put on their best suits and posed stiffly, speaking rhetorically as if addressing a meeting. But my generation, conditioned by watching television all the time, think it quite normal to give their opinions in public.

Way back in the Fifties, I was a member of the *Brain's Trust*. At the old Lime Grove studios, a team of three or four people first dined in a room mocked up in panelled wood like a stately home. We were then filmed while engaged in forty minutes of would-be intellectual conversation. I enjoyed the people I met more than the conversations. I remember Edith Sitwell treating me as if I was a dangerous teenager. For a time, I also appeared in some of the satirical TV shows of the Sixties, *That Was the Week that Was* and *Not so Much a Programme . . .*; also on Radio's *Any Questions*. All this was clearly a drug for an exhibitionist. Fortunately, my theatre work took up more and more of my life and prevented me from becoming too involved.

I've always loved interviewing people and drawing them out. But I quickly discovered that my pleasure in public speaking and the delight I take in communicating to a live audience had very little to do with what was needed in a studio. Talking to a television camera is extraordinarily difficult. Very few people can do it and look natural. I can't. The camera cannot be treated as a public meeting, because it is intimate; cannot be ignored because it is close to your very eyes. Every flicker of discomfort, every tension, is visible. To read an autocue without looking mesmerised is, for me, almost impossible.

I am much better improvising whatever needs to be said.

In the early Seventies I took over fronting *Aquarius*, the LWT arts magazine; and for those two years I never felt easy talking to the camera, though I was completely happy talking to the succession of fascinating people I interviewed. I remember especially two long conversations with Rubinstein when he spoke of his passions: music and women.

I suspect that I enjoy holding forth because I am enormously stimulated by having to think aloud on my feet. It helps me to share my discoveries as I make them. And that, after all, is exactly what I do at my rehearsals, whether they are for plays or operas or films.

PART SIX

Extravagant Hopes?

– 1 –

I emerged from fifteen years at the National with a great deal of energy that I wanted to put to use. I formed an independent theatre company and called it, with shameless arrogance, the Peter Hall Company. It was, to begin with, backed by Duncan Weldon's commercial set-up, Triumph Productions. Our first venture was *Orpheus Descending*, Tennessee Williams's underrated Gothic masterpiece. It is an imperfect giant of a play which contains the essence of its creator. I had always wanted to stage it, and once Vanessa Redgrave agreed to play Lady (a part she was born for) I pressed ahead.

At the RSC I had directed Vanessa early in her career in *A Midsummer Night's Dream*, *Coriolanus*, and *The Taming of the Shrew* – but not since then. From the very beginning, she was a special creature, a golden girl who seemed to share with everyone in the audience her own youth and hopes for the future. I was briefly in love with her.

Now, thirty years later, in *Orpheus Descending*, I found her the most complete actress. She had the same daring I had seen in Ralph Richardson and Edith Evans. She rehearsed in a totally absorbed way, taking every suggestion, following every hint that she received from her instinct or mine. She seemed to be wired into the truth. I could only ever reject what she offered if I thought its meaning was not right for the play; never because it was false as acting. She worked without vanity or inhibition. Every day was an extraordinary adventure.

Although such endless creativity is exciting, by the time a play opens it is usual for the director and cast to have reached a solution for each scene, which then goes on developing through the run. Vanessa's explorations are so intense that she is quite likely to change radically in performance and hardly know she has done it. But since these are changes produced by a strongly inventive imagination, it is hardly possible to object. If, though, her director has not visited a production for a couple of months, he or she may be in for a few surprises.

After a successful London run, *Orpheus* went to Broadway. For the first time, I was able to direct a Tennessee Williams play with a mainly American cast. I was amazed that, initially, they were more resistant to his rhythms than English actors, finding it difficult to sustain his long sentences right to the end. They wanted to split them up into short colloquial phrases in order to make them sound 'real'. The result was to make them sound ordinary.

Astonishingly, casting had taken me just a day and a half. I left Glyndebourne – where I was rehearsing the Simon Rattle *Figaro* – early one Saturday morning, boarded Concorde, and arrived in New York in time for auditions at 10.30 a.m. I auditioned all morning, all afternoon, and on the Sunday morning. By lunchtime I was on Concorde going home, and back at Glyndebourne ready for work on Monday.

There is nothing remarkable about this particular lunacy, except that I managed to select so fast an almost perfect company. It was true that I already had Kevin Anderson as well as Vanessa; but to have been able to add players such as Tammy Grimes and Anne Twomey was miraculous. There is a dispiriting reason for this: good actors are readily available in New York because so few plays are being done. It is certainly not possible to cast with such ease in London.

We had great difficulty in getting a theatre on Broadway, and this, I'm sure, was because of Vanessa's very vocal support of the Palestinians. Broadway is fundamentally a Jewish province, and I went through several agonising meetings where no theatre owner was courageous enough to admit this. Other reasons for not doing the play were given. Suddenly the set was too big, or the cast too numerous. One, bafflingly, said that when he saw the play in London he had hoped for some real Tennessee Williams writing but hadn't heard any. I pointed to Frank Rich's *New York Times* notice of the London *Orpheus* which was a fanfare for Vanessa as a great actress. He answered that Rich can break a production but not make one, and that anyway there were several American actresses who could do the part just as well. I stuck to my guns, and in the end Jimmy Nederlander presented the play with panache and enthusiasm.

Something else caused me trouble. There is now hardly a play on Broadway, even in the smallest theatre, that does not use amplified sound. This is needed mainly because of the appallingly loud air conditioning. So loud was it at the Neil Simon Theatre for the first preview of *Orpheus* that I had it turned off. Unfortunately, this coincided with a warm Fall evening. By the interval, the temperature was stifling and as the second act began there was an eruption from the stalls with much waving of programmes and cries of: 'Turn up the air conditioning.'

I ran down the aisle, leapt on the stage, and conducted an impromptu public meeting. The indignation subsided only when I suggested taking a vote on whether the audience would prefer to hear the play or be cool. Fifteen people stalked out, but the majority were for staying and sweating.

Next day there was a story in the *New York Times* about the air-conditioning riots. To my delight, men arrived and carried out maintenance at the Neil Simon Theatre for the first time in years. I like to think this was my contribution towards quieter and better-serviced installations on Broadway.

– 2 –

Before we began rehearsing *Orpheus*, and during the height of my midsummer madness with Nicki, I had been telephoned by Dustin Hoffman. He was in England and we met. He said he needed some advice: did I think he could play Shakespeare? I said he had a rich and resonant voice, a fine sense of rhythm, and providing he first developed the technique and didn't just hurl himself into the task on a tide of feeling, he ought to do it brilliantly. He looked at me with those big, streetwise eyes: 'Do you think I could play Hamlet?' 'No,' I replied. '*No?*' He was surprised. 'You're too old for Hamlet, and anyway an American actor who thinks he can take on Hamlet as his first Shakespearean role is like a hill climber who thinks he can shin up Everest.'

He was delighted. 'It's so good to get a frank opinion,' he said.

I told him that if he wanted to do Shakespeare he should pick one of the really showy character parts which are not play-carrying. The rest of the cast do the work for you, and you make all the effect. I suggested that he should look at Shylock and Malvolio, and Angelo in *Measure for Measure*.

We chose *The Merchant of Venice*, though there was a little flurry of liberal anxiety in Dustin about the play's supposed anti-Semitism. It is not taught in many American schools for that reason – which is insane. The very heart of the play is a vivid demonstration of the perils of racism, and how it can poison the persecutor as well as the persecuted.

Dustin is as obsessed as Vanessa, living and breathing his work twenty-four hours a day. He rehearsed as if he were performing, as if the cameras were always rolling on him. At the end of a six-hour rehearsal he was completely shattered. But he would go home, shower and rest, and then return to the script, often calling me late at night to discuss some point or other.

He has a quick intelligence and a superb ear. Within a few hours he was moving around in Shakespeare's verse and making it his own. By the time he had played Shylock in London, and taken it to Broadway, he was giving the finest performance of the part I have seen. It balanced the tragic with the villainous, the mean with the comic, the pathetic with the predator. He was an entire and fallible man made evil by persecution.

I am saddened that I will not work with him again – for I do not think I will. Just before the end of the run in New York, he telephoned me and said he wanted to bring television cameras in to do a quick recording of the last two or three performances for video; the best takes from each would then be cut together. I explained that I hated the idea, it needed more time and care; and the video was stopped. This did not go down well. Dustin returned to Hollywood and the world of mega-millions and I have never heard from him since. Phone calls are not returned and letters go unanswered. Sam Cohn, my agent, remarked about the reigning stars of Hollywood that you don't fuck with them lightly.

The Merchant, also presented by Jimmy Nederlander, was a sell-out on Broadway for seventeen weeks. Its success, as in London, was largely due to Dustin; but, as well, to a group of actors, particularly Geraldine James as Portia, who made the text immediate and lucid. At an early performance in New York I heard a woman behind me say: 'Of course it's been modernised, I can understand it.'

– 3 –

In October 1988 both my parents died in the same week.

My mother was very ill in hospital; cancer had destroyed her with extreme speed. She knew – for her intelligence still burned brightly – that this was the end, and the knowledge made her demented and angry. She struck a nurse quite viciously with the walking stick that hung from the head of her bed. It had to be taken away.

When she fell into a coma, the doctors suggested I tell my father that, though she might just regain consciousness, she would almost certainly die within ten days. I did this, and asked him to come and live with me in London after she had gone, while we sorted everything out.

'I don't want to talk about that now,' he said. 'I'd prefer just to get through the next few days.'

I arranged to collect him the following Sunday and drive him across to Oxford to see my mother. Father always took a little nap after lunch. On the Saturday, he took his nap and didn't wake up. He died in his sleep of a heart attack and was found sitting peacefully in his chair.

My mother died on the day of my father's funeral.

He never knew of my mother's death and she never knew of his. She had not regained consciousness. They went together, after many years of fuss and flurry on her part, but not on his.

I think my mother's happiest years were when she and Father ran the general store and post office at

Kessingland on the Suffolk coast, after he had taken
early retirement from the railway. He was chairman
of the parish council and the local school. My mother
knew everybody, talked to everybody, and became the
presiding mother-hen of the village. She complained
about it, of course. She was fed up with hearing everybody else's troubles; and she never stopped saying how
little they made from the proceeds of the shop, and how
hard they worked. But she didn't fool me; she enjoyed it
all.

I worry sometimes when I remember the hours my parents spent watching epics by Shakespeare, not to speak
of long elaborate operas. Mother, I suspect, put up with
them as she'd put up with my reading so many books.
To her, the plays and the operas, like the books, were
evidence of success. I'm not so sure about Father. My
parents liked the theatre rather as they liked strolling
through a luxurious department store. It was exciting,
even attractive; but not really for them. In the same way,
though they could easily have done so in their later years,
they never went abroad.

My father was revered by my children as someone
particularly kind and wise. And they always adored my
mother. She was very well cast as the grandmother.
She continued to cook to the end, making something
hot for Father every day, including huge, sweet cakes
and battalions of scones.

It took me time to appreciate her. For most of my adult
life I did not love her. She was pretentious, wayward and
bossy; but she had a very sharp mind and an instinct for
exactly what was going on which rarely let her down. If
I'd had brothers or sisters, she could have shared her
energy. I think she would have been happier. But then, I
suppose, I would have had less of her; and perhaps never
been given the chances to do all that I burned to do. I was
lucky to have had her.

My father was eighty-six when he died. Did he decide,
after he knew Mother was dying, that life was no longer

worth living? I suspect so. People can die because they want to.

I find it hard to describe my father, hard to pin him down. And perhaps that was his attraction to his son and to his grandchildren, particularly the boys. We all knew that there was something perceptive and very shrewd going on behind his mask of decency and tolerance, but we couldn't quite define what it was.

He encouraged me and was proud of me, though not as vociferous about it as my mother. He was moved when I was given my knighthood, but no more prepared for it than I was.

The first step to receiving an honour is a cautious letter to those chosen asking if they would accept, should it be decided that they are offered it. Because of some mistake, my letter went to my parents' house, and Father phoned me. 'I've got a very official-looking letter here, boy,' he said. 'Have you been in trouble with the police or something?'

Anxiously, I asked him to open the envelope. He read me what the letter said and very nearly broke down. 'A's a great honour, a's all I can say. A's a great honour,' he kept repeating.

Mother and Father had loved and bickered for nearly sixty years. They had never been separated, not even by the war, and I don't think either of them could have contemplated life without the other.

I felt their loss in ways I would never have suspected. Once your parents die, if you are an only child there is no-one of your blood to lean on, to find refuge with, to go home to. There is instead the naked and alarming feeling that you are next in line, there is no-one between you and mortality.

In his later years, I learnt to love my father deeply all over again. I almost achieved the same with my mother; but I suppose we were too alike to find complete peace.

– 4 –

The Peter Hall Company had started off with the idea that Alan Ayckbourn would be in partnership with me and do alternate productions. A big, large-cast play Alan wanted to direct was, however, turned down by Duncan Weldon as too expensive. Duncan was entirely within his rights, but he never fully explained his reasons to Alan, who resigned. He was a huge loss.

Thelma Holt was the producer for the Peter Hall Company. I love Thelma because she is quintessentially of the theatre. She trained as an actress, but fell into administration, and she had been with me at the National, where I was careful to give her a little empire of her own – including foreign tours and transfers – and let her get on with it. She is a noisy, one-woman band, not a collaborator. Duncan, at first, had grave reservations about employing her: producers don't usually like other producers around. When, though, he found she took an absolute delight in getting stuck into crises, however unpleasant, he began to rely on her more and more.

Thelma is a born trouble-shooter. She will often, if there is no trouble to shoot, imagine some, so that she can go on shooting. She spent the first months of my association with Duncan telling me how difficult he was, while telling him how difficult I was. She was quite right in both instances. But it didn't help. And the relationship between Duncan and me deteriorated. In the end, Thelma left to be on her own as an independent producer.

There was another problem. I had joined Duncan on the understanding that my company would occupy the Theatre Royal in the Haymarket. I wanted an identifiable home for my plays. But just before I signed the deal, the words 'or a comparable theatre' were added to the contract. I was uneasy, but I signed it.

As it turned out, only *Orpheus* was given at the Haymarket.

The Wild Duck is one of my top dozen plays. It remains, for me, the first masterpiece of family drama; perhaps the inspiration of Chekhov. It is also, in places, painfully funny. I love Ibsen's mordant sense of humour. His plays exploit black comedy, yet this frequently gets lost in English versions. A translated text can easily make the director feel that he is looking at the play through a frosted-glass window; he can't quite *see* the original. As with *John Gabriel Borkman* at the National, I worked on the translation of *The Wild Duck* with Inga-Stina Ewbank, a Norwegian-speaking Scandinavian who, because she is a great Shakespearean scholar, is astonishingly sensitive to the nuances of English.

Norwegian is a language with a very small vocabulary. Ibsen uses the same words repeatedly to great dramatic and often comic effect. Too many English translations lose these repetitions by employing the wealth of English synonyms to give variety. Inga-Stina taught me to trust the same words; she taught me, as well, what was beneath the text.

I followed *The Wild Duck* with a revival of *The Homecoming*, twenty-five years after staging its premiere for the RSC. At the first rehearsal we all met with Harold to read the play. Before we began, he announced he had made a change in the text: would everybody please turn to page thirty-seven. In an atmosphere tense with anticipation, we did as he asked.

Harold said: 'You will see the line: "And if you don't like it, you can flake off." I would like you to cross out the word "flake" and substitute for it the word "fuck".'

The actors dutifully wrote 'fuck' in their scripts. There was a pause. Then Warren Mitchell, who was playing Max, said: 'I rather prefer "flake".' ' "Fuck" is what I meant,' said Harold. The Lord Chamberlain had been busy in 1965.

– 5 –

At the beginning of 1991, my association with Duncan having collapsed, Jeffrey Archer offered me the Playhouse, which he owned, as a permanent base for my company. I accepted at once. It is a lovely theatre, almost on the Embankment, and had been newly decorated. We had a successful season. Within twelve months we had presented Felicity Kendal, Paul Eddington and John Sessions in *Tartuffe*; Julie Walters and Ken Stott in *The Rose Tattoo*; Eric Porter and Maria Miles in *Twelfth Night*; and Deborah Warner's Abbey Theatre production of *Hedda Gabler* with Fiona Shaw.

But half-way through the season, Jeffrey telephoned me to say that he had decided to sell the theatre. I was staggered and felt as if I was just part of the furniture and fittings. By the end of the year I was homeless again.

It is not, I am glad to say, difficult to find a West End stage for my work. But I still dream of a theatre I can think of as home. I know from my RSC and National years that if a theatre is associated with one policy, the place defines the work and audience loyalty grows, which is not only an economic but a creative security.

The last decade has seen ticket prices more than double in the West End, and the subsidised houses pressured by the Arts Council to charge prices as high as the market will bear. This has not yet reduced the size of the audience – but its composition has changed. Many young people can no longer afford good seats, so it is increasingly a problem to reach a new public. All the signs are that theatre going will soon be not a regular habit, but a tourist attraction or just an occasional treat.

On the other hand, the general level of creativity has increased: productions are more daring and actors more prepared to take risks than when I started out in the theatre. And if audiences are no longer as young, they are more sophisticated than they were. The serious London theatre audience has been made by the Royal Court, the RSC and the National. There is a core audience of 50,000 to 100,000 people that I know I can depend on when I do a play.

I am sure that Jeffrey Archer wanted me to raise the profile of the Playhouse. But it was a big shock to lose it just as I was beginning. However, soon afterwards came the great joy of directing *Four Baboons Adoring the Sun* at New York's Lincoln Center, and finding in its author, John Guare, a new friend.

When I was sent the first draft, I was very interested in what John was trying to do but not entirely sure I was reading it right. I telephoned him and asked some basic questions. He hopped on the next plane to London and we spent two days locked in conversation. The result was one of the happiest collaborations of my life.

John told me on the first night that only two pages of the original script remained unaltered from the beginning of rehearsals. We had made the piece on our feet. And for the first time in all the years I have worked in New York I felt that what mattered was the play, not the dollar.

Four Baboons worked on the frontiers of dramatic technique. It mixed direct audience address with naturalistic wise-cracking scenes; and a commentator – the God Eros – interpreted the follies of the characters through twenty-eight short musical numbers. We received the blessing of Broadway – a clutch of Tony nominations – but the play only ran its allotted time at the Lincoln

Center and didn't, alas, move elsewhere. I know, none-theless, that I shall be living for years on the things I discovered while directing it.

In 1992, I directed at Stratford with the RSC for the first time in twenty-five years. The play was one I had always wanted to do, *All's Well That Ends Well*, a complex piece of Shakespearean chamber music. The theatre was the Swan, where I had hoped to work ever since it opened in 1986. The brainchild of Trevor Nunn and the architect/designer Michael Reardon, this is the beautiful, galleried auditorium set in that part of the original old Stratford theatre which survived the fire of 1926.

The Swan lived up to my expectations in almost all respects. Its greatest virtue is its sound. Acoustically it is virtually perfect. Actors can whisper from its stage as well as shout, and the wooden interior gives a warm bloom to the voice. I didn't, in the end, enjoy the thrust stage because it thrusts too much. It is like an enormous diving board: wonderful to progress down, but then the actor is stuck. There is nothing he can do except turn round and go back again.

The recently discovered foundations of the Rose Theatre show beyond doubt that the Elizabethan play-house had a traverse, *not* a thrust stage. I have always believed this in my heart. How, I thought, could subtle verbal theatre be presented on a stage where half the audience was unable at any one moment either to see or hear the actor? The vitality of the thrust stages at Stratford, Ontario, and at Chichester comes from the constant need to keep the actors on the move, so that they are able to share out their faces and their words. But to the audience round them, restlessness damages understanding and verbal nuance. This was a happy challenge for Tyrone Guthrie (who built the stage in Ontario) because he was a genius at stage movement and had a talent for energising old texts with physical excitement. But he, too, often gave a swirling general effect, rather than specific meaning. The problem is not as bad at the Swan because the scale is so small; but it is there.

It was strange working in Stratford again – the town where such an important chapter of my life had started – and in the Swan, which stands where our enormous rehearsal room had once been. The town was changed. It was packed with tourists and noisy with the amplified voices of the guides on the coaches. But the theatre was the same, and the river, and the gardens opposite the Dirty Duck. The willow tree where I used to tie up my boat when I came by water to summer rehearsals was there still, but now huge, thick-trunked and leaning over. At every corner, I expected to see Peggy Ashcroft coming towards me, or Michel St Denis puffing his pipe. I had been back often to see plays, but not since 1968 had I worked there. And the absence of old friends made it hard to bear.

But this time at Stratford marked the arrival of someone new. It was while I was rehearsing *All's Well* that curly-headed Emma was born, Nicki's first child and my sixth.

Back in London, there were other new beginnings. I called on Bill Kenwright, the prolific and enthusiastic producer, and we decided to work together: he would finance the Peter Hall Company.

Our first offering was a new play by Stephen Poliakoff, *Sienna Red*. As is usual with Stephen, it was bursting with relevance and irony. Sadly, however, it didn't speak to the audience. Whether this was the fault of my production or the text I found difficult to assess; it was probably a bit of both. We did not bring it into the West End after its short tour.

This was a nasty jolt for Stephen and me; and an expensive one for Bill Kenwright. It says much for his belief in me, and his generosity, that we surmounted such a hurdle and went on from there to present Wilde,

Shaffer, Rattigan, Goldsmith and Aristophanes. The list of plays I want to direct seems to stretch out for ever . . .

And there are films. . . Not long ago I was in Hollywood. Many meetings took place at which the person I was meeting had telephone calls. In between, he or she would listen politely to my ideas. But nothing happened. Nothing, that is, until last summer when my American agent called me in some excitement. He said a film script was on its way by special delivery from Hollywood and it was an offer. He would say no more. As soon as the script arrived, I sat down and read it eagerly. It began: *'Interior, Kensington Palace. Night. Charles and Di are curled up on the sofa watching a video of their wedding in St Paul's Cathedral.'* I decided to pass.

– 6 –

As a boy, I was told that life speeded up as you got older. I didn't believe it. I was young and in another country. But these days I have a sense of time running out, and of so much left to do. A vivid indication of this is my mania for books. I buy them compulsively, but already as I pass the thousands of volumes I have accumulated – too many even for the yards upon yards of bookshelves in my house – I wonder whether I shall ever open those that are still unread or reread those that I have half forgotten. I begin to think, too, of the pieces of music I will never hear, the countries I will never visit, and – of course – the plays I will never direct.

I am often appalled at the punishing pace at which I live. I hate to waste time, hate not to be doing. Why does this drive continue? Mainly, I suppose, because my adrenalin addiction makes me happy only when it is coursing through my veins. And I have the perfect job to feed that.

For six or seven hours a day I am usually rehearsing with a group of talented actors who potentially terrify me. It is up to me to hold their interest, to inspire them, and I must give unsparingly of my energy. Rehearsing is for me the habit of a lifetime, something I like to do every day. It is almost an erotic passion.

My entire working life has been – and still is – spent trying to understand the power of the theatre. The audience at a play or opera are not only involved in one of the few live experiences left that is not about passive watching and passive listening; they are being actively invited to use their imaginations in a potent game of make-believe. No good performance leaves its audience untouched. It challenges them, provokes them and makes them understand their own lives a little better. This heightened awareness is not necessarily serious, and it is certainly not always intellectual. It is visceral. A farce by Feydeau can produce it as readily as a tragedy by Aeschylus.

This communion has a slyer, sexier side. The sense of excitement, of expectation that comes before seduction, is there at the beginning of any performance. Good theatre teases and titillates. The eyes of the audience are turned on to a small space, and their gaze is frank and uncompromising – not the veiled or deferential look given to strangers during the ordinary business of life, but rather the look of ownership the lover gives to the loved one. There is lust in it, and corresponding disappointment if what is looked at fails to rouse the expected interest and attraction. All this is intensified by the darkness of the modern theatre, which helps its private and concentrated purpose.

The theatre trades in sex and sexuality. Stars are not essentially defined by acting talent. They are those with extraordinary physical presence, those whom the men and women in the audience are drawn to watch and find desirable. And the performers' sex can be confused; in fact, some of the greatest stars seem androgynous.

We are only now starting to admit how much the waking hours of the normal adult are spent thinking about sex. To look at an attractive person is to imagine possession – and this is a feeling the stage encourages. Breasts are emphasised, legs flaunted, bottoms (particularly in the ballet) raised. Always there is the hope, the tease, of even more exposure. In the Sixties, much fashionable theatre used this tension by having actors strip off at the slightest excuse in the name of truth and honesty.

Of course, sexual excitement does not necessarily make good theatre. If it did, a strip show would be a rich experience. But I believe there is no good theatre that is not also sexual. It is no wonder the Puritans hated and feared it. The erotic may not be the end of the experience, but it certainly has to be there.

Movies – with their huge close-ups, idealised stars and dark concentration – can, to many, be sexier than the theatre: the scale is hypnotic. But to me, theatre has the edge. It is alive and now. Anything might happen.

– 7 –

I have had the good fortune to be able to remake myself from time to time, by the process of constant work.

At first, I was a director of new writing, the champion of Samuel Beckett, of Tennessee Williams, of John Whiting. By the mid Sixties I was regarded as a Shakespearean, and the director of Pinter. Soon after, I was seen as a fantasist because of my work in Baroque opera, while my scrutiny of Mozart and success in persuading singers to behave like human beings were heralded as a revolution. Then, as productions became more and more subjective and concept-based, I began to be thought of as a 'realistic' director, interested only in naturalism. From being someone who, it was said, stripped the varnish off well-loved pictures, I came, to my surprise, to be labelled a traditionalist.

The same thing has happened in response to my staging of Shakespeare. I used to be known as a radical, but am considered today a classicist who is rigorous about the verse. It's true, I do not now cut Shakespeare's plays with the abandon that I did in the Sixties, but I cannot say my essential approach has changed – except that I hope it is better executed. I find it isn't in me to trim my beliefs or check my instincts in order to meet the ebb and flow of fashion. My only course, providing the world will let me, is to keep working.

Though tempted when near the edge, I have never been psychoanalysed. My appetite for work does, I know, lead to recklessness and depression. I am told that people like me attempt to keep death at bay by over-achieving. Possibly. I think about death every day. But achieving is something I relish; and it is not done for power, nor for influence, nor, above all, for money.

When I was a child my family was very conscious of money – or rather the lack of it. Perhaps that is why I have never allowed it to rule my own life. I think of it as a tool that helps me to follow my obsessions, as something that buys me the luxury of being able to do this in some degree of comfort.

Though my years in the profession have brought me wonderful comradeship and loyalties, I realise that my greed for work has caused resentments and made me enemies. Many people, particularly men, have found it difficult to stomach my ambition. The subsidised arts have gradually become a branch of politics where two-facedness, hypocrisy and bad-mouthing are constant. In the theatre, however, such hostilities are often only skin deep.

– 8 –

The world has improved during my crowded lifetime. Stupidity is still the enemy of progress, but I have seen a Fascist empire defeated, and a Russian empire (perhaps the most awful oppression in history) demolished. But my own country has become sadder and smaller. The doctrine of market forces has sanctified greed, and art and education have suffered as a consequence. We think we live in a democracy, but we do nothing of the kind. We pay for our politics by allowing special interests to dominate them – big business finances the Tory Party and the Unions finance Labour. Market forces, as a result, are bound to influence each party's manifesto. While the country is largely moderate, our absurd first-past-the-post system produces extremes which do not at all reflect the wishes of the electorate. The idiotic conventions of adversarial politics bombard the public with half-truths and misrepresentations. Neither party can risk being honest; they must rather score points off each other. The mindlessness of television has reduced literacy and blunted sensibility; paradoxically, it has also increased awareness and knowledge. It is harder now for politicians to lie without being found out, or to conduct horrible little wars without arousing world concern.

The British are dangerously indifferent about preserving their freedoms and their institutions. Will things have to get much worse before they wake up to what they are losing?

In all this muddle, it has been refreshing to work in the arts. Art is absolute. It provides unquestionable integrity and inescapable standards.

– 9 –

Looking back, I see that I, the only child of a small-time country stationmaster with a family, on both sides, of farm labourers and odd-job men, have been blessed with marvellous chances. So much so that actors often accuse me of being born with a silver spoon in my mouth. Since I was born with next to nothing in my mouth I have always, I hope, worn lightly whatever successes and good fortune I have had.

Sometimes I try to trace music or theatre in my ancestry. There isn't a sign of either, unless you count my father cheerfully singing Gilbert and Sullivan. Where this passion came from, this love for the uncertain world I ran to embrace in my early teens, remains a mystery.

I have occasionally thought how difficult it would be – since I am an atheist – to have a child who wished to be a parson; or one who hated music, or went into a world I could not possibly understand such as advanced physics. Though parents love their children no matter what, children do not always love their parents. I have been extraordinarily lucky because my children share my obsessions. And pride in our children's abilities can be forthright; there is no need for modesty.

I have described the particular talents of Jenny and Rebecca. Christopher, my eldest, having paced himself carefully, is now emerging as a leading television and film producer. Edward is a gambler, like me, but has already made a mark as a director in the theatre and is bursting with plans. Lucy is a stage designer and is, so far, the only one of the five to refuse to work with me. She says she is not yet ready to cope. She has designed at

Chichester, the Royal Court, the Gate and various reps, and is a complete original.

Then there is Emma, one year old as I write this. She, Nicki and I live in a tall, four-storey Victorian house. The other day Emma, excited by a new-found ability to crawl, pounded up the stairs from the basement to her own room at the very top. I walked behind, flight after flight, to be sure she wouldn't tumble backwards. After she had arrived, triumphant, I carried her back to the basement. She immediately set off again and climbed once more right to the top of the house. I took her back. She climbed yet again.

Very small children are the most fascinating creatures in the world. They are unpredictable, often moving, suddenly perceptive and very funny. To have had thirty-five years of them has been a constant nourishment.

Though my life remains crammed, hectic and as full of anxiety as of hope, my one sadness is that it seems to have passed in a flash. I would like it to have gone more slowly. I would even like to start again – providing I could do the same job. My work stays so great a joy that I still speed to it every day as if I were going on holiday. And, as I go, I see Emma setting off again, determined to go on climbing.

— LIST OF PRODUCTIONS —

For obvious reasons I could write about only some of the plays, operas and films I have directed. Just in case any reader might be interested to fill the gaps, here is a full list of my productions up to 1993. The years given are of the first performance. Revivals and tours are omitted.

P.H.

PLAYS AND OPERAS

1953	THE LETTER (professional debut)	Somerset Maugham	Theatre Royal, Windsor
1954	BLOOD WEDDING (London debut)	Lorca	Arts, London
	THE IMPRESARIO FROM SMYRNA	Goldoni	Arts, London
	THE IMMORALIST	Gide	Arts, London
	LISTEN TO THE WIND (children's musical)	Vivian Ellis	Arts, London
1955	THE LESSON	Ionesco	Arts, London
	SOUTH	Julien Green	Arts, London
	MOURNING BECOMES ELECTRA	O'Neill	Arts, London
	WAITING FOR GODOT	Beckett	Arts, London
	THE BURNT FLOWER-BED	Ugo Betti	Arts, London
	SUMMERTIME	Ugo Betti	Apollo, London
1956	THE WALTZ OF THE TOREADORS	Anouilh	Arts, London
	GIGI	Colette	New, now Albery, London
	LOVE'S LABOUR'S LOST	Shakespeare	Stratford-on-Avon
	THE GATES OF SUMMER	John Whiting	New, Oxford
1957	CAMINO REAL	Tennessee Williams	Phoenix, London
	THE MOON AND SIXPENCE (opera)	John Gardner	Sadler's Wells
	CYMBELINE	Shakespeare	Stratford-on-Avon
	THE ROPE DANCERS (NY debut)	Morton Wishengrad	Cort Theatre, NY

401

1958	CAT ON A HOT TIN ROOF	Tennessee Williams	Comedy, London
	TWELFTH NIGHT	Shakespeare	Stratford-on-Avon
	BROUHAHA	George Tabori	Aldwych, London
	SHADOW OF HEROES	Robert Ardrey	Piccadilly, London
1959	MADAME DE . . .	Anouilh	Arts, London
	TRAVELLER WITHOUT LUGGAGE	Anouilh	Arts, London
	A MIDSUMMER NIGHT'S DREAM	Shakespeare	Stratford-on-Avon
	CORIOLANUS	Shakespeare	Stratford-on-Avon
	THE WRONG SIDE OF THE PARK	John Mortimer	Cambridge Theatre, London
1960	THE TWO GENTLEMEN OF VERONA	Shakespeare	Stratford-on-Avon
	TWELFTH NIGHT	Shakespeare	Stratford-on-Avon
	TROILUS AND CRESSIDA	Shakespeare	Stratford-on-Avon
1961	ONDINE	Giraudoux	RSC
	BECKET	Anouilh	RSC
	ROMEO AND JULIET	Shakespeare	RSC
1962	A MIDSUMMER NIGHT'S DREAM	Shakespeare	RSC
	THE COLLECTION	Pinter (who also co-directed)	RSC
	TROILUS AND CRESSIDA	Shakespeare	RSC
1963	THE WARS OF THE ROSES (a trilogy, adapted with John Barton from Henry VI Parts 1, 2, 3 & Richard III)	Shakespeare	RSC
1964	RICHARD II	Shakespeare	RSC
	HENRY IV, Parts 1 & 2	Shakespeare	RSC
	HENRY V	Shakespeare	RSC
	EH?	Henry Livings	RSC
1965	THE HOMECOMING	Pinter	RSC
	MOSES AND AARON (opera)	Shoenberg	Covent Garden
	HAMLET	Shakespeare	RSC
1966	THE GOVERNMENT INSPECTOR	Gogol	RSC
	THE MAGIC FLUTE (opera)	Mozart	Covent Garden
	STAIRCASE	Charles Wood	RSC

402

List of Productions

Year	Title	Author	Company
1967	MACBETH	Shakespeare	RSC
1969	A DELICATE BALANCE	Albee	RSC
	DUTCH UNCLE	Simon Gray	RSC
	LANDSCAPE & SILENCE	Pinter	RSC
1970	THE KNOT GARDEN (opera)	Tippett	Covent Garden
	LANDSCHAST (German language version of Landscape)	Pinter	Hamburg
	LA CALISTO (opera)	Cavalli	Glyndebourne
	THE BATTLE OF SHRIVINGS	Shaffer	Lyric, London
1971	EUGENE ONEGIN (opera)	Tchaikovsky	Covent Garden
	OLD TIMES	Pinter	RSC
	TRISTAN UND ISOLDE (opera)	Wagner	Covent Garden
1972	ALL OVER	Albee	RSC
	ALTE ZEITEN	Pinter	Vienna
	IL RITORNO D'ULISSE (oprea)	Monteverdi	Glyndebourne
	VIA GALACTICA (musical)	Galt MacDermot	New York
1973	THE MARRIAGE OF FIGARO (opera)	Mozart	Glyndebourne
	THE TEMPEST	Shakespeare	NT
1974	JOHN GABRIEL BORKMAN	Ibsen	NT
	HAPPY DAYS	Beckett	NT
1975	NO MAN'S LAND	Pinter	NT
	HAMLET	Shakespeare	NT
	JUDGEMENT	Barry Collins	NT
	NIEMANSLAND (German language version of No Man's Land)	Pinter	Hamburg
1976	TAMBURLAINE THE GREAT	Marlowe	NT
1977	BEDROOM FARCE	Ayckbourn (who also co-directed)	NT
	DON GIOVANNI (opera)	Mozart	Glyndebourne
	VOLPONE	Jonson	NT
	THE COUNTRY WIFE	Wycherley	NT
1978	COSI FAN TUTTE (opera)	Mozart	Glyndebourne
	THE CHERRY ORCHARD	Chekhov	NT
	MACBETH	Shakespeare	NT
	BETRAYAL	Pinter	NT
1979	FIDELIO (opera)	Beethoven	Glyndebourne
	AMADEUS	Shaffer	NT
1980	OTHELLO	Shakespeare	NT

1981	A MIDSUMMER NIGHT'S DREAM (opera)	Britten	Glyndebourne
	THE ORESTEIA	the trilogy by Aeschylus	NT
1982	ORFEO ET EURYDICE (opera)	Gluck	Glyndebourne
	THE IMPORTANCE OF BEING EARNEST	Wilde	NT
	MACBETH (opera)	Verdi	Metropolitan Opera House, NY
	OTHER PLACES	Pinter	NT
1983	DER RING DES NIBELUNGEN (opera)	Wagner	Bayreuth
	JEAN SEBERG (musical)	Hamlisch/ Barry/Adler	NT
1984	ANIMAL FARM	Orwell/Hall	NT
	CORIOLANUS	Shakespeare	NT
	L'INCORONAZIONE DI POPPEA (opera)	Monteverdi	Glyndebourne
1985	YONADAB	Shaffer	NT
	CARMEN (opera)	Bizet	Glyndebourne
	ALBERT HERRING (opera)	Britten	Glyndebourne
1986	THE PETITION	Clark	NT
	SIMON BOCCANEGRA (opera)	Verdi	Glyndebourne
	SALOME (opera)	Strauss	Los Angeles
	COMING INTO LAND	Poliakoff	NT
1987	ANTONY AND CLEOPATRA	Shakespeare	NT
	LA TRAVIATA (opera)	Verdi	Glyndebourne
	ENTERTAINING STRANGERS	Edgar	NT
1988	CYMBELINE	Shakespeare	NT
	THE WINTER'S TALE	Shakespeare	NT
	THE TEMPEST	Shakespeare	NT
	FALSTAFF (opera)	Verdi	Glyndebourne
	COSI FAN TUTTE (opera)	Mozart	Glyndebourne
	ORPHEUS DESCENDING	Tennessee Williams	PHCo/Theatre Royal Haymarket
1989	THE MERCHANT OF VENICE	Shakespeare	PHCo/Phoenix
	NEW YEAR (opera)	Tippett	Houston
	THE MARRIAGE OF FIGARO (opera)	Mozart	Glyndebourne
1990	THE WILD DUCK	Ibsen/Hall/ Ewbank	PHCo/Phoenix

	BORN AGAIN (musical)	Ionesco/Barry/Carr	PHCo/Chichester
	THE HOMECOMING	Pinter	PHCo/Comedy
1991	TWELFTH NIGHT	Shakespeare	PHCo/Playhouse
	THE ROSE TATTOO	Tennessee Williams	PHCo/Playhouse
	TARTUFFE	Molière/Bolt	PHCo/Playhouse
1992	FOUR BABOONS ADORING THE SUN	Guare	Lincoln Center, NY
	SIENNA RED	Poliakoff	PHCo/L'pool
	ALL'S WELL THAT ENDS WELL	Shakespeare	RSC
	THE GIFT OF THE GORGON	Shaffer	RSC/Wyndhams
1993	THE MAGIC FLUTE (opera)	Mozart	Los Angeles
	SEPARATE TABLES	Rattigan	PHCo/Albery
	LYSISTRATA	Aristophanes/Bolt	PHCo/Old Vic
	SHE STOOPS TO CONQUER	Goldsmith	PHCo/Queen's

FILMS

WORK IS A FOUR LETTER WORD (1968)
A MIDSUMMER NIGHT'S DREAM (1969)
THREE INTO TWO WON'T GO (1969)
PERFECT FRIDAY (1971)
THE HOMECOMING (1973)
AKENFIELD (1974)
SHE'S BEEN AWAY (for BBC TV, 1989)
ORPHEUS DESCENDING (for Turner TV, USA, 1990)
THE CAMOMILE LAWN (for C4, 1991)

VIDEOS
(adapted from stage productions)

THE WARS OF THE ROSES (1965)
IL RITORNO D'ULISSE IN PATRIA (opera, 1972)
THE MARRIAGE OF FIGARO (opera, 1973)
DON GIOVANNI (opera, 1977)
FIDELIO (opera, 1979)
A MIDSUMMER NIGHT'S DREAM (opera, 1981)
L'INCORONAZIONE DI POPPEA (opera, 1984)
CARMEN (opera, 1985)
ALBERT HERRING (opera, 1985)
THE ORESTEIA (1986)
LA TRAVIATA (opera, 1987)
THE MARRIAGE OF FIGARO (opera, 1989)
SALOME (opera, 1992)

— INDEX —

407

Index

Index

Index

production of *Othello* 166−7; in Hall's production of *No Man's Land* 167, 193, 269

Gift of the Gorgon, The 303

Gigi 110−1; film 119−20, 122

Gilbert, W.S. 41, 398

Gilbertson, Geoffrey 237

Gilliatt, Penelope 155

Gingold, Hermione 120

Giraudoux, Jean 163, 173, 322

Giulini, Carlo Maria 221

Globe Theatre 78

Gluck, Christoph 239

Glyndebourne 62−3, 210, 213−8, 228, 230, 232−3, 235−9, 248−52, 254−6, 261, 268, 276−7, 292, 299, 301, 335, 350, 366

Gobbi, Tito 221

Godard, Jean-Luc 357

Godfrey, Derek 155, 364

God Save the Queen 278

Gogol, Nikolai 182, 185

Goldoni, Carlo 94−5, 98, 100, 278, 281

Goldsmith, Oliver 393

Gone With the Wind 29, 357

Gonne, Maud 53

Goodbody, Buzz 316

Goodman, Arnold 170, 207−9, 261, 269, 273, 332, 336

Goodwin, John 145, 174, 198, 204, 269, 315, 323, 347−8

Gorbachev, Mikhail 349

Goring, Marius 51

Gorky, Maxim 287

Gorky Theatre, Leningrad 142

Gostelow, Gordon 93

Gough, Michael 99

Government Inspector, The 185, 300

Gowrie, Grey 327−9

Grade, Michael 371

Graham-Jones, Sebastian 291

Grand Hotel 184−5

Grand Manoeuvres 268

Granta 70

Granville-Barker, Harley 50, 55, 79, 99, 265, 281

Gray, Simon 261, 296

Gray, Terence 50

Greater London Council 286, 307, 314, 329

Green, Julien 99, 102

Gregory, Lady Isabella 53

Griffiths, Hugh 109

Griffiths, Trevor 291

Grimes, Tammy 380

Grock 63

Grotowski, Jan 199

Grunwald, Dimitri de 363

Guardian, The 104, 273, 294, 320, 350

Guare, John 390

Gui, Vittorio 215

Guildhall School of Music 232

Guinness, Alec 79, 102

Gulbenkian Foundation 217

Gulliver's Travels 325

Gunter, John 255

Guthrie, Tyrone 391

Guys and Dolls 316−18, 321

Haitink, Bernard 230, 249−50, 255, 299

Hall, Christopher 53, 111, 115, 119, 121−2, 181−3, 186, 209, 398

Hall, Edward (Tudor chronicler) 174

Hall, Edward 187, 284, 292, 304, 398

Hall, Emma 346, 392, 398−9

Hall, Grace 3−4, 6−11, 15−16, 19, 21, 23, 28−35, 37−40, 43−5, 49−50, 64, 75, 89, 111, 347, 351, 375, 384−6

Hall, Jennifer 111, 119, 121, 181−3, 186, 345−6, 398

Hall, Lucy 187, 284, 292, 304, 398

Hall, Mahala 44

Hall, Peter: Childhood 3−42; Family 3−4, 6−23, 26−38; Early experiences of theatre 19−20, 28, 44−5, 50−1, 54−8, 64−5; University 54−5, 60, 68−82, 84−89, 96; National Service 55−68; Early love affairs 65−7, 69, 73, 75, 80, 89, 96−7, 110−1, 173; Early experiences of directing − at Cambridge 82−9; − in rep 90−93, − at the Arts Theatre Club 94−6, 98−109; − at Stratford 109, 112−13, 117, 119, 126, 129−30, 134−5; Marriages 97, 11−12, 118, 121, 130, 158−9, 171−3, 177−8, 180−7, 239−42, 290, 292, 299−300, 304, 318, 345−6, 349−52; Children 53, 111, 115, 119, 172, 181−3, 185−7, 209, 241, 284, 304, 318, 344, 347, 349, 373, 392, 398−9; at the RSC 101, 130−1, 146−51, 153−9, 161−6, 168−80, 185, 187−92, 194−210, 222, 249, 259, 266, 285, 287, 322, 340, 361, 363, 379, 388−9, 391−2; illnesses 177−8, 208, 349; and Covent Garden 185, 196, 221−30; at the National Theatre 101, 186, 200, 209−10, 235, 242, 246, 248, 253−4, 259, 261−98, 300−52, 366−7, 379, 388−9; at Glyndebourne 210, 213−18, 230, 233, 235−41, 248−51, 254−6, 292, 299, 334, 348, 366, 380; at Bayreuth 243−8; and *Peter Hall's Diaries* 265, 272, 305, 322−4, 340; and

411

Index

Index

417

Index

Index